TO COMMEMORATE THE 40th YEAR OF I.I.P.A, NEW DELHI

LANDMARKS IN KARNATAKA ADMINISTRATION

LANDMARKS
IN
KARNATAKA ADMINISTRATION

Editor

S. Ramanathan, *IAS* (Retd.)

Chairman

Indian Institute of Public Administration

Karnataka Regional Branch

Bangalore

Published for

Indian Institute of Public Administration

Karnataka Regional Branch

Bangalore: 560008

UPPAL PUBLISHING HOUSE

NEW DELHI-110002 (INDIA)

UPPAL PUBLISHING HOUSE
3, Ansari Road, Daryaganj, New Delhi-110 002
Phones : Off. 3273756, 3286571, Res. 2242884

First Published 1998
ISBN 81-85565-98-8

Printed in India

Published by B. S. Uppal for Uppal Publishing House, 3, Ansari Road, Daryaganj, New Delhi and Laser typesetting by DV Graphic Prints (P) Ltd., Karol Bagh, New Delhi and Printed by Mehra Offset Press, Daryaganj, New Delhi - 110002

CMP/148/98.

BANGALORE-560001

DATED. 13.2.98

J.H. PATEL
CHIEF MINISTER

FOREWORD

It was a pleasure for me to browse through the book **LANDMARKS IN KANATAKA ADMINISTRATION** being brought out by the Karnataka Regional Branch of Indian Institute of Public Administration to celebrate completion of four decades of IIPA, New Delhi.

The authors have chronicled their subjects authoritatively and the indepth research and painstaking efforts are clearly evident in enunciation of their topics. They have spotlighted the developments and evolutionary trends in the administrative set-up of Karnataka, and have succeeded in depicting the State, which since a very long time has been a frontrunner in administrative and allied fields, in its true perspective.

The suggested measures for further improvement and more efficient programme implementation are sure to steer the State through the complexities of effective administration.

The book, I am sure, will be a useful reference guide to administrators, academics, students of public administration, universities and general public.

I congratulate Shri S. Ramanathan, Chairman, Karnataka Regional Branch of the Indian Institute Public Administration, for the excellent work he has done to edit the book and the authors for their stupendous performance.

J.H. PATEL

PREFACE

This volume on **Landmarks in Karnataka Administration** owes its origin to the decision taken by the Indian Institute of Public Administration (IIPA), New Delhi, to commemorate the 40th anniversary of the Institute. The IIPA decided that it would be appropriate if a few Regional Branches were assigned the task of bringing out the volumes on the landmarks in public administration of the states since independence. The Karnataka Regional Branch of the IIPA was one of the few Regional Branches selected for undertaking such a study.

It is relevant to highlight the point here that this study is not based on research or in-depth analysis of the policies and programmes of the Karnataka Government in the various areas of socio-economic administration. On the contrary, based on the guidelines for conducting the study suggested by the IIPA, New Delhi, an attempt has been made to spotlight the evolutionary trends in the selected areas of Karnataka administration since independence/reorganisation of the state, resulting from legislative enactments or programmes formulated during the several Five Year Plans. In addition, a broad review of the changing policies and programmes over the decades has been made, and suggestions offered for improvements in policy formulation and programme implementation.

I

The State of Karnataka, which, earlier, was named as 'State of Mysore' when it was formed on 1st November 1956, had its territories dispersed in four states viz., the erstwhile Part-A States of Bombay and Madras, and the Part-B States of Mysore and Hyderabad. In addition, there was the centrally administered small territory of Coorg which retained its separate identity till its merger in the new Mysore State.

All the integrated areas of the new State, had, even prior to 1947, followed the British pattern of administration at all levels, viz., from the Secretariat down to the divisional, district, sub-division, taluk and village levels. They had established a fairly good administrative system and apparatus and in fact, the administration in the erstwhile Bombay and Madras Presidencies was hailed as one of the best in the country. Further, in various sectors of socio-economic development, the erstwhile princely Mysore State and Bombay and Madras Presidencies were far ahead compared to the Hyderabad State. Even in the more important area of popular participation in government, the erstwhile Mysore State and Bombay and Madras Presidencies had established through various legislations, statutory Assemblies/Councils with people's representatives both directly elected and nominated, which had a say in the policies and programmes of the government. This, however, was not the case in Hyderabad State. Even till independence, a representative assembly of the people did not exist. In such a scenario, the IIPA, Karnataka Regional Branch, had necessarily to examine the scope of the study keeping in view the literature that has been published during the last 40 years on various aspects of Karnataka State's administration. It was a daunting task and the Executive Committee of the Branch set up an Editorial Committee for the purpose of selecting the topics which, in the contemporary context, would be of great interest and relevance to those who are interested in the present status of public administration. Hence, after careful deliberations, the Editorial Committee finalised the list of topics to be included in the study. It was evident that the study had to be necessarily selective with focus on the topics which, as stated above, are important in the present context.

Twentyeight authors have contributed 20 chapters in the volume which have been broadly grouped under eight major headings. These are: 1) Evolution of Administration; 2) Decentralisation and Local

Government; 3) Agricultural and Industrial Administration; 4) Financial Administration; 5) Environmental Administration; 6) Law and Order Administration; 7) Social Welfare Administration; and 8) Administrative Reforms.

II

The volume begins with a paper by Suryanath Kamath and S. Ramanathan on the **"Evolution of Administration in Karnataka".** In order to understand the present day administrative organisation, the authors felt it necessary to trace the evolution of administration from the 19th century to the present day in the four principal branches of administration viz., General, Revenue, Police and Judiciary. They have highlighted the influence of the British pattern of administration in the princely states which developed, barring minor exceptions, administrative organisations needed for the transaction of government business in the four principal areas of administration. They have also traced the development of representative people's institutions in which both elected and nominated members served as people's representatives to voice their opinion on the policies and programmes of the government.

They have referred to the emerging political scenario, especially after the 60s, and the split in the Indian National Congress, and the emergence of regional parties. In the sections dealing with the revenue, police and judicial administrations, the authors have discussed the organisationl set up which, with suitable changes from time to time, discharges government business in these important areas of public administration and the enactments for codification of laws and the reforms introduced in administration.

Finally, the authors have referred to the recent decision of the Government to create seven new districts based on the recommendations made by the three expert committees which were appointed at different points of time to make recommendations for recorganisation of the districts.

III

The section on **"Decentralisation and Local Government"** has two papers, viz., 1) **"Panchayat Raj in Karnataka"** by M. Umapathy and

S. Ramanathan, and 2) **"Urban Administration"** by A. Ravindra. M. Umapathy and S. Ramanathan, in their paper, state that the Karnataka Panchayat Raj model system has been recognised as one of the best models in the country which can be taken as a suggestive model for other states with a leverage to permit modifications in each state depending on its requirements.

The credit for this, according to them, goes to the then Janatha government (1983), which implemented the recommendations of the Ashok Mehta Committee report. Subsequently, however, with the change in government, a modified version of the Panchayat Raj Act, known as **Karnataka Panchayat Raj Act 1993,** based on the 73rd Amendment to the Constitution of India, was enacted, during the Congress Government, which is currently in operation. The authors, have analysed the developments in the last two years, particularly with reference to the changes required in the Act, based on the recommendation of the Expert Committee and discussed certain emerging issues of contemporary relevance.

A. Ravindra, in his paper, **"Urban Administration",** emphasizes the point that the 74th Constitutional Amendment can be considered as a landmark in the history of local government as it introduced far reaching legislative changes for strengthening urban local bodies. He adds that the future development in the urban sector must be viewed in the context of changes envisaged in the Act. He has presented a profile of urban bodies and the emerging policies that are needed for making urban and civic administration efficient and more responsive to the public need and growing concerns. He has referred to the role of citizen's organisations, resident's associations and NGOs in managing and maintaining many civic services and amenities.

IV

In the section on **"Agricultural and Industrial Administraion"** there are four papers. The first paper, **"Agricultural Administration"** by R. Dwarakinath, B.A. Poonacha and D.S. Murigappa Sreshty, discusses the development of agricultural administration in three phases. The first phase was noted for the introduction of land reforms, improved agriculture practices and agricultural education. In the second phase, the Department of Agriculture was restructured to meet the changing needs and extension services were strengthened. In the third phase, many programmes for target groups like scheduled caste and tribal farmers, small and marginal farmers continued to receive special attention. This was the period of agricultural stagnation and attempts were made to remedy the situation. During this period, Panchayat Raj Institutions were involved in agricultural development programmes. In conclusion, the authors spotlight both the constraints and the areas which, in their considered view, should be taken note of by the Department of Agriculture while formulating the agricultural programmes and policies for the State's Ninth Plan.

The second paper in this section, **"Industrial Development"** by A. Indira and Vinod Vyasulu traces the industrial development in Karnataka. The authors point out that at the time of the states reorganisation in 1956, Karnataka had grown to have a fairly wide, diversified industrial sector. They have referred to the industrial development of the state during the last 40 years and the establishment of the financial institutions for providing industrial finance. They have highlighted the problems created by the concentration of industries in and around Bangalore area and initiatives taken under various industrial policy resolutions for attracting industries in backward areas, and fiscal and financial incentives provided by the state. In particular, they have referred to the prominent role played by the Karnataka State Industrial Investment and Development Corporation and the Karnataka State Financial Corporation for promoting industrial development. They mention the role played by research institutes and laboratories which gave impetus to the growth of industry. They observe that the Karnataka Government had a positive approach towards industrial development and also understood the need for technical knowledge and strong R&D base. In conclusion, they lament on the failure of the state government to invest sufficiently in infrastructure, especially in power and trans-port - two areas in which severe shortages have impeded the growth of industry for nearly two decades.

The third paper, **"Public Undertakings"** by A. Ramaswamy highlights the pioneering role played by the erstwhile Mysore State which had set up many public undertakings. Tracing further the development of the public sector in the state since re-organisation, the author has referred to a large number of undertakings that have been set up in the areas of agriculture and allied activities, in power and industrial development. On the current scenario of the public undertakings, he refers to the unhappy situation in which a large number of public undertakings are incurring losses. He has outlined the measures, which, in the present day context of liberalisation and disinvestment, are needed for restructuring and re-vitalising the state's public undertakings. Finally, he has argued the case for the establishment of a separate department of public enterprises to formulate and implement all policy matters pertaining to the public undertakings in the state.

The last paper in this section, **"Industrial Relations"** by B.R. Patil and P.D. Shenoy while discussing different aspects of industrial relations states that the contemporary industrial relation scenario in Karnataka in the last few years is, by and large, quite peaceful and cordial with the exception of traditional industries like textiles and cement.

In the field of information technology, electronics and telecommunications, where the employers and employees have a stake in the growth and development of the organisation, the industrial relation is of a different kind. It takes the form of human resources management with emphasis on employee development and employee relations. Consequently, the co-operation between labour and management has been increasing. However, in other traditional industries, in spite of the various measures evolved to maintain cordial industrial relations, instances are not wanting of industrial conflict due to both internal and external factors.

In conclusion, the authors state that co-operation between labour and management is becoming more common than conflict; human resource management and development are fast replacing personnel management, and labour relations are changing to employee relations.

V

The section on **"Financial Administration"** has 3 papers. The paper on **"Planning in Karnataka State and Sub-State Levels"** by D.M. Nanjundappa discusses the interface of market and planning and type of issues that concern planning at the state and sub-state levels, planning in Karnataka, decentralised planning and problems and issues involved in sub-state level planning. The author states that the development planning must necessarily consist of a mixture of price type and quality type instruments. He also focusses on the need for recognition of major planning functions by reducing rural and urban imbalance, inequality and removal of institutional obstacles. As regards planning in Karnataka State, the author refers to the plan outlays during the various plans and the mobilisation of resources by the state and the administrative set up that has been created both at the state level and currently, in the Panchayat Raj institutions for the formulation of the state and district plans. Finally, he has referred to the basic instruments of decentralised planning - an area in which in the current context of formulation and implementation of programmes by the PRI institutions, there is need for studies for refining the methodology of planning at the district level.

B.K. Bhattacharya's paper **"State Government and the New Economic Policy"** highlights the challenges faced by the state government and its institutions in the present era of liberalisation and their response to these challenges. It is obvious that satisfactory solutions have not been found to many of the problems such as mobilisation of resources, taxation reform, public sector reforms etc. He stresses the point that the adoption of fiscal and trade policy correctives, abolition of 'Licence - Permit' raj and reforms in the banking sector and taxation polices will not alone be sufficient to convert the Indian 'Lamb' into another Asian 'Tiger'.

According to the author, before the central and state governments go beyond this exercise of liberalisation and globalisation, it is necessary to make the nation invest heavily in the social sector by speeding up the programmes for removing illiteracy, under-nourishment, ill-health and social inequalities. In this way, the author shares the widely held view that investment in social infrastructure will expand opportunities and make the very large section of the population productive in order to contribute their might for the development of the country. The real challenge before the Central and state governments in the coming years will be to undertake this neglected exercise and going beyond liberalisation. Unavoidably, there will be financial implications of such an exercise. This must be carefully examined.

G. Thimmaiah, in his paper on **"Tax Administration in Karnataka"**, discusses the evolution of major taxes in Karnataka and the administrative set up for mobilising and collecting tax revenues from different sources. He refers to the areas in which reforms are needed particularly for ensuring efficiency in the functioning of various departments. Some of these are: changes in the mode of recruitment, modernisation of tax design, reorganisation of tax structure, improvements in training and research in tax administration. He also refers to the need for attitudinal changes on the part of officials towards the tax payers.

VI

In the paper on **"Environmental Administration"**, M.V. Nadkarni discusses the evolution of environmental administration and assesses the present situation. He refers to the instruments through which environmental control is exercised and points out that in view of the increasing concern on ecology and environment, there is a growing awareness both on the part of the government, NGOs and the people of the measures needed for tightening environmental control and involvement of the local people dealing with environmental pollution or degradation. However, the author regrets that enforcement of environmental laws is inadequate even in the highly polluting category of industries. Regarding conservation and improvement of forests, the author states that it is being affected by the political struggle between competing interest groups.

VII

S. Krishnamurthy in the paper on **"Law and Order Administration"**, highlights the complex nature of police administration. Initially, it was mostly concerned with controlling criminal activities, but now its scope has totally changed with increasing work load with- a large population and with new tasks such as civil rights enforcement, intelligence, oppression of weaker sections, terrorist containment, insurgency protecting railways, gender violence etc. Added to this, training the police personnel in modern investigation methods, application of scientific techniques in criminal investigation and many innovative measures have also been introduced. Women police personnel are also taking active participation in law and order administration.

In today's democratic set up, the outlook of the police has to be people-oriented. Since welfare of the police is directly linked with their efficient functioning, many welfare measures are being introduced for them.

In view of the vast changes in the scope and complexion of the work of the police force referred to above, there is need to re-orient the fuctioning of the police administration. In this context, the author suggests the need for redefining the duties, powers and responsibilities of the police, and good personnel policy, improvement in the working conditions of the police, modernisation of the police force and creating an authority to assess police performance.

In conclusion, he states that irrespective of whatever is done to modernise the police force, no force can discharge the duties without fear or favour unless there is a political will not to interfere with the working of the force.

VIII

The section on **"Social Welfare Administration"** has four papers. The paper on **"Administration of Health Services"** by P. Hanumantha Rayappa and T.V.Sekher states that there has been a rapid expansion of medical facilities in the state during the last three decades, both in the government and private sectors. The authors make the point that poor utilisation of government health services underlines the fact that mere expansion of health services will not yield the desired results and what is required is improvement in the qualitative aspects of the health care system. They state that the reluctance of health functionaries to work in the rural areas is also affecting the health services.

They mention that the private sector is more visible in the medical service as a consequence of inadequate public health care system and that it is the responsibility of the state to strengthen the efficiency of the state health services which calls for better management and planning.

According to them, the ongoing structural adjustment policies will have significant repurcussions on the health sector as this sector is more vulnerable to cut in public expenditure in the process of restructuring of the economy. They appreciate the initiative taken by the Karnataka state to involve the voluntary organisations in implementing the programmes. What is needed today is a better co-ordination of various health programmes with active involvement of government, private and public sectors.

A.S. Seetharamu's paper on **"State and Education"** comprehensively deals with all the areas of education, namely, school, higher, technical, medical, adult, and non-formal. In all these areas the author has traced the development of the policies and programmes initiated by the government and analysed some of the current issues in each area of education. According to the author, the role of education has been changing over the years which has evolved in three distinct phases: a) welfare; b) regulatory; and c) promotional. Even though in the field of primary education the state has taken a lead by initiating the **Compulsory Primary Education Act 1961,** much remains to be done. The state government would have to suitably initiate measures for introducing compulsory primary education. In regard to higher education, an area in which private sector has come to play a major role, the author highlights the regulatory role of the government in regard to the growth and development of higher education. According to him, the measures taken by the government have not succeeded so far. Finally, the author refers to the transfer of school adult non-formal education and libraries to Zilla Panchayats under the **Karnataka Panchayat Raj Act 1993**.

The regulatory role of the government both in promoting and regulating the institutions which administer education has been highlighted by the author.

Anita Kaul's paper on **"Women and Children"** highlights the current situation regarding the status of women and children in terms of their access to education, employment and other rights under various legislations. With the help of the latest census data, the author has focussed the issues which are of great concern for improving the education of children and in raising the health status of women and reviewed the programmes such as Community Development Programme, Mahila Mandals, Training and Visit, Vocational Education, Dwarca, Trysem, monetary incentive schemes, income generation and other poverty alleviation for women, and ICDS, Akshaya Yojana, Vidya Vikas schemes and District Primary Education Project for children. She highlights the weaknesses of these programmes and also states that the welfare approach started in the 1950s is still continuing without any change in the policy. She also refers to the field problems in implementing the programmes for children and women and states that the major landmark decision taken by the government to reserve 33 per cent of the seats in the Panchayat Raj Institutions for women, and the political participation of women in these institutions may lead to formulation and implementation more effectively of the programmes meant for the welfare of women and children. This, supplemented by other legislations intended to provide joint landholdings, sites and houses and assets, will lead to economic empowerment of women and improve their lot. She concludes that the recent achievements and experience gained in implementing the programme for children and women may hopefully provide some answers to the question of women and child development and general quality.

To sum up, she says that the few initiatives taken in recent years through special projects, such as WYTEP, DPEP, Tlc, Mahila Samakhya, Panchayat Raj training may not perhaps give us the final answers to the question of women and child development and equality between men and women, but they do nevertheless, provide directions for us to move along.

N. Sivanna, in his paper, **"Other Services: Housing, Water Supply and Sanitation, and Public Distribution System"**, examines the services like housing, water supply and sanitation and public distribution system in different sectors, and their impact on the living standards in the state of Karnataka. On housing, he highlights the various schemes that are being implemented and the provisions made for weaker sections and the poor. He points out that non-involvement of beneficiaries, wrong selection, construction of houses by contractors rather than by the beneficiaries and lack of adequate manpower to supervise and assist the beneficiaries are some of the functional flaws in the programme. The author says that the achievement in both rural and urban area is far from satisfactory.

Regarding water supply and sanitation, the author states that although several schemes are being implemented for augmenting rural water supply, there has been unsatisfactory maintenance of the assets created. He states that at present the maintenance of rural water supply is under the purview of the Zilla Panchayat which have not been able to give adequate attention to the maintenance of the schemes. Therefore, he suggests that the maintenance of the scheme should be entrusted to the Village Panchayats which can give immediate attention to the problems, making the administrative process a responsive, people-friendly, reciprocative and committed one.

Although the rural sanitation programme has been in operation since 1984-85, it has not been received well by the public due to unsatisfactory implementation process. The government is urging to treat this programme as a "Movement" but this requires greater participation of the people, elected representatives etc. There is need to educate and motivate the people in keeping their environment clean.

As far as the public distribution system is concerned, the author states that in spite of all the merits and demerits of having PDS, it acts as an effective delivery system to the poor and weaker sections. According to the author, an interesting feature of PDS in Karnataka is that the distribution system is mostly confined to the co-operative section and state institutions excepting in areas where these institutions have not been able to undertake the distribution. The author makes a case for the re-establishment of the "Food Enforcement Cell" to prevent sluggishness in the procurement of grains. The author also suggests that because of the weak administrative structure at the sub-state level, it has become necessary to hand over the operation of PDS to the Panchayats.

In the overview, the author states in spite of certain functional flaws, there is some satisfaction when the state level performance is compared with all India performances of these services.

IX

A.K.M. Nayak, in his paper, **"Administrative Reforms in Karnataka"** outlines the measures taken to reorganise the State Secretariat and the creation of four administrative divisions to provide an effective system of administration. He also refers to the legislation enacted for the abolition of heriditary village officers and the creation of the Department of Admir:strative Reforms with the responsibility of looking after administrative reforms, organisation and method activities, mechanisation of administration, simplification of procedures and emphasis on training. In these areas, he discusses the efforts made for streamlining the work of government, improving efficiency, protecting the interests of public servants, the introduction of modern office procedures and systems, and computers for data processing, rendering services to government departments and autonomous bodies. He has rightly stressed the importance of training of government functionaries at all levels, and the important role the Administrative Training Institute at Mysore and the District Training Centres are playing for providing training to all categories of government servants for upgrading their knowledge, skills and enhancing their capabilities and efficiency for ensuring speedy disposal of government business.

He also refers to the institution of Lok Ayukta and other redressal measures that have been set up for attending to the grievances of public servants.

K.H. Cheluva Raju, in his paper on **"The Study of Political Science and Public Administration in Karnataka Universities"**, traces the development of the study of public administration in Karnataka Universities and laments that even after fifty years of independence such an important discipline as public administration has still to take roots in the universities. In one form or other, the subject is being taught in all the universities, but it has not yet been accorded the status of an independent discipline. Although a Department of Public Administration was started in Mysore University in 1954, it was merged with the Department of Political Science in 1958, and since then public adminstration is taught as a paper in political science. The opposition from the Political Science Department and the problem of employment of post-graduate degree holders in public administration seem to have been the causes for this development.

As regards the teaching of Public Administration in the universities, he says that Public Administration is not being offered at the pre-university level, but offered as a paper at the degree and post-graduate levels. The author has complimented the Mysore University for the landmark decision taken to start a full fledged M.A. Course in Public Administration from 1966.

All the six universities are offering opportunities for research, and a number of students have taken Ph.D in the Political Science in the area of Karnataka public administration, at M.Phil and Ph.D levels.

In order to encourage teaching of, and research in, public administration, the author has, in conclusion, emphasized the need to establish departments of public administration in the Universities and a Karnataka Social Science Research Centre. He has also stressed the important role of the IIPA, New Delhi, and the Karnataka Regional Branch of the IIPA, in establishing rapport with the Universities and for organising conferences and seminars in collaboration with them.

S.K. Hajra and V.S. Angadi, in their paper on **"Training in Karnataka: An Analytical Framework"**, state that training as an instrument of change is a dynamic activity through which the capability of personnel can be improved to meet the present and future performance needs in terms of knowledge, skills and attitudes. The administration has a special responsibility for promoting creative abilities and innovational attitudes of the personnel for fostering motivation and commitment for change on a continual basis. In the light of this recognition, Karnataka took a decision way back in 1967 to start an Administrative Training Institute in Mysore. Thereafter, a District Training Institute has been set up in each district.

The authors have discussed the identification of training needs, formulation of training objective and methodology, and also touched on the importance of training of trainers.

A problem which needs attention is the regional imbalance in the training coverage. There is need for sensitising officials at various levels to the importance of data management in the domain of administrative and public services.

The authors stress the need for networking among training institutes, and have highlighted the role of the Department of Personnel and Administrative Reforms in framing the training policy of the state government. In conclusion, the authors state that despite the growing concern for training of public personnel, it is being increasingly realised that development of administrators has been either inadequate or **ad hoc** especially in the context of the role of administrators in the new emerging areas of public administration such as science and technology, environment and ecology, and structural reforms with emphasis on liberalisation and globalisation.

The last paper, **"State Policy and Social Science Research"** by P.V. Shenoi and A.S. Seetharamu, refers to the founding of the premier Bangalore based Institute for Social Economic Change by the internationally well known economist late Dr. V.K.R.V. Rao. Prior to the setting up of the Institute, there was not a single academic body, by and large, exclusively concentrating on the study and research in various aspects of Karnataka administration. This lacuna was overcome when this Institute was set up. The authors have elaborated the studies, workshops and research conducted on the socio-economic aspects of Karnataka such as agricultural and rural development, infra-structure, decentralisation, planning and administration, industries, education, demography, urban water supply, housing, programmes for the benefit of SC/ST and weaker section of the society. The authors have referred to the consultancy studies undertaken on behalf of the Government of Karnataka, which have led to either changes in the existing policies or initiation of new policies by the government.

X

In conclusion, it may be noted that the papers which are included in the volume have spotlighted the landmarks in the policy formulation and programme implementation in the various fields of Karnataka State's public administration and drawn attention to the difficulties and weaknesses in the existing policy formulation and programme implementation, and recommended the changes, which, on a priority basis, are needed in the policies, and suggested the measures for efficient programme implementation.

S. RAMANATHAN

ACKNOWLEDGEMENTS

The Karnataka Regional Branch of the Indian Institute of Public Administration is very grateful to Shri J.H. Patel, Chief Minister of Karnataka, for his befittingly thoughtful Foreword to this book. His words of appreciation of the work done by the Branch is a great source of encouragement. We hope to subsequently cover the areas/sectors of Karnataka Administration not dealt with in the present volume.

In preparing this volume, the Government of Karnataka and several individuals have actively participated and assisted the Branch. The Branch is grateful to the Government of Karnataka for the special grant of Rs. 3 lakhs for undertaking the study. In particular, the Branch would like to acknowledge with gratitude the active support received from the former and present Chief Secretaries of the State, Principal Secretary to the Government of Karnataka, Finance Department, and Secretary to the Government, Department of Personnel and Administrative Reforms. The Branch places on record the guidance and help it has received from the members of the Editorial Committee. The Branch would like to thank all the contributors of papers and the referees who have gone through some of the papers and have made valuable suggestions.

Finally, the Branch would like to thank M/s. Uppal Publishing House for bringing out this volume at extremely short notice and Sri V.S. Parathasarthy for the editorial assistance received from him.

S. Ramanathan

List of Contributors

1) *Sri V.S. Angadi,*
Faculty (Economics and Planning),
Administrative Training Institute, Mysore.

2) *Sri B.K. Bhattacharaya, IAS*
Addtional Secretary & Principal Secretary to Government,
Finance Department,
Government of Karnataka.
Bangalore

3) *Dr. R. Dwarakinath,*
Former Vice-Chancellor,
University of Agricultural Sciences, & Former Director of Agriculture,
Government of Karnataka.
Bangalore

4) *Sri S.K. Hajra, IAS,*
Director-General,
Administrative Training Institute, Mysore.

5) *Mrs A. Indira,*
Dy. Director, Technology, Informatic, Design and Endeavour Development Research Foundation (TIDE), Bangalore.

6) *Dr. Suryanath Kamath,*
Former Chief Editor,
Karnataka Gazetteer.
Bangalore.

7) *Smt. Anita Kaul, IAS,*
Director,
District Primary Education Programme,
Government of Karnataka,
Bangalore.

8) *Dr. S. Krishnamurthy,*
Additional DGP (EO),
Government of Karnataka,
Nrupanthunga Road,
Bangalore.

9) *Dr. M.V. Nadkarni,*
Prof. and Head,
Ecology Economics Unit,
Institute for Social and Economic Change,
Bangalore.

10) *Dr. D.M. Nanjundappa,* Deputy Chairman, State Planning Board, Government of Karnataka, Bangalore and Chairman, Indian Council of Social Science Research, New Delhi.

11) *Sri A.K.M. Nayak, IAS,* Secretary to Government, Department of Personnel and Administrative Reforms, Government of Karnataka, Bangalore.

12) *Sri. B.R. Patil,* Professor, Indian Institute of Management, Bangalore.

13) *Sri B.A. Poonacha,* Addl. Dir. of Agriculture (Retd.), Government of Karnataka, Bangalore.

14) *Dr. K.H. Cheluva Raju,* Former Vice–Chancellor, Gulbarga University, Gulbarga.

15) *Sri. S. Ramanathan, IAS (Retd.),* Former Secretary to the Government of India, and Chairman, IIPA, Karnataka Regional Branch, Bangalore.

16) *Sri A. Ramaswamy, IAS,* Director, Karnataka State Bureau of Public Enterprises & Ex-officio, Secretary to Government (DPAR), Government of Karnataka, Banglore.

17) *Dr. A. Ravindra, IAS,* Secretary to Government, Forest, Ecology and Environment Department, Government of Karnataka. Bangalore

18) *Dr. P. Hanumantha Rayappa,* Professor and Head, Population Research Centre, Institute for Social and Economic Change, Bangalore.

19) *Sri G.S. Sastry,* Asst. Professor, Ecology Economics Unit, Institute for Social and Economic Change, Bangalore.

20) *Dr. A.S. Seetharamu,* Professor and Head, Education Unit, Institute for Social and Economic Change, Bangalore.

21) *Sri T.V.Sekher,*
Asst. Professor,
Population Research
Centre, Institute for Social
and Economic Change,
Bangalore.

22) *Dr. P.V. Shenoi,*
Director,
Institute for Social and
Economic Change,
Bangalore.

23) *Dr. P.D. Shenoy, IAS,*
Chairman & Director,
Mysore Lamp Works,
Bangalore.

24) *Dr. N. Sivanna,*
Dy. Project Director,
Decentralisation - Training,
Institue for Social and
Economic Change,
Bangalore.

25) *Sri D.S. Murigappa Sreshty,*
Dy. Director of Agriculture
(Retd),
Government of Karnataka,
Bangalore

26) *Dr. G. Thimmaiah,*
Member, Planning
Commission, New Delhi.

27) *Dr. M. Umapathy,*
Professor,
Dept. of Studies in Political
Science, University of Mysore,
Manasagangotri, Mysore.

28) *Dr. Vinod Vyasulu,*
Consulting Economist,
Bangalore.

CONTENTS

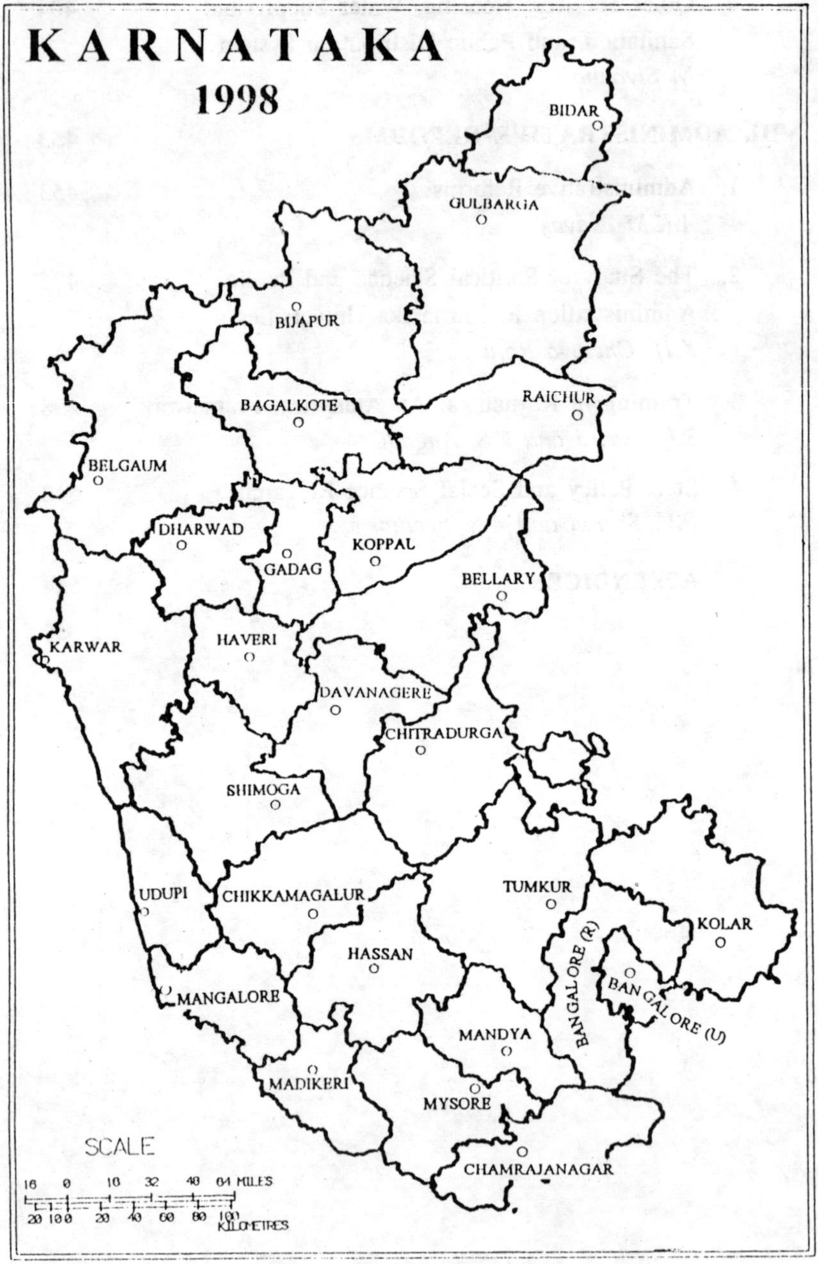

* This map is not an official map issued by the state Government.

I

EVOLUTION OF ADMINISTRATION IN KARNATAKA

Suryanath Kamath
and S. Ramanathan

Movement for Unification of Karnataka: Since the demand for formation of linguistic states intensified following the establishment of Andhra Pradesh in 1952, it would be pertinent to refer to the demand for the establishment of a Kannada speaking state not only in the old Mysore state but also in the districts of the erstwhile Bombay state which, became the base of operations for the unification of Karnataka. In fact, the first unification conference was held in Belgaum in 1924. The movement for the formation of the state was the outcome of renaissance that Karnataka had evidenced. It was essentially a movement of intellectuals to begin with. It was nurtured by poets, writers and journalists. The politicians also accepted this as it provided the necessary emotional urge for freedom from British Raj. The momentum also gained from the neglect of the Kannada speaking people not only in Bombay-Karnataka area but also in the various princely states, many of which were ruled by Marathi speaking princes. Kannada speaking people were in a minority in the state's administration. Dharwad was, in fact, the seat of the unification movement and intellectuals, writers, poets, and politicians all stepped up the campaign. Eminent people and the press provided the necessary intellectual and emotional urge. In 1937, the Congress in its election manifesto declared itself in favour of the formation of Andhra and Karnataka. However, even this did not yield results and this led to a series of agitations in the Bombay—Karnataka area, some of which turned violent. Finally, the Central Government appointed a States Reorganisation Commission which recommended, **inter-alia,** formation of a new state on a linguistic basis. This new state was named State of Mysore on 1st November 1956.

The present state, which was in 1973, renamed as the State of Karnataka, comprises the following territories of the integrated areas:

1. The pre-1956-B State of Mysore including Bellary District, which was integrated in October 1953 from the erstwhile Madras State.

2. Belgaum, Dharwar, Bijapur and North Kanara districts from the erstwhile Bombay State.

3. Gulbarga, Raichur and Bidar districts of the erstwhile Part-B state of Hyderabad.

4. South Kanara district, and Kollegal taluk from the Coimbatore district of the erstwhile Madras State.

5. Part-C State of Coorg.

It may be mentioned that in the areas from the erstwhile Madras, Bombay and Hyderabad states, there were many princely states predominantly populated by Kannada speaking people, which after the abolition of princely states, had merged in the districts of the erstwhile states. Sandur state, with 23 villages was merged in Bellary district and became a taluk. The princely states of Jamakhandi, Mudhol, Aundh, (Gundal group of villages), areas of Sangli state (areas around Banhatti), Miraj state (around Terdal) came to be merged in Bijapur district. Twentyfive villages of Ramdurg taluk were merged in Badami taluk of Bijapur district. Twentyeight villages of Ramdurg and 20 villages of Wadgaon (Junior Kurundwad) states, 54 villages of Sangli state around Ugar Khurd (7 villages) were merged in Belgaum district.

Some villages from Kurundwad state (18 to Belgaum taluk and three to Athani taluk) and from Kolhapur state (31 villages around Raibag), 14 near Ramdurg and 11 villages around Khadaklat, now in Chikodi taluk, were transferred to Belgaum district. Jamkhandi, and Mudhol became taluk headquarters in Bijapur district and Ramdurg and Raibag in Belgaum district.

Kundgol from Jamkhandi state (17 villages and 3 towns), Lakshmeshwar from Miraj (14 villages and one town), Shirahatti area from Sangli (72 villages and 1 town), Gudgeri etc., from Junior Miraj (14 villages) and the whole of Savanur state (23 villages) and 12 villages of the Raichur district (of the erstwhile Hyderabad state now in Ron taluk) were merged in Dharwar district and Kundgol became part of Dharwad district. Savanur and Shirhatti became taluk headquarters.

Evolution of Administration: The four areas of administration that evolved during the 19th century both in the erstwhile states and the British administered provinces were as follows:-

1. General Administration (including establishment of nominated and elected Representative Assembly/Legislative Council in Mysore and Legislative Assembly and Legislature Council in Madras/Bombay Presidencies).

2. Revenue Administration

3. Police Administration.

4. Judicial Administration.

Though this study on Karnataka administration is primarily concerned with the developments in the post-independence period, an attempt has been made purposely to outline briefly the main features of the evolution of administration in the these four areas from the 19th century to the present time.

1. General Administration: So far as the erstwhile Mysore State is concerned, evolution of the modern administration can be traced back to the year 1799 when Tipu Sultan was defeated by the British forces. During the minority of Krishna Raja Wodeyar III (1799-1811), the administration of Mysore was run by Poorniah who was nominated as the Dewan by the British with full executive control over the affairs of Mysore. Apart from organising, at the field level, the revenue and police administration, he made a beginning by organising and administering the functions of the government through government departments such as finance, revenue and miscellaneous. The state was divided into three 'Subhas' each under a Subedar. However, due to the misrule of Maharaja, the administration of Mysore was entrusted in 1831 to a Board of Commissioners, and later, in the following year, to one sole Commissioner.

During the administration from 1834 to 1878, two great administrators, namely, Sir Mark Cubbon and Mr. Lewin Bowring left an indelible impression on the state's administration by good and industrious work. The general administration of Mysore was modernised during this period and various reforms were introduced in the areas of law and order, revenue, police and welfare administrations. During Cubbon's time, the new Secretariat building known as 'Athara Kacheri' was built to house the Secretariat departments. During Bowring's tenure the state was divided into eight districts and further reforms were introduced in the area of law and order and civil and criminal justice administration. Local self-governing institutions were also established and measures were also started to promote and encourage education on a large scale by starting schools. The well/known Central College building in Bangalore (1860) was a creation of his time.

After the rendition in 1881, the administration of the state was returned to the young Maharaja. From that time onwards, the state administration was headed by a series of very eminent, competent and devoted administrators who served as Dewans of the state, starting with Dewan Rangacharlu in 1881 to Sri Arcot Ramaswamy Mudaliar in 1946. They were Sarvashri K. Sheshadri Iyer, P.N. Krishnamurthy, V.P. Madhava Rao, T. Ananda Rao, M. Visvesvaraya, Sardar Kantharaj Urs, M. Mirza Ismail and N. Madhava Rao. They all made significant contribution to the development of the state's administration. It was during the tenure of Dewan Rangacharlu that some sort of Representative Assembly was established in 1881 at the time of Dasara when the policy of the government and statement of expenses were brought to the notice of the members. In fact, it appears that this was the first arrangement of its kind in India as such a representative body did not exist even in the British Presidency. Mysore state became a pioneer in starting many industrial undertakings in the public sector which, in the post independence period served as a foundation for expanding the industrial base of Karnataka. It was Sir M. Visvesvaraya who launched many schemes for the economic and rural development of the state such as rural electrification, irrigation projects, hospitals, dispensaries, primary, secondary and collegiate education. He also gave fillip to strengthening the local self-governing institutions. No wonder he was hailed as the 'Maker of Modern Mysore'.

In Bombay and Madras Presidencies, the general administration of the state had followed a uniform pattern during the 19th century with the Governor as the executive head of the state. The Secretariat organisation was headed by the Chief Secretary to government. He was assisted by Secretaries to government and field departments headed by heads of departments. Bombay Presidency was divided into four administrative divisions each under a Divisional Commissioner. The district head was known as the District Collector. Various departments of the government also had their field level officers in the divisons/ districts. The District Collector was the kingpin of the district administration and the activities practically of all the departments were co-ordinated and supervised by him. In Madras state, there were no Divisonal Commissioners. Instead, it had a Board of Revenue at Madras.

In Hyderabad-Karnataka, the administration was directly under the ruler viz., the Nizam of Hyderabad. Prior to 1947, under the Nizam there was a Prime Minister and Ministers, a few of them being Britishers. The Secretariat was headed by the Chief Secretary and the departments by the Secretaries to government.

So far as Kodagu is concerned, the administration of the district was taken over by the British in 1834 and this continued for almost 143 years, i.e., right till independence in 1947. A reference to the administration of the district has been made elsewhere in the chapter.

Representative Institutions — People's Participation in Government : Representative political structures have been historically the result of either attempts by the rulers to legitimise themselves or to seek public purpose as a helpful input, or the efforts of the ruled to control the ruler in terms of legislative participation. Quite often, both these factors have converged in order to bring about the establishment of representative institutions.

The growth of such institutions in Karnataka has been both quantitatively and qualitatively an uneven historical process because of the fact that Karnataka, prior to 1956, was divided into five political administrative units. However, the representative structures in the Bombay and Madras-Karnataka areas were a response to participatory demands from below, whereas the representative structures in the erstwhile princely state of Mysore were a response to motivations from above. But, within these units there were differences.

The history of represenfive institutions in Bombay and Madras-Karnataka and Kodagu is part of the history of constitutional development in British Indian states as a whole. In Bombay and Madras-Karnataka, represenfive institutions developed earlier and more systematically in response to the pressures radiating from the increased tempo of nationalist movement. Beginning from the introduction of local self-government on a limited scale under Lord Ripon's reforms in the late 19th century, an increasing quantum of self-government was granted to the Indians by the **Government of India Acts of 1909, 1919, 1935.** The system of responsive and represenfive government was more substantial in old Mysore even though the electoral and representative principle extended only to a limited and narrow population. However, in considering the relative traditions of the represenfive institutions in different areas in Karnataka, it must be noted that they were far more significantly democratised in Bombay and Madras Presidencies than in old Mysore. In Kodagu, though a British administered territory, democratisation was slightly lower because of the fact that its size and unique history combined to gain for it a lesser administrative status both under the British and in independent India.

Hyderabad-Karnataka was politically the least democratised part of Karnataka prior to independence. Here, due to the autocratic administration of the Nizam, democratic and representative structure even in the normal sense, appeared only after the police action in 1948. After independence, Hyderabad-Karnataka tended to converge towards the full democratic political system envisaged in the Constitution.

In the erstwhile Mysore state, a beginning in the development of popular participation in government was made when soon after the rendition, Dewan Rangacharlu established in 1881 some sort of a Representative Assembly with 144 members who were representatives of Local Boards and Municipal Boards, merchants, planters and agriculturists, who assembled at the Dasara Durbar. Though it was not a statutory body, the policies of the government and the statement of expenses were brought to their notice at its annual meeting. In fact, it was the first arrangement of its kind in India as such representative body did not exist even in the British Presidency. The veteran freedom fighter and patriot, Sri Bal Gangadhar Tilak, wrote in 1882 in the "Maratha" that the "British Government might do well to take a lesson from the enlightened Maharaja of Mysore".

Dewan K. Sheshadri Iyer, who succeeded Dewan Rangacharlu, encouraged the development of the Representative Assembly by gazetting the names of its members from 1887. From 1891, members came to be chosen by election, with high property qualification for voters being fixed. Graduates also secured the right of voting. From 1894, a tenure of three years was fixed for the members.

In 1914, separate representations were allowed for sub-taluks. In 1918, the electorate was broadened with certain qualifications. In 1919, the Assembly was allowed to have a second session in June called the budget session. In 1920, provision was made for by-election. In 1923, the Representative Assembly was given a constitutional status on the basis of recommendation of the Seal Committee. The Assembly was empowered to pass resolutions on matters of public administration and also on the principles and policy of the budget. The strength of the Assembly was to be 250 to 255. In 1923, women were given voting powers. Standing Committees consisting of members of the Representative Assembly and the Legislative Council were to be constituted to advise the government. Thirtyfive seats were set apart for representation of minorities interest like Muslims, Indians Christians and Depressed Classes. This reform formally separated the Executive from the Legislature within the Constitution in which the executive, the legislature and judiciary were separated.

Legislative Council: During the dewanship of Shri V.P. Madhava Rao, a major step towards responsible government was taken by the establishment of the Legislative Council in 1907. This was done with a view to associating with it a certain number of non-official members with practical knowledge and experience in legislation. This Council was to have not less than ten and not more than fifteen additional members to the existing strength of three Executive Councillors including the dewan and, of this, not less than three fifths were to be non-officials. Two members were to be elected by the Representative Assembly to the Council.

During Dewan Sir M. Visveswaraya's tenure, the Legislative Council came to be expanded (in 1913) by increasing its membership from eighteen to twentyfour. Three members were to be elected from the Representative Assembly and four others from the eight districts. The Council was given powers to discuss the budget.

In 1923, the strength of the Council was raised to fifty and of this, twentyeight were allotted to nominated members (twenty official and eight non-official) and twentytwo elected members (elective principle being introduced for the first time). The powers of the Legislative Council were enlarged to increase the elected element to provide for special interest and minorities.

The Council had powers to vote on the state budget. A Standing Committee of the Legislative Council was formed in 1923 in order to help the government in an advisory capacity. No legislative measure could be introduced in the Council without the previous sanction of the Dewan.

Movement for Constitutional Reforms: As this did not establish a responsible government, there was a demand made in an all party conference for the establishment of responsible government. A political party known as Praja Paksha, which later became Praja Samyukta Paksha, was started in 1934, and subsequently in 1937, it became the Mysore Congress. This Congress stepped up the agitation for the demand for constitutinal reforms.

In 1938, K.R. Srinivas Iyengar Committee was appointed to look into the demand for constitutional reforms. By the Act of 1940, the government partially accepted the recommendations of the Iyengar Committee. A sixtyeight member Council and three hundred and ten member Assembly were founded. Seats were reserved for Muslims, Christians and women. The non-official members in the newly appointed Cabinet were not actually responsible to the legislature. The Congress, while continuing to agitate against the new arrangements, contested the elections to the Representative Assembly and won a sizeable number of seats in 1941.

With the intensification of the freedom struggle and the 'Quit India' movement launched by Mahatma Gandhi in 1942 and the arrest and imprisonment of the Congress leaders all over the country, the British Government had no alternative but to hold negotiations for India's independence. By the close of 1946 it was almost certain that the British were leaving India. India became an independent country in August 1947 and a new chapter in India's history began and the Central Government under the Prime Minister Pandit Jawaharlal Nehru, ably assisted by the Home Minister, Sardar Vallabhai Patel, initiated discussions for the abolition of the princely states. The Constituent Asembly met in Delhi in December 1947 to frame the new Constitution of India.

Post-1956 - Constitution of Government of Karnataka: As laid down in the Indian Constitution, the State of Karnataka is being administered by the Governor with the help of the Chief Minister and his Council of Ministers.

Governor: The Governor is the constitutional head of the state and the government is carried on in his name. He is appointed by the President of India for five years. The Governor has to act according to the advice of the Council of Ministers (Cabinet) except in so far as required under the constitution to exercise the powers at his discretion. He is vested with the power of making ordinances during the recess of the state legislature. The state Bills require the assent of the Governor and in certain cases he has powers for reserving them for consideration of the President. No Act passed without his consent becomes operative. All the powers which he enjoys will have to be exercised as the constitutional head of the state and not in his own discretion or in his individual capacity.

State Legislature: The State Legislature consists of two Houses viz., Legislative Assembly (Lower House) and Legislative Council (Upper House). The Legislative Assembly consists of elected members and one member nominated by the Governor to represent the Anglo-Indian community. In 1983, the Assembly consisted of 224 elected members who were elected through adult franchise. The term of members is five years. The Assembly sessions are presided over by the Speaker who is elected by the Assembly.

In 1956, the strength of the Legislative Council was 63. Of this, 21 were elected by the Assembly, 21 by Local bodies, 6 by registered teachers, 6 by registered graduates, and rest nominated by the Governor. In 1966, the Council's strength increased to 75, of which 25 were elected from the Legislative Assembly, 25 by local bodies, 7 by the registered graduates, 7 by registered teachers and 11 nominated by the Governor. The Council elects its own Chairman.

Council of Ministers: The Constitution provides for a Council of Ministers with the Chief Minister as the head, to aid and advise the Governor in the exercise of his functions. The Chief Minister, who is normally the leader of the majority party, is appointed by the Governor and other Ministers are appointed on Chief Minister's advice. The Council of Ministers, which is collectively called the Cabinet, consists of Cabinet Ministers, Ministers of State and Deputy Ministers.

Secretariat: The organisation of the Executive Wing of the Government under the Secretariat in old Mysore can be traced back to 1881. There were then four departmental Secretaries in the Mysore Secretariat viz., Chief Secretary to Government in the General and Revenue Department, Secretary to Government in the Public Works Department, Secretary to Government in the Education Department and the Military Secretary to the Maharaja. The Muzrai Secretariat was formed in 1891. The Maharaja reconstituted the Executive Council in 1895 and the Secretariat was reorganised by bifurcating the general and revenue departments - the Revenue department under the Chief Secretary, and the General department under the General Secretary. In 1895, the office of the Chief Secretary was abolished and another post viz., the post of the Revenue Secretary was created. The post of Chief Secretary was later revived in 1923-24.

In Madras and Bombay Presidencies, the organisation of government business under the Secretariat with its various departments except for minor changes, has remained unchanged for over a century. The Chief Secretary is the head of the State Secretariat departments. The conduct of business through manuals, instructions, standing orders was efficiently arranged and in administration, these two states came to be recognised as among the best in British administered India. Further, healthy tradition in the discharge of government business and public duties rested on the shoulders of the officers of the Indian Civil Service and the provincial service and it is primarily due to the hard work and devotion to duty and integrity of the officers that very high standards of administration were obtaining in the two Presidencies.

Kodagu, as stated earlier, was directly administered by the British with the Chief Commissioner as the head of the administration. He was assisted by the first and second Assistant Commissioners. These officials were responsible for the work of the number of departments under their charge.

The three major functionaries of the state are: (1) The Ministers; (2) The Secretary to Government; and (3) The Executive Head of the Department. The Chief Minister, the Ministers and the Secretaries are all served by the Secretariat organisation.

After the formation of the new State, next to the Chief Secretary in rank were the Development Commissoner and Ex-officio Agricultural Production Commissioner, Secretaries to Government and various executive Heads of departments. However, in 1980, a post of Additionsl Chief Secretary was created to assist the Chief Secretary, with specific terms of work allocated tc him. A second post of an Additional Chief Secretary was created and the Commissioner of Finance and Secretary to Government, Finance department, was appointed and designated as the Additional Chief Secretary.

The number of Secretariat departments has increased over the years, with the introduction of new legislative enactments, new development programmes sponsored by the Centre and the state and emphasis on emerging concerns relating to social welfare, ecology and environment, energy, science and technology, health and family welfare, women and children, education, especially primary education. It became necessary therefore to create new Secretariat departments. In 1982, there were 18 government departments. Again, between 1983 and 1996, there was an increase in the number of Secretariat departments due to reshuffle of portfolios.

As on 31st January 1997, there are 28 Secretariat Departments. They are: 1) Agriculture and Horticulture, 2) Animal Husbandary, Veterinary Services and Fisheries, 3) Co-operation, 4) Education, 5) Energy, 6) Finance, 7) Food and Civil Supplies, 8) Forest, Ecology and Environment, 9) Health and Family Welfare, 10) Home and Transport, 11) Housing, 12) Urban Development, 13) Industries and Commerce, 14) Information, Tourism and Youth Service, 15) Irrigation, 16) Kannada and Culture, 17) Labour, 18) Law, 19) Parliamentary Affairs, 20) The Legislature Secretariat, 21) Personnel and Administrative Reforms, 22) Planning, Institutional Finance and Statistics, Science and Technology 23) Public Works, 24) Revenue, 25) Rural Development and Panchayat Raj, 26) Social Welfare 27) Infrastructure, 28) Women and Child Development.

In order to provide promotional avenues to IAS officers, a few posts of Secretaries have been re-designated as Principal Secretaries to Government. Currently, the number is 8 in the rank of Additional

Secretary to Government of India. In some departments where the load is heavy there is a second Secretary known as Secretary II. Some departments have, in addition, Additional and Joint Secretaries. In all the departments, there is the Secretariat hierarchy consisting of Deputy Secretaries and Under Secretaries.

At the head of the Secretariat, the Chief Secretary is responsible for the proper and efficient running of the administrative set up in the state.

Creation of Indian Administrative Service: When India became independent in 1947, a large number of British officers of the ICS either went back to England or were given posting by the British Government in other British administered colonies. A large number of Muslim officers of ICS opted to Pakistan. Hence, a big vacuum was created in the civil service. Due to the farsighted and pragmatic decision taken by Sardar Vallabhai Patel, the Central Government announced the creation of Indian Administrative Service. The first All India competitive examination for recruitment to the service was held soon after independence and the first batch of officers joined the service in 1948. Many of them were posted to the erstwhile British administered states. In the part-B State of Mysore there was no intake of direct recruits to the State Cadre till 1951. Preference was given to the nomination to the service of the officers of Mysore Civil Service, who were found suitable. Hence, during the period 1947-51, all the IAS officers in the Part-B State were selected from the Mysore Civil Service. With the re-organisation of states, the Central Government decided on the strength of IAS cadre in the new state and a few officers both directly recruited and nominated to the service were allotted to the new cadre of Mysore state from the integrating areas. Despite the varying administrative ethos and traditions prevailing in the districts of the integrated areas, there were no problems of officers getting adjusted to the work as well as the administrative ethos of the erstwhile princlly State of Mysore.

Political Parties A crystallised party structure first appeared when the Karnataka Provincial Congress Committee (KPCC) was installed as a result of organisational changes in the Indian National Congress in 1920. It exercised jurisdiction originally over the Bombay-Karnataka and Madras-Karnataka and Kodagu regions. Its physical and political centre was Bombay—Karnataka with headquarters first at Gadag and later, at Hubli. Prior to 1956, it dominated the politics of these areas through three separate legislatures. After 1956, and by the time of the second General Elections in 1957, Karnataka Pradesh Congress Committee (KPCC) became the sole Congress Party in the new state, after incorporating the Congress units in the other two sub regions. The Hyderabad Pradesh Congress Committee had started the democratic movement in 1937. But it had a federal set up, which implied a very loose association between the three linguistic sub-units. Finally, after 1956, the KPCC became the sole dominant party in the new state.

Post Reorganisation: From 1956 to 1969, it was the undivided Indian National Congress that ruled the state. From 1969 to 1970, it was the Congress (O), one of the two breakaway parties from the original Congress. After a brief spell of non-party rule under the Governor from 1972 to 1978, the other breakaway Congress Party Congress (R) dominated. From mid 1972 till mid 1979, it was the Congress (I) which governed the state.

But, in 1979, the ruling Congress (I), after some dissidents left it, got converted into Congress (U) under the leadership of Sri Devaraj Urs, who continued to be the Chief Minister of the state. Early in January 1980, as a result of the Lok Sabha elections, the state reverted to Congress (I) on the basis of massive defection back into the party. This domination of the Congress (I) ended with the election to the Assembly in 1983, when the Janata Party came to power and Sri Ramakrishna Hegde became the Chief Minister. However, due to imposition of the President's rule, there was another election to the State Assembly in 1985 when the Janata Party was again returned to power with an overwhelming majority under the Chief Ministership of Sri Ramakrishna Hegde. However, the wind turned in favour of the Indian National Congress in the Legislative Assembly elections when the party under the leadership of Sri Veerendra Patil captured 176 seats out of 226 seats in 1989. Subsequently, there was a change of leadership and Sri Bangarappa became the Chief Minister. In the elections to the Legislative Assembly in 1994, the Janata Dal came to power capturing 116 seats out of 224 under the Chief Ministership of Sri H.D. Deva Gowda.

The Janata Government is still in power though with Sri J.H.Patel as the Chief Minister consequent on Sri H.D.Deve Gowda being sworn in as the Prime Minister of India on 1st June 1996.

From the information given above, it is obvious that in the early decades and after the second general elections, the political party system of Karnataka was predominantly a one party dominant type. However, there has been, due to various political and other socio-economic developments, rise in the popularity of the Janata Dal, which has been twice in power. What is also significant is the emergence of Janata Dal in 1994 elections as the largest party owing primarily to the formation of a breakaway independent party known as Karnataka Congress Party by Sri S. Bangarappa, which captured 10 seats in the elections.

In December 1996, the Congress, in view of the factionalism and infighting in the Indian National Congress , demanded the resignation of Sri P.V.Narasimha Rao as Congres President and leader of the Congres Parliamentary Party. With the nomination of Sri Sitaram Kesri as the Congress President and the merger of the splinter parties founded by Congress defectors, it is difficult to predict the political scenario of the state when the next general elections to the Legislative Assembly are held in 1999. Currently, the three main political parties which have an all India base are the Janata Dal, the Indian National Congress and the BJP. All other parties, which contested elections have not fared well. It is noteworthy that neither the CPI (M) nor the CPI has secured any seat in the elections held to the State Assembly from 1989 to 1994. Unlike in some other states, no regional party has been able to play any positive role in the state.

2. Revenue Administration: The revenue administration had come to occupy till independence, a unique place in the history of Indian administration. Whether it was under the ancient Hindu Kings or later, under the Mughul rulers or during the British administration, land revenue was the major source of income of the government. Though, prior to 1799, different systems of land revenue fixation were followed, on the restoration of Mysore state to the Wodeyar royal family in 1799, Dewan Purnaiah brought about some order in the revenue system by rationalisation and stabilisation of various rates of assessment and bringing the whole system of revenue administration under the direct management of the government. During Sir Mark Cubbon's administration of Mysore, from 1834 and 1861, the system followed in revenue matters was the ryotwari system that was laid down in British provinces. During Lewin Bowring's tenure of office (1862-1870), a major landmark was the promulgation based on the **Bombay Acts I of 1865 and IV of 1868** with suitable changes and by framing of the Survey and Settlement Rules. Based on the experience gained in the implementation of the scheme, the government decided to codify the land revenue system and it was decided to base the codification on the **Bombay Land Revenue Code** which was found suitable. Accordingly, the draft of the **Mysore Land Revenue Code** was examined, debated both by the officers and in the Mysore Representative Assembly and the final regulations called **the Mysore Land Revenue Code of 1888** was promulgated in 1899 during Sir K. Sheshadri Iyer's tenure as Dewan. Further, amendments to this Code took place on several occasions. The rules were framed under the **Land Revenue Code** and in August 1902, the Land Revenue Commissioner was appointed as the head of the Revenue department.

In the Bombay Presidency, the principle of land settlement possessed a definite statute which regulated survey assessment and other matters. In addition, it had reached the stage at which first re-settlement had been completed under Section 48 of the **Bombay Land Revenue Code of 1879.** Over a period of time, based on periodic survey and re-settlements, the assessment of land revenue for different types of lands was defined.

In Bellary district of the erstwhile Madras state, the ryotwari system was introduced and here also, based on the changes made during re-settlements, the administration of land revenue stablised. The owner of the land was given patta, which indicated the extent and assessment of each survey number and the portion of land that was in his occupation.

In Dakshina Kannada district, the ryotwari system was established and based on survey and settlement carried out during the last decades of 19th century, and in the first decade of this century, two surcharges were levied on lands - one, on all lands at a uniform rate of 12 per cent, and the other, on large holdings paying an assessment of over Rs. 500/-. The surcharges continued even after reorganisation of the state till the end of 1960-61.

In Kodagu, which was under the direct administration of the British, a summary settlement was first undertaken in 1896 and another survey was done between the years 1907 and 1912. The lands were divided into two main categories, namely, those held by private individuals and those held by the government. Private lands were divided into four main classes and varying rates of assessment were levied depending upon the nature of the crop grown on the land.

In the Hyderabad-Karnataka area, the land records system was reformed in 1919, on the basis prevailing in British India. The record of rights was first introduced in Hyderabad State in 1936 and the Land Records Department with a Commissioner was set up in 1937. The rate of assessment varied according to the category of land, viz., dry, wet or garden. The two Departments of Land Records and Record of Rights were amalgamated in 1945.

Post 1956-Reforms in Land Revenue Administration

(a) Enactment of the Mysore Land Revenue Act 1964: After the formation of the new State of Mysore, the government took a landmark decision to codify the entire land revenue system and introduce a uniform Land Revenue Code for the state. Since different land revenue systems were prevalent in different parts of the state, the government, based on the recommendations made by the Deputy Commissioner of Settlement, enacted the **Mysore Land Revenue Act of 1964** which introduced uniformity in the procedures of the settlement throughout the state. A fresh revenue settlement was carried out and enforced from 1965 with the new uniform systems.

The Code set out the principles for zoning for settlement operations, fixation of standard rates, grouping of areas, maintenance of land revenue accounts including annual accounts, jamabandhi, realisation of land revenue and remissions etc.

(b) Land Reforms: There was a pressing demand for examining afresh the tenancy problems in detail and for adoption of a uniform measure throughout Karnataka. Therefore, a Committee called the Mysore Tenancy and Agriculture Land Laws Committee was appointed in 1957 under the Chairmanship of Sri B. D. Jatti. This Committee went into the question of fixation of rent, security of tenure, right to resumption of land by landholders for personal cultivation, right to purchase of land by tenants and payment of compensation to landlords, ceilings and landholdings and other related matters. The Committee submitted its report in September 1957. **The Karnataka Land Reforms Bill** in 1958 was referred for examination to the Joint Select Committee and a Bill was finally enacted in 1962. But, its implementation was held up as certain amendments to certain provisions of the Act were needed. It was only in 1965 that the amendments were enacted and it was brought into force in the state with effect from 2nd October 1965.

The enactment has made comprehensive provisions in respect of tenant's rights, ceiling limits of existing holdings and future acquisitions and payment of compensation. Based on the experience gained in implementing the act, the **Karnataka Land Reforms (Amendment) Act 1973** was enacted with radical changes made in the 1961 Act. The Act terminated the landlord tenant relationship, provided for ownership of land by the tenants, and also set up Land Tribunals for taking decision on tenancy and the eligibility of payment for occupancy rights. The Act also provided for the mode of rent fixation and compensation payable to landlords, payment of premium by tenants and also ceiling of landholdings and distribution of surplus lands to specified categories of landless people. By 1981, due to the initiatives taken by the government, 90 per cent of land reforms work had been completed.

(c) Karnataka Prevention of Fragmentation and Consolidation of Holdings Act 1 1964: The third landmark in the revenue administration was the enactment of the legislation to prevent sub-division and fragmentation of holdings. It had long been recognised that one of the causes responsible for making agriculture an unprofitable industry was the sub-division of land and fragmentation of holdings. The first step to prevent fragmentation of holdings and promote consolidation was taken in the **Bombay State when Bombay Prevention of Fragmentation and Consolidation of the Holdings Act** was enacted in 1947. Thereafter, only in 1964, the **Karnataka Prevention of Fragmentation and Consolidation of Holdings Act 1964** was introduced throughout Karnataka.

d) Abolition of Inams/Jahgirs: Practically, in all the areas forming the new state, various categories of persons who rendered services to the state or village community were granted lands. Lands were also granted for religious, charitable or other purposes. These lands, known as Jodi, Vatans, Inams or Jahgirs, were continued to be enjoyed on a hereditary basis. These inam lands continued till independence and one of the major reforms in the post-independence period and especially after the formation of the new state under the Indian Constitution was to abolish the various classes of inams, irrespective of whether they were granted for services rendered to the state or in the village to the hereditary village officers known as Shanbog, Patel, Deshpande, Kulkarni, Village Karnam or Village Munsiff.

In erstwhile Mysore state, **the Mysore (Personal and Miscellaneous) Inams Abolition Act 1954** and **Mysore Religious and Charitable Inams ACt 1955** were passed. In Hyderabad-Karnataka area, **the Abolition of Jahgir Regulation of 1949** came into force on 15th August 1949. In Madras area, **the Madras Estates Abolition and Conversion Ryotwari Act** was passed in October 1948. The inams to which this Act did not apply in Bellary District and Kollegal Taluk of Coimbatore district were abolished by the **Karnataka Certain Inams Abolition Act of 1977.**

In Bombay-Karnataka area, the various types of inams, including the two Saramjams of Hebli and Gajendragad were abolished by three Acts **(1) Bombay Personal Inams Abolition Act of 1952, (2) Bombay Service Inams (Useful to the Community) Abolition Act of 1953, and (3) Bombay Parganas and Kulkarni Vatans Act of 1950.** Legislation was also passed to abolish inams/jahgirs extending to the small princely states which merged in the districts of the Bombay-

Karnataka and in Bellary district. It can be mentioned that there were no zamindari estates or inams in Dakshina Kannada district as they had been resumed earlier by Hyder Ali and Tipu Sultan.

Field Level Administrative Organisation

Administration Divisions: In order to establish an effective system of administration in the field, the state, after reorganisation was divided into four divisions, viz., 1) Bangalore Divison with Kolar, Tumkur, Shimoga, Chitradurga and Bangalore districts; 2) Mysore Divison with Mandya, Mysore, Kodagu, Dakshina Kannada, Chikamagulur and Hassan districts; 3) Belgaum Division, with Uttara Kannada, Dharwad, Belgaum and Bijapur districts; and 4) Gulbarga Division with Bellary, Raichur, Gulbarga and Bidar districts.

The revenue Division is headed by the Divisional Commissioner, the district by the Deputy Commissioner, the sub-division by the Assistant Commissioner, and the taluk by the Tahsildar. Under the Tahsildar, villages are grouped into Revenue Circles under Revenue Inspectors. In the village, there is the usual set up of village accountant and village patel.

Though the Divisional Commissioner is primarily the head of revenue administration in the Division, he was also till the establishment of Panchayat Raj institutions, the chief co-ordinating authority for all departments at the divisional level. He was also the sanctioning authority for various programmes and works. However, after the introduction of **Panchayat Raj Act 1993,** he is no longer directly associated with development administration.

District: The district has been, right from the mid 19th century, when the area acquired by the British was administered by the East India Company from 1765 to 1858, the key administrative unit of the field of the revenue and general administration in India. During the administration of the East India Company, the district collector's precursor was the "Supervisor", who was appointed when there were problems in the dual administration set up by Robert Clive, in which 'natives' were utilised to collect land revenue. The Supervisor's tasks included preparation of the rent roll, regulating revenue and supervising collection, investigating all titles to land and administering justice. Above all, he was to be the friend of the owner/cultivator of the land. However, the supervisors of the East India Company indulged in private trade and did not perform their duties satisfactorily. In 1771, the Company became `the Dewan' and opted to collect taxes directly. In 1772, Warren Hastings designated the post `district collector'. From 1787, the powers of administration in revenue, civil justice and magistracy were fully and unambiguously vested with the Collector and the district became the unit of revenue, police and judicial administration. The district collector became very powerful. In 1783, Lord Cornwallis divested the Collector of judicial powers and made him only the collecting agency. However, after the **Regulations of 1813 and 1814,** the Collector's position as the authority for both revenue collection and as a magistrate of civil justice returned. In spite of minor changes introduced in some states, based on local situations, the Collector by the mid 19th century became the principal agent of the government in the district. He came to be recognised as the `Maa Baap' of the district, to whom practically all sections of society whether living in the towns or villages, looked up for rendering justice either formally within the framework of the law or informally as an impartial administrator in whom people had trust and people voluntarily sought his decision in settling family disputes or personal problems.

In Madras and Bombay Presidencies, the District Collector was till the early years of this century, mostly a British Officer borne on the Indian Civil Service, which had come to be recognised as one of the most efficient civil services in the world. In fact, it was called the 'steel frame' of the Indian administration. In the early decades of this century, with the induction of Indian officers in the Indian Civil Services, a number of districts in the two Presidencies and elsewhere came to be manned by Indian officers.

In erstwhile Mysore state, a beginning was made during the tenure of Bowring to reorganise the district administration on the pattern of the administration in British Indian Provinces. In 1861, the head of the district was known as Deputy Superintendent. In 1869, he was designated as Deputy Commissioner of the District. In 1879, the posts of Commissioners of Divisions were abolished and there was only the Deputy Commissioner of the districts and below him the Assistant Commissioner in charge of sub-division and the Amildar in charge of Taluk.

In the erstwhile Hyderabad state, there were five revenue sub-divisions and 17 districts. The head of the division was the Subedar, the district head was the Talukdar and under him, there were sub-divisional officers known as 2nd or 3rd Talukdars on the basis of their grade and service. The Tahsildar was in charge of Tehsil (same as Taluk). After the police action in 1948, the head of the district was designated as the District Collector and under him, there was an Assistant/Deputy Collector in charge of the Division and Tahsildar in charge of Taluk.

So far as Kodagu is concerned, from 1834 when the administration of Kodagu was taken over by the British, till the year of independence, it was directly administered through a Commissioner who, in 1869, was redesignated as the Chief Commissioner. He was assisted by a 1st and 2nd Assistant Commissioner. It is interesting to note that the office of the Chief Commissioner functioned from Bangalore till 1840, when it was shifted to Madikere.

No. of Districts: The number of districts till July 1997 in the state were 20. They were 8 between 1862 and 1939 and 9 till 1956, when the States reorganisation took place. Since then there were 19 till the Bangalore District was bifurcated into Bangalore Rural and Bangalore Urban Districts in 1986. In August 1997, the number of districts increased to 27 with the creation of 7 new districts.

Size: In terms of size and population, the districts in Karnataka vary widely. Bijapur, with an area of 17,000 square kilometers is the largest in size, while the Bangalore Urban District with 2,100 square kilometers and Kodagu with 4,102 square kilometers are the smallest urban and rural districts respectively. The Bangalore Urban district with its population of 4,839,000, is the most populous district in Karnataka. Among rural districts, while Belgaum with a population of 3,584,000 is the biggest, Kodagu with a population of 489,000 is the smallest (DES 1995:11)

In terms of the number of sub-divisions, taluks, hoblis, villages and towns and corporations into which the district is sub-divided for administrative purposes, the districts in Karnataka vary much. In the number of sub-divisions, while Dharward and Bijapur have 4 sub-divisions each, Kodagu has only one.

In the number of taluks, Dharwad with 17 taluks is the biggest, whereas Kodagu with only 3 Taluks is the smallest. In the number of hoblis (Circles of revenue villages), while Kolar district stands first with 53, Kodagu with 16 hoblis is the lowest. In the number of villages, Tumkur district tops with 2,537 inhabited and 181 uninhabited villages, Kodagu with only 291 inhabited and 5 uninhabited villages is again at the bottom. In terms of towns and urban agglomerations, while Belgaum and Dharwad, each with 20 of them, are on the top, Bidar, with only 5, is at the bottom, and, in terms of the number of Municipalities and Corporations, Dharwad district with 19 of them is on the top, and Kodagu with only one Municipality is again at the bottom (DES 1995:12)

The Deputy Commissioner who is the head of the district administration is the kingpin of the revenue and general administration in the district. His range of functions is very extensive. As the revenue head of district, he is the chief representive of the government. He has played and continues to play even now today a prominent and pivotal roles, in all aspects of administration. His main function may be broadly classified as 1) Revenue, 2) Law and Order, 3) Development, 4) Co-ordination, and 5) Public Welfare, in general.

As the District Magistrate, he is responsible for the maintenance of law and order within the district. He exercises functions under various enactments of the state such as those dealing with distribution of food, essential commodities, excise, elections, municipal and development work, issues of licence for arms, explosives etc. Even after the advent of Panchayat Raj, he played a very constructive and co-ordinating role as the Chairman of the District Development council set up under the **Karnataka Local Boards and Village Panchayat Act 1958.** In fact, through the decades, his moral authority as the co-ordinating head enabled him not only to assist the district officers of other departments in implementation of the programme but also in taking up with the heads of departments at the state level and Secretaries to Government, issues and problems of those departments for the purposes of assisting them in getting sanctions or approvals to schemes/programmes. Subsequently, under the **Karnataka Zilla Panchayat, Taluk Samithis, Mandal Panchayat and Nyaya Panchayats Act of 1983,** the Deputy Commissioner has ceased to be in charge of development administration in the district. However, he continues to play a useful supporting role in assisting the Zilla Panchayat and the Chief Executive of Zilla Panchayat in all matters which need the help of the revenue administration for implementing development works. His moral authority even today for doing public good is immense and instances are not wanting of dynamic Deputy Commissioners who have taken initiative and interest in specific areas of development administration and earned a good name for themselves and the government.

Under the Deputy Commissioner there is an Assistant Comissioner who is in charge of a Revenue sub-division comprising of a number of taluks. He is the appellate authority as well as supervisory officer in respect of taluks under him. Under the Assistant Commissioner is the Tahsildar, who is in charge of the Taluk and below him is the Revenue Inspector who supervises the work of village officers of group of villages placed under his charge. In the village there is now a stipendiary Village Accountant and Village Patel.

It may be stated that though the revenue administration in terms of residuary work such as collection of land revenue, maintenance of the record of rights, settlement of land disputes are still the important functions of the principal officers connected with land revenue administration, viz., Deputy Commissioner, Assistant Commissioner and Tahsildar, land revenue as a percentage of total revenue of the state has become insignificant compared to other principal sources such as excise and sales tax.

District Reorganisation: In India, after indpendence and especially after the reorganisation of the states in 1956, reorganisation of the districts in many states has been taking place with emphasis on bifurcation of large districts for more effective general and development administration. For example, in Tamil Nadu, Bihar, Madhya Pradesh, districts have been reorganised with the creation of new districts, sub-divisions and taluks. In Karnataka, there has been demand for a long time for the reorganisation of the districts having regard to their geographical size, population, proximity of the people to the administrative headquarters, and the administrative difficulties in running the districts etc. It was felt that smaller and compact districts would go a long way in ensuring effective general and development administration.

In Karnataka, two regional planners, viz., V.L.S. Prakasa Rao and L.S. Bhatt were the first to suggest in 1950 the reorganisation of states in terms of the planning region for better implementation of development programmes. Later, the Government of Karnataka appointed three Committees to study the reorganisation of the districts and taluks. They are: 1) Vasudeva Rao Committee in 1963 which submitted its report in 1975; 2) Hundekar Committee in 1984 which submitted its report in 1986; and 3) The Guddigowdar Committee in August 1986 which submitted its report in June 1987. All these Committees recommended reorganisation of districts, and sub-divisions and taluks and increasing their number as under:-

District Reorganisation Committees Reports at a Glance Abstract

Si. No.	Unit Nos.	Existing Nos.	Vasudev Rao Committee	Hundekar Committee	Guddigowdar Committee
1	Taluks	175	186	202	205
2	Sub-divisions	49	56	70	70
3	Districts	19	21	27	28
4	Divisions	4	4	7	7

Source: GOK 1987:597-600

The new divisions and districts out of the 28 suggested by the Guddigowdar Committee were:-

1) Nanjangud/Chamarajanagar, 2) Udupi, 3) Bangalore City, 4) Davanagere, 5) Bagalkot, 6) Gadag, 7) Gokak, 8) Koppal and 9) Yadgir.

The additional 3 Divisions suggested were 1) Shimoga, 2) Dharwad and 3) Mangalore. The number of sub-divisions and taluks suggested by them is large as may be seen from the abstract.

There was no doubt an urgent need for reorganisation of the districts as some of them were geographically very large, a more compact and mangeable size of district is conducive to more efficient general and developmental administration.

The issue of district reorganisation has been hanging fire during the last two decades and no political party in power has taken a bold policy decision to find an acceptable solution to this issue. In fact, a convenient strategy of deferring a decision was taken by appointing two committees. There was a lot of discussion in the legislature on the action proposed to be taken by the Government of Karnataka on this issue and the legislators and politicians hailing from the districts which are proposed for reorganisation have, on their part, added fuel to the fire by mobilising public opinion at the field level. Unfortunativ, the statement made recently by the Chief Minister Sri J.H. Patel on 10th December 96. on the occasion of the completion of the two years of Janta Dal's government in the state that there would be no problems in creating five new districts viz., Chamarajanagar, Davanagere, Koppla, Gadag and Bagalkot, and the names of the other two districts would be announced later had provoked both controversy and violence in Haveri and Gadag.

The delay in taking a final decision only complicated the problem. In view of the pressing demands from legislators and ornanisations representing various interests in the proposed new districts, the Government issued the draft notifications in June 1997 inviting objections and suggestions for the creation of the new districts of Chamrajanagar, Davanagere, Bagalkote, Gadag, Koppal, Haveri, and Udupi. After consideration of the objections and suggestions, the State government issued the final notification on 2nd August 1997 creating the new districts with headquarters at Chamrajanagar, Davanagere, Bagalkote, Gadag, Haveri and Udupi and second notification on 4th August 1997 creation the new district of Koppal. Government has not taken the final decision on the creation of new districts from out of Belgaum and Gulbarga districts to the opposition from legislators and other organisations. It is necessary that a decision is taken room on the creation of the new districts out of Belgaum and Gulbarga districts. It may be mentioned that the High Court granted a stay against inclusion of Sindhanoor Taluk in the new Koppal District. Similarly, a stay has been obtained from the High Court against the inclusion of Channagiri and Honnali Taluks in the new Davanagere district.

The Government has already appointed the Deputy Commissioners of the new districts. The Supertendentants of Police have also been appointed. However, as regards the Zilla Panchayats the Government has decided to constitute them for the new districts in the financial year commencing, 1st April 1998. The creation of the new districts will bring in its wake transitional problems in the areas of revenue, law and order and development administration. It is hoped that within a couple of years, the administration departments and panchayat raj institutions get geared to the task of providing efficient administration in the new districts.

3. Police Administration: In a report given by Sir Mark Cubbon in 1838, it is said that under the rulers of Mysore, the duties of police were performed by Talwars, Totis, Nirgantis, Kavalgars, Kattabidi Peons, Paikas, Umbilidars, Amargars, Hulagavals, Ankamalas and Kalla Koramars, Patels and Shanbhogs and these denominations were continued with little variations under the rule of Tipu Sultan and Purnaiah in princely Mysore.

During Dewan Purnaiah's tenure, Kandachar peons were appointed for doing police work. In 1834, the Kandachar peons were made exclusively police peons though employed in rotation in the collection of land revenue.

The first step towards reforms was the introduction of the **Police Act of 1861** to Bangalore district and the appointment of an officer of the Madras Police to be in charge of the district. The task of remodelling the village police was begun by government on the scheme drawn up by Mr. Mangles, Judicial Commissioner.

In 1856, the Judicial Commissioner was appointed and he became the ex-officio Inspector General of Police. In the districts, the Deputy Commissioner was the ex-officio head of police. In 1879, the Chief Commissioner was in charge of the police.

By January, 1881, the reorganisation of police had been carried out and the Chief Commissioner issued a circular conveying instructions as to the scope and extent of the powers to be exercised by the Deputy Commissioners and Amildars.

The recruitment to the post of Asst. Superintendent of Police in erstwhile Mysote state was through nomination. At the district level subordinate police officers were appointed by the Superintendent of Police.

In Hyderabad-Karnataka area, there was no well organised police force till 1853. In 1856, regular police was raised and placed under the revenue authority. In 1869, a special Sadar-Ul-Moham or Police Minister was appointed for Hyderabad state. In the state, the recruitment for the post of Assistant Superintendent of Police was through nomination and the subordinate police at the sub-district levels were also by nomination. There were two separate police forces functioning, that is, the Diwani Police and the Jahgir Police. The Diwani Police was of the Nizam government's, while Jahgiri police was of the individual Jahgirdars. Gulbarga was the divisional headquarters for the four districts with Gulbarga, Bidar, Raichur and Osmanabad. After the accession of Hyderabad State to the Indian Union in 1948, Jahgirs were abolished and the entire police administration was taken over by the Diwani Police.

From 1948, the princely state of Hyderabad adopted the pattern of police administration prevailing in other states of the country. There was an I.G.P. assisted by a Deputy Inspector General of the division, Deputy Superintendents of Police of the district, Assistant Supertendent/ Deputy Supertendent at the sub-division and Circle Inspector, Sub-Inspector at the Police Stations. Gulbarga had a DIG in charge of Raichur, Gulbarga and Bidar districts.

In Bombay and Madras-Karnataka areas, as in other states, directly under British administration, importance was given to the organisation of police administration during the 19th century, since law and order was the primary concern of the British Government. Hence, as in the areas of general and revenue administration, the British Government recognised the need to have an organised and disciplined police force at all levels - the State, Divisional, District and Taluk and the Village.

In Bombay-Karnataka area, in 1827, a regular police force was organised under the administrative control of the district magistrate with the **Bombay Regulation XII of 1827.** Under this Act, the police administration was reconstituted, defining the powers and functions of the police officers. This Act was, however, repealed by the **Bombay Police Act of 1890,** which provided in more exhaustive terms, the rules governing the performance of police duties and maintenance of the police force. **The Act of 1890** continued to be in force till 1951, when a consolidated and comprehensive legislation known as the **Bombay Police Act of 1951** came into being. Till the reorganisation of the state, **the Act of 1951** was in force in the four districts of Bombay-Karnataka area. Under that set up, there was an IGP in Bombay, a Deputy IGP in charge of the Belgaum Division, District Superintendent of Police in the district, Assistant Superintendent/Deputy Superintendent of Police in the sub-division and Circle Inspector and Sub-Inspector and sub-ordinate police at the Police Stations. Prior to the integration, the District Superintendents and police forces of the district were under the control of District Magistrate. All questions of policy and of the administration of the law within the district were administered by the District Magistrate.

In Madras-Karnataka area, prior to British rule, the police administration was the ancient Kaval system (watch system). Under this, Talaiyaris (watchmen) in each village sub-ordinate to the Kavalgars (head watchmen) in charge of group of villages were appointed by local Chieftains. However, after the advent of British rule in the Presidency, a uniform pattern of administration was introduced with an Inspector General of Police at the state level, Divisional Inspector General of Police at the division, District Supertendent of Police at the district, and Assistant Commissioners/Deputy Superintendent of Police at the sub-division and with Inspector, Sub-Inspector and Head Constable at the police station.

Recruitment to Police Service: It may be mentioned that even prior to the formation of the Indian Police Service after independence, there was, like the Indian Civil Service, a service known as Indian Police (IP) to which recuritment was made by the British Government. Normally, the post of Inspector General of Police/Deputy Inspectors General of Police and Superintendent of Police were held by the officers of Indian Police (IP). After independence, all these posts were encadred statewise for officers of the Indian Police Service.

Enactment of the Police Act of 1963: As different Police Acts were in force in the territories forming part of the new state of Mysore, it became necessary to remove this diversity in police administration and to ensure uniformity by the enactment of a common Police Act. Hence, the **Police Act of 1963** was enacted replacing as many as 19 legislations enumerated in schedule IV of the said Act. The Act was brought into force on 2nd April 1965. A Police Manual was compiled in three volumes. **The Act of 1963** deals with regulation, control and discipline of police, police regulations, special measures for maintenance of public order and safety of the state, dispersal of gangs and harmful persons convicted of certain offences, executive powers and duties of police, prevention of offences, punishments, State Reserve Police etc.

4. Judicial Administration: After the takeover of the administration of the erstwhile princely State by the British in 1831, the following

Courts were established: (1) The Amils, (2) Town Munsiffs, (3) Sadar Munsiff, (4) The Principal Sadar Munsiff, and (5) The Court of European Superintendents. From the decision of the Principal Sadar Munsiff appeal lay to the Superintendent of the Division or to the Huzur Adalat.

By 1862, the Huzur Adalat and the Munsiff's Court were abolished and the judicial hierarchy consisted of the Judicial Commissioner, the Superintendents of Divisions, the Deputy Superintendents and Amildars of Taluks. As regards criminal justice, the Judicial Commissioner, the Superintendents of Dewans, Deputy Superintendents of Districts and Amildars of taluks were conferred with criminal jurisdiction also. **The Criminal Procedure code (Act of 1872)** was introduced in the state. Thereafter, in 1899, the Munsiffs were invested with the power of Taluk Magistrates. The hierarchy of criminal courts established were Session Judges and Assistant Judges, District Magistrates and Magistrates. In 1884, the Mysore Chief Court was constituted and later, renamed as High Court in the same year by the **Mysore Chief Court Amending Regulation of 1884.**

In Bombay and Madras States where the British judicial system prevailed, there were District Judges, Civil Judges and Munsiffs for civil matters and the Service Judges and Magistrates for criminal matters. Village Committees dispensed with petty crimes and disputes. There were High Court, Federal Court and Privy Council in England as Courts of Appeal.

In Hyderabad-Karnataka area, a scheme of separation of judiciary from the executive was implemented in 1922, Munsiff Magistrates were appointed for each taluk with magisterial powers on the criminal side. For the whole area of Gulbarga division, there was only a District Court presided over by a District Judge. In April 1951, a District and Sessions Court for each district was established. The **Hyderabad Civil Court Act** was enacted in 1954 and Courts of (1) District Judge or Additional District Judge, (2) Subordinate Judge, and (3) Munsiff or Additional Munsiff were established.

Post 1956: High Court: After the unification, the High Court came to be constituted with effect from 1-11-1956 under Section-52 of **States Reorganisation Act.** The High Court has, under the Constitution, extra-ordinary jurisdiction, viz., (1) power to issue writs for enforcement of fundamental and other legal rights, and (2) power of superintendence over all Courts and Tribunals in the state. In addition, it is the highest court of criminal and civil appeal and revision.

Civil Courts Act of 1964: After the new state came into being there was a need to introduce uniformity of the civil judicial system and the **Civil Courts Act 1964** was enacted. Under the provisions of this enactment, a three-tier system of Courts with uniform designation was provided for, viz., (1) District Court for each District, (2) Civil Judge's Court for a District or a smaller area as may be provided for, and (3) Court of Munsiff.

Karnataka Small Causes Courts Act 1964: With a view to enacting uniform law relating to the courts of small causes in the new state, the **Karnataka Small Causes Courts Act 1964** was enacted. Under the Act, a Judicial Officer of the rank of Civil Judge is required to be nominated as a Small Causes Judge.

Criminal Procedure Code 1973: The set up of courts and criminal procedures established under the **Criminal Procedure Code** continued in the new state until it was replaced by the **Criminal Procedure Code of 1973.** Under this Code, besides the High Court, the class of criminals courts provided for are; (1) The Court of Sessions, (2) Judicial Magistrate of First Class, and in Metropolitan areas, Metropolitan Magistrates and Judicial Magistrates of the second class.

Special Tribunals: Apart from the hierarchy of Civil Courts invested with the jurisdiction to try ordinary civil cases, having regard to the various types of cases coming under innumerable socio-economic legislation enacted by the legislature in the implementation of the Directive Principle of State Policy, special tribunals were constituted with the exclusive jurisdiction to try certain types of cases in order to ensure speedy determination of claims under the respective laws. Examples are: Land Tribunals, Labour Courts, Karnataka Appellate

Tribunal, Karnataka Administrative Tribunal, Consumer Redressal Forums, etc.

The Adovcate General is the Chief Legal Advisor and Adovcate for the state. There is a Directorate of Prosecutions functioning with Prosecutors, Asst. Public Prosecutors assisting at the taluk level in respect of the government cases. Lok Ayuktha (1986) (formerly Vigilance Commission founded in 1948) looks into the cases against the public servants.

Since 40 per cent of the total number of civil cases arising in the state are from Bangalore, it was considered necessary to have a two-tier system for the purpose of speedy disposal of cases. Accordingly, the **Bangalore City Civil Courts Act 1980** was enacted. Under the Act, in the Metropolitan City of Bangalore, City Civil Courts were established.

As on 31-3-1992, there were 24 Judges in the High Court, 35 District Judges including Additional Judges, two Judges of Family Courts, 73 Civil Judges, 20 Judges of Small Causes Courts, 209 Munsiffs, 35 District and Sessions Judges, 28 Metropolitian Magistrates and 247 Magistrates in the state in various courts. The total sanctioned strength of staff in the High Court was 1,117, and Subordinate Courts was 10,506, as on March 92.

As in 1992-93, the total number of Civil cases for disposal in the High Court was 150,510 and of which, 32,808 cases were disposed off, and out of 5,562 criminal cases for disposal, 3,014, cases were disposed off, similarly, 625,689 Civil cases were to be disposed of in 1992-93 in all other courts in the state, of which 179,139 cases were disposed off. Out of 544,242 criminal cases, 282,805 cases were disposed off. In addition, in Bangalore City, as in 1992-93, 134,810 Civil cases were to be disposed off, of which 48,272 cases were disposed and out of 366,311 criminal cases, 101,086 cases were disposed.

There are about 10,000 advocates in the state of whom about 40 per cent are in Bangalore City. There are the Advocate's Associations and Bar Council of India, Karnataka Branch, both with Bangalore as their Central office.

REFERENCES

Directorate of Economics and Statistics (DES) (1995). **Karnataka at a Glance.** Bangalore: Government of Karnataka.

Government of India (1992). **Karnataka State Gazetter.** Part I. .Bangalore: Government of Karnataka.

Government of India (1993). **Karnataka State Gazetter**. Part II. .Bangalore: Government of Karnataka.

II

DECENTRALISATION AND LOCAL GOVERNMENT

1
PANCHAYAT RAJ IN KARNATAKA

- M. Umapathy and
S. Ramanathan

Karnataka's Panchayat Raj model system has been recognised as one of the best models in the country which can be taken as a suggestive model for other states with a leverage to permit modifications in each state, depending on its requirements. The objective is to carve out a third tier of government, viz., district government through the enactment of the **Karnataka Panchayat Act 1993**, consequent on the 73rd Amendment to the Constitution of India. With the enactment of the Act, the foundation has been laid for the effective functioning of the three-tiers of the system, viz., Zilla Panchayat (ZP), Taluk Panchayat (TP), and Village Panchayat (VP). It must be said that from 1959 when the **Karnataka Local Boards and Village Panchayats Act** was enacted to 1993 when the **Karnataka Panchayat Act** was enacted, the movement for democratic decentralisation has faced many problems and hurdles such as inadequate transfer of functions or finances, lack of political will to establish statutory elected ZPs, postponement of elections, appointment of official administrators, withdrawal of powers and functions and the lukewarm and often negative attitude of different political parties in power either in the state or in the Centre. Some of these factors have been referred to at the appropriate places in this chapter. In spite of these negative factors what has finally emerged under the **Act of 1993** is a Panchayat Raj system whose constituent units are conceived as units of government and thus giving concrete shape to the concept of democratic decentralisation from bottom to top, viz., from the Gram Sabha (Village level) to the Lok Sabha (Parliament.)

Act of 1959 : Soon after the new state of Karnataka was formed in 1956, the Balwant Rai Mehta Committee submitted its epoch making report in 1957 on democratic decentralisation. The Committee made out a strong case for the establishment of Panchayat Raj Institutions (PRIs). The Government of Karnataka, in pursuance of the report, enacted the **Mysore Village Panchayats and Local Boards Act** in 1959 under which a three-tier structure was introduced, viz., directly elected bodies at the village and taluk levels and indirectly constituted body at the district level with the objective of transferring power and responsibility to these institutions and to achieve certain well defined objectives of planned programme.

Under this Act, a Village Panchayat (VP) was constituted for every village or a group of villages with an average population of 2,500. The members of the VP were directly elected. Constitution of Town Panchayats, as a part of rural local self-government, was a salient feature of the Act. There was a reservation for SCs and STs and for women. The VP discharged two types of functions, namely, obligatory and dicretionery. The VP received 30 per cent of land revenue collection of the village and 10 per cent of the same as discretionery grants. VP was also empowered to levy tax on lands, fees on bus stands, markets, cartstands etc. The VP performed limited municipal functions and they had also limited resources.

In every Taluk, there was a Taluk Development Board (TDB) whose members were also directly elected. The number of members ranged from 11 to 19. The Board also had obligatory and discretionery functions.

In the VP and TDB, the members elected the office bearers. The Members of the State Legislature and the Members of the Parliament had a right to vote but not to hold office.

The District Development Council (DDC) was a body consisting of the official, the nominated and indirectly elected members. The Deputy Commissioner of the district was the ex-officio Chairman of the Council. The members consisted of members of the State Legislature/Parliament and Presidents of TDBs. There was a provision to nominate one SC or one ST member and a woman member to the DDC.

The TDB was empowered to levy surcharge on stamp duty. The government transferred 50 per cent of land revenue collected in the local areas and 10 per cent of the total collection in the state to the TDBs and VPs. But, in view of the low rates of land revenue and concessions of various kinds, these institutions did not have adequate funds. They had only limited fiscal independence and most of these funds came from the government.

It may be stated that the PRIs set up under this Act did not fully conform to the model suggested by the Balwant Rai Mehta report. Both the TDB and DDC were indirectly constituted and the middle-tier was constituted not at the block level but at the taluk level, mostly on grounds of administrative convenience.

The evaluation studies conducted at that time showed that the TDBs functioned reasonably well within the ambit of the functions transferred to them and the funds available. They served as good training grounds for a new cadre of elected non-officials who, subsequently, also became members of State Legislature and other bodies. Many of them demonstrated qualities of leadership and administrative competence in planning and implementation of development programmes. However, it was apparent that the full-potential of the PRIs could not be developed due to inadequate transfer of functions and finances and also, often, the lack of political support, lack of planning expertise and organisations.

Following the death of Pandit Jawaharlal Nehru in 1964, there appears to have been a decline in the commitment to PR in many states. In Karnataka also, the elections to PRIs due in 1964 were postponed to 1968. Meanwhile, the Kondajji Basappa Committee which submitted its report in 1963, recommended the setting up of elected Zilla Parishads, exclusion of MPs and MLAs from the PRIs and establishment of Nyaya panchayats. A bill based on the recommendations of the Committee was introduced in the State Legislature. But, as the Congress Legislature Party in power was not in its favour, it was allowed to lapse. Elections, were due again in 1972, and in 1975, TDBs and many Village Panchayats were superseded and placed under administrators. It was only in 1978 that elections were held, but in 1983 these bodies were dissolved once again.

Act of 1983: When the Janata Government came to power in 1977 in the Centre, it appointed the Ashok Mehta Committee. The recommendations made by the Committee in 1978 were not implemented. In 1983, when the Janata Party came to power in the state there was a revival of interest in PR with genuine devolution of powers and functions. This was a commitment made in the election manifesto of the Party. The new government headed by Sri Ramakrishna Hegde enacted **the Zilla Parishads, Taluk Panchayat Samithis, Mandal Panchayats and Nyaya Panchayats Act, 1983.** However, there was delay in obtaining the President's assent to the bill because of the negative attitude of the Congress Party in power at the centre. Elections were, therefore, held under the new law only in January 1987 and the elected Panchayat Raj Institutions, viz., Zilla Parishads (ZP), Mandal Panchayats (MP), Taluk Panchayat Samithi (TP) and Village Panchayats (VP) started functioning. Elections to the newly constituted ZPs and MPs were conducted on party lines.

It has been said that the **Act of 1983** could be regarded as a landmark in the history of democratic decentralisation as it demonstrated the willingess of the state government to divest itself of substantial powers and functions in favour of PRIs. The new set up under the Act was modelled on the lines of Ashok Mehta Report with a two-tier structure — Zilla Parishads at the district level and Mandal Panchayats, for a group of villages - with direct elections to both the bodies.

The ZP became, under the Act, the primary body as the district was considered as a development unit large enough for it to be fairly self-sufficient in administrative and technical capabilities — a pre-requisite for effective decentralisation. The ZP was fully responsible for planning and implementation of all the development programmes in the districts. The MP was entrusted with a number of development schemes.

The ZP was directly elected with 25 per cent of the seats earmarked for women and seats reserved for SC and ST in proportion to their population (with a minimum of 18 per cent of the seats for them). The MLAs and MPs belonging to the district were entitled to take part in the proceedings, could vote, but not hold office.

The President and Vice-President of the ZP were given the status and salary of the Ministers of State and Deputy Ministers of the state government respectively. In order to establish an effective official hierarchy to assist the elected representatives of the ZP, the government appointed an executive head called the 'Chief Secretary' drawn from the Indian Administrative Service. As a matter of deliberate policy, the Chief Executive officer was to be a person senior in service to the Deputy Commissioner of the district. The district level officers and staff of the development departments functioned under the ZP. A planning unit under a Chief Planning Officer with four or five subject matter specialists was also set up.

Apart from the overall planning and co-ordination of development schemes and preparation of a district plan, the ZPs had specific responsibilities in respect of the schemes transferred to them in the areas of agriculture, horticulture, soil conservation, animal husbandry, fisheries, forest, rural development, minor irrigation, roads and bridges, nutrition, primary and secondary education, rural health, family welfare, welfare of the scheduled castes and scheduled tribes, and backward classes, minorities, social welfare, housing, sericulture, small scale industries, sports and new services. Government also issued detailed instructions specifying the scheme/programme and the personnel of each department transferred to the ZPs.

As regards finances, the state government allocated the plan and non-plan budget provisions, sectorwise and districtwise. In 1987-8, which was the first year of functioning, 28.3 per cent of the state's own plan outlay (37.2 per cent inclusive of Centrally sponsored schemes) were transferred to the district sector. On the non-plan side, the transfer amounted to over 20 per cent. As regards personnel, about 30 per cent of government employees came under the administrative control of the ZP.

It may be mentioned here that the Deputy Commissioner of the district, who, for decades was the chief co-ordinating authority for all development programmes was, for the first time, kept out of the PR system. The government felt that with his position as chief representative of the district at the district level, equation between him and PR bodies would be based on mutual respect and appreciation of the complementarity of each other's roles to secure the maximum public good.

The second-tier of the direct elected body, viz., the MP was constituted for a group of villages with a population from 8 to 12 thousand, and with a population of 4 thousand in the hill districts. It consisted of elected members at the rate of one member for a population of 400 with reservation for women, SCs and STs. The ZP appointed a whole time Secretary for the MP who functioned as the chief executive.

The MPs had 27 schemes exclusively transferred to them for implementation. A list of the schemes transferred to them under various sectors of development was also notified.

While the ZPs and MPs were the two pillars of the system, a co-ordinating and monitoring body known as the Taluk Panchayat Samithi was set up at the taluk level. It is interesting to note that the MLA, representing the major segment of the Taluk, was made the head of the TP. The members of the ZPs elected from the taluk, MLAs and

MLCs representing any part of the taluk (excluding urban centres) and the Pradhans of MPs were members of the Samithi. There was also a provision for co-opting five members. The BDO functioned as the Secretary and Chief Executive of the TP. The TP was a co-ordinating body with no executive powers.

A landmark feature of **1983 Act** was the setting up of gram sabha for each village consisting of the adults of the village. This sabha was expected to meet at least twice in a year to discuss the implementation of the development programmes in the villages and to approve new programmes of development including the selection of the beneficiaries. The gram sabha was also expected to promote unity and integrity at the village level.

As regards finances, the state government had effected from a budget a massive transfer of funds to the ZPs which did not have powers to tax. The MPs had the usual powers to levy property tax, tax on vehicles etc. The state government gave a per capita grant of Rs. 10 per annum, three fourths of which accrued to the MPs and the balance to the ZPs. The intention was that this grant would meet the administrative expenditure of ZPs and MPs and leave some funds with the latter for local development activity. The state government provided grants for both plan and non-plan programmes.

As regards planning at the district level, the ZP was entrusted with this responsibility. In order to enable the ZPs to perform the task, the government issued elaborate instructions regarding the procedures and methodology to be followed for preparing the plan, taking also into account the MP plans. The ZPs would prepare the district plan and send it to the government. The state government would then discuss the plans with the Presidents of ZPs. Thereafter, the district plans would get incorporated in the state plan for submission to the Planning Commission.

It could be said that the PR system under the **Act of 1983** had broken distinctively new ground. The PRIs were conceived as units of government in the district and sub units. The status and pay given to the President and Vice-President of ZPs, appointment of an IAS officer as Chief Secretary (who was senior in service to the Deputy Commissioner), the transfer of staff of development departments, the allocation of a district budget were all indicative of the government's political commitment to ensure the successful functioning of the three units of government.

Another innovative feature was the setting up of the State Development Council with the Chief Minister as Chairperson and all the ZP Presidents as members. The Minister of Rural Development and few other Ministers were also included as members. The Council was to serve as a forum for continuous review and direct the PR movement in the state, in addition to serving as a sounding board for policy and procedural formulation and interaction between the political, executive and the PR System.

The 1983 Act also provided for a Finance Commission to recommend to the government the pattern of assistance to the ZPs and the principles which should govern the grants in and from the government to ZPs and MPs.

Review of the Functioning of PRIs: The ZPs and MPs, which started functioning in 1987, had to face many problems in the beginning. However, within a couple of years they settled down to work. Studies carried out after two or three years of their functioning, disclosed that, by and large, they had performed well. A young and educated leadership had emerged in the institutions. What is significant is that there was a sizeable representation of landless persons at both the levels.

The functioning of primary schools, primary health services and housing programmes also showed improvement and there was a good mobilisation of local resources. The understanding between the elected representatives and officials also showed improvement. On the negative side, it was noted that the two dominant castes, viz., Lingayats and Vokkaligas, had secured more than their proportionate share of membership and offices. The participation in discussion and decision making of SC/ST members and women representatives was rather limited. It was also seen that there was a shift of priorities towards social services but due to lack of resources the ZPs had little freedom in the determination of priorities. MPs were administratively weak and depended on the staff of ZPs. In spite of these difficulties, the functioning of these bodies indicated that democratic decentralisation could become a reality.

The report of the State Finance Commission, submitted in 1989, covered plan and non-plan expenditure, per capita, discretionery and incentive grants. However, no action was taken, as interest in PR started waning. By 1988, factionalism within the Janata Party had set in and not many ministers and legislators including those outside the Janata Party were committed to the ideals of PR. As a result, the ZPs became weaker due to withdrawl of powers and functions. With the assumption of office by the Congress Party in 1990, the ZPs ceased to have any role, for instance, in the area of co-operation, horticulture and public distribution system. The bureaucracy, especially in the technical departments, was not also fully reconciled to working under local political masters. Ultimately, in 1992, when elections were due, the state government superseded the ZPs and MPs and appointed administrators. This decision was contested in the Courts, right up to the Supreme Court, which directed that fresh elections to ZPs must be held before the end of June 1993. A similar directive was given by the Karnataka High Court in respect of MPs.

73rd Constitution Amendment Act 1992: The new Congress government headed by Sri Rajiv Gandhi, noting the dismal situation in many states of the country regarding the lack of political commitment on the part of the party in power for strengthening the PR and the non-holding of elections, supersession of PRIs, enacted the **73rd Constitution Amendment Act 1992,** making it mandatory to establish a directly elected three-tier structure of PRIs. The states, under the Act, were required to modify their existing PR legislation and replacing them with the requirements incorporated in the **Constitution Amendment Act.** In view of this development, the Karnataka state government enacted altogether a fresh piece of legislation called the **Karnataka Panchayat Raj Act 1993.**

Panchayat Raj Act 1993: Under the new Act of 1993, a 3-tier PR system has been established in the state with elected bodies at the village, taluk, and zilla levels. The Act provided for Gram Panchayats

(GP) at the village level, a Taluk Panchayat (TP) at the taluk level and Zilla Panchayat (ZP) at the district level with direct election to all the three bodies. It stipulates that election to Gram Panchayats should not be on party lines. The elections are to be conducted by the newly created State Election Commssion constituted under the Act.

Gram Panchayats: The state government has formed 5,640 Gram Panchayats for which elections were held in December 1993. The average population of each Gram Panchayat is 5,300 as compared to about 10,000 in the case of Mandal Panchayat according to 1991 census. Of the total number of members of 80,627 in all the Gram Panchayats, 35,305 (43.8 %) are women. The categorywise break up is as follows:

SC 17,918, (22.2%), of which 7,372 are women (41 %).

ST 7.575, (9.4%), of which 5,933 are women (75%).

BC 26.878, (33.27%), of which 10,722 are women (40%).

General 28,306, (35%), of which 11,278 are women (40%).

Total 80,627, of which 35,305 are women (43.8%).

As per the provisions of the Act, the offices of Adhyaksha and Upadhyaksha of Gram Panchayats have also been reserved. The breakup is as follows:

SC 1,025, of which 342 are women (33.36%).

ST 295, of which 99 are women (33,56%).

BC 1,880, of which 626 are women (33.36%).

General 2,440, of which 813 are women (33.32%).

Total 5,640, of which 1860 are women (33.33%).

This reservation will conform to the reservation pattern for different categories as envisaged in the Act.

Taluk Panchayats: For each Taluk, a Taluk Panchayat has been constituted. It consists of elected members at the rate of one member for every 10,000 population or part thereof. However, Taluks having a population of not exceeding 1.00 lakh will have 11 elected members.

Elections to all the 175 Taluk Panchayats in the state were held during 13th-18th March, 1995, on party basis. The categorywise elected members are as follows:

SC 601, (18%), of which 261 are women (45.0%).

ST 169, (5%), of which 104 are women (61.5%).

BC- A 894, (26.25%), of which 389 are women (48.5%).

BC- B 223, (6.68%), of which 52 are women (23.3%).

General 1,453, (43.5%), of which 537 are women (36.95%).

Total 3,340, of which 1,343 are women (40.2%).

The offices of Adhyaksha and Upadhyaksha of Taluk Panchayats have been reserved to different categories as follows:

SC 32, of which 11 are women.

ST 9, of which 3 are women.

BC-A 46, of which 15 are women.

BC-B 12, of which 4 are women.

General 76, of which 26 are women.

Total 175, of which 59 are women (33.71%).

Zilla Panchayats: There are 20 Zilla Panchayats in the state. Each Zilla Panchayat shall consist of elected members at the rate of one member for every 40,000 population and part thereof (1 member for 30,000 population in Chickmagalur and North Kannada districts and 1 member for 18,000 population in Kodagu district). The M.L.A and M.Ps representing part of the area and the M.L.Cs and Rajya Sabha Members who are electors in the district are ex-officio members. Besides, all the Adhyakshas of Taluk Panchayats are also ex-officio members of Zilla Panchayats.

Elections to all the Zilla Panchayats were held during 13th-18th March, 1995 on party basis. The categorywise elected members are as follows:-

1) SCs 165, (18%), of which 63 are women (35%).

2) STs 57, (5%), of which 22 are women (40.5%).

3) BCs-A 243, (26.4%), of which 89 are women (36.6%).

4) BCs-B 63, (6.7%), of which 19 are women (30%).

5) General 401, (43.6%), of which 142 are women (35.4%).

Total 919, of which 335 are women (36.5%).

The elections to the offices of Adhyaksha and Upadhyyaksha were held during 3rd-10th April, 1995. The categorywise reservation of these offices is indicated below:-

1) SC 4, of which 2 are women.

2) ST 1.

3) BC-A, 6, of which 2 are women.

4) BC-B 1.

5) General 8, of which 3 are women.

Total 20, of which 7 are women.

Here also the Adhyaksha and Upadhyaksha have been elected from among the elected members of Zilla Panchayats. The Zilla Panchayats meet at least once in 2 months for the transaction of business.

Under the Act, practically all the programmes of various departments - both plan and non-plan - in the state have been entrusted to the PR bodies. The TPs have been rightly accorded primacy as the implementing agency for practically all schemes which fall within the geographical boundaries of the taluk. Annexure-I indicates briefly the functions to be performed by GPs, TPs and ZPs.

As regards finance, the GPs will derive funds from taxes on houses, shandies, share of cess on land revenue, grant of Rs.1.00 lakh by government every year and allocation under Jawahar Rozgar Yojana.

As regards TPs, it may be stated that they have no power to raise resources through taxation. Under Section 207 of the Act, the government shall make a grant to every TP to cover all revenue expenses of the Panchayat. Government can also make dicretionary grant for specific purposes.

It may be noted that the ZPs have no power to levy tax for raising resources. The government will provide them establishment grant to cover the expenses of establishment. Otherwise, the ZP will depend on the resources allocated by government for implementing plan and non-plan schemes. The other sources are income from immoveable assets, if any, 20 per cent allocation under the Jawahar Rozgar Yojana and dicretionary grant, if any, provided by the government.

The ZPs would be in charge of all programmes which cater to the needs of more than one taluk and certain other major activities.

A feature, which some pundits have termed as retrograde, is that under the **1993 Act,** the state government has now reserved considerable powers of supervision and control over the PRIs at all levels. These include control over suspension of resolutions and issue of directives and supersessions. Considerable confusion was also caused by not indicating the status of Adhyakshas and Upadyhakshas in the Act. However, by an amendment to the Act in 1996, the Adhyaksha has been designated as the executive head of the ZP. However, the Act has strengthened the position of the Chief Executive Officer and the position is the same at the taluk level. The power to transfer officials vests with the state government.

Under Section 10 of the Act, a District Planning Committee has to be constituted which will consist of MPs, members of the State Legislature, Adhyakshas of ZPs, Mayor or President of the district headquarters municipal body. The other members are to be elected from among the members of ZPs and municipal bodies in proportion to the populations of rural and urban areas in the districts. The District Planning Committee is responsible for consolidating the plans prepared by the Panchayats and Municipal bodies and to prepare a draft development plan for the district as a whole. Recently, the government has decided to set up District Planning Committees (DPC), the size of which varies, depending on the size of the panchayat raj institutions and municipal bodies. One of the elected members would be chosen as the President of the DPC. The Minister has stated that care would be taken to see that DPC would not emerge as a rival centre of power and no infrastructure was being provided to the bodies, the function of which would be limited to holding periodical meetings.

In order to conduct the election to the new bodies, a State Election Commission, under Section 308 of the Act, has been constituted with a retired IAS Officer as State Election Commissioner. Elections were conducted for 5,000 to 5,640 Gram Panchayats during December 1993. However, there was a delay in holding elections to TPs and ZPs, and in spite of the time limit stipulated by the Supreme Court, there was a delay in conducting the elections. Ultimately, the elections to TPs, and ZPs were held during the period 13th-18th March 1995.

This was a reflection on the lack of political commitment to hold the elections in time, a feature which was so common earlier and which was the prime reason for the initiative taken by the Central Government, headed by Prime Minister Rajiv Gandhi, to enact the **73rd Constitution Amendment Act.**

The allocations made sector-wise and district-wise in the district plan budget 1996-97 of the state government may be seen in Annexure-II. A total sectoral outlay of the plan and non-plan schemes for ZPs is Rs. 1,272 crores, of which Rs. 732 crores is in the state sector and Rs. 540 crores in the Central sector. The districtwise outlays and the tentative allocation among the three bodies may be seen in Annexure-III and IV. It may be seen that in 1996-97, the average percentage of the total allocation of Central and state budgetary provisions is 41 per cent for ZPs, 44 per cent for TPs and 15 per cent for VPs.

The 1993 PR Act attracted criticism from various quarters. A considerable part of the criticism stemmed from what is perceived to be the overiding power given to bureaucracy over the elected bodies. It has been mentioned that the **1983 Act**, in this regard, was more progressive with greater autonomy to PRIs. This concept of the **1983 Act** was discussed in the State Legislature and has also been the subject of suggestions by activists in the field of PR and democratic decentralisation and the elected representatives of ZPs and TPs. Having regard to this criticism, the Government constituted an Expert Committee to review the **(Karnataka Act 1993)** under the Chairmanship of Dr. K.S.Krishnaswamy in February 1995. Subsequently, Sri P.R.Nayak, IAS (Retd.), was appointed as Chairman of the Committee. The terms of reference of this committee were as under:

(1) To review the **Karnataka Panchayat Raj Act, 1993** and to recommend changes that may be necessary in the Act to enable Panchayats to function effectively as institutions of self-government with special reference to:

(a) the powers and functions of the elected bodies vis-a-vis government officials;

(b) the powers of dissolution and control of lower level Panchayats by the higher level Panchayats;

(c) the principles of allocation of powers and functions between different levels of Panchayats and whether such powers and functions should be delegated by the Legislature;

(d) The Constitution of a Panchayat Council with Chief Minister as the Chairman;

(e) empowering Panchayats with necessary judicial and police powers to settle petty cases both of civil and criminal nature; and

(f) decentralised planning and implementation.

(2) To examine the reservation system for ensuring greater equity and justice in the representation of people in the Panchayat Raj Institutions and the Committees thereof bearing in mind the Constitutional provisions.

(3) To recommend a scientific mode for determining the delineation of the Constituencies.

(4) To consider any other relevant aspects as may be found necessary for making the Karnataka Panchayat Raj system more

effective and to promote the objectives of decentralised local self-government.

The Committee took evidence from all persons who were active in the PR movement and representatives of the PRIs, NGOs, academics and administrators. The major recommendations of this committee, **inter-alia**, are as under:

a) When there is a default in the performance of duty by a PRI, only the next higher PRI (or government in the case of Zilla Panchayat) should order the performance of such duty.

b) The existing power of the government officer of suspending any order of PRI for the reason that it is unlawful or will be injurious to the public or will lead to a breach of peace should be withdrawn and vested in the next higher PRI.

c) The Adhyaksha of the Zilla Panchayat should be declared as the executive head. The position should be the same with regard to the Adhyaksha of the Taluk Panchayat. The Chief Executive Officer/Executive Officer shall exercise his powers subject to the general powers of the Adhyaksha.

d) The government should initiate steps to permanently transfer government personnel of Group 'C' and 'D' to PRIs; constitute a PRI service with linkage with the State Service to provide mobility at higher levels and concurrently curtail further recruitment of government personnel meant for PRI work.

e) Rules of Business for conducting the business of PRIs should be prescribed under the Act's rule-making power.

f) The exercise of executive power by the Adhyaksha and other elected non-officials and officials alike should be governed by the Rules of Business.

g) The government needs to keep itself fully informed of the functioning of the PRIs, as it continues to be answerable to the legislature in that respect.

h) In order to ensure all-round accountability, a duty should be imposed on the Chief Executive Officer/Executive Officer to advise the ZP or any of its Committees or any authority of the Panchayat in writing with regard to any inconsistency between a proposed resolution or order and the position in law, financial regulations, budget provisions etc; and, if the resolution or order is passed without resolving the inconsistency, to forward it to the government along with the written advice.

i) The power of removal from office of an Adhyaksha or Upadhyaksha for misconduct or for being persistently remiss in the discharge of his/her duties is a power which should, at this juncture, be used only by the government.

j) A PRI or government can initiate action for the removal of the Adhyaksha or Upadhyaksha of any lower PRI but the government may take action, in respect of the office-bearers of the GP or the TP only after receiving the recommendation of the next higher PRI and, in the case of the office-bearers of the GP, also of the ZP.

k) The District Planning process should move away from the current methodology of dealing separately with each of the social development sectors, such as, health, education, social welfare, water and sanitation to a system of integrated area planning starting from the Gram Sabha. A beginning may be made in this direction in selected Taluk Panchayats and Gram Panchayats.

l) Women members of the PRIs should be represented on all Standing Committees, as far as possible, at one-third of the total committee membership.

m) The Act should provide for the formal constitution of the Gram Sabha. The Adhyaksha of the Gram Panchayat should be duty bound to convene at least two meetings of the Gram Sabha during the financial year at which a quorum of ten per cent registered voters should be present. The Gram Panchayat should have a Standing Committee for each village consisting of the Gram Panchayat members elected from that village.

n) A substantial number of schemes under the ZP are appropriate to the TP, some of which may even be planned by the GP and implemented by the TP. It is necessary for the government to reclassify the schemes under the three Schedules to the Act.

o) A State Panchayat Council should be constituted under the Act and should be chaired by the Chief Minister. Any alteration in the activities assigned to the three tiers, as also in the Rules of Business, should be discussed by the Council. The Council should address itself to policy issues and avoid individual complaints of omission or commission.

In order to discuss the recommendations of the committee and to elicit the opinion of the experts, Presidents of ZPs, TPs, VPs, academics and serving officers, the government had organised a Workshop at the state level on 21-11-1996. It was noted that the Committee had drawn heavily on the provisions contained in the **1983 Act,** regarding the supremacy of the elected bodies while making several recommendations for rejuvenation and revitalisation of PR. In particular, they observed that the elected body should be supreme in order to reduce scope for bureaucratic interference which can, at times, be prompted by political considerations. It was their recommendation that in a three-tier structure, it is the higher body which should really supervise the working of the lower body and take appropriate action in case there has been failure or omission in the discharge of the functions entrusted to the lower body. According to the Committee, the role of the government officials within the PRIs should be facilitative and executive rather than authoritative. In order to put on a sound footing the system of working in the PRIs, the Committee has rightly felt the need for framing rules of business by each institution.

Another point which also has been adequately treated by the Committee relates to organisational linkages between higher level bodies and lower level bodies. The underlying principle is that the PRIs should be able to adopt a self regulatory mechanism so that authority goes well with accountability. The Committee also has suggested the constitution under the Act of a State Development Council which was created as an informal body earlier. This body should address itself to policy issues and also discuss matters relating to changes in the activities assigned to the PRIs.

The Nayak Committee examined the allocation made in ZP sector in the budget of 1995-96 and felt that a reclassification of the schemes under the 3 schedules is needed as there are several functions which are appropriate to the TPs. As reclassification of schemes and their implementation will take some time, the Committee recommended that in order to enhance the capability of the Zilla Panchayats to render assistance to lower Panchayats for the implementation of the schemes and facilitate effective view by the ZP, the ZP should exhibit in their plan all programmes in the Districts/Taluks with their allocations GP wise under whichever P.R. level they may have been classified. This process, according to the Committee, will generate a sense of oneness among the P.R. levels and a common feeling that the entire District/Taluk programme is their responsibility and that the failure of any ZP is also the failure of TP/ZP.

A contentious issue arose from the amendment made to the Act limiting the terms of Adyakshas and Upadyakshas of ZPs and TPs from five years to 20 months and rotating them on the basis of reservation to provide a chance to women and members of SC/ST and Backward classes to function as Adhyakshas and Upadhyakshas. This was challenged in the Karnataka High Court by the Presidents of ZPs and TPs. However, the High Court has upheld the decision of the government to limit the terms of Adhyakshas and Upadhyakshas to these bodies for 20 months. While, no doubt, the government has taken this decision on grounds of providing an opportunity to women and members of SC/ST and other backward classes to function as Adhyakshas and Upadhyakshas, it is debatable whether as Adhyakshas or Upadhyakshas they will be in a position during the short tenure of 20 months to understand fully the working of the ZPs/TPs, establish working relationship with the Chief Executive officers and other government officials and provide leadership that is needed for mobilising public support and implementing successfully the development plans. In fact, the Nayak Committee which had examined this question had recommended that such a move would be counter productive and normally whether in government or outside an executive head requires at least 3 years for the purpose of acquainting himself with a nature of work and gaining confidence and experience in the discharge to his duties. There is considerable force and merit in this recommendation. However, in view of the decision of the High Court judgement and the government intention to implement the decision, it will be interesting to study in due course of time whether the Adhyakshas and Upadhyakshas are able during the tenure of 20 months to provide leadership, enlist the co-operation of other elected members of the bodies and Chief executives and other officials and oversee effectively the implementation of the development programmes.

Another important recommendation which has been made by the Committee and which can cause political ripples is the abolition of Area Development Boards, which have been constituted by government. The Committee has rightly observed that there is no place for such boards when the PRIs in the district can take care of all the development works in the districts as the principal development agency.

It has to be recognised that the new PR system will work only if there is political will and commitment from the party in power and legislators to strengthen the working of these institutions and not to interfere with their functioning but to hold them accountable for the discharge of the functions entrusted to them. On their part, the elected representatives of the PRIs and especially those who are elected as Adhyakshas and Upadyakshas should realise that the institutions are training grounds of democracy and if they do well and gain a reputation for effective functioning of these institutions they will certainly develop a public image and popularity which will stand them in good stead when they aspire to become legislators at the state and Central levels.

The Minister of Rural Development and Panchayat Raj has stated that a set of comprehensive amendments would be incorporated in the **Act of 1993** for greater and effective devolution of power.

It will be interesting to closely watch the contribution that will be made by the women representatives in the PRIs. Many of them are occupying the offices of Adhyakshas and Upadhyakshas in all the three levels. Many of them have undergone the training course organised by training institutes at the behest of the government. Their contribution to policy making and more particularly in overseeing the effective implementation of the programmes meant for welfare for women and children and the SC, ST, and BCs will be closely watched. The greater their involvement, ability and capacity to plug the loopholes in implementation of programmes and ensure effectiveness of delivery systems, the better the chances of ensuring that the PRIs become effective units of decentralised government.

There has been, now and then, criticism or complaints about the misuse of funds due to both political interference by elected representative and connivance between them and the officials. There have been charges that schemes are not being properly implemented and the funds allocated for the purpose are being misused resulting in either poor quality work or the benefits not reaching the persons for whom it is intended. Financial irregularities in the purchases made by ZPs have also come to light. When more than Rs.1,000 crores are allocated for district plans in the state budget, there is no doubt a temptation for misuse of funds at all three levels. While financial accounting and control systems and the rules for transaction of business would, no doubt, be properly formulated on paper, it is essential in order to minimise the scope for corruption and misuse of funds to provide for the right to information to public and the community in regard to the manner in which the funds are being spent under various schemes and works. In Rajasthan, NGOs and villages have asserted their right to information on use of funds and have exposed corruption and the misuse of the funds in VPs. They have demanded the right to inspect records, construction sites, muster rolls, bills and vouchers for development works carried out in their villages. The barrier to information is the single leading cause for corruption in society. The Mazdoor Kisan Samiti Sangathan's campaign for right to information and right to look into records and documents and arrange for public hearings is noteworthy and a step in the right direction.

It is essential that the right to information in decision making process of PRIs and on the amount spent on schemes and works is made available to NGOs or individuals or other oganisations which are anxious to ensure that public money is spent wisely and fruitfully for the economic betterment of the people and improving their standard of living.

The National Institute of Rural Development which conducted a case study of the Mysore Zilla Panchayat has observed that the Karnataka model is the 'best model'. However, it may be stated that it is rather early to assess and evaluate the working and performance of the PRIs as they have functioned for over just an year.

Perhaps, in 1998, the government should constitute an expert committee to make a mid-term appraisal of the working of the PRIs and to take such remedial measures as may be necessary, to ensure that the PRIs are on the right track.

To sum up, it may be stated that the Karnataka Panchayat Raj Act is a progressive piece of legislation designed to ensure that the PRIs function as units of government at the district and sub-levels. It is hoped that the Karnataka PR system will provide a foundation for the growth of full-fledged grass root democracy.

ANNEXURE I

jarnataka Panchayat Act 1993

Functions of Gram Panchayat: The Gram Panchayats have to perform a large number of functions which was listed in Schedule-I of the Act. The important ones are:-

(i) Maintenance of drinking water schemes.

(ii) Providing street lights.

(iii) Rural Sanitation.

(iv) House site distribution within Gramathana limits.

(v) Construction and maintenance of village roads, drains and Primary school buildings.

(vi) Adult education.

(vii) Afforestation.

(viii) Maintenance of Gomal and other Govt. lands entrusted to it.

(ix) Village libraries and reading rooms.

(x) Monitoring the public distribution system.

(xi) Construction and maintenance of cattle pounds, slaughter houses, public parks, play grounds etc.

Functions of Taluk Panchayat:

The important functions of Taluk Panchayats as listed in Schedule-II are as follows:

(a) Maintenance of agriculture and horticulture farms and nurseries.

(b) Training of farmers and Extension activities.

(c) Implementation of community and individual irrigation works.

(d) Maintenance of veterinary services and improvement of breed of cattles, poultry and other livestock.

(e) Promotion of rural and cottage industries.

Functions of Zilla Panchayat:

The functions of Zilla Panchayat normally included those programmes which cater to the needs of more than one Taluk and certain other major activities. The important functions are as follows:-

a) Establishment and maintenance of agricultural, horticultural and commercial farms.

(b) Organising agricultural fairs and exhibitions, construction, renovation and maintenance of minor irrigation works.

(c) Watershed development programmes.

(d) Development of groundwater resources.

(e) Improvement of breed of cattle, poultry and other livestock.

(f) Prevention of epidemic and contagious diseases.

(g) Establishment and management of training-com-production centres and organising marketing facilities.

(h) Development of waste land.

(i) Construction of and maintenance of district roads.

Annexure-II

Annual Plan 1996 & 1997

Sectorwise Outlays under the Zilla Panchayat Sector

(Rs. in lakhs)

Sl.No.	Sector	State	Centre	Total
1.	Primary and Secondary Education Genral Education-2202	13,995.00	2,642.86	16,637.86
2.	Adult Education-2202 General Education-04	116.00	88.35	204.35
3.	Sports and Youth Service-2204	325.00	-	325.00
4.	Health and Public Health Services. Rural Health-2210	4,092.50	-	4.092.50
5.	Indian Systems of Medicine-2210	343.00	-	343.00
6.	Family Walfare Programme-2211	102.00	6,009.00	6,111.00
7.	Rural Water Supply-2215	5,187.50	10,320.50	15,508.00
8.	Welfare of SCs and STs (Social Welfare)-2225	3,548.00	1,534.07	5,082.07
9.	Special Component Plan-2225	3,641.00	954.54	4595.54
10.	Welfare of BCM-2225	1,713.50	...	1,713.50
11.	Welfare of Women and Children-2235	531.05	4716.68	5247.72
12.	Nutrition-2234	3,389.50	...	3,389.50
13.	Agriculture-2401	584.50	1.252.84	1,837.34
14.	Horticulture-2401	483.00	...	483.00
15.	Animal Husbandry-2403	2,555.00	...	2,555.00
16.	Fisheries-2405	339.00	41.77	380.77

(Contd.)

(Rs. in lakhs)

Sl.No.	Sector	State	Centre	Total
17.	Forest (including Soil Conservation)-2408	1,146.50	1,095.97	2,242.47
18.	Co-operation-2230, 2425, 3456, 4250, 4425, 4575, 6425 & 7475	268.50	...	268.50
19.	Labour & Employment-Rehabilitation of Bonded Labourers-2230	1.00	1.00	2.00
20.	RDP-Rural Development Special Programmes			
	(a) IRDP (Monitoring)	435.50	435.50	871.00
	(b) IRDP (Subsidy)	2,685.50	2,585.50	5,271.00
	(c) TRYSEM (Training) -2501	270.00	270.00	540.00
	(d) DWACRA (Devt. of Women & Children in Rural Area)-2501	55.96	111.92	167.88
	(e) Drought Prone Area Programme-2501	1,281.50	1,697.50	2,979.00
	(f) Integrated Rural Energy Programme-2501	258.50	...	258.50
Total (21)		**4,986.50**	**5,100.42**	**10,087.38**
21.	Rural Employment (Jawahar Rozgar Yojna)-2505	4,599.50	18,398.00	22,997.50

(Contd.)

(Rs. in lakhs)

Sl.No.	Sector	State	Centre	Total
22.	Other RDPR Programmes			
	(a) Grants to Zilla, Taluk and Grama Panchayats-2515	14,816.00	...	14,816.00
	(b) District Level Sub-Plan-2515	188.00	...	188.00
	(c) Western Ghats Development Programmes-2551	...	1,231.08	1,231.08
Total (22)		**15,004.00**	**1,231.08**	**16,235.08**
23.	Minor Irrigation-2702	1,157.50	...	1,157.50
24.	Village and Small Scale Industries-2851	349.00	...	349.00
25.	Sericulture-2851	450.50	...	450.50
26.	Roads and Bridges-3054 & 5055	3,353.50	...	3,353.50
27.	Secretariat Economic Services Dt. Planning Unit-3451	75.50	...	75.50
28.	Tribal Sub Plan-2225	660.00	695.29	1,355.29
29.	Village and Small Industries-Handlooms 2851	202.00	1.45	203.45
Grand Total		**73,200.00**	**54.084.32**	**1,27,284.32**

Annexure-III

Annual Plan 1996-97

Districtwise Outlays under the Zilla Panchayat Sector

(Rs. in lakhs)

Sl.No.	District	State	Centre	Total
1.	Bangalore Urban	1,816.95	1478.99	3,295.94
2.	Bangalore Rural	3,139.90	2,595.26	5,735.16
3.	Chitradurga	3,777.02	3,263.71	7,040.73
4.	Kolar	3,786.69	3,662.54	7,449.23
5.	Shimoga	3,172.62	2,848.62	6,021.24
6.	Tumkur	4,042.59	3,588.66	7,631.25
7.	Mysore	4,658.82	3,344.90	8,003.72
8.	Chikmgalur	2,499.46	1,770.30	4,269.76
9.	Daksihna Kannada	3,511.03	2,870.55	6,381.58
10.	Hassan	2,974.51	2,004.52	4,979.03
11.	Kodagu	1,266.87	1,042.28	2,309.15
12.	Mandya	2,784.47	1,828.97	4,613.44
13.	Belgaum	4,976.64	3,461.73	8,438.37
14.	Bijapur	4,620.22	3,397.19	8,017.41
15.	Dharwad	4,491.31	3,941.61	8,432.92
16.	Uttara Kannada	2,270.58	1,875.35	4,145.93
17.	Gulbarga	4,437.72	3,715.89	8,153.61
18.	Bellary	3,170.74	3,111,33	6,282.07
19.	Bidar	2,423.64	1,779.18	4,202.82
20.	Raichur	3,834.22	2,502.74	6,336.96
21.	Lumpsum	5,544.00	...	5,544.00
	Grand Total	**73,200.00**	**54,084.32**	**127.284.32**

Annexure IV

District Sector Allocation among ZPs, TPs and GPs – 1995-96 and 1996-97

(Rs. in lakhs)

Sl. No.	Institution	1995-96 State	%	Central	%	Total Allocation	%	1996-97 State	%	Central	%	Total Allocation	%
1.	Zilla Panchayat	22,446,720	36	24,000,830	50	46,447,550	42	24,825,280	36	25,955,710	48	50,780,990	41
2.	Taluk Panchayat	30,376,260	49	15,690,360	33	46,068,720	42	37,870,360	50	19,991,170	37	57,861,530	44
3.	Grama Panchayat	9,175,020	15	8,340,080	17	17,515,100	16	10,504,360	14	8,137,440	15	18,641,800	15
	Total	62,000,000	100	48,031,270	100	110,031,370	100	73,200,080	100	54,084,320	100	127,284,320	100

REFERENCES

1. Directorate of Economics and Statistics. (DES) (1995). **Karnataka at a Glance 1993-94.** Bangalore: Government of Karnataka.
2. Government of Karnataka (GOK), (1993). **Kanataka State Gazetteer,** Part II. Bangalore: Government of Press
3. Government of Karnataka (GOK). (1987). **Report on Reorganisation of Districts and Taluks in Karnataka State 1984-87.** Bangalore:
4. Government of Karnataka (GOK). (1988a). **Mysore Disrict-Karnataka State Gazetter.** Bangalore : Government of Karnataka.
5. Government of Karnataka (GOK). (1989b). **District Governments and Decentralised Planning.** Bangalore : Government of Karnataka
6. Institute of Social Sciences. (1995). **Status of Panchayat Raj in the States of India. 1994.** New Delhi : Concept.
7. Maheswari. S.R. (1990). **Indian Administration.** New Delhi: Orient Longman.
8. Sadashivan. S.N. (ed). (1988). **District Administration: A National Perspective.** New Delhi: IIPA.
9. Satyamurthy. D.M. Rajasekara Reddy and G. Rajani Kanth (1995). Panchayati Raj Insitutions in Karnataka - A case Study of Mysore Zilla Panchayat. In S.P. Jani (ed), **Panchayati Raj Institutions in India: An Appraisal.** Hyderabad: NIRD.
10. Umapathy.M. (1995), **A History of Local-Self Governement in Rural Karnataka.** Mysore: Prasranga, University of Mysore.
11. Umapathy.M. (1995) Panchayati Raj in Karnataka: Status Report. **In Souenior of the Indian Public Administration Association 15th Annual Conference.** Mysore. University of Mysore.

2

URBAN ADMINISTRATION*

A. Ravindra

Evolution - Pre-Independence Era: Karnataka, like several other states in India, has a long history of local government. The process of converting village settlements into towns began with the organising of shandies or fairs. Gradually, town assemblies came to be formed with representation to different sections of the population. The founders of towns in medieval times used to be rewarded by the office of the headship of the town.

Modern self-governing institutions, however, came to be established during the British rule. In Karnataka (then princely state of Mysore), the foundation of local government was laid during the period of the Commissioner's rule between 1831 and 1881. **The Government of India Act XXVI of 1850 (The Improvement of Town Act)** was made applicable to Mysore state, and Municipal Boards were constituted for the first time in 1862 for towns like Bangalore and Mysore. For smaller towns, Municipal Committees were constituted by about 1870. **The Bangalore Town Municipal Regulation,** passed in 1871, authorised levy of taxes like octroi, taxes on houses, buildings and lands, professions, trades, carriages, bricks and tiles, and licence fees.

In Bangalore, elections were introduced in 1882 but only those who paid property tax were entitled to vote and contest elections. Initially, the Deputy Commissioner was the President of the Municipality. **The**

---

* This paper reflects the personal views of the author, not of the government.

Mysore Regulation VI of 1906 gave the Municipalities a statutory footing and the Regulated Municipalities, as they were called, comprised 15 councillors, of whom one third were ex-officio members and the others were nominated. These Municipalities were headed by Amildars. The tenure of Municipal Councillors was three years, extendable by another year. **The Act of 1906** was repealed in 1933 and three separate legislations were passed, viz., (1) **The Mysore City Municipalities Act**; (2) **The Mysore Town Municipal Act**; and (3) **The Mysore Minor Municipalities Act.** The Municipalities came to be classified into three categories based on the population of the area and its importance. **The Bangalore City Improvement Trust Act** was passed in 1945 to provide for the improvement and further expansion of the City of Bangalore. In 1949, Bangalore City and the Civil Station were combined into a single Corporation under the **City of Bangalore Municipal Corporation Act.** The office of Mayor and Deputy Mayor were created under the Act and Bangalore City was divided into fifty divisions or wards. The distinction between major and minor Municipalities was removed with the repeal of the **1933 Act** and the enactment of the **Mysore Town Municipalities Act in 1951.**

Position in the Integrated Areas: The present state of Karnataka is carved out of areas comprising the old princely state of Mysore and the districts which formed part of the adjoining states of Bombay, Hyderabad, Madras and Coorg. The position that prevailed in these parts before they merged into the new Karnataka is described below.

In Bombay-Karnataka area, Municipalities were constituted under the **Bombay District Municipalities Act** (III of 1901). The term of Municipalities was three years, extendable by one year. Provision was made for the constitution of managing committees for a municipality, and pilgrm committees in areas specially notified by the government. The Director of Local Authorities and District Collectors exercised control over the Municipal bodies. In 1925, some of the Municipalities were upgraded to Borough Municipalities which enjoyed greater powers. At the time of re-organisation of states, the Municipal bodies in the Bombay state were functioning under the **Bombay Municipal Boroughs Act, 1920.**

In the Madras area covering Dakshina Kannada, Bellary District and Kollegal Taluk, the Municipalities were created under the **Town Improvement Act X of 1865.** However, it was the **Madras District Municipalities Act IV of 1884** which provided for the constitution of Municipal Councils. The Council was to consist of not less than 12 persons of whom three-fourth were to be elected by tax payers and the rest appointed by the government. A modified Act of 1930 increased the elected proportion of the councillors and provided for the reservation of seats for Indian Christians, Muslims, Europeans, Anglo-Indians, women and Harijans. Women were also eligible to contest for election.

In the Hyderabad area comprising the districts of Gulbarga, Bidar and Raichur, the **Local Cess Act of 1900** made provision for the constitution of Sanitation Committees in towns with a population exceeding 5,000. The Sanitation Committees were replaced by Municipal Committees in 1924 in the district headquarters and other bigger towns. These committees consisted of 16 members, of whom 12 were non-officials, while Town Committees consisted of 5 members with 3 officials and 2 non-officials. The peculiarity of the local fund administration in Hyderabad state in 1929 was that the district and town finances were combined.

In Kodagu area, which was under the rule of Commissioners for over a century, i.e., 1834 to 1947, Municipal Committees were established in 1890 at Madikeri and Virajpet. There were also Notified Area Committees in the small towns headed by Revenue Officers.

Post-Independence Developments: Although India achieved independence in 1947, the municipal systems evolved during the British period continued for quite some time. With the re-organisation of states in 1956, the different Municipal laws which were in existence in the erstwhile states of Mysore, Bombay, Hyderabad and Madras continued to be in force in the respective areas. It was only in 1964 that a uniform law, viz., **the Karnataka Municipalities Act,** applicable throughout the state came into force. Subsequently, the need was felt to have a separate legislation for the larger cities, viz., the Corporations, and the **Karnataka Municipal Corporation Act 1976** was enacted.

Constitution of Municipalities : Urban local bodies in Karnataka were classified into the following four categories under the **Municipalities Act of 1964:**

1. Local area with a population of more than 10,000 and less than 50,000 - Town Municipalities;

2. Local area with a population of more than 50,000 and less than 2 lakhs - City Municipalities;

3. Local area with a population of 2 lakhs and above and with an annual income of not less than Rs.1.00 crore - City Corporation ; and

4. Notified Area Committee/ Sanitary Board - where improved arrangements are required to be provided for a specified area.

There are 6 Municipal Corporations, 39 City Municipal Councils, and 82 Town Municipal Councils apart from 87 Town Panchayats, totaling 214 urban local bodies in the state. Notified Area Committees and Sanitary Boards were abolished recently.

The number of councillors to be elected for each Municipal Council ranges between 15 and 35 depending on the population. For the Corporations, the number of councillors has been fixed between 50 and 100. Reservation has been provided for the Scheduled Castes and Scheduled Tribes in proportion to their population. For the first time, reservation for women was introduced by amending the Municipal Acts in 1983, to the extent of 20 per cent of the total number of seats. This must be considered a very significant development in the history of local government in the state.

Every Corporation has a Mayor and a Deputy Mayor elected by the Councillors for a period of one year. For Municipal Council, there is a President and Vice-President. In Corporations, Standing Committees are constituted for different subjects like Taxation and Finance, Public Health and Works. In Bangalore, Standing Committees are also constituted for Town Planning and Improvement, Education and Accounts. In Municipal Councils, there can be one or a maximum of three Standing Committees. The members of the Standing Committees are elected every year according to the principle of proportionate representation by means of single transferable vote.

A Commissioner is appointed to perform the executive functions in Corporations and City Municipal Councils, and in Town Municipal Councils, the Chief Officer performs these functions. The Mayor or President presides over the meetings of the Council and discharges other ceremonial duties.

The Divisional Commissioner acts as the Chief Controlling authority over Municipal Councils. In respect of Corporations, the state government can exercise control by calling for records, giving directions and through revisionary powers.

Personnel: The Municipal Corporation Act provides for the appointment of officers from the State Administrative Services to head various departments like Engineering, Health, Revenue and Accounts in the Corporations. The Commissioner is usually an officer of the Indian Administrative Service. The Municipal Acts also provide for the appointment of officers from the Karnataka Municipal Administrative Service for certain posts like Chief Officer or any specified post. This service was created in 1970 with a view to providing qualified personnel to the Municipal Organisations. The Commissioner or Chief Officer exercises control over the staff working under him. The Commissioner, who is vested with executive powers, is responsible for carrying out the provisions of the Municipal law. He also enjoys wide powers in an emergency to safeguard the property of the Municipality or the safety of the public. It is only the Commissioner who is authorised to carry on correspondence with the public.

74th Constitution Amendment Act, 1992: The 74th Constitution Amendment Act, passed by the Parliament in 1992, must be considered a landmark in the history of local government in India. It has introduced far reaching changes with the objective of strengthening urban local bodies and enabling them to function effectively as democratic units of local self-government. The major reforms proposed are as follows:

1. Municipalities will be constituted at three levels, viz., Municipal Corporations for larger urban areas, Municipal Councils for smaller urban areas, and Nagara Panchayats for areas in transition from rural

to urban. There is no provision to set up Notified Area Committees or Sanitary Boards but industrial townships may be established.

2. Elections to local bodies shall be held at regular intervals and no municipal area shall be without an elected government for a period exceeding six months. A State Election Commission shall be constituted to conduct elections.

3. There shall be reservation of seats not only for Scheduled Castes/Scheduled Tribes but also for women which will not be less than one-third of the total number of seats. The State Legislatures are also given discretion to provide for reservation for Backward Classes.

4. A State Finance Commission shall be constituted to review the financial position of the Municipalities and to suggest measures to improve their resources.

5. A District Planning Committee and a Metropolitan Planning Committee shall be constituted to consolidate the plans prepared by the Municipalities and the panchayats and prepare a District Development Plan and Metropolitan Development Plan.

6. In cities, with population exceeding three lakhs, Ward Committees shall be constituted to promote decentralisation.

The Government of Karnataka has amended the **Karnataka Municipalities Act** and the **Municipal Corporations Act** to bring them in conformity with the Constitutional provisions. It has also taken steps to give effect to some of the provisions of the **Amendment Act.** As already noted earlier, reservation for women had been introduced in Karnataka even before the **Constitution Amendment Act** came into force. However, the extent of reservation has been raised from 20 per cent to 33 per cent. Similarly, the State Election Commission had already been set up in Karnataka much earlier. The State Finance Commission was set up in 1995 and it has already submitted its recommendations. Reservation for backward classes has now been provided to the extent of 30 per cent. Reservation has also been provided to the post of Mayor and Deputy Mayor, President and Vice-President, and Chairman of the Standing Committee. However, Karnataka is yet to implement certain important provisions of the **74th**

Amendment Act like constitution of Ward Committees, District Planning Committees and Metropolitan Planning Committees.

Functions of Municipalities: Municipalities are expected to perform obligatory functions and discretionary functions. The obligatory functions include cleaning of public streets and public places, removal of garbage, construction and maintenance of drains, the lighting of public streets, naming and numbering of streets, maintenance of burial grounds, provision for public parks, and gardens, prevention of spread of dangerous diseases etc. The discretionary functions include organisation and maintenance of maternity and infant care centres, institutions for blind and other handicapped children, swimming pools, provision for shelter for destitute persons and any other measure likely to promote public safety and health.

The 74th Amendment Act has enlarged the functional domain of Municipalities. The 12th schedule to the Constitution lists 18 subjects which can be entrusted to the urban local bodies (Annexure-A). It includes subjects like urban planning, planning for economic and social development, urban forestry and protection of environment, slum improvement, urban poverty alleviation and promotion of cultural, educational and aesthetic aspects. The functions listed in the 12th schedule are, however, not mandatory and it is left to the discretion of the State Legislatures to bestow on the Municipalities such powers and functions as they deem fit.

A broad assessment of performance of Municipalities during the last 45 years would show that while a number of civic improvements have come about, there has been deficiency in the discharge of obligatory functions. Provision of basic amenities like water supply, sanitation, street lighting and even construction and maintenance of roads and pavements has not been satisfactory. Some cities like Bangalore and Mysore may present a better appearance, but the services cannot be said to be up to the mark. At times, it is observed that some Municipalities tend to perform discretionary functions to the neglect of obligatory duties.

Urbanisation in Karnataka: The level of urbanisation in Karnataka is relatively high, with nearly 31 per cent of the state's population living in urban areas compared to 25.7 per cent for India as a whole. The urban population of the state went up from 5.2 million in 1961 to 13.4 million in 1991, an increase of over 250 per cent in a period of thirty years, whereas the total population registered a growth of only 90 per cent during the same period (Table-1).

It is interesting to note that while there has been a significant growth in the urban population of the state, the rise in number of urban centres has been modest from 213 in 1961 to 254 in 1991. The distribution of population in different size-class cities shows that nearly 65 per cent of the total urban population is concentrated in 21 class I cities, i.e., cities with a population of a lakh and above (Table-2). While some of the class II towns are in the process of attaining class I status, the very small towns, viz., class V and VI are declining in importance.

Bangalore occupies a dominant position, accounting for as much as 29.5 per cent of the state's urban population. It is six times larger than the second largest city, Mysore, which had a population of 0.62 million in 1991. Bangalore is not only the capital of Karnataka but an important metropolis of India attracting migrants from all over the country. Its rapid growth has also contributed to the imbalance in the urbanisation pattern of the state.

The pace of industrialisation and urbanisation in Karnataka has resulted in severe pressure on services and infrastructural facilities like water, power, housing, roads etc. It has also led to unauthorised settlements and proliferation of slums. Karnataka was one of the first states to launch planned development of towns, especially in respect of Bangalore and Mysore as far back as the late 19th century. The Dewans of Mysore evinced keen interest in developing cities with broad roads, pavements, parks and in providing civic amenities.

Urban Planning and Development: Urban administration is a part of the process of urban planning and urban development. Modern town planning is based on the models evolved in Western countries. In Karnataka, the legal framework for planned development of urban areas was provided by the **Karnataka Town and Country Planning Act**

which came into force in 1961. This law aimed at achieving the following objectives:

(i) To create conditions favourable for planning and replanning of the urban/rural areas in the state with a view to providing full civic and social amenities for the people; (ii) To stop uncontrolled development of land due to land speculation and profiteering in land;

(iii) To preserve and improve existing recreational facilities and other amenities, contributing towards balanced use of land; and

(iv) To direct the future growth of populated areas in the state, with a view to ensuring desirable standards of environmental health and hygiene, and creating facilities for the orderly growth of industry and commerce, thereby promoting generally standards of living in the state.

The administrative machinery envisaged under the Act comprises the Directorate of Town Planning, the State Town Planning Board and the Local Planning Authorities. The Town Planning Board is only an advisory body set up to advise the state government on planning and policies for achieving the balanced development of the state. A Planning Authority is constituted for a Local Planning Area declared as such under the **Town Planning Act** and is made responsible for the preparation and implementation of plans. Planning Authorities have been constituted in 18 towns and cities of the state.

The planning process visualised under the Town Planning law involves the following three stages:

i) Preparation of Outline Development Plan (ODP);

ii) Preparation of Comprehensive Development Plan (CDP) ; and

iii) Preparation and implementation of Town Planning Schemes by the Town Planning Authorities.

Karnataka has made significant progress in the preparation of plans for major cities. Till March 1996, Outline Development Plans had been prepared for eight urban areas and Comprehensive Development Plan for sixteen cities. In respect of Bangalore, a revised CDP was prepared in 1995 taking into account the recent growth and developments of the city. However, no Planning Authority has prepared and implemented town planning schemes visualised under the Town Planning Act.

Establishment of Parastatal Agencies: With the growth of cities, the capacity of the Municipal bodies to deliver services have come under severe pressure. Investments in capital projects suffered on account of lack of resources. The government, therefore, began to set up statutory bodies independent of the municipalities for specific services. The Bangalore Water Supply and Sewerage Board was set up in 1964, charged with the responsibility of production and distribution of water and providing sewerage facilities to the Bangalore Metropolitan area, divesting the Bangalore City Corporation of this function. Another such body, namely, the Karnataka Urban Water Supply and Drainage Board was created in 1975 to cater to the water supply and drainage requirements of the other cities in the state.

In order to meet the housing needs of the public, the Karnataka Housing Board was established in the year 1956. It catered mostly to the requirements of urban areas outside the state capital, whereas for Bangalore, the City Improvement Trust Board (CITB) had been constituted as far back as 1945. This Board played an important role in creating a number of new residential extensions in the city. The CITB and the Planning Board for Bangalore were merged and a new body called Bangalore Development Authority (BDA) was established in 1976, which combined in itself planning and development functions. The **Karnataka Urban Development Authorities Act** was passed in 1987 providing for the establishment of Urban Development Authorities in other cities of the state and 22 such authorities have already been set up. With a view to devoting special attention to the needs of the slum dwellers and the weaker sections of the society, the Karnataka Slum Improvement and Clearance Board was set up in 1975.

These parastatal agencies have played a significant role in the urban development of Karnataka state. The Bangalore Water Supply and Sewerage Board, for instance, has been responsible for the execution of Cauvery Water Supply Schemes (Stages 1, 2 and 3) resulting in augmentation of water supply to the extent of 540 million liters per day to Bangalore City. The CITB and BDA have contributed to the development of Bangalore City by establishing a number of well-planned residential layouts and allotting about 65,000 house sites to different categories of people. The Urban Development Authorities have provided over 10,000 sites for residential and commercial purposes in the other urban centres. The Karnataka Housing Board has played a key role in adding to the housing stock in the state. It has constructed about one lakh houses in various urban centres since its inception. The contribution of Slum Improvement and Clearance Board to housing has been a modest 12,000 - but it has implemented a number of schemes to improve the living conditions of slum dwellers like provision of water supply, electricity and sanitary facilities. There are about 1,600 slums in the state with a population of nearly 16 lakhs.

It can be argued that the parastatal agencies have not been able to meet the growing demands of the public and in that sense, the performance has fallen short of expectations. The reasons are not far to seek. These bodies also suffer from weaknesses such as lack of adequate resources and functional autonomy as also managerial deficiencies. As statutory authorities, they are expected to be autonomous institutions but in reality they are subject to the control of government in a number of ways. The appointment of the senior personnel and revision of tariffs, for instance, requires the approval of government. In any case, with increasing urbanisation and the pressure of population, governmental agencies will be hard put to provide urban infrastructure all on their own.

Resources of the Urban Local Bodies: The resources of the urban local bodies are derived from the following sources:

1. Municipal taxes.
2. Grant-in-aid and inter-governmental transfers.
3. User charges.
4. Other fees and levies

Taxes levied by Municipalities include octroi, property tax and in some states, profession tax. Octroi, a tax levied on goods entering a city was a major and promising source of revenue for a long time but it was abolished in Karnataka in 1979 on the ground that it was an obnoxious levy. Except in a few states like Maharashtra and Gujarat, other states have abolished this tax. Consequently, property tax now constitutes the major source of revenue for the Municipal bodies. However, the system of property tax as it exists now suffers from a number of drawbacks. The assessment of the property is to be done on the basis of annual rental value which is again linked to the standard rent under the **Rent Control Act.** The yield, particularly from the older properties, is, therefore, very low. The total revenue from property tax of all municipal bodies in the state during 1994-95 amounted to about Rs. 50 crores, of which a lion's share of Rs. 30 crores was accounted for by Bangalore City Corporation. One reason for the low growth of revenue from this source is that Municipal authorities are reluctant to undertake revision of tax. Moreover, the valuation of property is not free from arbitrariness.

The grant-in-aid and transfers from the state government to the local bodies constitute the largest source of revenue to the Municipalities. The most important is the octroi compensation grant. To begin with, an annual increase of 5 per cent was allowed and it has gradually risen to 15 per cent. Even so, it is often argued that it does not really compensate the revenue from the abolition of octroi. Receipts from entertainment tax, motor vehicle tax and stamp duty are shared with the local government on percentage basis or in terms or fixed amount. For instance, 90 per cent of the revenue derived from entertainment tax is transferred to the local bodies whereas only a small amount from out of the motor vehicle tax is given to them. Bangalore City Corporation gets Rs. 75 lakhs per annum and other cities much less. The total devolution of funds to the municipal bodies from the state government during 1995-96 was of the order of Rs. 217.60 crores comprising octroi grants (Rs. 126.30 crores), entertainment tax (Rs. 48.60 crores), motor vehicle tax grant (Rs. 8.10 crores), stamp duty charges (Rs. 18.10 crores) and development grants to the tune of Rs.18.50 crores.

User charges are levied on services like supply of water and power. However, the full costs of providing the services are not recovered. In

Bangalore, drinking water up to 25,000 litres was being supplied free of cost till recently. Even now, the Bangalore Water Supply and Sewerage Board (BWSSB) is able to recover hardly 50 per cent of the cost of production of water. Sewerage services were provided free of cost for a long time. Only in 1987, a sanitary cess came to be levied in Bangalore at ten per cent of the water supply charges which has since been raised to 30 per cent.

Certain other charges and fees levied by local bodies include building licence fee, market fee and advertisement tax. The revenue from these charges are not high except in big cities like Bangalore.

Resources for capital projects are obtained from financial institutions like HUDCO, LIC etc., and through government contribution. The Karnataka Urban Infrastructural Finance Development Corporation was set up in 1993 to assist the local authorities in mobilising funds for infrastructural projects and also in providing expertise.

Emerging Policy Changes: The future development in the urban sector must be viewed in the context of the changes envisaged in the **74th Constitution Amendment Act** and the economic reforms heralding a greater role for the private sector. The former has given a constitutional status to the municipal governments in India and aims to make democratic decentralisation a reality. In future, elections to local bodies will have to be held regularly and they cannot be superseded by the state government. The constitution of Ward Committees in larger cities is expected to promote people's participation in the decision-making process at the grass root level. The Planning Committees at the district and metropolitan levels will impart democratic character to the planning process. The state legislature may consider bestowing more powers on the municipalities to make them stronger self-governing units but whether they will do so will depend on the willingness of the state government to part with their own powers. The possibility of introducing a cabinet system of government at the city level where accountability rests in the political executive can also be explored. In view of the key role envisaged by the Constitution for the municipal government, it would be necessary to redefine the role of the parastatal agencies like the planning and development authorities, the Water Supply Boards etc.

Urban management essentially involves delivery of civic services to the people. Till now, this function has been the monopoly of governmental or civic agencies. Liberalisation of the economy has opened the doors to the private sector to participate in the process of managing and developing cities, especially in infrastructure development. The following areas can be considered for private participation:

a) Contracting out Solid Waste Management - services like cleaning of streets and drains, garbage collection and disposal.

b) Billing of water, power charges and collection of revenue therefrom.

c) Public transport - allow private sector to compete with the public sector Road Transport Corporations.

d) Capital intensive projects like water supply systems, waste water treatment plants etc.

e) Public-Private partnerships can be encouraged, especially in housing sector.

The need to augment the financial resources of the local government cannot be overemphasised. This calls for bold fiscal reforms which would include a rethinking of provision of subsidised services. The pricing policy should recognize the need to recover the cost of providing services like water, power and public transport. Property tax system should be rationalised by de-linking it from rent control evolving proper valuation methods. Urban land must be treated as a resource and its revenue yielding potential fully exploited. Urban development policies must aim at achieving a balance between the goals of efficiency and equity.

Dealing with the changed context calls for suitable legal and institutional reforms. Legislations relating to urban administration will have to be amended with a view to enabling the urban authorities to function more effectively, free from excessive controls of government. Rules and procedures, especially those relating to land use controls, building regulations etc., need to be rationalised and simplified. Provision must be made for innovative methods of land acquisition like land readjustment and guided development so that land is released speedily for the purpose of housing and infrastructure development. A proper regulatory framework has to be evolved to regulate the activities of the private sector in urban development.

Institutional capacity building is of crucial importance for effective service delivery and the success of plans and schemes. A proper system of recruitment and training at different levels of local bodies must be devised and implemented. Training in areas like financial management and project planning and implementation is particularly important. Elected representatives should also be exposed to training in local laws so that they gain an appreciation of the intricacies of urban administration.

Finally, it is necessary to stress the importance of citizen participation in civic affairs. Voluntary and non-governmental organizations can play a vital role in promoting citizen awareness and in assisting the authorities in better environmental management. Protection of the environment and promotion of ecological aspects have been included in the 12th schedule to the Constitution as one of the functions that may be assigned to the municipalities. Apart from the efforts of the local bodies, the co-operation of the people is essential in protecting and improving the urban environment. A number of NGOs have come up in Karnataka like the Centre for Environment Education, AVAS, Wastewise etc., who are actively involved in improving the city environment including the plight of the urban poor. Government at the state and local levels would do well to recognize the role of the community in addressing the urban environmental problems and re-orient their policies and strategies to create 'environmentally sustainable cities'.

ANNEXURE A

TWELTH SCHEDULE

(1) Urban Planning including town planning;

(2) Regulation of land use and construction of buildings;

(3) Planning for economic and social development;

(4) Roads and bridges;

(5) Water supply for domestic, industrial and commercial purposes;

(6) Public health, sanitation, conservancy and solid waste management;

(7) Fire services;

(8) Urban forestry, protection of the environment and promotion of ecological aspects;

(9) Safeguarding the interest of weaker sections of society, including the handicapped and mentally retarded:

(10) Slum improvement and upgradation;

(11) Urban poverty alleviation;

(12) Provision of urban amenities and facilities such as parks, gardens, playgrounds;

(13) Promotion of cultural, educational and aesthetic aspects;

(14) Burials and burial grounds; cremations, cremation grounds and electric crematoriums;

(15) Cattle pounds; prevention of cruelty to animals;

(16) Vital statistics including registration of births and deaths;

(17) Public amenities including street lighting, parking lots, bus-stops and public convenience.

Table-1

Urban Population in Karnataka: Decadal Growth

Year	No. of Towns	Total Population	Urban Population	% of Urban to Total Population	% Growth or Urban Population
1961	213	23,486,772	5,266,493	22.33	18.26
1971	227	29,299,014	7,122,093	24.31	35.23
1981	250	37,043,345	10,711,103	28.91	50.39
1991	254	44,806,468	13,850,702	30.91	29.09

Source: Census of India

Table:2

Percentage Distribution of Urban Population in Different Size-Class Cities in Karnataka

Class of Town	1981	1971	1991
I	58.60	51.32	41.37
II	6.46	8.40	12.76
III	17.75	15.38	15.95
IV	13.74	19.05	19.50
V	2.87	4.62	8.04
V	0.58	11.23	2.38

Source: Census of India

REFERENCES

1. **Annual Reports,** Housing and Urban Development Department, Government of Karnataka.

2. **Census of India Reports.**

3. **Karnataka State Gazetteer,** Part II, Government of Karnataka, Bangalore, 1983.

4. Venkatarangaiya, M. And M. Pattabhiram (eds.) (1969); **Local Goverment of India : Select Reading** Bombay: Allied Publishing.

5. **74th Constitution Amendment Act, 1972 and the Karnataka Amendment Acts.**

III

AGRICULTURAL AND INDUSTRIAL ADMINISTRATION

1

AGRICULTURAL ADMINISTRATION

R. Dwarakinath,
B.A. Poonacha and
D.S. Murigappa Sreshty

Introduction: When the new state of Mysore was formed on 1st November 1956, it inherited an agricultural administrative system in the integrated districts as they existed in their erstwhile states. There was in the districts from the integrated areas a fairly uniform administrative set up at the district level with a District Agricultural Officer, who was normally a class II officer. He was assisted by Agricultural Officers, Agricultural Demonstrators at the taluk level. In addition, there were Divisional Deputy Directors of Agriculture, based at Dharwad and Raichur respectively. Depending upon the special agricultural programmes that were being implemented in different areas, specialist agricultural officers were also functioning, e.g., a Divisional Soil Conservation Officer in Bijapur and Agricultural Extension Officers in the command area of the Tungabhadra project in Raichur district. Besides, there was an agricultural college at

Dharwad established in 1956. There were also many agricultural research stations/farms in the integrated areas.

While the entire set up of the department of agriculture in erstwhile Mysore remained intact along with that of Coorg. the systems coming from the former states of Bombay, Madras and Hyderabad, had to be integrated into a single unified department in the new state. Hence, as a matter of priority, attention was first devoted to streamlining the administrative system under the Director of Agriculture at the state level. The state was divided into four divisions, each under a Deputy Director of Agriculture, Senior (Class I). At the district level, there was a District Agricultural Officer (Class II). With the creation of the post of Deputy Director of Agriculture at the Divisional level, some measure of decentralisation in administration became possible with the Divisional Heads being in overall charge of all agricultural programmes.

With the formulation of the Second Five Year Plan at a time when the new State came into being, there were a number of new schemes that were sanctioned with additional staff. There was a new thrust for growing commercial crops and hence, by 1990, two posts of Joint Directors were created to assist the Director of Agriculture.

Three Phases of Development

The efforts toward agricultural development along with the steps taken to strengthen and decentralise administration may be seen in three distinct phases, namely, the first phase from 1956 to 1966, the second phase from 1966 to 1980, and third, from 1980 to 1996.

The prominent developments witnessed during these three phases are briefly discussed below:-

First Phase 1956-1966: In this phase the main emphasis was on increasing food production not only to meet the prevailing deficit but also to meet the increasing population. The focus was on programmes yielding quick results. Schemes which were basically launched during this period could be broadly classified into (i) land development, (ii) educational development, (iii) popularisation of manures and fertilisers, (iv) promoting improved seeds, (v) advising plant protection measures,

(vi) diffusion of improved agricultural practices, (vii) emphasis on intensive cultivation practices, and (viii) supporting schemes.

Land Reforms in Karnataka: Though in the erstwhile state after independence, reforms had been initiated in 1961, a major landmark in agricultural development took place in 1996 when the Karnataka Land Reforms Act was enacted as a uniform law relating to agrarian relations, conferment of ownership on tenants, ceiling on holdings and related matters. Based on the concept of land to the tiller, occupancy rights were granted to 1.18 lakh tenants on 46 lakh acres of lands.

Land Development: Another important agricultural programme was that of land development by way of reclamation of lands and water and soil conservation. For land reclamation and land development, tractors and bulldozers were made available from the department. Soil conservation work also got accelerated.

Irrigation: Since the irrigated area in the new state was only 7.3 per cent of the cultivated area it became imperative to develop irrigation resources. Apart from stepping up minor irrigation schemes, the only major irrigation project in the state was the area irrigated from the Krishnarajasagar Dam in Mysore. The Tungabhadra project was, at the time of reorganisation of states, in the final stage of completion. Further, in the subsequent years new projects such as Ghataprabha, Malaprabha, Kabini, Harangi, Hemavathi and Upper Krishna were taken up as major irrigation projects. However, the utilisation in the first phase was very low mainly because the field channels had not been constructed and technical assistance had also to be stepped up for developing land for irrigation by providing subsidy and technical services.

Though these projects, at enormous cost, created valuable irrigation potential, the progress in agricultural development in the command area was disturbingly slow. In order to bring about all-round development under the large irrigation projects, the state government passed the **CADA Act in 1972,** constituting the "Command Area Development Authority (CADA)" for major projects and river basins.

Fertilisers and Manures: In 1956, the fertilisers use in the state was just about 5,600 tonnes in terms of nutrients which rose to 5.5. lakh tonnes in 1986-87. As a result of the extension efforts along with subsidies, consumption of fertilisers increased gradually, specially in the irrigated areas. Presently, the state average is slightly above the national average.

With the increased use of fertilisers, adulteration has become a problem. Steps have been initiated, therefore, aimed at quality control in fertilisers. As such, Fertiliser Control Laboratories have been established at strategic places in the state on the basis of Fertiliser Control Order. Similarly, Soil Testing Laboratories have been established to test the soils and recommend balanced use of fertilisers. Efforts have been initiated to educate farmers on quality aspects of organic manures and their proper preparation and use. Special schemes have been undertaken to increase the production of rural as well as urban compost.

Improved Seeds: Seed is the most important input in crop production. The improved seeds were multiplied through the Registered Seed Growers under the technical supervision of the departmental staff. These seed growers were encouraged to sell the seed directly at a small premimum. During the II plan, a chain of state seed farms were established to produce 'foundation seed' using the 'nucleus seed' obtained from the research stations. The foundation seed was then distributed to registered seed growers. During this period, 56 seed farms were established. Another 27 were established during the Third plan. Subsequently, however, some of these farms were closed leaving ultimately only 62 with the department.

As this arrangement was also found inadequate, leading to a rethinking on the seed policy, a Seed Corporation was set up, to begin with, as a subsidiary of the State Agro-Industries Corporation. Subsequently, it became an independent Corporation. In the meantime, a Seed Certification scheme was initiated to ensure quality seed supply to farmers. The **Seeds Act of 1966** as a Central Act was passed in 1966 and relevant rules were framed by 1968. Later, in 1974, a Seed Certification Agency, as an autonomous body, was also established.

Plant Protection: With the crop losses due to pests and diseases becoming considerable, estimated at 8 to 10 per cent of production, scientific methods of plant protection also entered the scene, more rapidly with the commercial crops. In order to lead the farmers in this regard, plant protection schemes were taken up, supplying plant protection chemicals and equipment on concessional terms. Gradually, chemcial control became quite popular, particularly on the high value crops. Thus, the area treated with plant protection measures which was around 5,200 hectares in 1956-57 increased to about 2.24 lakh hectares by 1965-66. For ensuring the quality of pesticides, the **Insecticides Act** was also passed as a Central Act. An Insecticide Testing Laboratory was established at Bangalore to back-up quality control measures.

Strategies to Improve Farming: The Japanese method of paddy cultivation was such a programme initiated in 1950s to increase rice productivity. This programme continued after 1956 also with the special staff. Kharif and rabi campaigns were initiated in 1959-60 to popularise improved cultivation practices of other food crops like jowar, ragi, bajra and wheat.

During the last four decades, experiments have been made with several strategies of agricultural extension as indicated below:

1) Pilot Extension Project - Community Development Project - National Extension Service, (1950-60).

2) Intensive Agricultural District Programme (IADP), Intensive Agricultural Area Programme (IAAP) (1961-70).

3) High Yielding Varieties Programme (1965-66).

4) Small Farmers Development Agency (SFDA) and Marginal Farmers and Agricultural Labour (MFAL) Programme.

5) Client - Specific Programmes such as:

a) Command Area Development Agency (CADA).

b) Drought Prone Area Programme (DPAP).

c) Integrated Dry and Agriculture Development (IDLAD).

6) Area-Specific Programmes such as:

a) Intensive Cotton Development Programme.

b) Intensive Oilseed Development Programme.

c) Intensive Cattle Development Programme.

7) Entrusting Nationalised Banks with agricultural lending responsibilities.

8) Other Programmes such as:

a) Integrated Rural Development Project (IADP).

b) Tribal Development.

c) Hill Area Development.

d) T & V Programme.

e) Special Component Programme.

f) National Pulse Development Programme (NRDP).

g) National Oilseeds Development Programme)NODP).

Raising Food Production: All these programmes cumulatively contributed to a notable increase in agricultural production in the state. The food grain production which was about 33.31 lakh tonnes in 1956-57 went up to 39.90 lakh tonnes by 1960-61 and to 48.39 lakh tonnes in 1964-65, and later, to 86 lakhs tonnes in 1992-93,. However, when the state faced one of the worst droughts, the production came down to 35.44 lakh tonnes. All the same, the potential for higher levels of production in normal years had been evidently built up in the state

Development of Commercial Crops: Karnataka is one of the leading states for commercial crops. In 1956, the important commercial and plantation crops were cotton, oilseeds (mainly groundnut), sugarcane, tobacco, coconut, coffee, arecanut, cashew, cardamom, pepper and fruit crops like oranges, banana, mangoes and grapes. In the new state, comprehensive development schemes for many of the above crops were formulated as Third Plan schemes (1961-66) with the specific object of increasing both the area and production. The main thrust was on supplying quality seeds and planting material, application of manures, popularising plant protection measures and developing irrigation facility.

In 1963, the government took a policy decision to transfer all schemes pertaining to horticulture, viz., fruits, spices and plantation crops, to the newly constituted state Horticulture Department. As a result, only cotton, sugarcane, oil seeds and tobacco remained with the Department of Agriculture.

Agricultural Education and Research: In 1956, when the new state came into being, it had two agricultural colleges, namely, Agricultural College, Bangalore, and College of Agriculture, Dharwad, with researach farms attached to them. There were also 45 other research stations and farms carrying out research on different crops and farming aspects. A number of **ad hoc** research schemes were also in operation. All these research schemes continued, as they were, during the Second Plan (1956-61). Based on the experience gained in implementing these schemes and considering the emerging research needs in the new state, the entire research set-up was restructured and strengthened as part of the Third Plan effort. Each major crop had a main research station, generally with two regional stations and four sub-stations, depending upon the situation in a given agro-climatic region. After 1956, both the colleges were strengthened with additional staff, equipment and building for increasing the intake of students to meet the rising demand for agricultural graduates.

During 1960s, institution building for agricultural development received a further impetus in the country, with the establishment of several State Agricultural Universities. Accordingly, the Karnataka Government began contemplating the formation of the University of Agricultural Sciences on the lines of Land Grant Colleges of USA. The **University of Agricultural Sciences Act** was passed in 1963. The University came into existence in 1964, taking over the two agricultural colleges, all the research stations dealing with agriculture, horticulture and animal husbandry, along with the veterinary college. A Fisheries College was established soon after. Consequently, the Department of Agriculture was left with a reduced responsibility for extension, ensuring input supply, farmers' training and related regulatory functions from 1965 onwards

Agricultural Schools: The Department of Agriculture placed considerable emphasis on educating farmers' sons and farmers in modern agriculture schools and their number increased to ten by the end of the Third Five Year Plan. In these schools, youngsters from farming families were provided practical training in modern agricultural practices.

Rural Development Training Centres: Community development programmes in the state needed in a large number the services of trained village level extension workers called Gramasevaks. Five Gramasevaks Training Centres were set-up to train Gramasevaks, initially, for a two-year duration and later, for one year duration. These training centres, earlier designated as Gramasevaks Training Centres, later came to be known as Rural Development Training Centres.

To sum up, some significant landmarks in agricultural development during this period are:

a) Formation of the Department of Agriculture for the new state of Mysore (1956) by integrating the staff, research and teaching institutions and training courses transferred from integrated areas.

b) Formulation of the Second Five Year Plan and implementation of a number of crop development, and extension schemes (1957-58).

c) Formulation of the Third Year Plan based on the needs of the new state.

d) Establishment of the University of Agricultural Sciences (1964-65).

e) Implementation of high yielding varieties programmes.

Second Phase - 1966-80: In order to cope with the challenges posed by the green revolution and the new technology, it became necessary to restructure the Department of Agriculture in 1967. Besides the two Joint Directors of Agriculture, one, for Development, and the other, for Soil & Conservation, a team of Extension Subject-matter Specialists in various special disciplines were created. At the field level, a Joint Director of Agriculture was posted at the Divisional headquarters. At the District level, a post of Deputy Director of Agriculture was created, who was assisted by subject matter specialists. Below the district level an Assistant Director of Agriculture was posted in a Sub-division and he was also assisted by subject-matter specialists.

The decade of 1960s was a period of significant technological growth. The hybrids and high yielding varieties of cereals made their debut in 1966-67 with a spectacular impact. The food production in the country till then being inadequate, the country had to depend heavily on imports, including PL-480 assistance from USA.

The agricultural scientists, plant breeders along with progressive farmers, rose to the occasion in developing and adopting certain strategic new agricultural technologies. The introduction of breeders succeeded in new hybrids or high yielding varieties in wheat, maize, bajra, jowar, rice and ragi, coupled with high grade fertilizers and irrigation facilities making the Green Revolution possible. Later, the hybrid cotton varieties gave a tremendous push to the commercial crops, as well.

At this stage, the Department of Agriculture, after the re-organisation, had not become well-settled, organisationally and operationally. The birth of the University of Agriculture Sciences in 1964 also warranted further readjustments. As such, the advent of new technology amounted to a new challenge. The extension work at the field level continued to be the responsibility of the Community Development Blocks, the Gramasevaks being the grass root level workers. Since these field workers were not very familiar with the new technology, the Department of Agriculture had to undertake the responsibility of upgrading the technical competence of the entire cadre.

In order to enable the Department of Agriculture to concentrate its efforts on extension and regulatory functions rather than on supplies and services, the Karnataka Agro Industries Corporation was established in 1967. Its responsibilities included not only the distribution of agricultural inputs but also providing services of tractors, bulldozers and well boring rigs.

Farmers' Training: Attention was also paid to training the farmers in acquiring knowledge and skills and eight Farmers' Education and Training Centres (FETC) were established under the Centrally sponsored schemes to train farmers. Further, agricultural schools for farmers' sons were also established in the districts where they did not exist earlier.

Multiple Cropping Programme: With the increase in irrigation facilities, attempts towards raising more than one crop in a year became a reality while raising three crops in a year became a possibility. Based on proper planning and choice of appropriate short duration varieties, farmers with year-round irrigation were able to raise three crops in a year. This was taken as a welcome opportunity when expansion of cultivated area had become impossible. Therefore, in support, pilot projects were taken up under Bhadra and Tungabhadra projects to effectively demonstrate multiple cropping patterns. This system was then extended to other irrigated areas in the state.

Demonstrations: For the purpose of spreading the new agricultural technology, the national demonstrations under the ICAR schemes were taken up on farmers' fields. In addition, under a state scheme, Block demonstrations were also launched in 1974 with a view to mobilising community efforts in large scale applications on recommended technologies. The demonstrations organised under both the schemes helped considerably in a rapid spread of the new technology in a short time and the cultivation of high yielding varieties was quite effective in increasing cereal production in the state.

In order to ensure the quality of hybrid seeds, fertilizers and plant protection chemicals, new quality control laboratories for seeds, insecticides and fertilizers were established. The seed industry witnessed a rapid growth during this period with increasing demand for new varieties of seeds. As the National Seeds Corporation by itself was unable to meet the demand, the Karnataka State Agro Seeds Corporation later on was set up. This Corporation which has been renamed as 'Karnataka Seeds Corporation Limited' now meets a substantial part of the demand for the seeds in the state. A Seed Certificate Agency was set up in 1974.

It was during this period from mid 1960 to late 1970s that green revolution was at its peak in the state. However, studies made during this period on the impact of the green revolution brought forth some disturbing findings. It was seen that though there was agricultural prosperity in general, the well-to-do farmers and those having irrigation facilities had prospered more. The new technology had not percolated to small and marginal farmers in general and to those in dry farming areas in particular. Further, while there was a substantial jump in cereal production, the position in the case of oil seeds and pulses was rather unsatisfactory. Hence, while formulating the Fifth Five Year Plan (1974-79), programmes for increasing the production of pulses and oilseeds were given special emphasis. Development programmes for farmers of SC (Special Component Plan), ST (Tribal Sub-plans) and small and marginal farmers were given priority. Integrated dry land development projects were taken up to demonstrate improved varieties suitable for dry land farming. Drought-prone areas were taken up for implementation in chronic drought affected areas and soil conservation works in arid regions.

Strengthening the Extension Service: During 1960s and 1970s, agricultural technology had taken great strides and the results of research had to be taken to the farmers. As such, programmes, like 'Lab to Land', were initiated to quickly transfer the new technologies to the fields. It was realised then that the existing extension system operating through CD Blocks and the multipurpose worker was unable to cope with the task of disseminating the new, and often complex technology to the farmers effectively. This was particularly so in reaching the target groups like Scheduled Castes and Tribal farmers, as also the small and marginal farmers.

It was also recognised that the multipurpose Gramasevak did not devote a major part of his working time for agricultural development as he was still loaded with non-agricultral activities. Taking these facts into consideration, along with the emerging needs of 1980s, a major restructuring of the Department of Agriculture was undertaken in 1979 with the assistance of the World Bank. Thus, T & V system of unified agricultural extension service was created by merging the agricultural staff working in the CD Blocks and those working in different crop development schemes. However, the soil conservation set up continued separately, as before.

In the new system, the Gramasevak was redesignated as Agricultural Assistant and was made solely responsible for agricultural development. At the taluk level, a post of Assistant Director of

Agriculture (Junior Class I) was created under this project who was made responsible for all agricultural development in the taluk. The taluk was divided into 4-5 agricultural ranges, each under an Agricultural Extension Officer, usually an agricultural graduate. He was required to guide and supervise the work of 5 to 6 Agricultural Assistants working under him. Each Agricultural Assistant was made responsible for about 400-800 farm families working through 'contact farmers'. For every cluster of taluks, a team of subject matter specialists was provided.

At the district level, the Principal Agricultural Officer of the rank of a Deputy Director of Agriculture was made responsible for implementing all the agricultural development programmes. He was assisted by a team of three subject matter specialists. Two or three districts constituted a division headed by a Joint Director of Agriculture.

This period witnessed the transfer of Agricultural Engineering wing to the Agro-Industries Corporation, intensification of Soil Conservation Schemes, establishment of Small and Marginal Farmers Development Agency and pilot projects in dryland development (1970). An independent seed certification agency to ensure production and supply of quality seeds to farmers was established in 1974. During 1974-75, sunflower as a major oil seed crop was introduced in the state. For the first time, food grain production in the state crossed 7 million tonnes. A major change in extension strategy was made through the implementation of training and visit system of extension under the World Bank assisted agricultural extension project (1978-79).

Third Phase - 1980-96: During this period, special programmes both Central and state sponsored, received greater attention. In 1990s, the Centre fielded the Oilseeds Technology Mission which is yet to increase oilseeds production. The programmes for target groups like Scheduled Castes and Tribal farmers, small and marginal farmers continued to receive special attention.

A notable landmark during this period was the exposure to farm women and farm youths new agriculture technology. A new project called WYTEP with DANIDA assistance was started in the state which is in operation from 1982.

Another landmark agriculture development project was the watershed development project. The watershed development started at Kabbalanala, Kanakapura Taluk in Bangalore District was a path finding effort. This venture served as the instrument for devising measures and standardising them as a package of improved land-use practices for the purpose of watershed development. A new project was started in areas having potential for watershed development. In 1991-92 the project was also extended to rainfed farming areas. By 1993-94, this programme was in operation in 19 Districts of the state in 85 watershed areas, benefiting around 82,000 hectares. In the projects, efforts were made to enlist people's participation, both or planning and implementation stages, and also mobilise and prepare them for the specific post-project responsibilities.

The most strategic programme that was initiated during this period was the dryland development project and the waterland development project. Dryland Development Boards were set up at the divisional level to undertake dryland development projects. By this time, the Ministry of Agriculture also got interested in this approach and came forward with the National Watershed Development Project. In short, during 1980s and 1990s dryland farming and watershed development programmes received greater attention then ever before.

The two Universities of Agricultural Sciences, one at Bangalore (1965) and the other at Dharwad (1986) provide a good agricultural research base and useful technology support for agricultural development in the state. Notable contributions have been made in dryland farming, watershed development, irrigation management, farm forestry, horticulture, poultry, vermiculture and hybrid rice. Commercial crops like cotton, chillies and sunflower have also received special attention.

The Report of the Expert Committee on Stagnation of Agricultural Productivity in Karnataka presented in 1993, turned out to be an event of far-reaching significance. The state had experienced some degree of stagnation, and even decline, both in the production and producitivity of the major seasonal crops during the preceding decade. In order to identify and analyse the problem and to come up with the necessary remedial measures the Government constituted an Expert Committee in 1992 with Sri T.R. Satish Chandran as the Chairman. A comprehensive examination of the issue by the Committee led to some practical recommendations.

The Committee noted that even the available agricultural technology was not being utilised adequately. The Committee emphasised the need for properly strengthening the extension programmes in the state. Further, the Committee noted that investments in agriculture both public and private, had come down shortly in later years. The credit support to agriculture had woefully fallen short of the requirements and even the input supply pattern had undergone several distortions. The Committee also highlighted the need for accelerating the pace of development of irrigation and improvements in water management.

As a follow up of the recommendations of the T.R. Satish Chandran Committee, the Department of Agriculture was reorganised, leading to the merger of two important services, viz., soil and water conservation and crop development programmes. Another major outcome was the formulation of the Draft Agriculture Policy Resolution (DAPR) through the instrumentality of the State Planning Board. The formulation of the DAPR (1995) was a landmark achievement as it embodied some bold and innovative concepts in agricultural development. The DAPR made far-reaching recommendations for improving agricultural productivity and creating a new climate for agricultural development.

The state has made a remarkable progress in encouraging private enterprise in Research and Development (R & D) work in agriculture. As a result, considerable headway has been made in tissue culture, seed production, floriculture and dryland horticulture. Sericulture too has registered a noteworthy progress.

During this period attention was also paid to export aspects in agriculture development with private enterprises coming into agriculture, seed production, oilseeds, dryland horticulture and floriculture.

The period also witnessed, as process of democratic decentralisation, the starting of the Panchayat Raj bodies, viz., Zilla, Taluk, Village Panchayats, established under the **Karnataka Panchayat Raj**

Act, 1993. Agricultural Development and implementation of programmes have become the responsibility of these bodies. Consequently, the Department of Agriculture had to rearrange its administrative operations in order to provide for the technical support and guidance to these bodies. It is hoped that the elected leaders of these bodies with proper orientation and training will discharge the agricultural responsibilities adequately and a more rapid comprehensive agricultural development may take place in their respective jurisdictions in the long run.

During this period the Department of Agriculture also reviewed the extension system for reorganising its structure and strategey to meet the emerging needs. The Government, therefore, brought about the integration of extension and soil conservation wings in 1995 and as a result, at present, there exists a unified agricultural development system in the state. Further, administrative reorganisation was also undertaken at the district level with each district being headed by a Joint Director of Agriculture except in the smaller districts of Bidar and Kodagu which are under the control of DDAs. The districts are divided into 2 or 3 divisions each under a Deputy Director of Agriculture assisted by two subject-matter specialists, one for crop production and another for plant protection.

LANDMARKS

The important landmarks in agricultural development could be briefly enumerated as below:-

1956—Formation of the Agriculture Department for the new state of Mysore (now Karnataka) by integrating the staff, research, teaching institutions and training centres transferred from integrated areas. 1957-58 Formulation of the Second Five Year Plan and implementation of a number of crop development and extension schemes.

1961-62—Formulation of the Third Five Year Plan based on the needs of the new state - restructuring of research framework development schemes.

1963—Transfer of schemes dealing with horticulture and plantation crops both research and development to the control of the Department of Horticulture, Lalbagh, Bangalore.

1964-65—Establishment of the University of Agricultural Sciences and transfer of all research schemes along with research stations and agricultural colleges from the Department to its control.

1966-67—Implementation of high yielding varieties programme - reorganisation of the Department of Agriculture - creation of a team of subject matter specialists at state level - creation of the post of Joint Director of Agriculture at divisional levels, Deputy Director of Agriculture at district levels with a team of three subject matter specialists, ADAs at sub-divisional level with a team of SMS, establishment of Agro-Industries Corporation to deal with supply and services.

1970—Transfer of Agricultural Engineering wing to Agro Industries Corporation. Intensification of soil conservation schemes, small and marginal farmers development agency, DPAP - Pilot projects on dryland development.

1974—Establishment of an independent seed certification agency to ensure production and supply of quality seeds to farmers.

1974-75—Formulation of Fifth Five Year Plan (1974-79) with emphasis on pulses and oilseeds - introduction of sunflower as a major oilseed crop.

1975-76—Food grains production crosses 70 lakh tonnes for the first time.

1978-79—Major change in extension strategy - implementation of Training and Visit System of extension under the World Bank assisted agricultural extension project - VLW brought under the direct supervision of the Department of Agriculture - major re-organisation of the Department of Agriculture - creation of a post of Assistant Director of Agriculture (Junior Class I) at taluk level who is made responsible for all agricultural development programmes - creation of agricultural ranges under AEOs - One AA for 400-800 families - Teams of SMS at cluster of taluks - Principal Agricultural Officer at district level with a three member SMS team - JDAs at divisional level for 2-3 districts.

1982—Sanction of WYTEP with DANIDA assistance.

1982-85—Constitution of Dryland Development Boards - implementation of dryland development projects - Watershed management concept brought into practice - implementation of National Agricultural Extension project - strengthening SMS team with soil and water management and farm management experts at district level, inputs at cluster taluk level and farm implements at divisional level.

1986-87—National Watershed Development Programme for rainfed agriculture.

1995—Reorganisation of the Department of Agriculture combining the soil conservation and crop production wings.

Conclusions

In spite of the progress made in several aspects of agriculture, there is yet a lot more to be achieved in certain areas. These areas are:

1) pulses and oilseeds where the state is deficient;

2) improving the efficiency in utilising the available irrigation resources and developing dryland farming;

3) increasing the investment in agriculture, both public and private;

4) developing agriculture as a means to reduce rural poverty; and

5) the need to make farm women and youth play a more productive role in farming.

A review of the development of agriculture so far brings out certain factors which are not conducive to increasing production. There was a time when farmers were reluctant to use chemical fertilisers and they had to be persuaded. However, now, there is indiscriminate fertiliser application which has resulted in the deterioration of soil health which has affected productivity. Similarly, indiscriminate use of plant-protection chemicals, over-use of irrigation water have proved counter-productive in farming.

The foregoing discussion of the agricultural scenario in Karnataka since independence brings out the fact that there is scope for accelerating agricultural development and productivity by attending to areas which need attention and by taking suitable corrective action to overcome a few serious constraints which often develop due to the very process of growth and act as impediments for further growth in agriculture. The areas which deserve attention are:

1. The Western-ghats receive heavy and assured rains. Karnataka being a water-starved state, the west flowing streams need to be harnessed both for power generation and for irrigation.

2. In the case of many major food crops, there are substantial and persisting yield gaps. Concerted efforts are needed to step up their productivity, so that the area under these crops is reduced, making room for other alternate crops.

3. The state is eminently suited for a variety of horticulture crops, both under irrigation and under rainfed conditions. The modest efforts made so far in this regard need to be systematically built up.

4. Being a premier sericulture state in the country, Karnataka has an established initial advantage in this enterprise. But, there is considerable scope for improving silk production in the state not only quantitatively but also qualitatively.

5. Not so long ago, the state was known for its crossbred animals. This lead seems to have been lost. There is room to improve this line of livestock development, in addition to further improving the dairy industry as well as the poultry industry.

6. There is considerable scope in the state for more development of the inland, coastal and marine fishing industry. Prawn cultivation also requires to be built up, but on scientific lines, taking note of the pitfalls encountered elsewhere.

7. To support a growing agriculture, an adequate infra-structure support is necessary. This has to be built up in the state, harnessing both the public and private investments.

8. Fostering a rapid growth of technical manpower is another matter that requires attention, to reinforce the development of agriculture.

As far as constraints are concerned, the following deserve attention at this stage of its development:-

1. Irrigation water being a scarce resource in the state, the matter of water-use efficiency needs to be given topmost attention both under public irrigation systems and private irrigation ventures.

2. Under some of the large irrigation systems in the state, considerable land areas are being thrown out of cultivation, mainly due to inappropriate water, soil and crop management practices. Urgent attention is warranted here both to contain the problem and to find remedial measures.

3. A rapid degradation of the environmental factors is seriously affecting normal agriculture in the state leading to expansion in drought-prone areas on the one hand, and to sinking groundwater levels, on the other. Effective measures to arrest and reverse this process is very necessary in the interest of sustainable agriculture.

4. The state is noted for its pioneering efforts in watershed development. But, it is estimated that it will take at least 30 years to cover all the vulnerable areas in the state under this scheme, going by the present rate of progress. Therefore, it is very important that appropriate dry farming techniques are devised combining soil and water conservation measures with improved crop production practices so that on-going degradation in dry land regions is impeded to some extent.

5. The progressive growth in agricultural production, specially in the case of seasonal crops, has come down in recent years due to the slowing down of research output. In the meanwhile, it is observed that the utilisation of available technology is found to be inadequate. Therefore, it is necessary that the agricultural extension system in the state is re-geared not only to make a better use of the available technology, but also to harness the beneficial indigenous technical knowledge.

6. The state has already made a substantial investment in building up the resources organisation needed for agriculture development. But, the returns from these investments seem to be declining in recent years,

mainly due to lack of effective management, external monitoring and social accountability.

7. A marked feature of the technical services in the state in recent times is its declining morale. Compared to the previous decades, administrative efforts toward recognition of technical talent, promotion of growth of technical competence and fostering of technical leadership seem to have suffered considerably. It is quite necessary in the larger interest that the technical services are not neglected or downgraded in any way.

8. Recent studies and observations indicate that the technical services could improve their contribution to growth very substantially, if the management component in their training is given due importance. In these days of fast moving developments, management of technical services merely on common sense has already proved inadequate.

It will be the paramount task of the Department to ensure that in the Ninth Plan of the state, some of these areas and constraints mentioned above are taken note of in the formulation of agricultural programmes and policies.

REFERENCES

Bowles, Chester (1964). **Who Owns the Land** (Inaugural address of the University of Agricultural Sciences, Bangalore). New Delhi: U.S.I.S.

Coleman, Leslie C. (1929). A Note on the Report of the Royal Commission on Agriculture in India. **Journal of Mysore and Experimental Union,** X (122).

Dwarakinath. R and Y. Chandra Shekar (1979). **Agricultural Zones in Karnataka State.** Bangalore: Department of Agriculture.

Dwarakinath. R and D.S. Murigappa Sreshty (1980). **Krishi Karnataka.** Bangalore: Department of Agriculture

Government of India (1975). **Gazetteer of India: Shimoga District.** New Delhi: Government of India.

Government of Karnataka (1976a). **Report of the National Commission on Agriculture - Summary of the Recommendations.** Bangalore: Department of Agriculture.

Government of Karnataka (1976b). **Block Demonstrations: An Effective Strategy to achieve Rapid Increase in Agricultural Production.** Bangalaore: Department of Agriculture.

Government of Karnataka (1977a). **Achievements in Minor Irrigation in Karnataka for Two Decades (1956-57 to 1975-77).** Bangalore: Public Works Department.

Government of Karnataka (1977b). **Irrigation Wells Sunk in Karnataka 1975-76.** Bangalore: Bureau of Economics and Statistics.

Government of Karnataka (1977c). **Annual Administrative Reports. 1900-76-77.** Bangalore: Department of Agriculture.

Government of Karnataka. (1978). **A Brief Note on the Development of Agriculture since Formation to 1975-76.** Bangalore: Department of Agriculture.

Government of Karnataka. (1988). **Karnataka Agriculture on the March. Platinum Jubilee Publication.** Bangalore: Department of Agriculture.

Government of Karnataka (1992a). **Trends in Area. Yield and Production of Principal Crops during 1960-80.** Bangalore: Directorate of Economics and Statistics.

Government of Karnataka (1992b). **Agriculture in Karnataka.** Bangalore: Department of Agriculture.

Government of Karnataka (1995). **Annual Report of the Department of Agriculture.** Bangalore: Department of Agriculture.

Government of Karnataka (1976). **Performance Budgets of the Department of Agriculture.** Bangalore: Department of Agriculture.

Government of Mysore (1939). **Agriculture in Mysore.** Bangalore: Department of Agriculture.

Government of Mysore (1958a). **Mysore Agricultural Calendar and Year Book.** Bangalore: Department of Agriculture.

Government of Mysore (1958b). **Second Five Year Plan - Programmes for 1958-59.** Bangalore: Planning Department.

Government of Mysore (1970a). An Analysis of Yield Components in Height Yielding Fields in Mysore State. **Advisers' Report.** Mandya Indo-Japanese Agricultural Extensive Centre.

Government of Mysore (1970b). **Long Term Training,** No.1. Mandya: Indo-Japanese Agricultural Extension Centre.

Government of Mysore (1970c). **Agricultural Progress in Karnataka: Facts and Figures.** Bangalore: Department of Agriculture.

Naik K.C. and A. Shankaran (1972). **History of Agricultural Universities in India.** New Delhi: Oxford & IBH.

Rao, P. Anantha Padmanabha (1954). **Crop Surveys in Mysore State. 1949-52 and 1953-54.** Bangalore: Department of Agriculture.

Sreshty. D.S. Murigappa (1979). **Manual of the Department of Agriculture.** Bangalore : Department of Agriculture.

Venkataramiah, B.P. and D.S. Murigappa Sreshty. (1977). **Early History and Organisation of the Department of Agriculture.** Bangalore: Department of Agriculture.

2

INDUSTRIAL DEVELOPMENT

A. Indira and Vinod Vyasulu

Introduction: The industrial development of present day Karnataka prior to the independence of the country in 1947, was very uneven due to historical circumstances. The erstwhile princely state of Mysore being comparatively autonomous since the Rendition in 1881, had evolved a definite economic development policy and programme and embarked on a programme of industrialisation. However, in the other entire areas of the state, industrial development was incidental and not on any planned basis. Thus, in 1958, Karnataka in India's industrial development, enjoyed the distinction of being a pioneer, thanks largely to the foresight and dynamism of the princely rulers and dewans of the erstwhile state of Mysore.

Economic History of the 18th Century: At the turn of the 18th century, there were significant changes in the Kingdom of Mysore. It was taken over by the British, who, once again installed the Wodeyars on the throne. In the initial years there were no major changes in the socio-economic system. However, during the time of Richard Wellesley, a personalized system of favouring and encouraging some speculators within the trading community was taken up as a policy. This brought in major differences between the different communities practising similar professions.[1]

This also gave rise to a mercantile capitalistic outlook where the middlemen reigned. Opening up of markets in British India made

1. For a more detailed discussion, see Pani et al 1985.

trading more favourable. So far, under Tipu Sultan there had been no trade with the rest of British India. Sandalwood and liquor were restored into the open market in reversal of policies existing from Tipu's time. In the same breath, the markets and factories established in the Gulf by Tipu were closed down.

The accent shifted to silks though cotton textiles co-existed side by side. The production of silks, however, followed a mercantile practice; most weavers were dependent on the middlemen who held the key to the whole business (Pani **et al** 1985). This strategy of encouraging trade within the existing system continued till around 1811, i.e., till the end of Dewan Purnaiah's tenure. The sandalwood and ivory accumulated during Tipu's regime helped raise much revenue Also, the large military garrison, maintained to protect British interests and property, helped to keep the price of grain high and as a result sums of money were drawn from the exchequer of the Madras government and put into circulation.

But slowly the inherent problems in the strategy followed by the British cleared the way for an economic breakdown. The personalized rule by giving specific concessions to the merchant class ensured increasing influence of merchant class and decreasing prosperity of the production systems. It destabilized the old system of administration.

From the year 1812, only a small garrison of the British was retained and hence, the prices of food grains fell. And last but not the least, the political and financial inexperience of the young King took a heavy toll. By 1830-31, the end was complete. There was an uprising of the ryots and the merchants. The British intervened under the clause of the Subsidiary Treaty, and reassumed direct management of the province and the Commissioner was installed.

Entrenchment of British: The picture of Bangalore changed after the coming of the English and their entrenchment with a Cantonment at Bangalore. Till this time the rule by the Maharaja of Mysore was an indirect rule of the British. A strict distinction was maintained between the Cantonment and the rest of the town. The occupation of the English so to say changed the course of Bangalore's history.

One of the first objectives of Sir Mark Cubbon's (the then Commissioner) economic strategy was to remove all remnants of extra economic coercion. Labour being paid in kind was discouraged and cash payment was enforced in its place. Another change was the standardization of weights and measures. With the regularisation of revenue, there was suitable tax cut for different communities.

The British policy of opening up the economy helped trade flourish but at the same time, it remained under direct British patronage. The cantonment became more a trading centre for goods of English tastes. The textile industry lost ground due to loss of patronage and market. A large proportion of the populace were dyers who were later replaced after the Cantonment was formed, by the upward mobility of the weaving castes. New forms of silks and cottons which suited the English were brought in with the various colonial tariffs against indigenously produced goods making it incompatible.

Complementarily, the making of gold laces, for which Mysore had made a mark, died out in 1870 due to imports of lace from France. Also, after the reign of Cubbon, the monopolies in trading of tobacco and betelnut were curbed. The possibility of merchant capital being diverted into industry was also restrained. However, by 1900 two large-scale textile mills came up, i.e, the Bangalore Woollen., Cotton and Silk Mills Ltd., in 1884 and the Mysore Spinning and Manufacturing Company Ltd., in 1894, both at Bangalore.

Dawn of New Era: With the ascent of Krishnaraja Wodeyar IV on to the throne a conscious decision was made to make Mysore a 'model state'. During the Dewanship of Sir K. Seshadri Iyer, rail track of up to 315 miles was laid by 1895. The Kolar Gold Mines was started in 1886. The King, in 1911, invited Sir M. Visveswaraya, who had already made his mark in the rest of the country, especially in taming the Musi river in the state of Hyderabad, to the Mysore durbar and gave him a free rein in running the administration.

At the time of Sir MV's taking charge there were several industries which were declining. Hand spinning which was a traditional activity was particularly hurt due to the advent of British-made mill yarn. The Government of Mysore sought to revive this as a cottage industry with the help of All India Spinner's Association.

The state had a history of iron and steel industry in the way of making wire-drawing for musical instruments. Brass casting and steel metal work were being carried on at Magadi, Nagamangala and Sravanabelagola. The industry was languishing in 1914. It declined because of crude technology and uneconomic manufacturing practices. Buchanan's (1807) description shows that the industry had not even a vague perception of a modern blast furnace.

Sir MV argued that the betterment of the people could only be done by preparing a detailed economic plan and implementing it. In this process, the government had a crucial role to play. Utmost importance was given to industries, particularly heavy industries, with emphasis on production of machinery and machine tools.

This is not to say there was no disagreement or differencs of opinion; Alfred Chatterton was a spokesperson of the view that the state should be fiscally conservative and stay away from industry which was the business of businessman - a view vastly different from that of Sir MV who felt that the state had to take a lead in this matter.

What is significant is that Sir MV's plan for the erstwhile Mysore State actually forethought a state-led industrial growth. There was an active encouragement to small-scale entreprenuers and the latest technology was brought from outside. Sir MV was deeply influenced by Japanese experience, and sought to implement the lessons he learnt from their experience. He realised that formal education was vital for any industrialisation. Towards this end, he helped set up the University of Mysore, and was also instrumental in opening up a new Industrial Training Institute in Bangalore. Sir MV helped in the growth of Tata Institute set up in 1909, which further helped promoting indigenous knowledge and other such efforts to gain ground towards a powerful environment.

Sir MV was the main brain behind the construction of the Krishnaraja Sagar dam for irrigation. The Sharavathi project was commissioned and completed within record time, paving way for a good power situation. This was the first time a state in pre-independent India had even realised the great potential in having a good energy source.

Sir MV anticipated the Indian Planning Commission in the Mysore Economic Conference which he set up in 1911. It had three main committees, agriculture, industry and commerce, and education. He was instrumental in getting a larger amount of freedom in the internal administration during the Instrument of Transfer signed in 1913. In January 1913, the Industries Department was founded.

The state endeavoured to support the handloom industry through a process of experimentation and research. The Government Textiles Institute adopted improved methods to local conditions. A new type of 'Pit Automatic Loom' was made whose output was double the ordinary loom.

Wool spinning and weaving were taken up too. 'Kamblies' (coarse blanket) were being made from days of yore. The two main sources of raw materials were shearings from sheep and the wet wool from tanneries. The quality of the product, however, was poor due to indigenous process of milling and finishing which were inefficient and laborious. Also, there was no process of grading of wool in vogue.

Sericulture as a subsidiary activity was century old. But this declined due to the dumping of silk from China and Japan. The main problems with the Indian variety was that the rearing period of the silk worm was longer. It required more mulberry leaves: hence, an increased expenditure on its food, and the percentage of silk produced was less. To add to this, the British gave tariff protection to the imported silks. Hence, there actually was dumping in the market, which relegated Indian silks to a corner. A separate department was set up in 1920 by the Government of Mysore. Since 1927-28, the government spent Rs. 22 lakhs on the rehabilitation. The annual expenditure amounted to Rs. 218,105 in 1937-38. The schemes started showing results in the Mysore filature. As a result, a silk weaving factory was started in 1931. The products earned a name for the very high grade fabrics produced. A lot of silkwaste and pierced cocoons were the by-products of this factory. A new factory, the Mysore Spun Silk Mills, was started which was the first of its kind in India, which made use of the silk waste. Carpet manufacturing as a cottage industry was also recognized.

A soap factory was started in 1918. Except for the locally available groundnut oil and 'hippe' oil, all the rest of the raw materials was procured from outside. Still, by 1935-36, the production of soap was 356 tons. The Mysore Iron Works at Bhadravati was started in 1918 and completed in 1922. It was designed to use charcoal, produced from the local forest resources. With the decline in forest area, and later decisions to change technology, the unit ran into trouble. The vision and foresight with which it was started could not be sustained.

The Mysore Paper Mills was started as a joint stock company in 1936. The resources were taken from the local forests in Bhadravati. As a private enterprise, gold mining in Kolar was started in the 1890s which was further promoted by giving power.

At the same time, the British as part of their war preparedness during the First and the Second World Wars, set up railway lines. A hauling system for railways was set up in Hubli, which later on grew to a good and large workshop station for rail wagons. Bangalore slowly gained ground as the strongest of military centres. An air-field was constructed at Jalahalli. A small workshop grew around it. The Walchand brothers came and set up a small aircraft maintenance factory during the course of the Second World War. The technology for an active foundry was built up to help the air-base. Another post-war boom was the coming up of Sri Krishnarajendra mills, a joint stock company in Mysore, and Minerva Mills in Bangalore. The Electro-Porcelain Factory was set up in 1932 which helped much in the early electrification of various industries.

In the Hyderabad-Bombay Karnataka, there was no industrial development as such on a planned basis. There were a few textile units that were started either with the patronage of state government or by private enterprises. At Gulbarga, M.S.K. Mills was established in 1884. However, it ran into difficulties and the state government of Karnataka took over the management in 1963. Later, in 1973, the mill was taken over by the National Textile Corporation.

In Bombay-Karnataka there was hardly any major industrial enterprise except for English owned textile mills established in 1889 at Gokak Falls and in 1898 at Hubli. In Bidar Taluk, there was a famous Bidriware craft work which had a good demand at the time. There were few handloom and spinning units in Bijapur, Belgaum and Dharwad districts. In the thirties and forties of this century, a few industries such as cement factories at Shahbad (Gulbarga District) and sugar factories in Bellary districts came up.

Dakshina Kannada had a few industrial units. Beedi manufacture grew as a cottage industry. Besides, thanks to the vision of a few enlightened persons with business acumen, many banks were started and by the time of the reorganisation of the state, some of them, especially the Vijaya Bank, Canara Bank and Syndicate Bank had already opened branches both in Karnataka and in other states.

The picture that emerged at the time of states reorganisation in 1956 was that Karnataka had grown to have a fairly wide diversified industrial sector. In terms of contribution to the country's total of value added from industry, Karnataka had occupied the fourth place in the forties and fifties. The point, however, that is to be kept in mind is that when one speaks of industrialization of Karnataka, most would mean only Bangalore and its growth as an important industrial town. And in this, except for the recent period, they would not be wrong.

Growth of Industrial Finance: A study of the economics of industrialization in the state would not be complete without understanding the pattern of industrial finance. No industry can be built without an investment. In Karnataka. The state understood this well and different forms of industrial finance were promoted. The Bank of Mysore was set up in 1913. In the beginning, there was neither structural differentiation nor functional specialization among banks. Slowly, the concept of banking came to be accepted. The patronage of the government towards industrial finance altered the portfolios of the banks. There came to be altogether 50 joint stock banks limited by shares and 16 banking institutions limited by guarantee in Mysore over time. The latter was exclusively for agricultural purposes. Non-agricultural credit societies, the earliest co-operative societies were started in Mysore. By 1934, there were 277 societies with a total membership of 52,588.

Mysore state was the pioneer in framing rules for introducing 'takavi' loans into practice, This won the encomium of Indian Industrial Commission for the effectiveness of its scheme. The state showed a paternalistic attitude - a policy of promotion and functional participation. There were many joint stock companies to promote private entrepreneurship.

Development of Industries - Post Independence: Using Sir MV's plan, the Congress Plaoning Committee (of which MV was a member) formulated the basic ideas of planning as a means for a state-led growth of the country. Nehru was the Chairman of this Committee. This was further taken forward by the exercise of the various plans under Mahalanobis[2]

With all the infrastructure built up over a decade, there was still a handicap in terms of scarcity of facilities of subsequent repairs and renewals of foreign imported machinery. This was a time of outside initiatives in Mysore; the state had yet to adjust to the changes of 1947. Bangalore was selected for its salubrious climate and the research base already existing, for the establishment of Indian Telephone Industries Limited. in 1948, Hindustan Machine Tools Limited in 1953, and Bharat Electronics Limited in 1954. The Hindustan Aeronautics Limited came into being by revamping the Walchand factory (1940).

The major public sector undertakings paved the growth of the city in two major ways. One, the growth of engineering colleges was further accelerated and two, with the rise in captive power generation, a mushrooming of small scale industries was later seen as an ancillary activity. This, in turn, attracted a lot of skilled labour from the adjoining states of Kerala and Tamil Nadu, especially in the public sector enterprises.

Developments after 1956: Efforts were made to integrate the various regions into a composite whole by investments in various fields. But, due to a great deal of difference in their levels of development, some

2. For a detailed analysis of similarities between MV and Nehru, see, Vyasulu 1989.

areas have grown faster than others. There had been some geographical dispersions in erstwhile Mysore state, but after the formation of Karnataka there has been a concentration in Bangalore.

During the First Five Year Plan, out of a total outlay of Rs. 196.89 lakhs, Rs. 122.96 lakhs were expended. The development of Government Electric Factory and the Porcelain Factory was taken up. The Mysore Iron & Steel Limited was also taken up for an expansion programme. The major difference was in the use of power, when it shifted from coal to electricity.

During the Second Five Year Plan, the development of Sandalwood factories at Shimoga and Mysore was taken up. The expansion of the Government Soap Factory was completed. The plan envisaged Rs. 10.39 crores for industries, of which Rs. 7.3 crores were expended. In 1959, Small Scale Industries and Handicrafts Board was constituted. The industrial estates programmes, giving infrastructural facilities like sheds and power were set up in different districts in the state. Today, the industrial estates are widespread in the districts of Bangalore, Belgaum, Bijapur, Bidar, Gulbarga, Bellary, Jamkhandi, Shimoga, Shiralkoppa, Chickmagalur, Kadur, Mercara, Mysore, Hassan, KGF, Mangalore, Muddenahalli, Mandya, Tumkur, Sira, Harihar, Hubli, Dandeli, Bykampady and Ramanagaram. The industrial estates programme did not help in the growth of the industrial sector in any exponential manner. It was plagued by the problems of insufficient infrastructure availability. The red-tapism in allotting the sheds created more handicaps to the entrepreneurs. Hence, in most cases, in the early stages, the estates did not show any commensurate performance when compared to a non-estate programme. The programme has been rejuvenated with the New Economic Policy in 1990s with more liberalization and the active initiative of NRIs, and external collaborative efforts, like the MOU with the Government of Singapore, in building the Software Technology Park. A new dynamism has been felt with the growth of information technology.

Growth of Karnataka as the Scientific Base: The 1960s saw the growth of many research institutes and laboratories, viz., Raman Research Institute, Central Power Research Institute, Indian Plywood Industries Training and Research Institute, Central Manufacturing

Technology Institute, National Aerospace Laboratories, Indian Institute of Astro Physics, National Institute for Mental Health and Neural Sciences, Central Food Technology Research Institute, etc. Another influential development was the coming of Indian Space Research Organisation, under the Ministry of Space, one of the only two GOI ministries to be outside New Delhi.

The Third Five Year Plan saw the setting up of Karnataka Industrial Investment and Development Corporation in 1964, and State Industrial Co-operative Bank in 1963. From the Fourth plan onwards emphasis has been laid on the growth and development of small industries. Towards this there was liberalization in many of the policies, and concessions/incentives given.

Currently, there are about 61 enterprises. Up to 1949, there were 12 state enterprises, mainly in iron and steel, and mining, manufacturing and consumer goods, electrical and machinery, chemicals and trading activities. During the 50s, only five enterprises were established and out of these two were of state initiative, Karnataka Housing Board and Karnataka Electricity Board. During the 1960s, there were 14 enterprises and they were evenly distributed in all the activities like construction, finance, mining, manufacturing, rural development, etc. The state actually saw surplus power position in the 1960s.

The 1970s saw a major break-through of public enterprises in Karnataka. Nearly 50 per cent of the enterprises were started during this decade. Major emphasis has been in the rural development and manufacturing. There was an added emphasis on the promotional institutions such as Karnataka State Tourism Development Corporation, TECSOK, etc. The target group-oriented enterprises during the 70s have been the establishment of KLIC, KSC and STDC and KBC and MDC. Many of the state enterprises were either merged or transferred to the bigger enterprises. Mysore Porcelain and REMCO were transferred to Bharat Heavy Electricals Limited. The KGF was transferred to Bharat Gold Mines. The State Bank of Mysore became affiliated to SBI and KIMCO was transferred to BEML.

The eighties saw the burgeoning of the state in the industries which were high-tech, namely, information technology, floriculture, horticulture, etc. There has been an increase in investment with respect to bio-tech industries like floriculture - encouraging entrepreneurs to export. Cold-storage facilities are being improved and quick lifting of goods through air has been provided. Many small scale industries specilalizing in software came into picture. Also, the MNCs started making their presence felt. Many now have their headquarters situated in Bangalore. But this industrialization is more centred in the capital than in other areas. Another interesting facet that is seen is that most MNCs use Bangalore only as their administrative headquarters and not a manufacturing base.

Infrastructure Development in the State: The growth of the overall industrial sector can be understood in terms of three major indicators: (a) the spread and growth of industrialization in all the districts; (b) the position in terms of capital and productivity, employment; and (c) competitive advantage with respect to the resources availability, power, interference/non-interference from state administration, and allied infrastructure like railways and communications for freight transport. An infrastructure Development Index (IDI) has been developed (Vyasulu 1992). The Index comprises of economic indicators such as power, irrigation, roads, post offices, banking, along with some social indicators such as health and education which has been constructed by the CMIE for the years 1966-67 to 1989-90. The IDI has a shortcoming for recent years, since rail-lines that have been converted from metre to broad guage in recent times have not been included.

The index for Karnataka shows an increase from 90 points in 1966-67 to 99 in 1989-90. With respect to roads, posts and telecommunications, Karnataka compares well with other states, but is poorly linked in terms of railways. In terms of power, the state has slid from a surplus position to huge deficits in the recent past. The power data on Karnataka highlights many important features. There has been an increase in demand. The installed capacity has increased from 191 MWs. to 2,656 MWs. between 1960-61 and 1990-91, though this increase is not commensurate with the demand. Power consumption has increased from 2,947 MWs. in 1970-71 to 11,688 MWs. in 1991-92. Correspondingly, the generation has increased from 1,058 MWs. to 12,430 MWs. in the same period. The skewed policies of free power to agricultural sector has been the ruin of the power sector in this state. Also, a sole dependency on hydel-power[3] resources at the cost of other sources has aggravated the situation.

The Index in the inter-district comparison shows that there is a striking disparity between Bangalore and the other districts. The Index was least in Bidar. Even between the first and the second rank holder, viz., Bangalore and Dakshina Kannada, the difference was nearly five times. The observation that infrastructural development is directly correlated to industrial development seems to hold good. Districts with a better IDI have shown a better growth in industries than their poor cousins. The first three districts in ranking are Bangalore, Dakshina Kannada and Belgaum respectively.

In a recent study (Vyasulu 1992), the growth of districts in the manufacturing sector in terms of number of factories, fixed capital, employment and value-added shows that the districts can be classified into following categories:

1. High growth rate of both fixed capital and employment;
2. High growth rate of fixed capital and low growth rate of employment;
3. Low growth rate of fixed capital and high growth rate of employment; and
4. Low growth rate of both fixed capital and employment.

The districts falling under each of these categories are:

1. Kolar/Tumkur/Kodagu, Chickmagalur, Raichur, Belgaum, Bijapur, Dharwad, Bangalore;
2. Shimoga, Mysore, Dakshina Kannada;
3. Bidar, Uttara Kannada, Mandya, Bellary, Hassan; and
4. Gulbarga, Chitradurga.

The results from the study confirm that the general growth in the state has taken place in clusters. The major growth centres that are

3. A massive hike of up to 30 per cent in the prices of power has been taken up and free agricultural power has been stopped forthwith from July 1, 1996, to fill the deficit in revenue account.

evolving are the Bijapur-Gulbarga region, which is a good source for lime-stone and now being exploited by having many integrated cement plants. The second region of industrial growth is Bellary-Hospet where steel is being manufactured. Mangalore is the third focal point where the refineries are helping in diversifying the industrial scenario in the region. Bangalore, of course, continues to be a growth centre, where more of the sunrise industries, like software, garments and other high-tech industries are located. The prospects of growth in other areas has improved with a massive reorganisation of rail network in the form of conversion of metre to broad gauge. The completion and opening of Konkan line has further increased the prospects of the coastal areas. However, the growth is much hampered by the environmental activists. It is necessary that the government and private sector work in concurrence with the environmentalists, otherwise, many projects can get bogged down by unnecessary litigations. The power sector is also very much gearing up to meet the requirements of the industry. Most new industries being commissioned or approved have co-generation or captive generation as a means towards energy self-sufficiency. In fact, in many cases the surplus power could in fact be fed into the main grid.

Industrial Growth: Karnataka has been one of the top three producers in a few industries in the country like 'wood and wood products' (15.25 per cent share in 1988-98), 'electrical machinery' (11.5 per cent in 1988-89), 'paper products' (8.9 per cent in 1988-90), and 'other manufacturing' category (11.9 per cent in 1988-90). At the end of 1994-95, electronics showed 3,836 units, automobiles 912. The largest jump was in job-work, repairs and servicing showing 11,137 units. However, food and beverages (23,817), textiles and garments (19,726), and wood-based (14,021) industries continued to lead the list in the same order. Within the state, more than 60 per cent of the value added is contributed to by food processing, electrical machinery, cotton textiles, basic metals and alloys, and transport equipment. In fact, the new industries to have entered the industrial production scenario in Karnataka are computers and electronic goods (Upendranath **et al** 1994).

The growth of small scale industries (SSI) was also largely encouraged by the fact that the government took the initiative in forming industrial estates and industrial areas. In 1988, the number of registered SSIs was 62,534. By 1992, this number had increased to 1.26 lakh units in the state with an investment of Rs.1,278 crores providing employment to 8.7 lakh persons. Bangalore (urban) accounts for about 18 per cent of the total number of units, the highest in the state. Mysore, Belgaum, Dharwad, Dakshina Kannada rank next to Bangalore in the same order. In backward areas of the state, there are 30,000 units under KUIC with an investment of Rs.47 crores providing employment to more there 4 lakh persons.

Further, more than 2.5 lakhs of people are engaged in handlooms and powerlooms. Sericulture is another industry which is very well developed in Karnataka. The state accounts for nearly half of the raw silk production in the country.

In the small sector, the employment growth was less compared to growth in the number of units, value-added and the value of output (Kumar 1996). This is because there has been a shift in the kind of industries in this sector. Many high-tech industries having less number of workers fall into this sector. During 1993-94, the total SSIs registered in the state was 12,614, having an investment of Rs. 19,890.56 lakhs with employment increasing to 69,563. With this, cumulatively, at the end of 1994-95, there were 163,524 units, having an investment of Rs. 93,616.78 lakhs, employing 1,076,512 persons.

The distribution of large and medium industries at the end of March 1992 stood as follows: 697 units with Rs. 5,659 crores providing employment to about 27 lakh persons. However, the figures are skewed in favour of Bangalore which accounts for about 144 per cent of the total. Mandya ranks second with 12 per cent, Dharwad third with 8 per cent. Although the total number of units is the largest in Bangalore, per unit investment is very low with Rs. 271 lakh and its rank in the state is sixteenth. With regard to the employment generated by these units, Bangalore has the largest share (144 per cent), followed by Kolar (10.17 per cent), Mandya (7.01 per cent), Bidar, Hassan, Kodagu having a very low share.

Though the employment figures in general show a good prospect, the census figures show a disturbing trend (Kumar et al 1995). In terms of the total rural workforce, the worker share in the primary sector has declined (84.64 per cent to 83.90 per cent), and instead of recording at least a minor improvement, the secondary sector employment has declined (8.39 per cent to 7.32 per cent). The increase was captured in the service sector. This is similar to the pattern visible at the all India level. In the urban workforce, unlike the all India pattern, the primary sector has witnessed a decline. The decline has been compensated by the increase in the urban service sector. In terms of the percentages, the share of the urban primary sector was 15.35 per cent for males and 27.94 per cent for females in the 1981 census and this declined to 13.77 per cent and 25.03 per cent respectively in the 1991 census. The tertiary sector recorded an increase from 49.74 per cent for males and 35.68 per cent for females to 52.93 per cent and 42.37 per cent respectively. Accordingly, the urban secondary sector declined from 34.91 per cent in the case of males and 36.38 per cent for females to 33.3 per cent. But this decline is not to be taken as a very negative feature because there has been a corresponding growth in the tertiary sector. In fact, this trend it seems would continue as the new industries coming up are fully mechanised systems, employing very few labourers, who are highly skilled. Hence, a shift in the skill structure in an industry would also be noticeable. The growth would hence tend to be in the service sector like ready-made food industry, transport for freight, cargo and passenger. The compound growth rates reveal that the change in the primary population is just equivalent to that of the population growth in Karnataka. The districts which witnessed highest growth in non-agricultural sector are Chickmagalur, Kolar and Bangalore.

Among the other industries gaining importance in Karnataka are the agro-based industries. Raichur has the maximum number of agro-based units constituting 18 per cent share in the state total. It is followed by Bangalore (14 per cent) and Dakshina Kannada (DK) (9.66 per cent). Still, Raichur has a low value-addition compared to Bangalore. Raichur also has a majority of the units processing grain mill products, Mandya and Belgaum have sugar producing units, and Bangalore has the largest number of units in bakery products, followed by canning, preservation of fruits and vegetables. Bijapur, Gulbarga, Raichur, Dharwad, Chitradurga and Tumkur stand first with respect to oil seeds production. But the oil production units are mainly situated in Dakshina Kannada (120 per cent), Dharwad (17 per cent) and Raichur (9.82 per cent). Tea-processing units are located mainly in Bangalore and Chickmagalur. Coffee is processed in Hassan, Dakshina Kannada, Kodagu and Mysore. Cotton ginning units are primarily situated in Dharwad, Raichur and Bijapur. Sericulture is also being promoted actively. There has been an increase in the total area under mulberry cultivation, and also in silk production. In terms of employment, Mysore has the largest share in the silk industry, though Bangalore accounts for 81 per cent of the total value-added. What is observed about the industries falling in the purview of other industries, other than manufacturing and core activities, is that they are constrained by their small sizes. One important suggestion would be to bring them out of the SSI sector so that large scale units can take up production which shall meet the economies of scale. However, if continued under SSI they would need a lot of governmental support in terms of infrastructure and markets, both of which cannot be undertaken by the units themselves (Upendranath **et al** 1996).

Industrial Finance in Karnataka: Growth and Structure: There has been an increasing awareness of the necessity of easy capital flow for investments. Bangalore is gaining ground slowly as a capital market. More foreign private banks are using Bangalore as a major base. The state has also had good rapport with all the financial institutions.

The expanding role of all financial Institutions (IDBI, IFCI, ICICI, SIDBI, IRBI, LIC, UTI, GIC, RCTC, TDICI, SCICI, SFCs and SIDCs) in facilitating the industrial growth in the state is indicated by five-fold growth of the industrial financing from Rs. 201.95 crores in 1980-91 to Rs.1,349 crores in 1991-92. But, the relative share of Karnataka in the country's total dropped from about 8.8 per cent in 1980-81 to 5.99 per cent in 1991-92. Next to IDBI which increased the sanctions from Rs. 126.13 crores in 1980-81 to Rs. 351 crores in 1991-92, SFC has emerged as a major institution in providing industrial finance to the state. Apart from the SFC, KSIIDC is another major state-level institution which is contributing its might to the industrial finance in the state. At the end of March 1995, the total sanction in all areas was Rs. 15,361.3 crores, and the corresponding disbursements for the same period was Rs. 10,198.0 crores.

A substantial amount of the disbursements of both KSFC and KSSIDC are in the area of large, medium scale and small scale industries, though the KSSIDC has confined itself more to SSIs. The narrower scope of KSSIDC is explained because it is a special agency catering to large and medium scale units. However, the rate of recovery of loans sanctioned by the KSSIDC is in the range of 35 to 43 per cent. KSFC is, however, the only SFC to get an investible credit rating from CRISIL and perhaps the only one to be considered for possible investment by major undertakings with surplus funds. The only discouraging fact, though it has a presence in all districts, however, is that the major bene-ficiary of all the sanctions is Bangalore.

Another important facet of the industrial climate in the state has been the encouragement given to women entrepreneurs. The KSFC has come forward to create opportunities for women to get intensive training in entrepreneurship and business development through governmental and NGO agencies[4].

Industrial Sickness: Another problem in any industrial town in India is the sickness, a misnomer for an unviable unit. At the end of September 1990, out of 1,467 non-SSI units in the country, Karnataka had 89 units accounting for a share of 6 per cent. The total number of SSI units found to be sick at the end of September 1990 was 10,982 with the amount outstanding touching Rs. 147.43 cores, thereby accounting for 4.8 per cent of the total number of sick units and 5.7 per cent of the total amount of outstanding in the country as a whole.

It was observed that sickness in non-SSI units was the highest in the case of engineering (12 units), followed by textiles (11), chemicals(9) and paper (8). In the case of SSI units, sickness was the highest in the case of engineering (410), textiles (136), chemical (102), electricals (78) and iron and steel (66). Of the total number of 59,469

4. A study report conducted by The Association of Women Enterpreneurs of Karnataka (AWAKE).

registered SIDO units in Karnataka in 1988, 14,268 were closed. Of these, 2,771 (18.94 per cent) were found in the metrpolitan areas, 7,871 (53.81 per cent) in urban areas and the rest 3,987 (27.25 per cent) in the rural areas. Food products acccounted for the highest number of closed units with 17 per cent followed by metal products with 13 per cent and chemical and chemical products with 9.7 per cent. Also most closed units were in the areas of Bijapur, Bellary and Raichur followed by Kolar, Mysore and Bangalore. The reasons for closure were also mainly financial problems and some due to marketing problems.

Industrial Policy: Realizing that Bangalore was getting concentrated at the cost of other districts, the government has consciously tried to have policies which encourage an even growth model among all the districts. The first package was announced for the period 1968-74. A number of concessions in terms of sales tax and octroi, electricity duty and others were offered for units set up outside Bangalore. In the second package of 1975-82, a review of the earlier package was made. It was found that the same trend of Bangalore heading the list continued. Hence, a renewed attempt at promoting fresh investment was made in the form of exemption of octroi for 7 years for the new units. Regions were identified for promotion. The third package for the years 1982-88 reiterated the second package. Further, four zones were clearly demarcated in the regions getting incentives and not getting incentives. The fourth package was to be for 1988-93. However, the government reviewd the industrial performance of the state against the 1983 package and announced a more comprehensive new industrial policy in September 1990. The focus on backward development continued. Also, concessions were announced for investment in thrust sectors such as electronics, telecommunication, informatics, agro-food processing, leather products, ready-made garments, sericulture-based industries and EOUs.

In line with the Industrial Policy incentives package initiated by the Government of India in 1991 for liberalisation, the state has been, more than any other state, able to pursue the economic policies by promoting various investments and setting up high-level committees to go into the different industrial proposals. To improve upon the previous policy of 1993, the Industrial Policy of 1996 has the following salient points:

1. **Active participation of Industry in the development of infrastruture:** Private investments in infrastructure areas such as the international airport, information technology park, Bangalore-Mysore express highway and several other projects. To continue this further, KSSIDC has been designated as the agency of the government to plan and formulate proposals for infrastructure development projects. The Government will consider such projects on BOO/BOOT/BOLT concepts.
2. **Emphasis on Infrastructure development**: To improve infrastructural facilities even in the existing industrial areas, etc.
3. **Development of Potential Growth Centres:** Government has already approved establishment of three growth centres at Dharwad, Raichur and Hassan with a total capital outlay of approximately Rs.120 crores.
4. **Encouragement of utilisation of non-conventional energy sources and co-generation.**
5. **Simplification/streamlining of rules and regulations and transparent administration.**

However, much cannot be said about incentives and cuts in duties, because concessions and subsidies have never helped the growth of any industry more so in a competitive environment as today. Power planning has been a major drawback in the state. Issues of conservation and efficiency need to be taken up (Reddy **et al** 1991).

Recent trends in investment proposals show that Karnataka has a marginal share, a little below that of what would be expected, in the total Industrial Entrepreneur Memoranda (IEM). Between August 1991 and May 1996, the total number of IEM cleared were 897, having an investment of Rs. 15,822 crores. Maharastra had the largest number of IEMs of 4,711 for the same period. But the picture is much brighter for single-window clearance of cases, and foreign collaboration cases. In the period August 1991 to November 1995, 263 units having an investment of Rs. 1,693.06 crores from foreign companies were clreared. Correspondingly, in the same period, the foreign technical collaborations also numbered 190. At the end of 1995-96, through single-window clearance procedure as many as 751 units were processed, with an investment of Rs. 534,278.44 lakhs and generating an employment of 109,925 numbers. The reasons for slow progress are many. The bureaucratic delays are frequently mentioned in most cases. Also, the infrastructural facilities like power and transport have not improved commensurately with the publicity generated inviting outsiders to come and invest in the state. Per unit cost of power is costliest in this state today. However, judged by the approvals given to the projects, it may be stated that the NEP has had a redeeming effect on the state's, economy.

Recently, in a workshop on 'new industrial policy - 1996 and incentives package' organised by the Department of Industry and Commerce, the State Minister for industrial development stated that the government was aware of some bottlenecks in the infrastrcture facilities of the state. He added, however, that the industrial policy would emphasise on private sector participation in the power sector. He mentioned that government had identified five satellite towns for the establishment of industries to discourage any new industry coming up in and around Bangalore and that all necessary infrastrcture would be provided in the proposed satellite towns. He also mentioned that the district level officers had been given powers to clear the projects in respect of small scale industry and procedures for allotment of plots and sheds at district level will be simplified through Karnataka Industrial Areas Development Board, Karnataka, Small Scale Industries Development Corporation and Karnataka State Electronics Development Corporation. He also made a reference to the large number of sick small scale units and the rehabilitation of sick S.S. units in the state which are about 15,000. The state government has now proposed to examine the suggestions made by the various industry associations and to set up panels to study issues concerning subsidy, labour, power and policy for sick small scale units.

CONCLUSIONS

While charting the industrial progress in the state, one tends to observe some positive points:

1. The state always had a positive approach towards industrial progress.
2. It has understood the need for technical knowledge and a strong R & D base and worked towards it.
3. It has always tried to forge a communication network with national and international agencies continuously.
4. Except for a brief time in the recent past when the severest crunch in terms of power has been felt all over the state, it has maintained its lead.
5. The state has realised the need for a national market. The Bangalore Stock Exchange is slowly making a mark in the national markets. It now has the Bangalore On-line Trading System by which it is linked to all the business.

However, there are equal number of negative points which need to be scrutinized:

1. The state has not made enough use of its rich natural resources potential.
2. The interactions with the R & D network and the academia an also lacking and this is evident in all the public and private sectors which have not fully utilised the full potential of the various research institutions in and around the capital.
3. With all the growth in its industrial sector, the state has not had the foresight to invest sufficiently in communications

(both information technology and other transport), as a result of which the state till today is badly connected between its various districts, and the outside regions.

4. Power is costly.

5. Future investments in power, and transport have never been in the agenda whose lacunae are showing up today.

6. Lack of local entrepreneurship has caused a skewed development with respect to the people investing, the people working in the various categories and the localities. This has adversely impacted on the social infrastructure in terms of local employment tussles, language issues being raised, etc.

REFERENCES

Buchanan, F.H. (1807) **A Journey through the Countries of Mysore Canara and Malabar**. London: W. Buhner and Company.

Indira, A. (1994) **Industrial R & D and Self-reliance: Case Studies in Technological Diffusion.** A Ph.d. thesis submitted to the Osmania University, Hyderabad.

Kumar, A.V. Arun (1996). Modern Small Industry in Karnataka - Growth and Structure. **Economic and Political weekly,** 31.

Kumar, A.V. Arun, B.P. Vani and Vinod Vyasulu, (1995). Structure of Employment as seen from 1981 and 1991 Censuses: a Preliminary Look. **Eeconomic and Political Weekly**, XXX (38): 2375-88.

Pani, Narendar, Tara Anand and Vinod Vyasulu (1985). **Impact of Colonialism on the Economic Structure of Indian Cities:** Bangalore 1800-1900. In K.S.C.S.T., **Essays on Bangalore**, vol 1. Bangalore: K.S.C.S.T and I.I.Sc.

Reddy, A.K.N. **et al** (1991). A Development-focussed End-use-oriented Electricity Scenario for Karnataka. **Economic and Political Weekly**, 26 (14 & 15) : 891-910 & 983 - 1001.

Upendranath. C., M. Vijayabhaskaran and Vinod Vyasulu (1994). Industrial Growth and Structure: Analaysis of Manufacturing Sector in Karnataka. **Economic and Political Weekly,** XXIX (48): M 157-64.

Vyasulu, Vinod (1989). Nehru and Visveswaraya Legacy. **Economic and Political Weekly,** XXIV (30):1700-4.

Vyasulu, Vinod (1992) **Industrial Policy in Karnataka** Bangalore: ISEC. Unpublished.

3

PUBLIC UNDERTAKINGS*

- A. Ramaswamy

Intoduction; Karnataka has a rich industrial tradition. The industrial history of erstwhile Mysore state was in many ways quite remarkable. The early rulers of Mysore had realised the fact that the growth of manufacturing industry was necessary in a largely populated country to absorb surplus population and put it to productive work. Dewan Rangacharlu had stated as early as 1881, his clear conviction that no country can prosper unless its agricultural and manufacturing industries were equally fostered. The later Dewans like Sir Seshadri Iyer, Sir M. Visvesvaraya and Sir Mirza Ismail also had the same conviction and formulated their policies based on it.

Industrialisation in Mysore may be said to have got off to a start as early as 1877, when the first textile mill was set up in the state. But records show that sugar was being manufactured in the state even as early as 1800. The establishment of Sivasamudram Hydroelectric Station in 1902, the first ever hydroelectric project in the country marked a new era in industrial development. Sir M. Visvesvaraya, who exhorted the nation 'industrialise or perish', was responsible for the establishment of an impressive array of basic and consumer industries dotting the landscape of the then Mysore state. The state enjoyed rich mineral resources, forest products and crops to support industrial activity. Even roads and railways had been provided to connect important towns for strtegic needs and administrative convenience.

---

* This paper reflects the personal views of the author, not of the government.

The erstwhile Mysore state, being comparatively autonomous since the Rendition in 1881, had evolved a definite economic policy resulting in the establishment of Kolar Gold Fields in 1880 by an English Mining Company (John Taylor and Sons), Bangalore Woollen, Cotton and Silk Mills Ltd. and the Mysore Spinning and Manufacturing Company in 1894.

The starting point of planned economic development as a concept and state policy began with the appointment of Sir M. Visvesvaraya as the Chief Engineer in 1909. The report of the Mysore Economic Conference in 1911 was a remarkable document regarding industrial development. A number of industrial opportunities were identified in the first ever survey conducted in 1912. The government accepted the recommendations of the Economic Conference and set up a Department of Industries and Commerce in 1913 which was a focal institution to advise, formulate and implement a number of industrial projects both in the public and joint sector. In fact, Sir M. Visvesvaraya dominated the industrial scene for over five decades. A special feature of the policy that emerged as a result of the Economic Conference and the survey was the concept of public or state enterprise and of joint sector enterprises in areas where private investment was not forth-coming either because of heavy capital investment or long gestation period. Among the early public undertakings were Mysore Chrome Tanning Company Ltd. (1908), Government Sandal Oil Factory at Mysore (1915), Government Soap Factory at Bangalore (1918), and The Iron Works at Bhadravathi (1923). In 1924, another government sponsored and supported Textile Mill came up (Sri Krishnarajendra Mills Ltd.) at Mysore.

During 1920s the total investment in the industrial sector was Rs. 500 lakhs employing 16,500 persons. The other notable industries outside the public sector during the period were the State Tobacco Manufacturing Company (1911), Imperial Tobacco Company Limited (1912), and Minerva Mills, all at Bangalore.

Prior to the State re-organisation in 1956, the decade 1931 to 1941 was the most active period in the economic scenario of the state. What Sir M. Visvesvaraya had envisaged in his remarkable publication

'Planned Economy for India' was put into action. The state's participation in industrial promotion ranging from token share to full ownership formed an active policy framework despite the Economic Depression of the late 1920s. The important industries set up during this period include the Mysore Industrial Testing Laboratory in 1931 in the field of pharmaceuticals, the Government Porcelain factory in 1932, the Mysore Match Company, Shimoga, the Government Silk Weaving Factory at Mysore in 1932, the Government Electric Factory in 1934 at Bangalore, the Mysore Sugar Company at Mandya in 1933, the Mysore Paper Mills Ltd. at Bhadravathi in 1936, the Mysore Spun Silk Mills at Channapatna in 1936, the Mysore Lamp Works Ltd. in 1936, the Mysore Stone Ware and Potteries Ltd, at Chickbanavara in 1937, the Mysore Tobacco Company in 1937, the Mysore Chemicals and Fertilizers Ltd. at Belagola in 1937, the Mysore Implements Factory at Hassan in 1939 (later known as Karnataka Implements and Machinery Company with the merger of Central Industrial Workshop in 1975), and Government Silk Filatures at Kollegal and Kanakapura in 1943. The total number of large industrial establishment during 1944 was 605 providing employment to about 77,518 persons. Some of the major units set up during the post war years before re-organisation of the states were Radio and Electrical Manufacturing Company Ltd. at Bangalore in 1946, the Mysore Lac and Paint Works Ltd. in Mysore and the Tungabhadra Steel Products Ltd. in 1952.

Though the state was well planned with considerable infrastructure, the political adjustment and loss of autonomy came in the way of any substantial investment in the first Five Year Plan 1951-56. The notable feature, however, during this period, was the introduction of Rural Industrialisation programme of Sir M. Visvesvaraya, aimed at the promotion of rural industries like handloom, handicrafts, blacksmithy, carpentry etc. A number of Artisan Training Institutions and Co-operative Societites came up during this period and in the subsequent second and third Five Year Plans. The Mysore Small Industries Ltd. (1960), which later became the Karnataka Small Industries Development Corporation for promoting industrial estates and providing essential raw material to small scale industries was also established. Other notable institutions set up during this period included Mysore

Small Scale Industries and Handicrafts Board (now known as Karnataka State Handicrafts Development Corporation), Mysore State Silk Handloom Weavers Central Co-operative Society (1956), and the Mysore State Cotton and Woollen Handloom Weavers Co-operative Society. In order to provide financial assistance to small scale and medium scale industries, the Mysore State Finance Corporation (presently Karnataka State Financial Corporation) was set up in 1952. A substantial expansion of the Government Electric Factory was made with the establishment of the New Government Electric Factory in 1961 with the technical collaboration with AEG Telefunken of West Germany. It has the most up to date manufacturing facilities with separate factories for transformers, switchgears, motors, silicon power diodes and rectifiers. During the First Plan, the outlay on Industries was Rs. 2.06 Crores against the actual expenditure of Rs.1.03 crores. Likewise, the actual expenditure on industries during the second plan was Rs. 8.87 crores against the outlay of Rs. 10.30 crores.

A major thrust in the Third Plan period was the channelisation of state's assistance jointly with the national level institutions like IDBI and IFCI with industrial institutions. The Mysore Industrial Investment and Development Corporation (presently known as KSIIDC) was set up in 1964 to provide equity participation, guarantee and loans to medium and large scale industrial enterprises. Simultaneously, the government took up modernisation, expansion and diversification schemes in public sector enterprises already set up during the Fourth and Fifth Five Year Plans. During the interim three years (1966-69) there were only Annual Plans. The policy of the government was to follow a progressive industrial policy incorporating new industries by providing necessary incentives and infrastructural facilities. However, the government continued to initiate industrial undertakings for which facilities were available and manage them till such time as they were able to stand on their legs.

In the larger interest of the state, some vital industries requiring huge capital and very technical skill were continued to be in the public sector. The incentives and concessions offered to industries and the infrastructure developed in selected areas, especially, around Bangalore, helped in the setting up of a number of private large scale and medium scale industries in the state. Most of these enterprises were either supported by state level institutions or joint sector projects. These institutions/companies floated subsidiaries also. The Mysore Electrical Industries was taken over by the government in order to revive the unit and protect the interests of labourers and creditors. The Hutti Gold Mines was also set up in 1963. The gross income from the sales of Sandal Oil Factories with its expansion at Shimoga, was Rs. 80.59 lakhs during 1956-57 and it rose to Rs. 145.65 lakhs by the end of the Second Five Year Plan. The other important measures included expansion of Government Soap Factory, setting up of Mysore Porecelains, and an additional unit of Mysore Implements Factory at Hassan. The Mysore Iron and Steel Works, the only steel producing unit in South India, at the time, with the installed capacity of 60,693 metric tonnes per annum of pig iron, diversified to the manufacture of slag granulated cement plant with a capacity of 18,289 tonnes per annum. The Karnataka Film Industries Development Corporation and Sree Kanteerava Studios were also set up in 1968.

The major expansion and diversification programmes undertaken during the Third Plan included Government Porecelain Factory for the manufacture of malleable foundry, modernisation of Government Silk Weaving Factory with 1,500 spindles, redistillation plant at Sandal Oil Factory at Mysore, expansion of mild steel production at Bhadravathi, manufacture of triacetate by the Mysore Acetate and Chemicals at Mandya, and establishment of State Industrial Co-operative Bank to assist artisans and entrepreneurs in the co-operative sector. The outlay for industries sector during the Third Plan was Rs. 13.55 crores, but the actual expenditure was Rs. 11.99 crores.

During the Annual Plan 1967 to 1969 the outlay and expenditure for industries sector were as shown below:

(Rs. in lakhs)

Year	Outlay	Expenditure
1966-67	166.00	227.00
1967-68	302.00	276.00
1968-69	160.00	346.00

The main objective during the period was the development of infrastructural facilities. The Mysore Industrial Area Development Board, which was created to acquire land and develop into plots to be allotted to entreprenuers, started to work in 11 growth centres identified by the state like Mysore-Belgola, Mysore-Nanjangud, Harihar-Davangere, Hubli-Dharwad, Shimoga-Bhadravathi, Bellary-Hospet, Dandeli, Belgaum, Gulbarga, around Bangalore and Mangalore. Further, feasibility studies for the following projects were also undertaken.

1) Steel Plant at Hospet.

2) Nitrogenous Fertilizer Project at Mysore.

3) Cement Asbestos Product at Holenarsipura.

In addition to this, pre-investment surveys were also made for structural fabrication, aluminum, foundry grade pig iron, stainless steel pipes and tubes, ferro chrome and pulp and newsprint.

In spite of these measures taken by the state, there has been imbalance in the development of industries - both area wise and product wise. While most of the new industries set up were concentrated in and around Bangalore, Mangalore, Mysore, Hubli, Dharwar, cotton spinning, edible oil, tobacco and sugar factories were concentrated in Northern Karnataka. With a view to set right the discrepancies, the plan efforts were put forth for equitable distribution of industries throughout the state during the subsequent plans.

Public Sector Undertakings: Subsequent to 1970, in order to provide succour to the artisans or to utilise the available raw materials and resources, the state government established a number of public sector agencies like Karnataka State Forest Industries Development Corporation in 1973, the Karnataka State Veneers Limited in 1974, Karnataka Vidyut Karkhane Limited in 1976, the Karnataka State Electronic Development Corporation in 1976, the Karnataka Silk Industries Corporation Limited in 1978, Karnataka Agro Industries Corporation in 1968 and Karnataka State Handloom Development Corporation in 1975, Karnataka Forest Development Corporation in 1971 and Mysore Sales International Limited. In the field of construction activity, Karnataka State Construction Corporation (1968),

Karnataka Land Army (1974) and Karnataka State Police Housing Corporation Limited 1985) were also established. Coming to the field of tourism, the Karnataka Tourism Development Corporation was set up in 1971, and Jungle Lodges and Resorts Ltd. in 1980.

Most of the corporations and boards set up were aimed at helping the artisans to get raw materials at a concessional rate with a direct marketing opportunity through the sales emporia.

Corporate Institutions for Socio Economic Activities: The importance of human element in economic development is a well recognised fact. Therefore, over and above the economic investments, there is yet another type of investment, namely, investment, in social welfare measures in order to improve the quality of the human element, upliftment of weaker sections of society, the backwards and minorities, women and children and so on. Though non-governmental agencies could perform a pivotal role in these fields, only to some extent, the need was felt for the state to set up certain agencies which could provide direct or indirect assistance in this important field. Keeping in view these objectives, the state government set up certain developmental enterprises like Karnataka SC/ST Development Corporation (1975), Karnataka Backward Classes Development Corporation (1977), Karnataka Minorities Development Corporation (1986) and Karnataka Women Development Corporation (1987). And yet another field of social services is the transport, where the Karnataka State Road Transport Corporation was set up in 1961 itself.

Agriculture and Allied Activities: The state of Karnataka can boast of good tradition of agriculture extension work commencing from the time of Dr. Leslie C. Coleman. The extension work also emphasises on the right input for each crop in the form of hybrid seeds, fertilizers, modern agricultural equipment, plant protection chemicals, and so on. Though there are a number of agencies in the field including the University extension service centres, the farmers have been assisted by few agencies set up at the state level like the Karnataka Agro Industries Corporation (1968), Karnataka Seeds Development Corporation (1974) and Karnataka Compost Development Corporation (1975). Further, in order to provide adequate food grains at affordable prices, especially to the poorer and weaker sections of the society, the state government established the Karnataka Food and Civil Supplies Corporation, which is the apex agency to procure the material both from the state as well as Centre and distribute these essential commodities through the fair price depots run under the supervision of Food and Civil Supplies Department.

Power: The source of material civilisation is power. There are three sources of power, namely, hydro-electric, coal, and oil. The princely state of Mysore was the pioneer in the country to tap the hydro-electric power as enumerated earlier. With the progress of industrialisation and consequent development in related fields, the state has to resort to thermal and diesel power. The need to resort to thermal and diesel power has arisen more due to the limited potential of hydro-electric power and the increasing demand from industries, agriculture and tertiary sectors. Therefore, the Karnataka Electricity Board, which was established in 1957 to generate and distribute power, was divested with the generation of power and this was entrusted to the Karnataka Power Corporation. The Power Corporation has taken up and implemented a number of projects with varying installed capacities like Kalinadi project, Varahi, Ghataprabha, Kadra Dam, and Power House etc., and Raichur Thermal Power Station. In addition to these, a number of major and minor projects are coming up both in the state sector as well as in private sector.

Karnataka State Bureau of Public Enterprises (KSBPE) : The Karnataka State Bureau of Public Enterprises was set up in July 1980. The main functions of the Bureau are to:

1) co-ordinate and monitor the performance of the PSEs in the state;
2) compile the needed information on terms and conditions of the employees of PSEs;
3) coordinate the work relating to the examination of the PSEs by the State Legislature Committee like COPU;
4) prepare Annual Reports on the functioning of the PSEs for presentation to the Legislature.

5) service the Public Enterprise Supervisory Board;

6) commission in-depth studies on areas of management in PSEs, as and when required; and,

7) co-ordinate management training for various levels of executives in the PSEs.

There are at present 76 state Public Enterprises coming under the purview of the Bureau of Public Enterprises.

Present Overview of the State PSEs: Over a period of time, both the pre-independence and post independence period, the Karnataka state made massive investments in the public sector in varied fields like industry, power, agriculture, animal husbandry, fisheries, transport, tourism, social welfare, irrigation and so on, touching every field of economic activity for varied objectives with the sole purpose, i.e., for the well-being of the people. During the early part of the period, the core sector was the main thrust but it gradually started penetrating to other areas as well, especially after the Third Five Year plan. This perhaps may be one of the main reasons for the poor return on investment, as the socio economic factor was an important issue that dominated the major investment decisions. A need has arisen now to take a holistic view on the performance and the benefits that accrued to the common man and evolve a policy framework to restructure and bring reforms, especially after the economic liberalisation policy adopted both at the Centre and the state, during the past five years.

As on date, the total investment in the 76 state PSEs that come under the purview of the Bureau of Public Enterprises is of the order of Rs. 9,059.85 crores as detailed below:

[A]	Contribution of Government of Karnataka		(Rs. in crores)
[a]	As Share Capital	...	1.812.78
[b]	As Loans	...	3,306.69
	Total [A]	...	5,119.47
[B}	Contribution of Others		
(a)	As Share Capital	...	150.06

(b)	As Loans	...	4,790.32
	Total (B)	...	4,940.38
	Total (A) + (B)	...	10,059.85

If the return on this massive investment is looked into, it is quite a dismal picture as given below:

Year	No.of PSEs/ Boards	Net Profit / Loss	[Rs. in crores]
1990-91	63	(+)	74.77
1991-92	64	(+)	110.63
1992-93	68	(-)	83.77
1993-94	69	(-)	55.00
1994-95	71	(+)	75.18

(Five enterprises had disclosed neither profit nor loss)

Statements showing the net profit/loss, accumulated loss, dividend declared etc., are given in Annexures I A to D.

In the manufacturing sector, however, 7 PSEs were referred to the Board for Industrial Finance and Reconstruction (BIFR) on their net worth becoming negative and the state government took quick action to put forth the rehabilitation proposals, and these are, at present, in various stages of implementation. The Datar Committee which took up the task of streamlining the PSEs in 1988, made certain suggestions which included winding up closure/rehabilitation of certain PSEs, but, for various reasons, the recommendations could not be put into operation.

The Committees appointed thereafter made several recommendations like winding up of certain PSEs which did not serve any useful purpose and were making continuous losses, avoid multiplicity of corporations in the welfare field, companies which were in the same field should be merged and so on. However, all these recommendations remained on paper only.

The State Committee on Public Undertakings also made some specific recommendation and expressed its displeasure on the inaction of the government.

The Committee also wanted to have professional people on the Board of Directors in the PSEs, introduce MOUs in the PSEs and positive role to be played by the Government Directors. In the meanwhile, the State Planning Board also made several recommendations including a return of 16 per cent on investment made on each PSEs within 3 years, stoppage of indiscriminative subsidy to PSEs, proper pricing policy, full autonomy to the Board of Directors and Chief Executives etc. With the plethora of recommendations and suggestions made by several committees since 1986, no serious attention was given by the government, and it wanted the State Bureau of Public Enterprises through the Public Enterprises Supervisory Board, to prepare a detailed policy paper for streamlining and restructuring of the state PSEs. The Bureau of Public Enterprises, after several rounds of meeting in the Public Enterprise Supervisory Board, finalised certain broad guidelines for restructuring and streamlining the state PSEs. These guidelines are broadly as under:

1. The PSEs were classified into five groups :

a. Enterprises which are in the priority sector of government and require substantial financial and administrative support from the government to achieve their socio-economic objectives.

b. Enterprises which are in the competitive sector and have good track record.

c. Enterprises which are incurring losses but have the potential of being turned around through private participation.

d. Enterprises which are not in the priority sector and which are not performing well.

e . Enterprises which can be considered suitable for merger with other PSEs.

In respect of these categories, the suggestions given were:

i) Group a - There shall be no dilution for the purpose of raising resources for the state.

ii) Group b - The PSEs in this category could go in for disinvestment, primarily as a revenue raising measure, to supplement the general revenues of the state with 51 per cent participation by government.

iii) Group c - The equities of these PSEs could be diluted in stages so as to convert them into joint sector projects with government holding 26 per cent or even up to 11 per cent.

iv) Group d - The PSEs could be considered for 100 per cent disinvestment or failing which, close down altogether.

v) Group e - Merger of PSEs with another in the same field or is a subsidiary of a major undertaking.

The details of the classification particulars are given in Annexures II A to E.

2. Disinvestment should not be looked upon merely as a revenue raising measure, but as a means of introducing greater professionalism and proper utilisation of funds.

3. The state should continue to play its role in service sector irrespective of loss. However, private enterprises could be allowed in the field of infrastructure.

4. The Memorandum of Understanding (MOU) system may be introduced for greater autonomy as well as responsibility to achieve the fixed target set forth.

5. A policy decision should be taken not to start any more new PSEs.

6. In view of the complexities involved in disinvestment, a financial agency to mastermind the process, attached to KSBPE, may be formed.

7. As a model employer, the government must keep the interest of labour also. If surplus labour could not be employed or absorbed in the PSEs or government, adequate compensation should be provided, if necessary, from the National Renewal Fund. While resorting to

partial disinvestment, at least 10 per cent of the share shall be earmarked to the labour force at a pre-determined price till a specified time.

8. There shall be total transparency with the processes of disinvestment or any other measures suggested for streamlining the PSE.

Conclusions : The KSBPE should be reorganised into a separate Department of Public Enterprises, somewhat in line with the Government of India pattern with the specified duties to be performed in guiding and extending assistance in the working of state PSEs, including matters relating to Standing Conference of Public Enterprises (SCOPE) and International Centre for Public Enterprises (ICPE). The whole process of streamlining and restructuring of the State PSEs should be overseen by the PBP functioning as a nodal agency of the government. In a nutshell, in view of the sweeping changes that have taken place in the socio economic sectors, the establishment of a Department of Public Enterprises which, incidentally, does not have any financial implication, will be an independent department of the government to formulate and implement all policy matters pertaining to the PSEs in the state.

The state government should consider the overall policy guidelines laid down as above and put the PSEs on a firm footing towards a new era in the growth and sustenance of public sector enterprises as envisaged by Sir M. Visvesvaraya and Pandit Jawaharlal Nehru.

ANNEXURE I A

Enterprises which have made Profits (Net Profits after Tax and prior year Adjustment) in 1994-95

	Name of the Enterprise	Net Profit (Rs. in Lakhs)
1.	B W S & S B	5,406.16*
2.	Karnataka Power Corporation Ltd	4,893.46
3.	Karnataka Electricity Board Ltd	4,632.00
4.	Karnataka State Financial Corporation Ltd	1,256.35
5.	Hutti Gold Mines Co Ltd	744.87
6.	Karnataka Forest Development Corporation Ltd	740.26
7.	K S I I D C Ltd	598.44
8.	Karnataka Co-op Milk Producers Federation Ltd	408.70
9.	Mysore Sugar Company Ltd	354.70
10.	Mysore Sales International Ltd	337.58
11.	Karnataka Vidyut Karkhane Ltd	256.63
12.	Karnataka State Construction Corporation Ltd	233.50
13.	Karnataka State Silk Marketing Board Ltd	154.90
14.	Karnataka Land Army Corporation Ltd	151.95
15.	Karnataka Housing Board	116.00
16.	Karnataka State Warehousing Corporation Ltd	68.10
17.	Karnataka Soaps and Detergents Ltd	65.10
18.	Karnataka Small Industries Marketing Corporation Ltd	58.95
19.	Mysore Paints and Varnish Ltd	57.00
20.	KEONICS	56.16
21.	Karnataka Silk Industries Corporation Ltd	54.83
22.	N G E F (Hubli) Ltd	52.87
23.	Karnataka Food & Civil Supplies Corporation Ltd	52.48
24.	K S S I D C Ltd	28.31

25.	Marketing Consultants and Agencies Ltd	27.95
26.	Karnataka State Seeds Corporation Ltd	25.44
27.	Karnataka State Handicrafts Development Corporation Ltd	20.50
28.	Karnataka State Agro Corporation Products Ltd	19.85
29.	Karnataka Coir Development Corporation Ltd	17.26
30.	Karnataka State Women's Development Corporation Ltd	10.45
31.	Mysore Electrical Industries Ltd	7.15
32.	Jungle Lodges and Resorts Ltd	6.63
33.	Karnataka Urban Information Development & Finance Corporation Ltd	6.31
34.	Karnataka Meat and Poultry Marketing Corporation Ltd	4.60
35.	K S T D C Ltd	2.84
36.	Karnataka Handloom Development Corporation Ltd	2.05
37.	Karnataka Compost Development Corporation Ltd	1.78
38.	D. Devaraja Urs Truck Terminals Ltd	0.27
	Total	**20,932.45**

* indicates income.

ANNEXURE I B

Enterprises which incurred losses in 1994-95

	Name of the Enterprise	Net Losses (Rs. in Lakhs)
1.	Karnataka State Road Transport Corporation	6,965.16
2.	N G E F Ltd	3,820.16
3.	K M C O Ltd	372.19
4.	Karnataka Agro Industries Corporation	326.07
5.	Mysore Minerals Ltd	302.15
6.	Karnataka Telecom Ltd	277.63
7.	Karnataka State Khadi and Village Industries	250.25*
8.	Mysore Acetates and Chemicals Ltd	202.69
9.	Mysore Lamp Works Ltd	190.11
10.	Karnataka Pulpwood Ltd	129.23
11.	Mysore Chrome Tanning Company	84.74
12.	Krishna Basin Lift Irrigation Corporation	74.10
13.	Cauvery Basin Lift Irrigation	72.30
14.	Karnataka SC/ST Development Corporation	64.09
15.	Karnataka State Textiles Ltd	60.48
16.	Karnataka Fisheries Development Corporation	46.97
17.	Karnataka Backward Classes Development Corporation	43.42
18.	LIDKAR	39.19
19.	Karnataka State Veneers Ltd	38.48
20.	Mysore Tobacco Co Ltd	27.88
21.	Karnataka Forest Industries Corporation Ltd	22.08

(contd).

22.	Karnataka Agro Protein Ltd	16.10
23.	Karnataka Film Industries Development. Corporation	11.69
24.	Mysore Cosmetics Ltd	10.09
25.	Karnataka Minorities Development Corporation	9.44
26.	Chamundi Machine Tools Ltd	8.89
27.	Karnataka Urban Water Supply & Drainage Board	6.64*
28.	Karnataka Cashew Development Corporation	4.97
29.	Sri Kanteerava Studios Ltd	4.62
30.	Karnataka Powerloom Development Corporation Ltd	3.56
31.	Karnataka Inland Fisheries Development Corporation	1.36
32.	Karnataka Urban Development Corporation	0.86
33.	Mysore Match Co Ltd	0.43
34.	Karnataka Milk Products Ltd	0.03
	TOTAL	**13,488.49**

* indicates deficit.

Enterprises which disclosed neither profit nor losses during 1994-95

1. Mysore Paper Mills Ltd.
2. Karnataka Police Housing Corporation.
3. Karnataka Tungsten Moly Ltd.
4. Krishna Bhagya Jala Nigama Ltd.

ANNEXURE I C

Enterprises with accumulated Losses at the End of 1994-95

	Name of the Public Sector Enterprise	Accumulated Loss (Rs. in lakhs)
1.	Karnataka State Road Transport Corporation	43,708.81
2.	Karnataka Electricity Board	11,168.00
3.	Karnataka Soaps & Detergents Ltd	9,430.77 [A]
4.	N G E F Ltd	9,383.16
5.	Karnataka Agro Industries Corporation Ltd	4,440.55 [A]
6.	Karnataka Urban Water Supply & Drainage Board	3,495.08 *
7.	B W S & S B	3,432.15* [A]
8.	K I M C O Ltd	2,893.17 [A]
9.	Karnataka Silk Industries Corporation Ltd	2,143.38 [A]
10.	Mysore Chrome Tanning Co Ltd	907.44 [A]
11.	Karnataka Co-op Milk Producers Federation Ltd	895.01
12.	KEONICS	824.07 [A]
13.	Mysore Tobacco Co Ltd	730.47 [A[
14.	LIDKAR	554.54 [A]
15.	Karnataka Land Army Corporation Ltd	523.95 [A]
16.	Cauvery Basin Lift Irrigation Corporation Ltd	511.61 [A]
17.	Karnataka Fisheries Development Corporation Ltd	402.08 [A]
18.	Karnataka State Textiles Ltd	386.88 [A]
19.	Karnataka Agro Proteins Ltd	375.86 [A]
20.	Karnataka Silk Marketing Board	347.49
21.	Karnataka Backward Classes Development Corporation	341.28
22.	Karnataka SC/ST Development Corporation	339.20

23.	Mysore Acetates and Chemicals Co Ltd	333.40	
24.	Chamundi Machine Tools Ltd	291.59	[A]
25.	Karnataka Pulpwood Ltd	282.80	[A]
26.	Karnataka Inland Fisheries Development Corporation	179.03	
27.	Karnataka Film Industries Development Corporation	176.67	[A]
28.	Karnataka State Handicrafts Development Corporation	169.02	
29.	Mysore Electrical Industries Ltd	152.73	
30.	Karnataka Cashew Development Corporation	101.51	
31.	Karnataka State Tourism Development Corporation Ltd	99.86	
32.	Karnataka Compost Development Corporation Ltd	99.24	[A]
33.	Karnataka State Forest Industries Corporation Ltd	77.00	
34.	Sri Kanteerava Studios	68.70	
35.	Karnataka Minorities Development Corporation	54.89	
36.	Mysore Cosmetics Ltd	53.33	[A]
37.	Jungle Lodges and Resorts Ltd	28.86	
38.	Mysore Match Co Ltd	15.26	[A]
39.	Karnataka Women's Development Ltd	10.61	
40.	Karnataka Coir Development Corporation Ltd	7.89	
41.	Karnataka State Veneers Ltd	6.56	
42.	Karnataka State Powerloom Development Corporation Ltd	3.56	
43.	Karnataka Urban Development Corporation Ltd	3.07	[A]
44.	Karnataka Milk Products Ltd	0.75	
	TOTAL	**94,411.28**	

[A]: In respect of these 21 Enterprises accumulated losses have exceeded their share capital, reserves and surplus

*: indicates the accumulated deficit

ANNEXURE I D

Enterprises which declared Dividend for 1994-95

		(Rs. in lakhs)
1.	Karnataka State Financial Corporation Ltd	417.65
2.	Karnataka Forest Development Corporation Ltd	100.83
3.	Karnataka State Small Industries Dev Corporation Ltd	16.81
4.	Mysore Sugar Company Ltd	54.69
5.	Hutti Gold Mines Company Ltd	29.62
6.	Mysore Sales International Ltd	24.00
7.	Marketing Consultants and Agencies Ltd	1.00
8.	Karnataka State Seeds Corporation Ltd (*)	3.91
9.	Karnataka Small Industries Corporation Ltd	34.20
10.	N.G.E.F. Ltd (HUBLI)*	0.01
	TOTAL	**682.72**

Note: (*) On Preference Shares

ANNEXURE II A

A. No Dilution - To be retained as they are

[A - Enterprises which are in the priority sector of government and require substantial financial and administrative support from the government to achieve their socio-economic objectives. There shall be no dilution for the purpose of raising additional resources for the state.]

1. Karnataka Electricity Board.
2. Karnataka State Road Transport Corporation.
3. Karnataka SC/ST Development Corporation Limited.
4. Karnataka Backward Classes Development Corporation Ltd.
5. Karnataka State Police Housing Corporation Ltd.
6. Karnataka State Minorities Development Corporation Ltd.
7. Karnataka State Women's Development Corporation Ltd.
8. Karnataka Agro Industries Corporation Ltd.
9. Karnataka Forest Development Corporation Ltd.
10. Karnataka Housing Board.
11. Karnataka State Warehousing Corporation.
12. Karnataka Urban Finance and Infrastructure Development Corporation Ltd.
13. Karnataka Food and Civil Supplies Corporation Ltd..
14. Karnataka Milk Federation.
15. Karnataka Land Army Corporation Ltd..
16. Krishna Bhagya Jala Nigama.
17. Bangalore Water Supply and Sewerage Board.
18. Karnataka Urban Water Supply and Drainage Board,
19. Karnataka State Khadi and Village Industries Board.

ANNEXURE II B.

B. Partial disinvestment - Controlling interest to be retained by the Government.

[B - Enterprises which are in competitive sector and have good track record. These could be considered for disinvestment in stages, subject to minimum holding of 51 per cent by the government, primarily as a revenue raising measure, to supplement the general revenues of the state

Name of PSE	Shareholdings pattern				NET Profit/Loss		
	GOK	PSE	Others	Total	1992-93	1993-94	1994-95
1	2	3	4	5	6	7	8
1. Karnataka Power Corporation Limited.	64,420.15	-	64,420.15-	1,124.4	3,058.02	4.893.46	
2. Karnataka Handicrafts Development Corpn. Ltd	200.00	-	55.31	255.31	-3.26	7.95	20.50

Name of PSE	Shareholdings pattern				NET Profit/Loss		
	GOK	PSE	Others	Total	1992-93	1993-94	1994-95
1	2	3	4	5	6	7	8
3. Karnataka Handloom Development Corpn. Ltd.	88.28	-	489.50	1,377.78	65.50	17.82	2.05
4. Karnataka Leather Industries Development Corpn. Ltd.	181.17	-	-	181.17	-52.61	-16.62	-39.19
5. Karnataka State Electronics Development Corpn. Ltd.	737.20	-	-	737.20	-330.99	46.73	56.16
6. Karnataka State Coir Development Corp. Ltd.	103.78	-	-	103.78	0.20	11.39	17.26
7. Mysore Paper Mills Ltd.	5,674.99	-	4,178.01	9,853.01	-	-	-

Name of PSE	Shareholdings pattern				NET Profit/Loss		
	GOK	PSE	Others	Total	1992-93	1993-94	1994-95
1	2	3	4	5	6	7	8
8. Mysore Lamp Works Ltd.	31.16	39.28	66.17	136.61	27.92	-53.17	-190.11
9. Mysore Minerals Ltd.	97.50	2.50	-	100.00	39.19	23.30	-302.15
10. Karnataka Agro Corn Products Ltd.	223.37	50.00	-	273.37	38.30	10.29	19.85
11. Karnataka Vidyuth Karkhane Ltd.,	390.96	-	-	390.96	30.02	277.26	256.63
12. Karnataka Silk Industries Corporation. Ltd.,	1,309.47	-	-	1,309.47	-9.58	66.77	54.83
13. Hutti Gold Mines Company Ltd.,	220.19	72.50	3.51	296.20	-272.66	4.58	744.87
14. Mysore Sales International Ltd.,	-	60.00	-	60.00	123.91	190.91	337.58

Name of PSE	Shareholdings pattern				NET Profit/Loss		
	GOK	PSE	Others	Total	1992-93	1993-94	1994-95
1	2	3	4	5	6	7	8
15. Jungle Lodges & Resorts Ltd.,	49.69	42.06	-	91.75	17.51	17.87	6.63
16. Karnataka State Financial Corporation. Ltd.,	5,320.19	-	2,989.81	8,310.00	1,254.90	859.92	1,256.36
17. Karnataka State Industrial Investment & Development Corporation Ltd.,	6,200.13	-	-	6,200.13	269.31	187.17	538.44
18. Karnataka State Small Development Corporation Ltd.,	2,056.36	10.00	-	2,066.36	42.06	47.75	28.31
19. Karnatka State Powerloom Development Corporation Ltd.,	50.00	-	-	50.00	-	-	-3.56

ANNEXURE II C.

C. Large Scale Disinvestment

To be converted into Joint Sector Enterprises, without Government retaining controlling Interest. Enterprises which are incurring losses but have the potential of being turned around - disinvestment could be permitted to a much larger extent leaving the government with a minimum holding of 26 per cent. The sale proceeds may be mainly utilised for rehabilitating the enterprise by diversifying its activites and/or improving the marketability of its products. (Rs. in Lakhs)

Rs. in Lakhs)

Name of the PSE	SHARE HOLDINGS PATTERN				NET PROFIT /LOSS		
	GOK	PSE	Others	Total	1992-93	1993-94	1994-95
1. Karnataka Film Industries Development Corporation Ltd.,	65.00	-	12.48	77.48	-11.45	-9.42	-11.69
2. Karnatka State Tourism Development Corporation Ltd.,	569.03	-	-	569.03	5.57	-12.41	2.84
3. D.Devaraj Urs Truck Terminals Ltd.,	15.01	-	14.00	29.01	5.62	6.70	0.27

(Rs. in Lakhs)

Name of the PSE	SHARE HOLDINGS PATTERN				NET PROFIT /LOSS		
	GOK	PSE	Others	Total	1992-93	1993-94	1994-95
4. Karnataka Meat and Poultry Marketing Corporation Ltd.,	44.00	-	109.50	153.50	-1.59	-3.58	4.60
5. Mysore Sugar Company Ltd.,	180.75	-	92.68	273.43	-203.32	213.51	354.70
6. Mysore Elect rical Industries Ltd.,	97.79	-	43.71	141.50	95.18	733.71	7.15
7. N.G.E.F	1,548.00	-	452.00	2,000.00	-2,089.05	-2,549.37	-3,820.60-
8. N.G.E.F (Hubli) Ltd.	-	300.00	-	300.00	-64.22	22.70	52.87
9. Karnataka Soaps and Detergents Ltd.	5.227.57	-	-	5,227.57	-978.74	-709.91	65.10
10. Karnataka State Textiles Ltd.	50.00	-	-	50.00	-96.13	-45.97	-60.48

(Rs. in Lakhs)

Name of the PSE	SHARE HOLDINGS PATTERN				NET PROFIT/LOSS		
	GOK	PSE	Others	Total	1992-93	1993-94	1994-95
11. Karnataka State Seeds Corporation Ltd.	43.41	-	154.53	197.94	41.18	28.98	25.44
13. Karnataka Silk Marketing Board Ltd.	2,245.00	-	-	2,245.00	-478.23	-132.28	154.90
14. Karnataka Compost Development Corporation Ltd.	-	50.00	-	50.00	-3.76	-3.40	1.78
15. Karnataka Telecom Ltd.	-	300.00	-	300.00	486.99	100.75	-277.62

ANNEXURE II D.

D. To be Totally Disinvested or Closed Down.

(Enterprises which are not in the priority sector and not performing well - these could be considered for outright sale to private parties through a privatisation Commission specifically set up for the purpose.) (Rs. in Lakhs)

(Rs. in Lakhs)

Name of the PSE	SHARE HOLDINGS PATTERN				NET PROFIT /LOSS		
	GOK	PSE	Others	Total	1992-93	1993-94	1994-95
1. Karnataka State Construction Corporation Ltd.	205.00	-	-	205.00	155.56	172.34	233.50
2. Krishna Basin Lift Irrigation Corporation Ltd.	55.00	-	-	55.00	-7.01	-194.73	-74.10
3. Cauvery Basin Lift Irrigation Corporation Ltd.	55.00	-	-	55.00	-89.57	-88.67	-72.30

(Rs. in Lakhs)

Name of the PSE	SHARE HOLDINGS PATTERN				NET PROFIT /LOSS		
	GOK	PSE	Others	Total	1992-93	1993-94	1994-95
4. Mysore Paints and Varnish Ltd.	67.73	-	8.92	76.65	9.61	29.62	57.00
5. Mysore Match Company Ltd.	0.50	2.95	1.55	5.00	-1.21	-1.46	-0.43
6. Mysore Acetate and Chemicals Company Ltd.	425.94	30.00	191.82	647.76	248.61	-122.89	-202.69
7. Mysore Cosmetics Ltd.	1.14	15.00	-	16.14	-15.90	9.29	-22.08
8. Karnataka State Forest Industries Corporation Ltd.	115.53	-	-	115.53	125.55	-64.12	-11.09
9. Karnataka State Veneers Ltd.	-	51.00	49.00	100.00	0.16	-26.21	-38.48
10. Chamundi Machine Tools Ltd.	63.50	-	-	63.50	-37.31	-29.87	-8.89

(Rs. in Lakhs)

Name of the PSE	SHARE HOLDINGS PATTERN				NET PROFIT /LOSS		
	GOK	PSE	Others	Total	1992-93	1993-94	1994-95
11. Karnataka Tungsten Moly Ltd.	-	0.01	-	0.01	-	-	-
12. Karnataka Inland Fisheries Development Corporation Ltd. (To be formally wound up. as assets have already been transferred to the Department).	184.30	-	-	184.30	-4.34	-2.44	-1.36
13. Mysore Tobacco Company Ltd.	2.00	11.05	5.81	18.86	-35.65	-34.10	-27.88
14. Karnataka Urban Development Corporation Ltd.	0.25	-	-	0.25	-0.31	-0.4	-0.86
15. K I M C O	525.34	-	-	535.34	-286.07	-267.17	-372.19

(Rs. in Lakhs)

Name of the PSE	SHARE HOLDINGS PATTERN				NET PROFIT /LOSS		
	GOK	PSE	Others	Total	1992-93	1993-94	1994-95
16. Mysore Chrome Tanning Company Ltd.	-	72.09	3.65	75.74	-64.81	-77.32	-84.74
17. Karnataka Fisheries Development Corporation Ltd.	239.65	-	-	239.65	-58.16	-26.96	-46.97
18. Karnataka Agro Proteins Ltd.	33.54	0.20	27.19	60.19	29.13	32.67	-16.10
19. Karnataka Milk Products Ltd.	201.62	-	-	201.62	-0.03	-0.03	-0.03

Note:- * Orders for closing down these enterprises have been issued by Government during 1992 and earlier.

@ Order for privatisation has been issued by Government in 1992.

These are to be formally wound up and assets transferred to the respective apex bodies in the co-operative sector.

ANNEXURE II E.

E. To be merged with Other PSEs.

(E - Enterprises which can be considered suitable for merger with other PSEs.) **(Rs. in Lakhs)**

Name of the PSE	SHARE HOLDINGS PATTERN				NET PROFIT /LOSS		
	GOK	PSE	Others	Total	1992-93	1993-94	1994-95
1. Marketing Consultants and Agencies Ltd., with MSIL.	–	5.00	–	5.00	5.92	12.55	27.95
2. Karnataka Small Industries Marketing Corporation Ltd., with KSSIDC.	136.00	35.00	–	171.00	15.38	54.52	58.95
3. Sree Kanteerava Studios Ltd., with Karnataka Film Industries Development Corporation.	63.60	–	5.90	69.50	–6.06	–9.69	–4.62
4. Karnataka Cashew Development Corporation Ltd., with Karnataka Forest Development Corporation Ltd.	387.03	–	44.00	431.03	-23.84	40.31	–4.97
5. Karnataka Pulpwood Ltd., with Karnataka Forest Development Corporation Ltd.	–	125.00	–	125.00	–	–147.26	–239.23

Note:-Orders for closing down these enterprises have been issued by the Government during 1992 and earlier.

4

INDUSTRIAL RELATIONS*

B.R. Patil and
P.D. Shenoy

Introduction: Industrial relations are interactions between labour and management and/or their representative organization reflecting the attitudes and positions the two take on issues of mutual and/or divergent interests and concerns. These positions and attitudes range from rigid, uncompromising, conflicting, and hostility to accommodative, co-operative, and collaborative. The industrial relations are evolving in nature and are not purely bipartite. The state is an interested party in promoting peaceful relations between the labour and management while protecting the interests of the weaker party by regulating their relations. The degree and extent of the state intervention determine the ultimate nature of industrial relations.

Whether industrial relations are bipartite or tripartite they are affected by the environment in which the parties live and interact. However, the management and labour can have some control over the internal environment and at times they may be able to mould it to their requirements. But, the ever changing and dynamic external environment does not allow any kind of manoeuvrability by either party. The state is supposed to provide a conducive and encouraging environment through economic/business, industrial and labour policies, the industrial and labour laws, and an impartial and independent industrial — relations machinery. In other words, the state is in a position to create a part of the environment that would affect the relations between the two.

---

* This paper reflects the personal views of the authors, not of the government.

This environment consists of economic, social, political and legal, technological and industrial, geographic and temporal environments. It is quite complex in its nature and impact. Hence, the industrial relations at any level - plant, enterprise, region, industry, industry-cum-region, sector, and nation - vary at any given point of time. The scenario that emerges and exists at one level and at one point of time does differ from the scenario at another level and at another point of time. The industrial relations scenario at the regional, industry, and sectoral levels may indicate certain discernible features and patterns.

After the declaration of the New Economic Policy (NEP) in July 1991, the environmental changes in India, specially the economic and business, have been quite phenomenal. Liberalisation, privatization, and the compulsions of becoming global have injected into industry an unprecedented dynamism. The organisations are restructuring themselves affecting the industrial relations in more than one ways.

While the employers and managements are happy about the changes taking place, the employees and their organisations are on the defensive and are meekly accepting the changes. The central and state governments have been trying to woo the multinationals to come to India by offering incentives and infrastructural facilities.

Objectives : Industrial relations are largely determined by the fast changing enviornment in India since 1991-92. There has been a general impression among the managements, trade unionists, the researchers and other students of industrial relations that the industrial relations in Indian industries are undergoing a change. But there has been no effort to empirically examine these impressions. Hence, a survey on industrial relations scenario in Karnataka was undertaken during 1995-96 with the following objectives to:

1) study the changing industrial relations in different industries and organizations in Karnataka to determine the nature of changing relations;

2) examine whether the changing industrial relations have promoted industrial peace or still the traditional form of relations characterized by conflict continue, and if so, what are the reasons for the continuing conflict;

3) find out whether the changing industrial relations have increased co-operation between labour and management enabling the organizations to gain competitive advantage; and

4) identify the trends in industrial relations and portray a total industrial relations scenario in the State .

Methodology : This is both an extensive and an intensive survey of the contemporary industrial relations in different industries and in different industrial centres in Karnataka. The industries covered in the survey are: aluminium, cement, electronics, engineering, fertilizer, information technology, leather products, paper, and textiles. The organisations in these industries were selected on the basis of the data gathered from the office of the Labour Commissioner, the Karnataka Employer's Association, and a few trade unions. The data from the selected organizations were collected by interviewing the personnel and industrial relations executives. Conciliation Officers in Bangalore, Belgaum, Mysore and Mangalore were interviewed. Both the professional and worker leaders were also interviewed to their views and opinions on the changing industrial relations scenario. All the interviews were unstructured. Data were also collected from the settlements and agreements signed during 1993-96, securing them either from the respective organizations or by taking extracts from the settlements registered in the office of the Commissioner of Labour.

The Industrial and Labour Policy of Karnataka: Liberalisation and globalisation in the present context have provided to the Indian industries, enterprises and organizations no options but to re-engineer their business and restructure their enterprises and organizations. While in the past, diversifications and expansion were the watchword of the corporate world, today's watchword is - identify core competency and divest/acquire/merge to gain the competitive edge. The Business Process Re-enigneering (BPR) has become a widespread practice and the enterprises and organizations are trying to define the vision, mission and objectives of their business. The Hindustan Brown Boveri, merging with Asea and becoming Asea Brown Boveri (ABB), the ABB taking over the ACC-Backcok and the latter becoming ABB - ABL, the Brooke Bond India and Liptons India Ltd. merging to become Brooke Bond Liption India Ltd (which have now merged with the Hindustan Lever Ltd.,) are some examples. At the same time, to enhance the organizational efficiency and to fix responsibilities of running the business viably the companies are being reorganised into the Strategic Business Units (SBUs). Each SBU is required to function as if it is an independent business enterprise and stand on its own. If it fails to sail in the turbulent business environment it has to wind up instead of being a liability on the Company.

Simultaneously, the managements are under pressure for updating their technologies and, if necesssry, to bring in the new technology and concentrate on the quality standards, acquire the international quality accreditations, and compete effectively in the global market. They are adopting clearly defined quality policy which is expected to be internalized by every one from top to bottom in the organization. The updated/new technology and the restructuring of orgnizations have far reaching implications for the people employed at different levels in the organization. In brief, the entire business operations in the present scenario are being reoriented and geared to achieve the objectives and realize the mission and vision within the targeted time.

Karnataka is one of the highly industralised states in India. Its industrial policy has been very progressive. The industrial scenario in the state is generally regarded as stimulating and encouraging both prior to and after independence. There is a heavy concentration of industrial establishments in the Bangalore region. However, of late, an increasingly large number of establishments are coming up in centres like Mangalore, Mysore, Hubli-Dharwad.

Karnataka is the home of several central and state public sector enterprises. Prominent among them are: Bharat Earth Movers Ltd. (BEML), Bharat Electronics Ltd. (BEL), Hindustan Aeronautics Ltd. (HAL), Hindustan Machine Tools (HMT), Indian Telephone Industries (ITI), Visvesvaraya Iron & Steel Ltd. (VISL), New Government Electric Factory (NGEF), Vikrant Tyres, Mysore Lamps, and Mysore Paper Mills. Karnataka is also the home of several banking companies, e.g., State Bank of Mysore, Canara Bank, Syndicate Bank, Vijaya Bank,

Corporation Bank, etc., in the public sector, and Vysya Bank in the private sector.

The 1980s saw Bangalore as a centre of information technology (IT) industry. And after July 1991, the state government has adopted a very encouraging industrial policy so as to induce the multi national companies (MNCs) to have their units in Bangalore, for e.g., Motorola, 3M, General Electric, Texas Instruments, Yokuguva, Smithkline Beechem, Hewlett Packard, IBM, Verifone, Digital Equipment, Huchison Max, etc. Similarly, for their establishment, some have moved their corporate offices too to Bangalore - Wipro, Britannia, GE Apar Lighting, Madura Coats, etc. The prime reasons for this high rate of industrialization are the availability of skilled and cheap labour, the raw materials, and a peaceful atmosphere.

Karnataka provides a very conducive environment to the IT industry. Bangalore is widely known as the Silicon Valley of India. The MNCs from the United States and Europe in the IT industry have already established their units in Bangalore. The government is planning to develop technology parks with the assistance of Australia, Japan and Singapore to attract more and more MNCs into the state.

Karnataka was perhaps first among the states to promote small scale industries in India on a large scale by establishing the largest industrial estate in Asia - the Peenya Industrial Estate with about 1,000 industrial sheds.

The co-operative and joint sector industries are also quite prominent in the state. A wide spectrum of industries, viz., heavy and light engineering, electronics, telecommunications, cement, silk synthetic, and cotton textile, consumer products, banking, oil refining, pharamaceuticals, chemicals and fertilizers, ports and docks, mining (including the precious metal), plantations, food processing, sugar, tobacco, brewing, software and hardware development, hotels, transport, etc., make the industrial scenario of the state. Industrial organizations vary widely in terms of their size employing less than ten to over ten thousand persons.

Increasing Industrial Sickness: Recent years have, however, witnessed an increasing rate of sickness in certain industries particularly textiles and small and medium scale establishments in the engineering industry. A large number of textile mills in Davanagere, and the KR Mills in Mysore have now been closed for a very long time. These mills not only lack capital, but more importantly suffer from obsolete technology and surplus labour. The problem is not confined to private mills but is also true of the NTC mills in Bangalore, Davanagere, and Gulbarga. While Renuka Mills, Davanagere, and MSK Mills, Gulbarga are fast pacing towards closure, Minerva Mills in Bangalore is in deep trouble. Despite introducing voluntary retirement scheme on a regular basis, the management finds a few hundred workers surplus.

Most of the state Public Sector undertakings are also sick. Prominent among them are the NGEF, Karnataka Soaps & Detergents Ltd., Vikrant Tyres, Mandya National Paper Mills, Mysore Lamps, and their cases are pending before the Board for Industrial and Financial Reconstruction (BIFR). However, the rate and extent of sickness in the organised medium scale organizations is much higher in the Mysore region.

Besides the managerial, financial problems, and obsolete technology, sickness is also attributed to acute shortage crisis of electricity. The organizations like the Indal Belgaum Works, Shimoga Steels, Mysore are forced to remain closed regularly for want of electricity. Considering this crisis, the government has given top priority for the generation of electricity. But it is a long way before the problem is solved to the satisfaction of the industry.

The Labour Policy of the State: During the last few years, the labour policy of the state has been encouraging, enabling, supportive, and responsive to the demands and needs of the industry and labour. The labour policy of the government has been very conducive right from the 1940s. The there government of Mysore had enacted the Mysore Labour Act in 1942 providing for one union one industry principle. Though this law does not exist today, the organizations and workers in the area comprising the erstwhile state of Mysore continue to be guided by it.

Till the beginning of the 1990s, the Government of Karnataka, like any other government in the country, sought to regulate and control the industrial relations. Following the examples of Tamil Nadu and Kerala, the government amended the Industrial Disputes Act in April 1988 to insert Section 10 (B) with a view to creating an atmosphere of cordiality in the organization during the pendency of adjudication of a dispute by laying down the terms and conditions of employment as a measure of interim relief. This amendment was strongly resented by employers. It was seen as a licence to assume blanket powers by the government in determining industrial disputes, as a step towards curbing collective bargaining, and as a step to pressurize the management to accept the views of the government. The new section was put to use in several disputes.

The Government of Karnataka has plans to bring forward a legislation for improving the working conditions of the unorganized labour, besides fixing minimum wages for different employments. Based on the Supreme Court judgment on contract labour, the government has directed the District authorities to supervise the abolition of contract labour.

Workers, Unions, Unionism and Union Leadership: The manpower availability in Karnataka is a strong inducement to the small, medium, and large scale industries and employers, private and public sector undertakings, labour intensive and high tech and sunrise industries, national and multinational companies and corporations. Unskilled to highly skilled and world class manpower with high productivity are available in the state enabling the industries to be globally competitive.

Industries in Bangalore region have drawn a majority of their workers from the neighbouring states. But, in other parts of the state and in traditional industries like textiles, cement, paper and engineering a majority of the workers are the local people. The staff and a majority of the managerial employees are, however, often brought from outside by the private sector employers. Employers complain that their workers lack the industrial and work culture and in industries like textiles and cement the rate of absenteeism is high posing several problems to the managements. But the workers in IT and other high-tech industries, who are labeled as the knowledge workers, are quite ambitious, have high aspirations and expectations from their organizations and managements. They are willing to take initiative and responsibility and work hard to rise to the expectations. They are enterprising and willing to take risks.

There is an increasing casualization and contractualization of labour. Every management has hired labourer through contractors to do the regular jobs. In many cases, the number of contract workers is 50 to 75 per cent of the regular workers and in one company, except the manager, every one is a contract worker. Only in one organization the contract and casual workers are covered under the settlement signed by the management with the unions extending the benefits on par with the regular workmen. In another organization the contract workers are organized by three separate unions.

The Trade Unions: The industrial labour in Karnataka is organized into small and big unions. Both in the public and private sectors the supervisory and managerial employees are also organized. The density of membership ranges from about 50 per cent in private sector enterprises to 100 per cent in the public sector undertakings. The labour unions are affiliated to the trade union federations like the AITUC, BMS, CITU, HMS, HMKP, and INTUC. But, in recent years, the number of independent and non-political unions is growing. In some industrial centres, the number of unions affiliated to BMS is far more than the unions affiliated to any other organization in centres like Mysore, Harihar-Davanagere, and Hubli-Dharwad. Many personnel executives in these centres stated that the BMS affiliated unions are more positive, reasonable and accommodative, interested in the survival of the organizations, do not make unreasonable demands, and are more democratic in internal functioning.

Extent of Unionization: Generally speaking, unionization of labour in Karnataka is low and the trade union members are apathetic to union activities. Available statistics reveal that during the period 1980-95, the total number of registered unions increased from 1,648 to 3,810 reflecting a 232.88 per cent rise (Table 1), an average of 15.52 per cent per year. But in terms of annualized increase, only during 1984 and 1987 there has been over 10 per cent growth; it was lowest in 1988, i.e., 1.41 per cent. In terms of membership too, the growth of unionization has been poor. Though the statistics on the membership of registered trade unions for all the years are not available, the figures for the period 1984-87 reveal that the membership increased from 4.15 lakhs in 1980 to 5.34 lakhs in 1987 revealing a 28.67 per cent increase during the period. It is also significant that only 21 per cent of the total labour force employed in the registered factories, motor transport, shops and commercial establishments, plantations, etc., are unionized.

The increasing number of unions clearly reveals the problem of multiplicity of unions. In some cases, the problem of duplicity of unions (two or more federation) also exists (ABB-ABL). But, the problem of multiplicity of unions is much less in Mysore region. The concerned managements have also played an important role in having a single union. They have a clear policy of not encouraging a second union.

The Changing Trade Union Leadership: With the increasing level of education the trade union leadership is passing on to the employees themselves. Yet, the professional leader is not extinct. He is now donning the role of an advisor on an increasing scale. The advisor is changed at the sweet will of the members often after a settlement is signed and specially when the workers feel that he is becoming appreciative of the management stand and not fighting for them. This trend is attributed to the greediness of the workers. A professional trade unionist observed: "at the bottom it is only indicative of the unlimited selfishness of the workers - to get the maximum out of the situation. This has now become the bane of trade union movement".

The Changing Trade Unionism: In the context of economic reforms, the trade unions cannot continue to be mere protest organizations and deploy the political means and weapons to achieve their objectives. Their main concern is to protect the jobs of their members while enabling the employers to continue in business. They need to move away from hostility and conflict to co-operation an collaboration.

Ever since the trade union movement took its root the philosophy of trade unionism has been 'unity of the working class'. But, trade unionism and trade union movement in India and Karnataka continue to be politically oriented, divided, subdivided and fragmented, failing to protect the interests of the labour, industry, and economy. The trade union movement has also shown its weaknesses in limiting itself to organized sectors. Trade unionism has reached stagnation. They have become self defensive and their concerns now are to save employment of their members and to maintain the existing level of facilities secured from the employers.

With the increasing percentage of knowledge workers in the labour force coupled with fast rise of high-tech industries there is a growing trend on the part of the workers to move away from the established pattern of trade unionism. The present day worker still finds the need for collective action but he wants his union not to be a mere protest organization. Consequently, the trade unions in the contemporary context do not want to be affiliated to the central trade union organizations. The old loyalties to the trade unions and the leaders are totally watered down. The workers and their unions change the leaders and affiliation overnight. The internal leadership is taking over the unions from the outsiders and playing a dominant role in the labour-management relations. Trade unionism today is limited to enterprise, companies and corporate organizations. Corporate trade unionism is growing at the cost of the united trade union movement. At the same time at hocism in trade unionism is increasing. Union and worker militancy is a bygone legacy.

Trade unionism in enterprises like the Gokak Mills is of a different kind. It is basically a gang war between two groups for the simple reason that the Mill is located in a reserved constituency and both the groups want to control the workers and their families for votes. But, these gang wars have affected industrial relations in the mill and have resulted in the loss of lives of innocent people. In Mangalore region, trade unions are dominated by the outsiders belonging to the dominant community. But, these persons belong to different political parties and the workers seek their leadership depending on which party is in power.

During the last few years, at the macro level, there is a better solidarity among the trade unions and other protest organizations. The non-trade union organizations like the Raita Sangha, Cine star's Fans Association etc., are extending their help to trade unions in their fight against managements. However, such organizations have assumed a determining role sidelining the trade unions. This is a development certainly harmful to the unions seeking their alliance, however temporary it may be.

Currently, collaboration between labour and management is gaining momentum. But the professional leaders are not willing to stomach this new development. They feel that the managements want the labour leaders to collaborate with them for specific purposes like increasing workload and productivity, acceptance of changes, rationalization and modernization. A section of the trade unionists feel that the next stage is employee control over the production processes leading to new forms of ownership and management.

The information technology and other high-tech industries are union free. These organizations have adopted human resources management and succeeded in developing one to one relations with the employees. However, in one IT organization the employees are the members of the union of the parent company, which has been very co-operative with the management; the management has full freedom to take decisions on any matter including technological changes. The employees in another IT company had formed a union when the company was not in a position to pay their salaries. After the company secured collaboration in 1989 with a French company, the management and the union signed an agreement for down-sizing the company through a Voluntary Retirement Scheme. Subsequently, the union vanished.

Reasons for No Unions: Several reasons have been identified for the industry being union free. These are:

1) The knowledge and professional workers constitute the force who can stand on their own not requiring a collectivity. Individual bargaining capacity of each employee is quite high; he need not depend on someone to fight his battle.

2) The average employee is young, mobile and independent. He has a greater desire and needs to learn more which makes him constantly keep looking for opportunities which are available on a

global level, and to avail them does not need an association of fellow employees.

3) The managements in IT industry have faith in people and they endeavour to be fair employers. They believe in pro-active approach to the concerns of employees.

4) Open systems, direct and free communication, informal work environment, and attractive compensation and facilities provided to the employees do not necessiate the formation of a union.

5) Organizations are small in size, the environment is development-oriented, decision-making is decentralised and pushed down to the lowest level enabling each one to participate in and influence decision-making.

6) Organizations take care of the employees in every possible manner to improve their quality of life.

The employee relations programmes and activities in this industry are, therefore, highly individual oriented giving recognition to excellent performance, creative thinking and contribution, and career interests. Different companies have different employee relations programmes and activities. The Japanese system of monitoring is adopted by many companies. The excellent performance of both the individuals and groups is recognized through rewards of different types, viz., the President's Club Award for all round performance, Excellence-in-Action awards, Stock ownership scheme, meeting with the CEO, rewards for suggestions, employee consultation, birth-day bashes, frequent get-to-gethers with families, provision of a computer and telephone at the employee's home etc,.

Besides IT and other high-tech organizations, in the enterprises that have elaborate and comprehensive human relations programmes and the managements take care of the quality of life of the employees and their families, the unions are absent. The best example in this regard is the Jindal Aluminium Ltd., Bangalore. Similarly, in flat organizations where the employees are empowered to work without supervision, and in the greenfield plants having a total belief in the employees, the workers have no reasons to form unions.

Employers' Organizations: The employers in the state are organized into both general and industrial associations. They include: the Federation of Karnataka Chamber of Commerce and Industries (FKCCI), the Greater Mysore Chamber of Industries (GMCI), the Karnataka Employers' Association (KEA), the Karnataka Planters' Association (KPA), the Peenya Industries' Association (PIA), the Human Resources Association (HRA), etc,. Barring the KEA, they do not, however, directly deal with the industrial relations matters and issues. They have generally been functioning as forums for lobbying, education of members, exchange of views and experiences through conferences and consultations.

Role of the State in Industrial Relations: During the last few years the role of the industrial relations (conciliation) machinery in promoting settlements is much reduced. Firstly, the industrial conflict has almost come to a naught and more and more organizations and trade unions prefer to register their agreements as settlements under Section 2(p) and 18 of the **Industrial Disputes Act.** Secondly, as Table 2 indicates, the number of withdrawals and failures are much more than the so called settlements. It only endorses the observation that collective bargaining is much preferred procedure for settling the issues, and conciliation is sought only to give a legal status to the agreements or to have adjudication.

Data from Table 2 also indicate that there is a persistent decline in the performance of the conciliation machinery. This could be attributed to the continuing practice of the labour unions and the managements, often with a mutual understanding and agreement, of seeking conciliation to convert their bipartite agreements into settlements for the benefits of Section 18(3) of the **Industrial Disputes Act.** So, if the bipartite agreements in a given year are more, the performance of the conciliation machinery is good, and if the number of agreements is less, the performance is poor. In other words, there is a direct relationship between bipartite agreements and the performance of the conciliation machinery.

Yet, it is a fact that the conciliation machinery has been highly constructive and cooperative with the managements and labour unions in developing bipartite relations and promoting industrial peace. It functions with restraint and encourages the development of bipartite relations. One could notice a trend/change in the functioning of the conciliation machinery which is certainly contributing to the development of good industrial relations. In many cases, the conciliation meetings are scheduled in the premises of the disputant companies when the managements communicate their inability to attend the conciliation meetings and all out efforts are made by the Conciliaton Officers (COs) to bring about amicable settlements. One finds a refreshingly new approach in the Failure Reports. The COs normally recommend the reference of the failed dispute for adjudication by an industrial tribunal or labour court and also frame the terms of reference. These terms of reference seek to provide relief to the workers when their actions are justifiable, and when not justifiable no relief for the concerned management is recommended. But now the COs have started framing the terms of reference which also seek to provide relief to the management if the actions of the workers/union are unjustifiable. The following example brings out this trend clearly:

1) Whether the strike by the Mangalore Chemicals and Fertilizers Workers is legal and justifiable?

2) If yes, to what relief are they entitled to?

3) If not, to what relief the management are entitled to?

In this case, the government concurred with the views of the CO and referred the dispute for adjudication on the same terms. Similarly, the labour enforcement machinery, in general, want to adopt refreshingly a fresh approach to labour problems. They are striving to educate the small scale employers on various labour laws so as to promote good industrial relations and to improve labour administration. This is what is needed and expected of the third party in ensuring a balance in labour-management relations in the changing industrial relations scenario.

Collective Bargaining and Industrial Relations: Collective bargaining, barring the non-union firms and the cement industry, has become a strong institution in industrial relations. There is an increasing realization by the workers and the unions that it is advantageous to negotiate an agreement and have the issues settled across the table instead of seeking the third party intervention. More importantly, collective bargaining is becoming a process of a **quid pro quo** transaction and mature with the increasing acceptance by the unions that in a competitive business environment the managements too have their demands. The negotiations based on the charter of demands and management "proposals" are increasing. The managements are now able to have most of their demands conceded by the unions and accepted by the workers subsequent to signing the settlement. When the managements and the unions seek the intervention of the COs they do it only after negotiating the major issues.

The increasing practice of recognizing the majority union or constituting a negotiating council consisting of major unions through secret ballot has largely contributed to the development and strengthening of collective bargaining. There is an increasing realization on the part of the workers and the trade unions that good bipartite relations could be developed through collective bargaining and a representative union determined through secret ballot. The agreements for referendum also provide for constituting the Joint Negotiating Councils (JNCs) in case no union gets a simple majority of the votes polled.

Recognizing unions through secret ballot has now become quite a common practice in the state and in many cases the initiative for a secret ballot is taken by the unions and they enter into agreements with the managements to conduct the referendum. In many cases the unions which took initiative to have the referandum conducted have failed to get elected. In such cases, the majority unions have accepted the verdict and have withdrawn from the active industrial relations situations. It was, however, found that a union that secured 34 per cent votes demanded the setting up of the bargaining council, the associate membership of the council and the privileges on part with the majority union. This union having had the patronage of the powers in Government was behaving as if it was the majority union. The management had allowed the things to take their own course since it wanted to have peace in the organization for some other reason.

There are also unions and managements in some regions which do not want to have a single union recognized as the representative union. Perhaps each union wants to represent its members and be active and the management wants to avoid recognizing particular unions that have an image of militancy. So, they continue to deal with all the unions.

An important trend in industrial relations has been that where the workers do not have a union and the organization is small the managements are negotiating with all the workers and making each one of them the signatories to the agreement. The number of such settlements is increasing. Another trend is that the individual contracts are being entered into with the workmen affected by the job loss due to disciplinary reasons, or conversion of dismissals into resignations with compensation. In MICO, the individual contracts involve voluntary retirement on the ground of ill health.

The Withering Industrial Conflict: Industrial conflict is a manifestation of divergent and conflicting interests, attitudes, approaches and positions the labour and management adopt toward each other to protect and promote their rights and interests **vis-a-vis** the other. The managements normally try to avoid conflict often by conceding the workers' demands and by buying peace. The causes and manifestations of industrial conflict change from time to time. According to the causes and manifestations of conflict have not changed despite a change in the environment and the compulsions created by that environment to go global and be competitive in terms of products, product quality and product pricing. Though there is an attempt on the part of the managements to impress upon the workers and the unions the necessity of working together in a competitive environment, the work stoppages and other forms of conflict continue to the a reality though their number and incidence are reduced.

In the contemporary scenario one finds prolonged work stoppages. The examples are: the Mangalore Chemicals & Fertilizers (MCF), and Goetz, Bangalore, the Gokak Mills etc. The work stoppages are caused for both industrial and non-industrial reasons. In Gokak Mills, there was violence and work stoppage for more than a month in 1994 and

1995 for reasons that cannot be considered as industrial. As stated earlier, it was a gang war between two political groups to grab the union and establish the supremacy of one over the other and secure the vote bank. In MCF, one union wanting to assert its majority status and control over the workers demanded the removal of a labour contractor from the company leading to lock-out also for over a month. In Vijaya Wires & Filaments, the workers were on strike for more than four months demanding the cancellation of the transfer of an employee from Mysore to Delhi. But the real issue involved was the recognition of the worker's right to form a union. In Escorts, the union went on strike over the wages which was unnecessary as it ultimately got very little over what the management had offered before the union resorted to strike. And from Table 3, it may be concluded that the number of strikes compared to lock-outs has sharply declined since 1992, and consequently the losses to both.

An analysis of the recent work stoppages reveals that they are caused by the following factors that are not different from the earlier ones:

1) Wrong perceptions by the workers about the work load they have to take on (e.g., Bata India Ltd).

2) Lack of confidence in the union leadership and absence of effective internal leadership (Triveni Engineering Ltd).

3) Inter-union rivalry (MCF).

4) Unions/workers picking up trivial and non-issues to fight the management or the rival union (MCF).

5) Non-acceptance of the rights of the managements to disipline workers (including the union office bearers) by the workers/unions and their desire to intensify the struggle to force the management to reverse their decision/actions or to take revenge on the management (Vijaya Wires &s Filaments).

6) Political rivalry and gang war between factional leaders supported by anti-social elements (Gokak Mills).

7) The desire of the professional (political) leaders to exploit the union and the workers to seek their personal ends (Escorts & Goetz).

8) The militant workforce (Canara Laminates).

9) The unchanging traditional attitudes and approaches of the professional leaders to labour-management issues, viz., fight and extract benefits (Escorts).

10) Failure of the managements to recruit workers with right attitudes and social background (Escorts).

11) Negative attitudes of the managements toward unions and the failure or unwillingness to recognize the rights of the workers to form unions (Vijaya Wires & Metals).

However, it is not enough to adopt new management techniques, procedures and systems without changing the conventional traditional attitudes toward workers and the unions. In the context of continuing traditions of industrial relations, the socio-legal environment and institutions, and the largely unchanging profiles of workers, it takes longer time and serious efforts to change from conflict to co-operation and collaboration. What the managements need is to create a mind set among the workers that the interests of both the management and labour need to converge in the competitive environment for the survival of both. This is an easy task in the case of young organizations but a difficult and time consuming process in the case of the older organizations. This is a compulsive imperative in the contemporary environment.

The Management Gains (Losses of Workers): A study of the agreements and settlements signed during 1995 and 1996 reveals that the unions and workers are conceding the rights of the managements to plan, direct and control the work processes and the management of the organization. The managements have now been able to gain job flexibility and productive work practices. The workers and the unions are also agreeing to the technological changes and methods improvement the managements desire to bring to become competitive in a global market. At the same time the workers are willing to undergo retraining in different jobs to reskill or multi-skill themselves and be redeployed wherever the management finds it necessary. In other words, the managements have regained many of their rights/prerog atives which they had lost in the past. Following are the gains the managements have been able to secure from the unions and the workers during the last couple of years through agreements and settlements:

1. Acceptance of technological and other changes.

2. Acceptance by the workers and unions the rights and responsibilities of the management in managing work and organization.

3. Modernization and rationalization of the organization and the production processes.

4. Co-operation in improving productivity and methods of production;

5. Job and worker's flexibility.

6. Workers' willingness to undergo training for multi-skills.

7. Control on wasteful and restrictive work practices.

8. Shop-floor discipline of workers.

The gains have certainly enabled the managements to go a long way in acquiring a competitive edge in the global market. It is now only a matter of time before the Indian industries go to the top.

From Participation to Involvement: Only in the high-tech and IT industry organizations efforts are made by the managements to involve the employees in the managerial processes and decision-making. The employees in these organizations are grouped into small work teams and those teams are empowered to take decisions. An important reason seems to be that they have started with human resources management and development as against traditional personnel managements and industrial relations in older organizations. The older organizations must continue to deal with the unions and transform them into business oriented organizations from their present political orientations. Yet one finds that in organizations like Indal Belgaum Works, the Works Committee, the Safety Committee and the Canteen Committee function effectively.

According to some trade unionists, the PSUs are moving towards industrial democracy from workers participation. But, there are no visible effects of it yet. In some private sector organisations, with a record of good industrial relations, the statutory joint committees are functioning. However, in the context of economic reforms and business restructuring, notwithstanding the joint committees, the trade union have been extending their co-operation to the extent the managements need to make the organizations competitive.

Conclusions: The contemporary industrial relations scenario reveals that the industrial relations in the last few years are quite peaceful and cordial. But, in traditional industries like textiles and cement the relations have not changed much despite the changing environment. The inability of the managements to replace the old technology and the non-acceptance of technological changes by the workers for fear of job loss are said to be the prime reasons for the unchanging relations. In the public sector enterprises, the workers and the unions continue to be concerned with the issues of wage increase and other monetary benefits. It is observed that the labour unions have not only not been taking interest in the implementation of agreements but a few are also violating the tripartite settlements. However, where the managements are determined the changes are noticed.

In the new industries and industrial organizations where both the employers and employees have a stake in the growth and development of the organization, the industrial relations are of a different kind. The best examples are the information technology, electronics and telecommunications. In IT industry the management of the people takes the form of human resource management and emphasizes employee development and employee relations. In electronics and telecommunications industries also the managements are progressively adopting the HRM philosophy and practices leaving behind the personnel management methods and techniques; co-operation between the management and labour is increasing.

In information technology and other high-tech industries, the employees are non-unionzed as they have individual bargaining capacity. The industrial relations in such firms take the form of one to one relation based on direct communication, involvement, better reward systems, etc. On the other hand, industrial relations in firms with independent unions are non-political and co-operative. But in firms with multiple unions and unions affiliated to central organizations the industrial relations have not changed.

The factors that contribute to cordial industrial relations are, of course, specific to organizations and localised. They include: professional management of the organization and the people, caring managements that provide for all kinds of needs of the employees, management's initiative in enabling the employees to have a single union, and training them in collective bargaining and leadership, internal leadership of the unions, and employee involvement in managerial processes.

Though, during the last few years, the overall industrial relations situation has been quite peaceful and cordial, co-operation between labour and management has been increasing, and the managements are progressively involving the employees in the managerial decisions, and the leadership of the unions is passing on to the workers themselves, industrial conflict continues to be an important form of labour-managemnt relations. Instances of prolonged strikes, violence and militancy are witnessed in medium and large scale organizations in the private sector. A close study of these instances points out that industrial conflict, as in the past, is a function of tradition, outside (political) leadership of the unions, and the rigid attitudes and position of the workers and the managements on the issues of common interests.

The professional leadership of unions is fast becoming a legacy of the past. Today, the professional leaders function more as advisors; they are changed at the sweet will of the workers and the internal leadership when they feel that the professional leader has become appreciative of the managements concerns. In the traditional industries, however, the professional leaders still dominate.

The high-tech and IT organizations are presently union free as they depend upon the knowledge/professional workers who have high individual bargaining capacity compared to their counterparts in other industries and their supply is much less than the demand of the industry. Hence, the situation will change once the employment opportunities in these industries shrink.

In sum, it may be stated that the industrial relations scenario is undergoing a change. Co-operation between labour and management is becoming more common than conflict; human resource management and development is fast replacing personnel management, and labour relations are changing to employee relations. At the same time, industrial relations in organizations with traditions of good industrial relations continue to be good. Similarly, the managements which are quick to respond to the changing environment have been able to retain their competitive position in the market. On the other hand, the labour unions are becoming more defensive and more concerned with protection of jobs. Yet, one finds instances of bad industrial relations in organizations where multiplicity of trade unions, inter and intra-union rivalry continue to be the characteristic features of trade unionism, dominant external leadership and/or weak internal leadership exists, and where managements are unwilling to recognize the freedom of workers to organize. In the changing environment caused by the economic reforms collective bargaining and employee involvement in managerial processes of decision-making are not only gaining ground but are becoming common. Even the smaller organizations where the employees are not organized the negotiations are undertaken periodically and settlements are signed making every employee a signatory. The workers are positively responding to the demands of the managements for improvement in production productivity and quality, job flexibility and shopfloor discipline. The managements are now in a position to buy back the lost prerogatives.

Table I

Number of Trade Unions on the Live Registers and the Annual Percentage Increases in Registered Unions and Membership of Unions

Year	Number of Unions on Live Registers	Percentage Increase per Annum	Membership (in Thousands)
1980	1,636	-	415
1981	1,763	7.76	-
1982	1,918	8.79	-
1983	2,048	6.78	-
1984	2,288	11.72	478
1985	2,476	8.21	499
1986	2,589	4.56	513
1987	2,913	12.51	534
1988	3,062	1.41	-
1989	3,139	2.51	-
1990	3,205	2.10	-
1991	3,444	7.45	-
1992	3,546	2.96	-
1993	3,635	2.51	-
1994	3,806	4.70	-
1995	3,810	0.00	-

Table 2

Functioning of the Conciliation Machinery During 1987-94

Year	Number of Disputes	Settled in Conciliation	Withdrawn	Failed	Pending
1980	1,631	843	123	345	320
1981	1,359	529	456	134	340
1982	1,756	546	144	548	518
1983	2,498	1022	205	678	593
1984	2,714	766	1073	241	634
1985	2,733	784	186	1065	698
1986	2,333	644	407	846	436
1987	2,485	619	133	1038	693
1988	3,131	751	670	881	829
1989	2,765	527	486	1100	552
1990	2,431	549	254	950	678
1991	2,386	578	815	316	677
1992	1,976	415	199	852	510
1993	1,716	417	205	483	611
1994	1,837	365	111	529	762
1995	1,899	309	203	611	776

Source: Office of the Commissioner of Labour,
Government of Karnataka, Bangalore.

IV

FINANCIAL ADMINISTRATION

1

PLANNING IN KARNATAKA STATE AND SUB-STATE LEVELS

D.M. Nanjundappa

The theme of planning at state and sub-state levels with special reference to Karnataka bringing out major issues at both the state level and the regional and decentralised planning is discussed in this paper in three Sections. Section I focuses on interface of the market and planning of the development process and the type of issues that confront planning at the state and sub-state levels. Section II deals with planning in Karnataka including investment planning and decentralised planning in Karnataka. Section III attempts to bring out the problems and issues involved in sub-state level planning, keeping in view the people's participation in the 3-tier Panchayat Raj system of decentralised planning.

I. Planning and Market

There has been a pervasive disenchantment with the crisis that developed in India about five years ago. Suddenly, a belief was generated that the market forces are better for deciding the direction and the optimum output, whereas the command system got discredited.

It is usually forgotten that there are and can be failures in government intervention just as the market failures predominate in certain sectors that are too crucial for the vast masses of the people. Therefore, development planning must necessarily consist of a mixture of price type and quality type instruments.

While the nature of mix can alter every time, so should the productive investment that is to be undertaken. In a country like India, the problems that require attention are health, water supply, education, nutrition, rural housing, agricultural growth, extension, research and market mechanism.

The major function of planning like, reducing rural and urban imbalance, inequality, protection to the infant and removal of institutional obstructions are to be clearly recognised. Planning, it is unfortunate, is being viewed as a major obstacle to institutional innovation and adaptation. The deeper understanding of the interface between market and planning is of strategic significance in ensuring a human existence for vast masses of people in the less prosperous countries. The planning process has to focus attention on the changes required. Hence, government intervention cannot be dispensed with but, at the same time, the advantages of market directions cannot be overlooked.

One important lesson to be learnt from Indian planning is that while it promoted regional development, reduction in regional imbalances, decentralised planning which was essential for the development of the villages and transforming the lives of the poor in the rural and urban areas took a back seat. Notwithstanding this, 2 or 3 states initiated regional and decentralised planning by formulating District plans, but both the formulation and their implementation suffered serious inadequacies for want of effective local self government institutions. Some of them introduced Panchayat Raj (PR) system and while doing so, the planned schemes which were to be in the local sector were transferred to the two-tier institutions like the Zilla Panchayat and Mandal, as in Karnataka in the past, or to the Zilla, Taluk and Village Panchayats as in West Bengal or Tamil Nadu. The **73rd and 74th amendments** to the Constitution made it mandatory to have three-tier Panchayat Raj institutions like Zilla Panchayat (ZP), Taluk Panchayat (TP) and the Village Panchayat (VP). Following this, Karnataka has also switched to three-tier system of Zilla, Taluk and Village Panchayats. This will go a long way in strengthening decentralisation, and a detailed micro level planning would be essential for integrated planning and implementation of the programmes at the three-tier local sectors.

The national objectives of planning have been:

1) increase in the rate of growth;

2) efficient use of resources and improved productivity;

3) removal of poverty and unemployment;

4) a speedy development of indigenous sources of energy and other resources with proper emphasis on conservation and maximisation of benefits;

5) strengthening the impulses of modernization for the achievement of economic and technological self-reliance;

6) improving the quality of life of the people, especially of the weaker sections of society through the provision of the minimum needs;

7) reduction of income inequalities;

8) reduction in regional and urban-rural inequalities and in the diffusion of technological benefits;

9) controlling the growth of population;

10) improving the ecological and environmental assets;

11) promoting the active involvement of all sections of the people in the process of development ; and

12) bringing about changes in attitudes and values of the people and the like.

Achieving these objectives is greatly constrained by the lack of clear perceptions of the various levels at which these objectives could be effectively pursued. The National Plan covers all the states, regions and sub-regions. The state and regional plans are to be guided by thc national plan objectives and priorites but the variations or peculiarities at the different levels are to be taken care of while maintaining consistency. It can also be seen that out of the objectives narrated above, a majority of them are very significant and relevant at the local level too.

In the preparation of the state plans and the National plan, the Planning Commission played a key role. The rate of growth and the inter-sectoral balances were sought to be achieved by the technical exercises before determining the investment outlay in the public sector shared between the Centre and the states according to the constitutional responsibilities. The total outlay was more dictated by the resource 'in sight'. For achieving specific priorities or orientation in sectors which came under the state plans, the Central sectors and the Centrally sponsored schemes were framed with varying patterns of funding or by offering incentives. The Central planning also provided for making a major contribution on obtaining external assistance for the projects of various states.

Broadly, the funding of state plans depended upon the generation of surplus from current revenues of the states and additional resource mobilisation (ARM). However, this was supplemented by central assistance which was passed on to the states as a Block Grant generally with a 30:70 ratio of grants to loans with exception for special category states. Also, the Centre regulated the market borrowings and the negotiated loans of the states from the national financial institutions. Target fixation was related to capital outlays. While this was an instrument for translating the policy objectives into what is to be put on the ground, excessive reliance on targetisation turned out to be one of the serious weaknesses of the Indian planning. While in theory, planning from below was emphasised, the scientific evolving of the village plans, block plans, district plans, based on the felt needs of the area and the local resource mobilisation effort were conspicuous more by their absence. One of the major causes for such a situation is that decentralised planning did not and could not start on a clean slate. The on-going schemes, indivisible projects and the statutory concern to ensure certain proportion of plan benefits to accrue to the target groups like SCs and STs, and Special Area Development Boards - all came in the way of systematic and effective decentralised planning and its dovetailment into the state and the National Plans.

Briefly, in the post-reform period, an Apex Policy making organisation like the State Planning Board or State Planning Commission in some states devote more of their energies to policy formulation, development of perspectives and bringing about decentralised planning and giving guidance in the preparation and integration of the local plans both vertically and horizontally. Thus, decentralised planning, an exciting discovery, stands in the forefront now.

Sub-State Level Planning: With the publication of the report of the Working Group on District Planning (1984), of the Planning Commission, the pressure on the need to resort to decentralisation of development effort, finances and institutional framework to suit the regions or areas have mounted. Also, the concept of decentralised planning has become somewhat synonymous with the concept of district planning. This may not be very appropriate. Decentralised planning connotes a better perception of the needs of the local areas, makes better informed decision-making possible, gives a greater voice in decision-making to the people for whom the development is meant, and serves to achieve better co-ordination and integration among programmes enabling the felt needs of the people to be taken into account. District planning is a kind of area based sub-state planning and arises from the need to supplement the national and the state plans with a more detailed examination of the resources, problems and potentials of local areas. The local area is accepted as the district, and the investment programmes are tailored accordingly. It is similar to that of area planning which assumes that the district is a sub-state decision-making unit within the system of multi-level planning. Therefore, in the process of decentralised planning, one lower level after the state is represented by planning at the district. Whether that is the most appropriate level and unit of planning and whether further tiers of decentralised planning are required, are to be determined by the constraints in the administrative system, paucity of required basic data and qualified personnel to undertake planning on a systematic basis.

In a broader sense, the move towards decentralised planning is the reaction to the following present day procedural aspects of centralised planning:

1) Carrying out the theoretical and applied exercise at the national level by the Planning Commission which has the overall responsibility for the planning process including formulation of national plans and the outlays of the state plans.

2) Determining at the Centre the share of the public and the private sector outlays in relation to the suitable objectives of the growth of the country.

3) Procedures followed for discussing the strategies, priorities, outlays (both of the Central and state plans), financing and implementation.

4) Approval of sectoral outlays of the state plans by the Planning Commission right up to the last insignificant head of development.

5) Imposition of Central Sector and Centrally-sponsored schemes without any discussions at the Working Group meetings with the State Teams.

While broadly keeping the national objectives, the over reliance on the sectoral planning, and tailoring uniform activities and patterns are to be replaced by a simultaneous process of planning at different levels enabling harmonisation and integration of one level with the other, achieving, **inter alia**, the establishing of inter and intra-sectoral linkages and the rural-urban integration.

II. Planning in Karnataka

The national objectives of the Five Year Plans need not necessarily conflict with the state Five Year Plan objectives in so far as at both the levels, we find a greater degree of convergence. In a state like Karnataka, the highest priority was given right from the beginning to irrigation and to power sectors for which more than 50 per cent outlay was allocated. Both irrigation and power programmes have been given 25 per cent allocation in most of the Five Year Plans and it is only in recent years that this proportion has slightly been reduced due to resource constraints. Power outlays are expected to be increased further by the flow of foreign capital to power sector, releasing more resources for the social sectors and also irrigation. Large scale and medium industries were considered relevant in the strategy of industrial development along with small scale industries and cottage industries. Karnataka's plans have accorded a higher priority to social justice realising that this approach would promote human resources development more effectively. Therefore, although the Planning Commission used to put a ceiling of 20-22 per cent for social services, this was invariably exceeded and the resources needed for financing larger outlays on social services were mobilised by additional taxation and by imposing appropriate user charges for the supply of economic inputs like water, power and the like. Perhaps, Karnataka was one of the earliest to impose a 'Betterment Levy' on the farm sector to mop up resources from the incremental land values resulting from irrigation facilities. The state recognised in the 1970s that the social injustice that had crept in irrigation investment, especially, large and medium irrigation projects, had to be corrected. This was considered all the more important considering the financial responsibility that was imposed on the small and marginal farmers who obtained funds to be repaid with interest for irrigation wells from the Banking system availing of one-third subsidy from the government. In the 1970s and until the mid 1980s, additional resources were mobilised to fulfil the objective of growth with social justice. It was also the first state to evolve a 'Housing Scheme' for the poor which has gained greater attention in recent years by both the Centre and the other states. Treating employment as an antidote to poverty, Karnataka introduced an 'Employment Affirmation Scheme' as early as 1973 which, later on, became the model for the 'National Rural Employment Scheme' introduced by the Planning Commission.

The per capita plan outlay in Karnataka has risen from about Rs. 25 in 1967-68 to Rs. 752 in 1995-96, the highest in the country. The pattern of growth of plan investment in the state is shown in Table 1.

Table 1

Investment (Public Sector) in Karnataka by Plan Periods

(Rs. Crores)

Sl. No.	Plan/Years	Investment *
1.	First Plan 1951-56	42.62
2.	Second Plan 1956-61	149.69
3.	Third Plan 1961-66	277.93
4.	Annual Plan 1966-69	290.93
5.	Fourth Plan 1969-74	481.19
6.	Fifth Plan 1974-78	1,231.57
7.	Annual Plan 1978-80	1,071.07
8.	Sixth Plan 1980-85	3,924.18
9.	Seventh Plan 1985-90	6,476.36
10.	Annual Plan 1990-92	3,857.77
11.	Eighth Plan 1992-97	14,620-07
12.	Total 1951-97	32,423.36

* Includes Centrally sponsored and Central Plan Schemes, direct investment by the Centre, non-plan capital outlay, Western Ghats Development Programme.

Source: Planning Department, Government of Karnataka.

The total state plan investment, which covers outlay on Centrally sponsored and Central schemes, direct investment by the Centre, non-plan capital outlay on irrigation projects and Western Ghats Development Programme, in addition to the state Plan outlay funded fully by the state resources on the plan side during 1951-97 is about Rs. 32,423 crores. The state Plan investment which was a meagre Rs. 43 crores in the First Plan reached Rs. 1,233 Crores in the Fifth Plan and touched Rs. 6,476 crores in the Seventh plan and went on to reach more than double this investment at Rs. 14,620 crores in the Eighth plan. Private sector investment in the state during 1951-97 is roughly estimated at Rs. 24,862 crores. Here also, before the Fifth plan, private sector investment varied from Rs. 87 crores in the First Plan to Rs. 722 crores in the Fourth Plan. From the Sixth Plan onwards, private sector investment showed a dramatic rise to Rs. 6,150 crores in the Eighth Plan. The public sector investment and the private sector investment taken together is estimated at Rs. 57,285 crores during 1951-97. No doubt, this massive investment has made it possible for the state to achieve an average growth rate of 4.5 to 5 per cent in the past two decades.

One important feature of Karnataka's Plan finance is that over the years, the share of Central assistance/resources for the state Plan investment almost stagnated around 20 per cent. This shows that nearly 80 per cent of the plan resources have been provided from the state resources alone. In a way, this has put a tremendous strain on the state's finances. A rough idea of the pattern of plan finance in the state may be seen from the Table 2.

Table 2.

Financing of Annual Plan 1995-96 (proposed) Karnataka

Item (1)	Rs. in crores (total outlay) (2)	As per cent of Col. 2 (3)
A. State's Own Resources		
1. Balance from current revenues	1,471.31	41.1
(of which ARM)*	(125.00)	(3.4)
2. Contribution of Public Enterprises	149.32	4.1
(a) State Electricity Board	156.05	4.3
(of which ARM)	280.92	7.8
(b) State Road Transport Corpn.	-	-
(of which ARM)	-	-
(c) Other Enterprises	-6.73	-0.16
(of which ARM)		
3. State Provident Funds	247.71	6.16
of which ARM raised through impounding of D.A. -	-	
4. Misc. Capital Receipts (net)	-414.85	-11.5
5. Share of Small Savings	450.00	12.5
6. Debenture/Bonds/others	543.28	15.1
7. ARM agreed at Dy.Chairman level discussions	-	-
8. Adjustments of Opening Deficit/ Surplus	-103.76	-2.8
Total A (1 to 8)	**2,343.01**	**65.5**
B. Central Support:		
9. Loans from market by state govt.	231.84	6.4
10. Negotiated loans and other finances	193.20	5.3
a) LIC/GIC	89.89	2.4
b) NABARD	0.49	

(Contd.)

c) REC		
d) IDBI	64.82	1.7
e) Others (specify)	38.00	1.0
11. Plan revenue deficit grant (NFC)	-	-
12. Central assistance (net)	358.15	10.0
i) Central assistance (gross)	358.15	10.0
ii) Adjustment of normal APA		
iii) Adjustment of relief APA		
13. Assistance for EAPs	448.80	12.5
14. Others (grants for spl. problems)	-	-
Total B (9 to 14)	**1,788.14**	**34.4**

C. Aggregate Plan Resources (A+B) 3,575.00

* Additional resources mobilisation (ARM)

Source: Planning Department, Government of Karnataka.

Out of the total outlay of Rs.12,300 crores approved (total investment Rs. 14,620 crores) for the VIII Five Year Plan at current prices, the Central assistance (normal and additional) is about Rs. 2,771 crores. Roughly, it forms about 22 per cent of the total plan outlay. Net Central assistance of Rs. 358 crores for 1995-96 Annual Plan accounted for hardly 10 per cent of the outlay approved.

Over these years, Central assistance has not increased significantly. The Government of India tried to show the funds of externally assisted projects also as Central assistance. In particular, Karnataka objected to such an aggregation. Consequently, assistance for externally assisted projects is now shown separately from Central assistance.

The plan finances depend heavily on the loans from the market, negotiated loans and assistance for externally assisted projects. Even then, market borrowings are yet to become a balancing factor in the scheme of plan finance. Karnataka has done the highest tax efforts when compared to all other states in the country. This has been so for several years, and even now it maintains that position. Karnataka's tax effort(proportion of tax revenues to per capita income) is 17.17 which is the highest in the whole country. The all state's average tax effort is 9.65.

Karnataka initiated the sub-state level planning right from the middle of 1970s. This was possible due to the establishment of one of the best Planning Departments in the country with seven functional divisions like Resources Analysis /Special Study, Perspective Planning, District and Regional Planning, Information and Monitoring, Evaluation, Project Formulation and Employment, and Manpower Planning. These Divisions are headed by 'subject experts' as Directors, supported by Research staff with designations like Assistant Director and Deputy Director. Their recruitment was done by a special committee, keeping these posts outside the purview of the Karnataka Public Service Commission. The main objective was to get experts for these functional divisions. They were also sent to the Planning Commission for training in the corresponding functional units of the Planning Commission. The Planning Department itself was headed, until recently, by a professional economist, functioning as Commissioner and Secretary to Government, Planning and Institutional Finance Departments. Such a set-up was helpful in not only introducing sophistication in the preparation of the Five Year and Annual Plans, but also in initiating decentralised planning. It is to be specially noted that Karnataka initiated the sub-state level planning right from the middle of 1970s after developing the required data base for Taluk/Tehsil/Block which helped in resources analysis, developing local strategy and formulation of programmes suited to the needs of local area.

In the absence of decentralised Panchayat Raj institutions like the ZP, TP and the VP and a State Level Finance Commission which decides on the District sector funds, the Planning Department took the initiative of classifying all plan schemes into 'divisible and indivisible' ones. The divisible schemes and their amount were considered for allocation to the District sector on the basis of a criteria which is given in Table 3.

Table 3

Criteria for Allocation of Fund to the District Sector

	Indicators	**Weights (%)**
1.	Population	50
2.	Backwardness in Agriculture as measured by the Value of Agricultural Output per Hectare	5
3.	Backwardness in Irrigation as measured by the Proportion of Irrigated Area to Net Area Sown	7
4.	Backwardness as measured by the Value of Industrial Output	5
5.	Backwardness in Communications as measured by Road and Railway Mileage per 100 sq.km. and per Lakh of Population	5
6.	Backwardness in Financial Infrastructure as measured by Size of Population served by each Commercial and Co-operative Bank	2
7.	Backwardness in Medical Health Facilities as measured by the Number of Hospitals per 1,000 Population/Bed Population Ratio.	5
8.	Backwardness in Power Supply as measured by the Proportion of Villages Electrified	5
9.	Problems of the Weaker Sections:	
	(a) as measured by the Proportion of SCs/STs in the Population	2
	(b) as measured by the Proportion of Landless Agricultural Labourers	2
10.	Special Problems of Malnad areas and Drought-Prone Areas;	
	(a) as measured by the Area under Forest	2
	(b) as measuredby the Rural Population of Drought-Prone Areas	2
11.	Literacy Percentage	5
12.	Performance in Family Planning Programme	3
	TOTAL	**100**

The above criteria cover allocation of plan funds among Zilla Panchayats. Similar, but simpler criteria have been fixed for determining the share of Taluk Panchayats out of the plan funds allocated to ZPs, and they are as shown below:-

	Indicators	Weights (%)
1.	Population	60
2.	Area	15
3.	Dry land Area	15
4.	Agricultural Labour Population	10

The indivisible items relate to areas like power projects, major irrigation projects, inter-district schemes, research and development and other state-wide activities which are to be handled at the state level only. The divisible items cover activities for which planning can be done at the district level and below, and their implementation can be carried out with the staff in those levels belonging to different departments. The tentative district sector allocation is communicated to the Deputy Commissioners on the basis of which a draft district sector plan is prepared. This was discussed at the state level with the District and Regional Planning division of the Planning Department and the final shape would be given thereafter. For such meetings, the Deputy Commissioner of the concerned district and other key personnel were required to be present. This procedure was followed until 1986-87 by which time Karnataka brought into existence two tier PR institusions consisting of the ZP, and Mandals. This was, in vogue, until the 73rd and 74th amendments were made to the Constitution of India by which it became mandatory for all the states to adopt uniformly a 3-tier Panchayat Raj set-up consisting of ZP, TP and VP. The former District sector has now become ZP sector and the Deputy Commissioner has been replaced by a Chief Executive Officer exclusively in-charge of the Zilla Panchayat.

For budgetary purposes and voting by the legislature, pending detailed exercise in consultation with the Accountant General, the state introduced the system of appending to the budget a separate document relating to the 'District Sector Plan' outlays and the various schemes there of relating to all the districts in the state. This, incidentally, helped overcoming the technical difficulty of moving the grants for vote in the Assembly by the concerned sector Minister. Even to this day, the same procedure is being followed. Radical changes are required in the financing and accounting procedures if real Sub-state Level Planning is to be done, about which, more will be discussed later.

To give an idea of the ZP sector outlays, in comparison with the state sector outlays, we may note here the position in the VIII Five Year Plan. The ZP sectoral allocation was Rs. 2,094 crores, forming 17.02 per cent of the total state's VIII Five Year Plan approved outlay of Rs. 12,300 crores. On the basis of the formula mentioned earlier, and adopting a slightly simpler but a similar formula for allocation of funds from the ZP to the TP and GP in the Annual Plan of 1995-96, the ZP sector outlay was about Rs. 620 crores, out of the total Annual Plan outlay of Rs. 3,725 crores. Keeping in view the urgency of meeting the pressing felt needs at the village level, Grama Panchayats were given a 'flat allocation' of Rs.2 lakhs each and this amount was deducted from the total ZP sector outlay and the balance was distributed to the ZP and the TP. An illustration of this allocation for 1995-96 Annual Plan is given in Table 4.

Table 4

Karnataka: District Sector Outlay 1995-96

Sl. No.	Name of the District	Amount Allocated	Grama Panchayat Allocation	Amount available for ZP & TP (Col. 3-4)	Allocation for Zilla for Panchayat	Allocation for Taluk for Panchayat
						(Rs.in lakhs)
1	**2**	**3**	**4**	**5**	**6**	**7**
1.	Bangalore(U)	1,650.34	163.22	1,497.12	743.56	743.56
2.	Bangalore(R)	2,874.09	313.31	2,560.78	1,280.39	1,280.39
3.	Chitradurga	3,452.42	391.59	3,060.83	1,530.41	1,530.42
4.	Kolar	3,462.06	437.10	3,024.96	1,512.48	1,512.46
5.	Shimoga	2,949.23	533.12	2,416.11	1,208.05	1,208.06
6.	Tumkur	3,690.83	434.00	3,256.83	1,628.42	1,628.41
7.	Mysore	4,257.97	499.30	3,758.67	1,879.33	1,879.34
8.	Chickmagalur	2,291.29	330.76	1,960.51	980.25	980.26
9.	D.Kannada	3,225.08	492.75	2,732.33	1,366.16	1,366.17
10.	Hassan	2,738.08	362.30	2,375.78	1,187.89	1,187.89
11.	Kodagu	1,152.38	137.52	1,014.86	507.43	507.43
12.	Mandya	2,554.46	323.49	2,230.97	1,115.49	1,115.48
13.	Belgaum	4,611.40	662.22	3,349.18	1,974.59	1,974.59
14.	Bijapur	4,228.45	512.95	3,715.50	1,857.75	1,857,75
15.	Dharwad	4,143.09	603.65	3,539.44	1,769.72	1,769.72
16.	U.Kannada	2,089.23	295.50	1,793.73	896.87	896.86
17.	Gulbarga	4,044.06	471.72	3,572.34	1,786.17	1,786.17
18.	Bellary	2,883.08	355.06	2,527.97	1,263.99	1,263.98
19.	Bidar	2,200.29	253.25	1,947.04	973.52	973.52
20.	Raichur	3,502.22	425.29	3,076.93	1,538.47	1,538.46
	Total	**62,000.00**	**7,998.12**	**54,001.88**	**27,000.94**	**27,000.94**

The major problems and the possible solutions arising from the decentralised and Sub-state level planning with Panchayat Raj institutions are discussed, in greater detail, in the remaining part of this paper.

III. Problems and Issues

Geographical Regions: As said earlier, in the process of decentralised planning, the district offers a sub-system or sub-region. It is possible to visualise all the feasible levels of planning within the state, instead of making a beeline for the district, perhaps for the convenience it offers. Undoubtedly, the district is a well recognised administrative unit and offers an established frame of reference of the functioning of various sectional activities, the administrative units concerning them and the institutional structure which goes with them. One could think of homogenous regions like water, forest and mineral resources etc., as units of decentralised planning. Some have argued that a Revenue Division may be taken as a level next to the state for decentralised planning. Possibly, a division may be more suited in some states but, on balance, wisdom seems to lie in the choice of the district as the third tier of planning, excepting in the states which are too small and do not stand in comparison with the average state in the country.

Hence, it will be seen that the choice and the number of levels of planning would turn out to be very important while developing the approach to decentralised planning. The infrastructure, the skills, the resources available and the awareness on the part of the people would be crucial factors.

Another major but highly neglected issue is of rural-urban integration. Somehow, so far, even while using district planning as synonymous with decentralised planning, the district plans are conceived as rural plans only. There are towns, both medium and large, where there is higher incidence of poverty or unemployment. Many activities which have rural-urban linkages are carried out in towns such as werehousing, dairying, agricultural research, manufacture of agricultural implements, industrial development, power generation and distribution, road ransport etc., which are implemented by either autonomous bodies or government departments. It may be necessary in decentralised planning at the district level to develop suitable integrating mechanism for bringing all these within the ambit of decentralised planning at the district level.

Determination of Activities/Programmes: The concept and methodology of decentralised planning will necessarily have to take note of the 'Local Sector' as distinct from the 'District Sector'. The local sector below the district level may be looked as one or more level below the district level where particular activity or a project can be formulated and implemented successfully utilising the instruments available with them. For example, a Block[1] or Taluk may be another unit of planning. Useful exercises have been done in states such as Karnataka, Maharashtra in this regard. Once this sector is defined, successful decentralised planning will call for a single stream of programmes assigned to them.

Linkages: The formulation of a consistent plan and its proper timely execution requires clear cut understanding of interdependance or the linkages of the different sectors of development. Getting an input from the other sectors linkage and supplying its own output to various other sectors either as raw material or as a finished product can be called as forward linkage. Experience has shown that the greatest single factor for poor performance of the plan programme has been the lack of establishing required linkages in ex-ante exercise and the lack of co-ordination among the various functionaries.

Instruments: The following areas can be visualised as the main instruments of decentralised planning:

a) Disaggregation of funds/allocation of funds.

b) Credit planning and its integration with district plan.

c) Institutional framework organisation.

d) Settlement patterns.

e) District Planning Committees.

f) Budgetary controls and accounting.

g) People's participation.

h) Change of power structure.

i) Evaluation.

1. A block is co-terminus with a revenue tehsil (taluk) in Karnataka (one or two big districts may be an exception)

Disaggreation of Funds/Allocation of Funds: Along with decentralisation at different levels there should be endowment of adequate fiscal powers or flow of funds to those levels to match their responsibilities. Against this background, the State Finance Commission, set up in each state as per statutory requirements, works out the general principles and transfer of resources to the Panchayat Raj bodies.

Under the state planning, efforts are made to disaggregate the programmes district-wise wherever possible, and on that basis, disaggreation of funds for the district plan is attempted. For example, in Karnataka's 1995-96 Annual Plan, Rs. 620 crores, out of a total outlay of Rs. 3,250 crores, were shown as district sector outlays covering all the 20 districts of the state. Within this Rs. 620 crores about 10 per cent would appear to be untied. According to the analysis made by the Karnataka Government's State Finance Commission, about 10.15 per cent of the fund recommended by them can be untied funds in 1995-96. A major impediment to decentralised planning arises at this level itself. If we are to adopt decentralised planning, the state plan outlays relating only to power, major industries, major transport and major irrigation may be in the domain of the Planning Commission and the rest should devolve to the state in a sectorally untied manner. Identification of those activities which can be planned and implemented at the state level and those which are relevant to the district is to be attempted. The basic point is that a lumpsum transfer of funds to each district is the first step in realising the objective of decentralised planning.

A question also arises regarding the mechanism for transfers of funds - should there be a statutory body like the Finance Commission at the state level for distribution of funds among the different districts with the 73rd and 74th amendments to the Constitution? It is obligatory for every state government to appoint a State Finance Commission and this has been complied with in states which have ushered in the PR system. There is merit in the setting of the State Finance Commission in as much as the Commission can bring about the transfer of resources on the basis of its own criteria which could broadly reflect the needs to devote more resources to districts which are relatively more backward and have special problems than the others. The point to be noted is that the formula that it adopts should be simple rather than being highly sophisticated which may give rise to continuous controversies. One special advantage of a statutory body like the State Finance Commission is that the legislature may not axe the allocation of funds on any political consideration.

Credit Planning and Its Integration with District Plan: With institutional credit being available from banks and financial institutions in a big way, the task of decentralised planning has become more demanding at the district level. The exercise in integrating the credit plans with the district plans is still imperfect. The point is that it is not enough that the credit component required for beneficiary-oriented programmes alone is taken care of. District credit plan should fully direct the district development plan and identify the areas which require credit support and extend the same. Probably, this is the only way of integrating credit plans with the district plans. If this is done, the full benefits of the district plan are likely to be realised.

It is likely that there may arise a clash between the banking culture and local government culture. These two cultures have to be dovetailed for the smooth functioning of the process of decentralised planning. There is considerable expertise with the banking community which has to be harnessed and co-ordinated with the skills and experience of those working in Zilla Panchayats and government offices attached to them. In the process, some further strengthening of the financial infrastructure may become necessary.

In short, the integration of credit plan and district plan depends upon how satisfactorily a district plan is prepared bringing within its compass all the developmental activities, including those for which institutional funds can be obtained from the banking system with or without subsidy. The success very much depends upon the expertise available in the planning body and the banks at the district levels and how much in advance the district plans become available with the banking institutions for preparing the credit plan.

Institutional Framework/Organisation: The institutional framework at the third tier must be such as to ensure integration of political, district administration and local institutions for determining the programme of development and their implementation at the district level. It is in this context that domestic institutions like PR institutions have come into prominence. While mini government status is given to the ZP, institutional framework is totally inadequate at the taluk and village levels, especially at the village panchayat level. This is an issue which needs to be debated for drawing up the guidelines for operationalising the district plan.

A major point which is often debated with the establishment of Zilla Panchayats is the role of the District Collector/Deputy Commissioner. Some argue that in view of the interdependence of law and order function and the development function the task of formulating and implementing development at the district will fail to take off without the active participation of the District Collector. In the Karnataka model, the Deputy Commissioner is exclusively for law and order and he is outside the Zilla Panchayat for which a senior officer is appointed as the Chief Executive Officer. The Deputy Commissionr has to attend to a large number of activities that will give him little time to provide initiative and guidance in the formulation of the plan, its integration into a district plan and implementation. Development has become more complex and with democratic process being enforced with full participation, it is in a way better to keep the law and order enforcing authority independent and insulated from the new decentralised democratic institutions.

Settlement Patterns: The careful choice of locations for the provision of facilities covered under the minimum needs programme and for the delivery of inputs is important for the successful implementation of the programmes. No doubt, this is a difficult task but not insurmountable if location specific programmes are carefully formulated.

District Planning Committees: In the context of decentralised planning at the district level the important task of planning assumes a special significance. As per the 74th amendment to the Constitution, there will be a District Planning Committee for each District/Zilla Panchayat. This committee will co-ordinate the programmes of the departments in the district and other agencies including urban and local governing institutions and area development boards. The responsibility of planning should be with one agency. This calls for expertise and therefore, the District Planning Committee, with a Chief Planning Officer should have a Technical Planning cell, with specialists in various disciplines. This cell should carry out technical exercises and based on their exercise prepare a draft integrated plan taking advice from the District Planning Committee and from the State Planning Division. To make micro planning effort more comprehensive it may be necessary to provide planning functionaries at the Taluk and Village Panchayat levels.

At the state level, in the light of the emphasis on decentralised planning, the State Department of Planning should be revamped and a Regional and District Planning Division with specialists and research staff should be set up, headed by a Director at the level of Joint Secretary. This Division will provide assistance and guidance to the District Planning Committee.

Budgetary Controls and Accounting: Another major instrument of decentralised planning which will require change is that of budgetary and accounting procedures. The present system of making budgetary allocations by head of accounts relating to departments which are in charge of different sectors has to be replaced by a different budgetary and control mechanism. If the funds are transferred to each district under the ZP set up, the amount can be shown in the budget as grants to ZP under a separate head like district plan schemes development. Financial controls to be exercised through concurrent audit, and the State Accounts Department has to get itself adapted to this method. The Audit Reports are to be placed before the legislature.

People's Participation: A strong feature of decentralised planning is that it enables the full involvement of the people in the decision process perhaps through their participation in planning, formulation and implementation. This will contribute to the development of a district style of development, responsive to the needs of the people. In addition, the association of voluntary organisations and associations of the poor and the unorganised with the PR bodies would be desirable. Constructive co-operation and understanding between the elected members of the PR institutions and the officials is a basic prerequisite for effective people's participation.

Power Structure Change is Imperative: It is now accepted that there is unequal distribution of power among people in so far as their participation at the district or lower levels of planning is concerned. People's participation at the different levels is primarily required to reduce unequal distribution of power and poverty. Generation of poverty is a function of concentration of power and the mobilisation of resources by rural elites or urban elites. People's participation at different local levels would lead to the redistribution of both the control of resources and the power in favour of the deprived and the poor. This task is not merely administrative or statutory process. Basically, it is a political process with which the administrative process is linked. There has to be a continuous dialogue among different levels, authorities and the various people. This continuous dialogue is the very heart of the decentralised process.

Evaluation: Monitoring and evaluation have now been recognised as essential parts of any organisational system. Their importance is all the more in planning at the state and sub-state levels and the Panchayat Raj institutions. Evaluation refers to the process of assessing the work done in the various activities and examining the worth of a project proposed to be undertaken or is being implemented. Monitoring is a component of evaluation. It deals with obtaining correct data and information periodically on the effects and progress of an activity **vis-a-vis** their predetermined objectives/targets in order to improve operational efficiency through timely detection of bottlenecks if any, and apply timely corrective action. There is need, therefore, to set up a Cell manned by experts at the district level preferably in the ZP which will report to the government through the Planning and Evaluation division of the State Planning department.

REFERENCES

Chakravarthy. S. (1987). **Development Planning: The Indian Experience.** Oxford: Oxford University Press.

Chakravarthy, S. (1991). **Development Planning: A Reappraisal,** Cambridge Journal of Economics, 15 (1): 15-20.

Government of India, Ministry of Rural Development (1994). **Powers and Functions of Panchayat Raj Institutions: A Framework,** New Delhi: Government of India.

Government of Karnataka (1988). **District Governments and Decentralised Planning.** Bangalore: Government of Karnataka.

ISEC. (1973). **District Planning** Bangalore: ISEC.

Lange, O. (1967). **Essays on Economic Planning.** Bombay: Asia Publishing House.

Little, I.M.D. (1982). **Economic Development: Theory, Policy and International Relations.** New York: Basic books.

Nadkarni, M.V. and R. Bharadwaj. (1992). **Planning for Social and Economic Development: Essays in Honour of Professor D.M.Nanjundappa).** New Delhi: Sage.

Nanjundapa, D.M. (1976). **Development to Social Justice.** New Delhi Oxford and IBH.

Nanjundappa, D.M. (1978). **Local Level Planning for Integrated Rural Development,** Bangkok: U.N. (Escap).

Nanjundappa,D.M. (1980). **Draft Guidelines for Local Level Planning for Blocks in Karnataka.** Bangkok: U.N.(ESCAP). Unpublished.

Nanjundappa, D.M. (1981). **Area Planning and Rural Development.** New Delhi: Associated Publishing House.

Nanjundappa, D.M. (1991). Concept, Approaches and Techniques of Decentralised Planning. In B.N. Yugandhar and Amita Mukherjee, Readings in Decentralised Planning, Vol. I. New Delhi: Concept.

Planning Commission. (1984). **Report of the Sub-group on District Planning.** New Delhi : Government of India.

Sundaram, K.V. (1977) **Urban and Regional Planning in India.** New Delhi: Vikas Publishing House.

Timbergern, J. (1967). **Development Planning**. London: Welfield Nicholson.

2

STATE GOVERNMENT AND THE NEW ECONOMIC POLICY*

B.K. Bhattacharya

Introduction: A major transformation of the Indian economy commenced during the financial year 1991-92. The immediately previous decade had seen 'the best of times, the worst of times' for the economy. In the mid 80s, it was generally believed that India was almost on the path of self-sustained and steady growth. During the 80s, GDP was growing at 5.5. per cent with the industrial growth rate averaging about 8 per cent. There was widespread expectation that India was finally breaking free of the constraint of the 'Hindu rate of growth' of 3.5 per cent per annum. However, the period August 90 to July 91 saw dramatic changes in the economics and politics of this country and by the time a new Government came to power in New Delhi and announced some dramatic changes in the economic policies in July 91 the country was supposed to be facing its worst financial crisis.

It is worth recalling here that the real sector of the economy was doing quite well just before the country entered its probably the worst ever financial crisis of mid 1991. To quote Bimal Jalan (1991), " As a result of an excellent monsoon agricultural production was at its peak. Industrial production was increasing at the rate of 8 per cent per annum and exports were doing well. The financial crisis was, however, of such magnitude that gains in the real sector were severely eroded by crisis of confidence and the shortage of international liquidity".

---

* This paper reflects the personal views of the author, not of the government.

During the Seventh Plan period, the resource position was subjected to exceptional strains. As a result, the fiscal deficit touched the record level of 8.4 per cent of GDP. The country was caught in a cobweb of inflation. The inflation rate, according to WPI, rose from 4.7 per cent in 1985-86 to 13.5 per cent in 1990-91. The rise in the prices of essential commodities seriously affected the daily life of common people.

However, the crisis was at its zenith in the external sector. The foreign exchange reserves had been decelerating at a fast rate. In February 1991, the foreign currency assets had declined to Rs. 2,382 crores. This was just sufficient to meet the import requirements for two weeks only. The problem had been accentuated by the outbreak of Gulf War. In the following days India had to borrow on the basis of pledge of actual gold reserve.

The mounting burden of external debt was a major factor in this crisis. At the end of March 1990 the volume of external debt was Rs. 96,429 crores which was 23.3 per cent of the GDP. There was a real danger of debt trap. It deteriorated further in 1992 and 1993. At the end of March 1993 the external debt had risen to Rs.213,508 crores which accounted for 32.4 per cent of the GDP.

Dr. Manmohan Singh, while presenting the Union Budget for 1992-93, had said:

"The fiscal year (1991-92) now drawing to a close has been a difficult one by any standards. It has been a year of crisis and of crisis management. It has also been a year of great economic challenges and bold initiatives.. ... we inherited an economy on the verge of collapse, inflation was accelerating rapidly. The balance of payments was in serious trouble. The foreign exchange reserves were barely enough for two weeks of imports. Foreign commercial banks had stopped lending to India. Non-Resident Indians were withdrawing their deposits. Shortage of foreign exchange had forced a massive import source, which had halted the rapid industrial growth of earlier years and had produced negative growth rates from May 1991 onwards..."

It was to tide over this crisis in the financial sector of the economy and also to give a fresh impetus to the growth process in the real sector that the Government of India announced a series of measures aimed at both macro-economic stabilisation and structural adjustment which have come to be known as the New Economic Policy (NEP) in India. It may be recalled in this connection that this new economic policy initiative was taken in India at a time when the centrally planned economies under the communist form of government had collapsed in Soviet Russia and Eastern Europe and these countries were also groping for ways to transform themselves from centrally planned economics to market economies. By that time a kind of Washington consensus (propounded by the IMF and World Bank) had also been developed about the right approach to correct the imperfections of the ailing economies of primarily the Latin American and African countries.

These policy packages mainly consisted of measures to reduce the government expenditure, devaluation, de-regulation of the economy, opening the economy to international competition etc. Around the same time, the world was taking notice of the remarkable economic development in the newly industrial countries (NICs) of Asia i.e., South Korea, Taiwan, Hong Kong, Singapore, Malaysia etc., and there was a general belief that the remarkable progress of these economies was a shining example of the beneficial effects of market economy and market-friendly policy intervention. Even in the arena of academic economics, recognition and encomiums (as for example, in the form of Award of Nobel Prize in Economics) were being showered on the economists who had used their tremendous intellectual abilities either to prove the futility of too much government intervention in economic activities or to clinically apply market-oriented logic to explain the relationships within the family or to provide rationale for an economic institution like slavery. It is in this background of national financial crisis and international turmoil in political and economic arena and the developments in academic theory and international economic policy formulations that the Central Government in July 1991 ushered in the New Economic Policy.

Essential features of the New Economic Policy: The NEP has two components: short run and long run. Short term measures focus on 'stabilisation' programmes while the long term measures are directed at policy and programmes for structural reforms.

The stabilisation policies are aimed at reducing the budgetary deficit by slashing the public expenditure. The areas mainly identified for reducing Central governmental expenditure including flow of funds to the state governments, allocation of resources to public sector, withdrawing or reducing subsidies to agriculture, fertiliser and export sectors in a phased manner, and reducing or pegging expenses on certain social sectors. It also aimed at securing a better macro economic management in terms of reduction in effective demand with the objective of curbing inflation and building up foreign exchange reserves. It also involved adjustment of exchange rate to meet the external liquidity crisis.

The structural reform policies are rooted in the concept of 'privatisation' and 'globalisation'. The industrial policy of 1991 opened up most parts of the economy to the private sector. The number of industries reserved for the public sector was reduced from 29 to 8. Trade policy has been liberalised, FERA is now almost non-existent. An open door policy for direct foreign investment has been initiated. Multinationals have been invited to invest and compete in the internal market. Reform of the banking sector has been initiated on the lines suggested by Narasimham Committee Report. Taxation reforms have been undertaken on the suggestions of Dr. Chelliah Committee. On the suggestions of Malhotra Committee, the Insurance sector may be opened up to the private sector. Implementation of the Dunkel proposal is expected to integrate the Indian economy with the global economy.

Financial Sector Reforms: The Narasimham Committee was set up to suggest financial sector reforms. The Committee made comprehensive recommendations for reform covering all aspects of banking, including the introduction of better capital adequacy norms, better provisioning for bad debts, rationalisation of the provisions for directed lending and the associated interest rate structure. The thrust of the Committee's recommendations is to move to a more efficient and competitive banking system including a larger role for the private sector. The Government took up the implementation of the Committee's recommendations in a phased manner:

a) Reducing the Statutory Liquidity Ratio to unlock large quantities of bank funds in relatively low yielding government securities. It was expected to reduce Central and state governments' dependence on borrowed funds from commercial banks and release funds for banks to expand credit to the private sector.

b) Both long term deposit (over 2 years) and term lending rates for over Rs.2.00 lakhs have been deregulated. Banks and financial institutions have now been given the freedom to fix the interest rates.

c) The Securities and Exchange Board of India (SEBI) was established; the office of the Controller of Capital Issues was abolished and premium fixation has been left to the companies approaching the capital market. The Government also granted permission to companies with good track record to issue debentures or equity abroad and extended tax benefits to these issues enabling domestic companies to tap the large pool of equity funds available in world capital markets. The Banking Nationalisation Act has been amended to permit public sector banks to raise resources from the capital markets. New private sector banks have been licensed.

The state governments are now borrowing from the markets at market related interest rates rather than borrowing from banks by stipulating reserve requirements. There is now an active market in government securities for 91 day and 364 day bills, and longer maturity securities are sold by auction.

Impact of the New Economic Policy on State Finances: Several of the measures referred to above had direct effect on the state government policy regarding financial management as well as policy towards development of agriculture, industry, infrastructure etc.

Transfer of Resources to the States: The state government has seen a slow down in the growth rate of resource transfers from the Centre. The Government of India has also reduced food and fertilizer subsidy, resulting in state governments being forced to step in with their own budgetary support to mitigate the hardships faced by the poor and the farmers. The NEP has thrown up another challenge before the state government in the form of increasing interest rates on the borrowings of the state government. The state government has been forced to explore new strategies for raising resources for various developmental projects, including investment in infrastructure development.

The Government of India's attempt at reducing fiscal deficit resulted in reduced transfers from the Government of India to the state on the plan account. Annexure - 1 gives a comparison between the periods 86-87 to 91-92 and 92-93 to budget estimates of 96-97. It is clear from the data that during the initial years of reforms, the plan assistance under the Gadgil- Mukherjee Formula almost stagnated and even showed a reduction in the year 94-95. Similarly, the market borrowings of the state governments saw a decreasing trend in the initial years of reforms. The average growth rate in market borrowings which stood at 17.59 per cent between 86-87 and 91-92 fell to as low as 6.42 per cent in 94-95. The receipt on the non-plan side, however, was not affected much (vide Annexure II).

The philosophy that public investment crowds out private investment led to slow down in the growth rate of market borrowings of the state permitted by the Central Government. As shown in Annexure-1, the net market borrowings in the initial years of reforms showed a negative growth. However, between 94-95 and 95-96, the growth rate was 16.65 per cent. But again in 96-97, the market borrowing has been maintained at the same level as in 95-96.

Increase in the Cost of Borrowing: The average cost of debt incurred by the state government has also increased. This is a fall-out of the Government of India's policy to have almost market determined rate for states' market borrowings and other loans to the state government like small savings and externally aided projects. For instance, the rate of interest on Central plan assistance and additional assistance for externally aided projects has gone up from 12 per cent to 13 per cent. The interest rate of market borrowings has also gone up from 12.5 per cent in 94-95 to 14 per cent in 95-96. The interest rates on direct borrowings from financial institutions have also gone up, and are now at 13 per cent. On the one hand, the share of Central plan grants has shown stagnation or low growth rate specially during the first three years of economic reforms whereby the states have been forced to finance their plan more and more from their own resources or borrowing, and on the other hand, the rate of interest on various types of borrowings of the state government has increased. This has led to a higher burden on the state government for debt servicing.

Compared to other states, the position of Karnataka seems to be somewhat comfortable in the matter of burden of debt servicing. The debt burden of the state, at the end of 94-95, stood at Rs. 8,704.01 crores. Out of this, Rs. 5,426.29 crores represented loans and advances from the Central Government. The ratio of interest payment to total revenue receipts for the state is approximately 10.43 per cent compared to the national average of 16.47 per cent. Similarly, debt servicing as a percentage of total receipt on revenue account for the state is 13.35 per cent compared to the national average of 21.23 per cent.

Food Subsidy: As a measure of reduction of the amount of food subsidy, the Government of India increased the issue price of food grains in the aftermath of economic liberalisation. For instance, the issue price of rice for public distribution system (PDS) has increased from Rs. 4.58 per kilogram to Rs. 6.48 per kilogram within a period of two years from 91-92. It is fairly well established that the food off take by the poor from the PDS saw a downfall during the initial years of the reforms. It is also established by empirical research that poverty ratio in rural areas is functionally related to the prices of foodgrains consumed by the rural poor. As such, there was no other option for the state government than to absorb some of the burden of increased prices of foodgrains supplied through public distribution system. The state government undertook to supply 10 kilograms of rice per tricolour (previously, it was called the 'green'card) ration card holder per month, at a price of Rs.3.20 per kilogram. These cards are specially supplied to the people below the poverty line in rural and urban areas. The state government has also undertaken to reduce the issue price of wheat supplied to these card holders from Rs. 2.95 per kilogram to Rs.2 per kilogram. As a result, the subsidy for food which stood at Rs. 48.08 cores in 92.93 has risen up to Rs. 220 crores in 95-96 and is expected to be Rs. 260 crores for the year 96-97.

Fertliser Subsidy: The Government of India decontrolled phosphatic and potassic (P&K) fertilisers whereby there was a substantial jump in the price of these fertilisers. That the use of fertiliser came down from 73.08 kilogram per hectare in 91-92 to 65 kilogram per hectare in 94-95 in Karnataka can be attributed partly to the rise in fertiliser prices. The fall in consumption was more pronounced for phosphatic and potassic fertilisers. There was a tendency to over-use nitrogenous fertiliser (N) as its price is still controlled and has not increased at the same rate as that of P & K. To check the overall fall in consumption and the imbalance in the use of various kinds of fertilisers, the state government has removed sales tax on all non-nitrogenous fertilisers.

Finance for Industries—specially Small Scale Industries: The major planks of financial sector reforms are the freeing of interest rates, the removal of subsidies or special financial assistance from the government to financial institutions coupled with inducing them to become market-oriented while raising resources and extending assistance, the promotion of competition between different categories and types of institutions and banks and the removal of priority sector restrictions.

Financial sector reform has placed unprecedented strain on the fragile finances of industries and principally on those of small units run by first generation entrepreneurs. The earlier approach was to provide separate, more or less exclusive, windows for project financing and working capital. A separate class of bankers - the Development Financial Institutions extended term finance at reasonable rates for periods of over a year to defray the costs of setting up a project, and commercial banks provided working capital (they also gave term finance). The resource structures of each of these two groups were adapted to meeting their specialised functions, especially that of financial institutions at the Central and state levels.

To enable term lending institutions to access funds and shelter them from temporary market fluctuations, the government was providing direct assistance through the Long Term Operations fund (LTO), the National Industrial Credit Fund, SLR bonds etc., as well as limited budgetary support. In keeping with the philosophy of withdrawal from the public sector and elimination of all special funding, under the New Economic Policy, LTO funds have stopped flowing and the financial institutions have to tend for themselves.

Financial institutions, therefore, are now looking to the market to raise resources. Theoretically, this appears desirable as the solvency, reputation for sound and prudent management and cost-consciousness of institutions, should determine the quantum and price of their resources. This philosophy, however, overlooks the practical problem associated with term lending institutions - finding long term investments. When markets are uncertain about the future, not necessarily because of fundamental economic reasons, such institutions become susceptible to every flutter and end up facing serious liquidity mismatches and exaggerated commitments to clients that they are unable to meet due to their inability to foresee market shortages. This has already happened. Several institutions like the IDBI and the ICICI have faced severe resource constraint in the second half of 1995-96 and have been forced to refuse or postpone disbursements on loans already sanctioned for industrial purposes.

Freeing interest rates has meant that the earlier Reserve Bank of India (RBI) determined rates for both term lending and working capital have been removed. The process started in October 1994 and now only lending rates for loans less than Rs.2.00 lakhs are fixed by the RBI. The sources that institutions depend on are so mercurial that the cost of funds keeps moving wildly. This has made institutions pass on the changes wholesale to clients in the form of floating rates, a practice that was not there in the past. Even when fixed rates are applied, these are frequently changed so that clients are unable to anticipate the rates likely to be applied to them as rates can change between sanctioned and disbursement. Between the first of April 1993 and the 31st of March 1996, refinance rates of the IDBI changed 7 times - 3 times upwards and 4 times downwards. For the industrialist and project planner this means a continuous adjustment of financial costs and a permanent atmosphere of uncertainty regarding the availability and cost of funds. This may not be conducive to planned implementation and industrial growth.

Transferring Risk of Bank Lending to State Government: In the Union Budget 1995-96, two new schemes had been announced. The shortfall in the priority sectors lending by the commercial banks are to be utilised to launch these two popular schemes. Under the first scheme, the funds from Khadi and Village Industries Corporation (KVIC) will be lent to Khadi and Village Industries Board (KVIB) against a state government guarantee at a rate of prime lending minus 1 per cent, which, at present is 14.5 per cent. Previously, KVIB was getting funds at a rate of interest varying from 0 to 4 per cent. Against this, the cost of funds now is 14.5 per cent. The KVIC is also permitted to debit the funds of the state government maintained with the RBI on notice, in case of default in repayments by KVIB. Twenty five per cent of the project cost will be provided as margin subsidy, which will be initially lent as interest free loan and later on, after 3 years if the units assisted are found to be functioning properly, it will be converted into a grant. On assuming 100 per cent conversion of subsidy element, the effective rate of interest would work out to 10.9 per cent. It is clear that the entire risk of commercial banks and the KVIC has been shifted to the KVIB and consequently to the state government along with the increase in the rate of interest.

Under the second scheme, the funds from commercial banks will be routed through the National Bank for Rural Development (NABARD) to the state governments for early completion of rural infrastructure especially minor irrigation schemes. The rate of interest is 13 per cent per annum with quarterly payments of interest (effective rate becomes 13.67 per cent). The NABARD is authorised to debit the funds of state governments maintained with the Reserve Bank of India on the issue of demand notice. Thus, the concerned banks are protected and the NABARD lending becomes risk free.

While the above two schemes ensure returns without risk to the lending agency, the risk is passed on totally to the state government. If the commercial banks were to do priority sector lending the risk will be that of the commercial banks. It is well known that the recovery rate was extremely poor in the priority sector. With the introduction of these two schemes, the risk has been passed on to the state government entirely.

STATE GOVERNMENT'S RESPONSES:

Market Borrowing by Public Utility Corporations: In the face of reduced Central Plan assistance and stagnation in open market borrowing limit by the state government directly, greater reliance in recent years is being placed on State Utility Corporations to raise their own resources for funding the plan. For example, the Krishna Bhagya Jala Nigam (The Corporation set up for implementing the Upper Krishna Project) has already raised Rs. 480 crores in two tranches during 95-96 and 96-97, and the Corporation plans to raise approximately Rs.2,000 crores from the Debt Market by 2000 A.D. for implementing the Upper Krishna Project and utilising the allocation of water made to Karnataka under the Bachawat Award. Similarly, Karnataka Power Corporation, Karnataka Electricity Board, Karnataka State Road Transport Corporation, Karnataka Urban Water Supply and Drainage Board, Karnataka Slum Clearance Board have been asked to increase their internal revenue and extra budgetary resources (borrowings) for meeting their plan expenditure. The total IEBR Internal and Extra Budgetary Resources for 95-96 is Rs.1,000.55 crores. The percentage has increased over the years from a level of about 3.76 per cent in 91-92 to as high as 23.34 per cent in 95-96. Since most of these utilities are not having enough internal resource generation, all these amounts of IEBR would practically come from extra budgetary resources i.e., from borrowings. As already explained earlier, the cost of borrowing has been going up and therefore, financing of plan projects of these utilities would be always at a higher cost.

This mode of financing of public utility projects is not feasible without charging the optimum user rates. If this is not done, the Public Utilities/Corporations/Boards will be faced with huge losses which will bring them to a grinding halt and they will not be able to repay the loans. It may be possible for such organisations to obtain loans from financial institutions/capital market on the basis of Government Guarantee, direct or indirect, for one year or so, but if the repayment liability actually devolves on the state government on account of the inability of the borrowing institutions to repay the loans, the state government will find the burden unbearable and the process will come to a halt. At the present rates of tariff, the Electricity Boards would incur huge losses. If immediate decision is not taken by the state government to increase power tariff and impose tariff on agricultural pumpsets, no further progress in energy sector will be feasible. It will be futile to expect that private sector power generating and distributing companies will be able to solve the power problems of the state which are being compounded by the public utilities. Unless the citizens of the state get fully reconciled to the idea that all sectors of power users will have to pay the economic price of power utilised by them, the private sector companies will fight shy of entering into this area as they will not be sure of getting adequate return on their investment.

Similar is the case with the Karnataka Urban Water Supply and Drainage Board. Non-collection of adequate user charge for water supply has resulted in - (a) the urban bodies defaulting in their repayments to the Board, (b) diversion of the funds by the Board to meet their establishment as well as debt servicing commitments. As a result, all projects have got delayed by 2-3 years resulting in cost escalations. The Board does not have enough funds to complete these schemes on time and the cash-strapped state government cannot find enough money to complete these projects, even if it is recognised that drinking water supply in rural as well as urban areas should get very high priority and people cannot survive without access to drinking water.

It should also be noted that in the capital market, the borrowing institutions have to operate on their own strength, armed with rating given by the Credit Rating Agencies. Such agencies will examine the resource generating and repaying ability of the borrowing institution and also the state government, if there is any partial commitment by the state government, to repay the loan before giving any credit rating.

If the institution is not inherently strong and if the state government takes more commitment than what it can comfortably fulfil, then the institution and the public issues will get poor rating and with such low rating the public utility organisations will find it impossible to raise funds in the market.

Bringing in Private Participation for Infrastructure Projects: There has been a growing realisation that infrastructure projects like power, road, industrial infrastructure, airport, tourism infrastructure etc., require large amounts of funds which cannot be provided out of the state budget. The Government of India have also permitted entry of private sector, domestic and foreign, in these areas. Necessary legislative changes to make it possible have either been undertaken (e.g.,Energy Sector) or in the process of being put in place (Highways). The state government has taken initiative to invite private sector investments in areas like Road Transport, setting up of Industrial Technology Parks, Power, Port, Airports, Tourism Complex, Group Housing etc. For example, in the Power Sector, the state government has permitted several private power projects like Cogentrix, small capacity multi-fuel projects, barge mounted power projects etc. In the Road Sector, the government has tried to attract private sector participation for the formation of Expressways and for the development of by-pass roads. MOUs (Memorandum of Understanding) have been signed for the development of Bangalore-Mysore and Bangalore-Hassan-Mangalore Expressways. Efforts are also going on for developing Bangalore-Devanahally International Airport Expressway and Hospet-Dharwad by-pass road with private sector participation. In some areas, the state government has also tried joint ventures in infrastructure. For example, the State Tourism Department, along with Taj Group, has entered into a joint venture. Similarly, the Karnataka Industrial Area Development Board, along with the Tatas and Singapore Development Corporation, have entered into a joint venture for the Industrial Technology Park (ITP Limited). A private consortium of Tatas - Singapore Authorities has been entrusted with the task of the development of an airport of international standards in Bangalore. This will be the first fully private airport of international standards in India.

However, there are several problems in infrastructure development through collaboration with private sector participants. The first and foremost problem area is the correct way of choosing private sector participants. The question involved here is whether we should follow the competitive bidding route or the MOU route. In principle, the competitive bidding route appears to be a more transparent procedure. It may involve some amount of delay. The other alternative, i.e., the MOU route can be relatively quicker but may lead to various types of complications. Another important problem which is involved in power projects is the finalisation of Power Purchase Agreement (PPA) and the finalisation of Guarantees. All private power projects insist on Power Purchase Agreement between them and the State Electricity Boards; the state government is also committed to give guarantee for payment in respect of the initial cases. The PPA is a detailed agreement on the rate at which the KEB will purchase power from these projects. The most contentious issue is to determine the per unit cost of power, minimum supply in different seasons, bonus, repatriation of profit, coverage of exchange risk fluctuations etc. After this, the PPA has to be backed by a guarantee of the government. The entire process of finalisation of PPA and that of a Guarantee (state government) and a counter guarantee (Central government) takes a long time as each and every provision of the agreement and its financial implications have to be gone into in detail.

The problems with the projects in the areas of roads and bridges are to find out which road should be used for private financing, how to make the road project viable, how to ensure that the road users are not exploited, how to fix the tariff rate etc. Probably, the constitution of a separate Regulatory Authority for roads may be the solution. Similar Regulatory Authority in other sectors also may be required to ensure justice to all the participating agents (owner of the system, public as consumer etc.)

Another point worth noting is that practically all cases of foreign investment in infrastructure projects needed clearance from various Government of India Ministries, Foreign Investment Promotion Board (FIPB) etc. It is expected that the philosophy of liberalisation, deregulation and decentralisation should permeate this area also. It will be worthwile to examine the Chinese practice in this regard, and see to what extent and with what safeguards similar policies may be adopted in India. It is a matter of concern that in spite of all the talk about the thousands of billions of dollars required to build infrastructure in this country, if our economy has to be globalised, precious little has been done in this matter during the last five years. Hopefully, the new government at the Centre will give serious attention to this matter and adopt a more decentralised policy (after studying the Chinese experience) in the matter of state governments seeking foreign investment in the infrastructure sector.

A new method of project financing initiated by the state government has been the introduction of a cess. For example, for the Bangalore Metropolitan Rail Transport System (BMRTS), a special cess known as BMRTS Cess has been introduced to raise funds as government contribution (for both equity and loan) for the Elevated Rail Transport System in Bangalore City. Even though the project will be implemented by a consortium of private sector companies, the economics of the project would need some [around 25 per cent of the project cost] contribution by the state government in the form of equity and sub-ordinate debt. This contribution is expected to be partially met out of the collection of BMRTS cess.

Rationalisation and Simplification of State Tax Structure: In order to integrate the entire country as a genuine common market, the Government of India, following the recommendation of Dr. Raja Chelliah Committee's Report, has been recommending introduction of Value Added Tax by all states and abolition of all other forms of commodity taxation by the state government (like Sales Tax, surcharge, Turnover Tax, Entry Tax etc). As a step in this direction, the Government of India took the initiative of convening meetings of State Finance Ministers and facilitating the development of a consensus about reducing the number of taxes, adhering to a minimum rate of tax on each commodity, stopping tax concession war among the states for attracting industrial investment etc.

The state government has taken several steps to rationalise and simplify the state tax structure. One of the important steps in this direction has been the bringing down of the number of tax rates. In two years, the tax rates have been brought down from 21 to 4. In this year's budget, about 98 per cent of the commodities have been brought under these four rates of taxes i.e., 2 per cent, 4 per cent, 8 per cent, and 12 per cent. However, there are some special rates for gold bullion, petroleum products, liquor etc. Another step has been grouping together related articles which were previously specified under different rates, under a common rate. The next important step for the state government will be to introduce the Value Added Tax System (VAT) in stages and abolition of other forms of taxes on commodities.

The state government, like other state governments, has been offering several types of tax incentives for various industries to be attracted to the state of Karnataka. Now, it is time to seriously consider the issue of phasing out these tax incentives which are making all state governments net losers and the gain to industries is not serving any socially desirable objective, as all the states are giving practically the same incentives for all the industries. In fact, by and large, the consensus among the state Finance Ministers was to abolish these incentives by April 1997.

Public Sector Enterprises Reforms: As on 31st March 1994, there were 70 Public Sector Enterprises (PSES) in Karnataka employing about 161,647 employees. The total investment in these public sector enterprises stood at Rs. 6,949 crores, out of which, the Government of Karnataka's contribution was Rs.3,338.71 crores (share capital Rs. 1,538.05 crores and loans Rs.1,800.66 crores). The accumulated losses as on 31.3.1994 stood at Rs. 852.71 crores. The dividend paid by the PSEs stood at Rs. 5.07 crores in the year 93-94.

The dividend and interest received during 91-92, 92-93 and 93-94 was 2 per cent, 2 per cent and 0.26 per cent of the aggregate investment in the respective years against an average rate of interest of 12.69 per cent paid by the government on its borrowings during these years.

It is clear from the above that the public sector enterprises have been yielding very low returns on the investment by the government. Many of them have entered the situation of a negative net worth, and are before the BIFR. Our attempt at restructuring the public sector enterprises has been three fold:

a) attempt at rehabilitating some PSEs like KSIC, KSDL and NGEF;

b) attempt to privatise some units like KTL, Chamundi Machine Tools; and

c) invite partial public participation in some units to expand their capital base and improve their performance.

There are some profit making public sector enterprises like Hutti Gold Mines and the Karnataka State Financial Corporation. There is a need to expand the capital base of these institutions to expand their operations. The government is examining the issue of allowing these public sector enterprises partially to go public i.e., to make public issue of equity shares with appropriate premium. Apart from enabling the enterprises to expand their activity with added capital base, such public participation is also expected to bring greater degree of professionalisation and expertise in the management of the units.

Reference has already been made to the problems faced by industries, specially small scale industries, in obtaining Term Loan in this era of liberalisation. The state government organisations like KSIIDC, KSFC have tried to mitigate the situation by resorting to innovative ways of tapping resources, and also by improving their own resource position by entering new areas like leasing, hire purchase, deferred payment guarantee, merchant banking etc. Even though equity participation by Central financial institutions (IDBI) in the state level institutions (KSFC) have remained frozen at the level prevailing five years ago, the state government has been providing equity support to these institutions with a view to supporting industrial development in the state, specially for providing finances for tiny, small and medium scale industries.

The New Agricultural Policy 1995: In 1995, the government of Karnataka announced its New Agricultural Policy which enunciates bold steps for agricultural sector reform. The main thrust has been towards:

(1) treating and extending the status of industry to agriculture, particularly in areas where agriculture is placed at a disadvantage **vis-a-vis,** industry;

(2) restructuring and revitalising credit institutions;

(3) bringing in the concept of farmers paying market prices for water and power consumed by them; and

(4) freeing of domestic and external market for agricultural produce.

Private sector investments would be welcome in areas of production activities such as seeds multiplication, high tech agriculture like floriculture, horticulture, sericulture, dairying, poultry and meat. Private sector investment in areas of marketing (such as setting up of warehouses and storage facilities) and agro-processing would be encouraged. Foreign capital will also be welcome in these areas with appropriate safeguards that protect the proprietary rights of farmers and subject to government approval. Public sector investment in agriculture would basically flow towards the creation of economic and social infrastructure, e.g., major and medium irrigation schemes, water harvesting structures, roads, agricultural markets, etc.

To meet the growing needs of credit in the agriculture sectors and to ensure timely and adequate credit supplies, the government is of the view that the subsidy incentive system may have to yield place to commercially viable interest and deposit rate structure. There may be no further interest or loan waiver or any interest or subsidy. The government is also considering the possibility of setting up a Karnataka Agricultural Finance Corporation to take care of the massive needs of credit for the agricultural sector.

With an intention to let market forces come into play in the agricultural sector, in future, the government also intends to free the domestic and internal market for agricultural produce. The government would like to ensure a free and fair play of agricultural markets that are devoid of any compulsory levies such as on sugar and rice. An associated issue will be to ask the farmers to pay appropriate prices for inputs like electricity and water consumed by them. The first attempt by the state would be to handover this responsibility of collecting the dues on water and electricity to farmer's organisations themselves on attractive commission basis. If they fail in this task then the private sector would be involved in the distribution of these critical inputs and collection of dues thereof.

CONCLUSIONS

An attempt has been made in this paper to highlight the challenges faced by the state government and its institutions in the present era of liberalisation and their response to these challenges. It is obvious that satisfactory solutions have not been found to many of the problems, e.g., problems of mobilisation of resources, high cost of mobilisation of such resources, problem of user-charges by public utilities, putting in place a regulatory body for private sector infrastructure projects, finances for small scale industries (which play a key role in the dispersal of industrial growth and generation of employment), taxation reform, public sector reform etc.

While further progress will be carried on in these areas in the coming years, we cannot be oblivious of one basic fact, that is, adoption of fiscal and trade policy measures, abolition of 'Licence-Permit Raj' and reforms in banking, insurance sectors and taxation policies will not be sufficient to convert the Indian 'Lamb' into another Asian 'Tiger'. While on the subject, it is worth recalling, what has been pointed out by Dreze and Sen (1995:181):

"The cage that keeps the Indian economy well tamed is not only that of bureaucracy and governmental overactivity, but also that of illiteracy, undernourishment, ill health, and social inequalities, and their causal antecedents: governmental neglect and public apathy.

"This recognition does not entail a dismissal of the diagnosis of bureaucratic overactivity, or a disputation of the need for basic economic reforms. ... We have tried to argue for a broader view of economic development, which has to be seen in terms of expanding social opportunities. While the removal of barriers to using markets can significantly enhance such opportunites, the sharing of certain basic capabilities - including those associated particularly with literacy and education (and also those connected with basic health, social security, gender equality, and rights, local democracy). The rapid expansion of these capabilities depends crucially on public action of a kind that has been severely neglected in India - both before and after the recent reforms. The real issue in uncaging the tiger is the need to go well beyand liberalization.

The real challenge before both the Central and the state governments in the coming years will be to undertake this neglected exercise of going beyond 'liberalisation' and unavoidably, there will be financial implications for such an exercise which have to be carefully examined.

ANNEXURE 1

Central Assistance for Plan Financing which saw Major Changes due to the New Economic Policy

(Rs. in lakhs)

ITEMS	86-87	87-88	88-89	89-90	90-91	91-92
1. Plan assistance	189.23	213.78	183.19	235.53	261.76	403.70
Under Gadgil - Mukharjee formula	149.73	182.75	159.81	190.73	203.85	265.25
EAP	39.50	31.03	23.39	44.80	57.91	139.45
2. a) Market borrowings (Net)	71.11	85.68	114.05	123.91	137.06	157.73
b) Market borrowings (Gross)	87.18	101.37	131.37	142.28	137.09	157.77
		Annual Growth Rates AAGR				
1. Plan assistance	12.97	-14.31	28.57	11.14	54.23	18.52
Under Gadgil - Mukharjee formulae	22.05	-12.55	19.35	6.88	30.12	13.17
EAP	-21.44	-24.62	91.53	29.26	140.80	43.11
2 a) Market borrowings (Net)	20.49	33.11	8.65	10.61	25.08	17.59
b) Market borrowings (Gross)	16.28	29.59	8.30	-3.65	15.08	13.12

ITEMS	92-93	93-94	94-95	95-96	96-97	
1 Plan assistance	563.11	622.90	625.60	660.65	810.07	
Under Gagil - Mukharjee formulae	266.32	278.85	275.60	372.65	372.65	
EAP	296.79	344.05	350.00	288.00	437.42	
2 a) Market Borrowings (Net)	159.25	154.12	181.61	211.62	211.62	
b) Market Borrowings (Gross)	168.49	179.19	181.84	243.47	212.34	
		Annual Growth Rates AAGR				
1 Plan assistance	39.49	10.62	0.43	5.60	22.62	
15.75						
Under Gadgil - Mukharjee formulae	0.40	4.70	-1.17	35.21	0.00	7.83
EAP	112.83	15.92	1.73	-17.71	51.88	32.93
2 a) Market borrowings (Net)	0.96	-3.22	17.84	16.52	0.00	6.42
b) Market borrowings (Gross)	6.79	6.35	1.48 3	3.89	-12.79	7.15

ANNEXURE IIA

ITEM	90-91	91-92	92-93	93-94	94-95	95-96	96-97
1 Non-Plan assistance	327.70	382.06	455.20	597.00	744.92	977.83	
73.00							
a) Revenue	302.46	353.85	424.47	574.62 7	24.58 9	53.19	70.94
b) Capital	25.24	28.21	30.62	23.17	20.35	24.64	2.06
			Annual Growth Rates AAGR				
1 Non-Plan assistance	16.59	19.14	31.33	24.61	31.27		24.59
a) Revenue	16.99	19.99	35.34	26.10	31.55		25.99
b) Capital	11.77	0.54	-24.33	-12.17	21.08		0.98

ANNEXURE IIB

ITEM		90-91	91-92	92-93	93-94	94-95	95-96	96-97
a)	Plan size	1487.02	1774.51	2032.95	2796.95	2861.28	3100.00	4300.00
	IEBR	-59.77	66.81	144.91	291.09	508.19	424.22	1000.55
	IEBR as % of Plan size	-4.02	3.76	7.13	10.55	1.7.76	23.34	22.37
				Annual Growth Rates				
Plan Size			19.33	14.56	37.58	2.80	8.34	

REFERENCES:

Gupta, S.P. (1995). Economic Reforms and Its Impact on Poor. **Economic and Political Weekly**, xxx(22):1295-1313.

Jalan, Bimal (1991) **India's Economic Crisis - the Way Ahead,** New Delhi : Oxford University Press.

Dreze, Jean and Amartya Sen. (1995). **Economic Development and Social Opportunity.** New Delhi: Oxford University Press.

3

TAX ADMINISTRATION

G. Thimmaiah

Introduction: Tax administration is generally understood as collection of taxes. Though this is a common man's understanding, in practice, the term 'tax administration' involves various stages of administrative, legal and accounting tasks. It even covers the sphere of management of government's finances. Before tax is collected, it has to be designed. Tax designing involves identification of tax base, determination of tax rates, preparation of tax law which should define the tax base (object on which tax is to be levied), indicate tax rates, exemptions if any, administrative machinery, powers and jurisdictions of tax collectors, penalties for delay in payment and evasion, machinery for redressing the grievances of tax payers, auditing etc. Once a tax is designed, the legislature has to approve the tax legislation. Then the government notifies to the public the date from which the tax becomes effective. Once the tax is put into operation, tax administration comes into picture.

Tax administrators have to identify the tax base, and the persons who own or transact in that tax base as defined in the law, determine the tax liability, collect the revenue and remit it to the government account. The tax administrators are also expected to keep watch on evasion of tax, and hardship caused to the tax payers and bring them to the notice of the appropriate authorities for modifying the legislative provisions or changing administrative procedures. After a reasonable period of time, tax administrators are supposed to identify the defects in the process of operation of tax law, difficulties faced by administrators as well as tax payers and suggest modifications in the tax structure either by changing the administrative procedure or tax law. This involves tax reforms (see, Thimmaiah 1978).

Economists have made significant contributions to the normative principles of tax administration right from the inception of economic thought as a body of knowledge. Notable among them is Adam Smith who has laid down five canons of taxation in Book V of his classic work: **An Inquiry into the Nature and Causes of Wealth of Nations** (1776). The first principle of taxation is intended to make the tax administration simple and easy. That is the canon of simplicity. This requires tax laws to be easily understandable and tax collection procedures to be transparent so that the tax payer is not put to unnecessary hardship while paying tax. The second principle is the canon of certainty. This requires that the government in power should levy such tax which is going to yield revenue without uncertainty. Reasonable certainty of collection of some revenue is very important as otherwise the government would be wasting its administrative resources.

The third principle is the canon of convenience. Any tax, in order to be acceptable to the tax payers, should be convenient for payment. This involves identification of the time of receiving income for income tax, and time of incurring expenditure for commodity tax so that it is convenient for the people to pay tax. It is also necessary to indicate thc time of collection convenient to tax administrators as, otherwise, it would impose additional cost on administration. The fourth principle is the canon of economy, that is, the tax which is levied and collected by the government should yield revenue more than the cost of collecting that tax.

The last principle is the canon of equity, that is, the tax which is levied should be fair in relation to the economic status of the tax payers so that it will not become oppressive on those who cannot afford to pay it. These essential features of tax administration have come to be accepted as universal and a number of other principles have been added to the list by later economists.

Background: Tax administration in Karnataka[1] is patterned on the model of tax administration which prevailed in the British India, particularly in the former Madras and Bombay Presidencies. It is true that all governments have to levy and collect some tax or the other for running their administration and meeting the cost of defence, welfare and developmental works, if any. This is a universal phenomenon. Therefore, some form of tax administration did exist at all times through the ages.

Karnataka was formed in 1956 by integrating the Kannada speaking areas of former Hyderabad state, Madras and Bombay provinces. Before the reorganisation of the state, tax administration in these areas was not different from the administration which existed in the erstwhile Mysore state except for some minor details. Though the erstwhile Mysore had the power to levy and collect income tax, customs duty, excise duty and also revenue from its own postal and railway departments, all these sources of revenue were surrendered to the Union government after the integration of the erstwhile Mysore state into the Indian Union in February 1950. After integration, the sources of revenue available to the former state of Mysore became very meagre. The state was given the status of Part 'B' state until the reorganisation of the states in 1956. From 1956, it has been a fulfledged state in the Indian Union enjoying the powers enumerated in the State List. Today, the tax powers of Karnataka government are derived from the State List of the Indian Constitution.

Until the reorganisation of states in 1956, the tax policy of the erstwhile Mysore state was guided by the objective of raising enough revenue to balance the budget. It should be mentioned in this context that though the prevailing ideas of the time were not radical as far as taxation was concerned, the erstwhile Mysore state was already

1. For a historical account of tax administration of erstwhile Mysore State, see, Rao 1984, Chapter II.

playing a prominent role in the field of economic development of the state. In addition to initiating several schemes of social welfare programmes like primary education, primary health services, construction of roads, bridges, the then state government had also undertaken several developnment programmes, prominent among them being construction of modern irrigation dams to increase the area under irrigation for the prosperity of agriculture, laying railway lines, producing electricity, starting industrial units in the public sector for utilising the available natural resources like sandalwood etc. All these activities invariably required more revenue. But the state government followed the policy of 'sound finance' approach to borrow money only for undertaking the works which involved creation of capital assets. And the public undertakings were also expected to yield adequate return which enabled the state government to maintain the overall tax burden at a modest level. The first Finance Minister of independent Mysore state, Sri H.C. Dasappa, after the integration of the state into the Indian Union, in his budget speech before the Representative Assembly on 2nd June, 1949, explained that the objective of his tax policy was 'progress with caution' (GOM 1949:3). According to this policy, all current expenditure of the government was met from current revenue which consisted of tax revenue and income from public undertakings. Capital outlay was undertaken to the extent that it could be financed from borrowings from the market. Thus the developmental activities depended upon the borrowings alone and taxation was used for meeting current expenditure of the government. The erstwhile Mysore government seems to have avoided running large budget deficits during these years thus scrupulously following the classical policy of 'sound finance'. The finances of the erstwhile Mysore state which are presented below from 1947-48 and 1950-51 indicate that the state government incurred very small deficits though in 1947-48 the magnitude of the deficit was considerable.

Table 1

Finance of the erstwhile Mysore State from 1947-48 to 1950-51

(Rs. in lakhs).

Budgetary Items	Year			
	1947-48	1948-49	1949-50	1950-51
Total Revenue	1,070.64	1,184.40	949.09	1,337.90
Total Expenditure	1,124.47	1,169.40	940.08	1,342.26
Surplus (+) or Deficit (-)	-53.83	+15.00	-00.99	-4.36

The state could maintain such low levels of budget deficits mainly because of its elastic sources of revenue which are shown in Table 2.

Table 2

Composition of Tax Revenue of the erstwhile Mysore State

(Rs. in lakhs).

Major Sources of Revenue	Yield in 1947-48
1. Land Revenue	138.86
2. Income Tax	172.34
3. Mining Revenue	174.56
4. Gold Duty	14.17
5. Stamp Duties	99.56
6. Registration Fees	36.87
7. Miscellaneous Taxes	7.50
Total	**643.86**

It may be mentioned here that state excise included not merely tax on liquors but also on other manufactured articles like match box, sugar, tobacco, vegetable products etc. After the integration of the state into the Indian Union, the state government lost what were known as federal source of revenue like income tax and excise on manufactured goods. Thus, by 1950-51, the composition of the state government tax revenues had changed substantially. This is evident from Table 3.

Table 3:

Composition of the Revenues after Financial Integration of the erstwhile Mysore State

(Rs. in lakhs).

Major Sources of Revenue	Yield in 1950-51
1. Land Revenue	129.00
2. State Excise	200.47
3. Sales Tax	141.14
4. Stamp Duties	49.33
5. Registration Fee	9.01
6. Entertainment Tax	1.08
7. Betting Tax	18.56
8. Motor Vehicles Tax	83.76
9. Irrigation Charges	180.84
10. Other Taxes and Duties	814.65

Thus, the composition of the state government's tax revenue changed because of the transfer of federal sources of revenue to the Union government. After losing income tax and excise on manufactured commodities, the state government realised that it should make good the loss by introducing new taxes. Accordingly, sales tax, entertainment tax, betting tax and motor vehicles tax were introduced. Even then it was not possible for the state government to balance the budget because of the increased expenditure on the one hand and limited buoyancy of new revenue sources on the other. Besides, the state government started losing revenue as a result of the extension of prohibition to some more districts in the state. No doubt, the Indian States Finances Revenue Enquiry Committee (1949) had recommended additional sources of revenue to meet the deficit. Further, the Committee had also recommended 'revenue gap' grant from the Union government to the state until 1955-56. In spite of all these, the state government could not balance its budget. The tax policy of the state did not aim at mobilising resources for development purpose nor was it designed to maintain overall stability through co-ordination with the tax policy of the Union government. The state government had not yet realised the use fullness of tax policy for achieving various other objectives like providing incentives to such economic activities as industries etc. Such policies had to wait for the national level planning era to start.

The launching of the Five Year Plans at the national level necessitated the co-ordination of policies of the Union and the state governments. They had to dovetail all their policies including tax policies in accordance with the objectives of planning. Though this need was recognised, it could not be achieved immediately. The desired co-ordination had to evolve over a long period of time on the recommendations of successive Finance Commissions, the Planning Commission and the initiative of the Union Government.

With the reorganisation of the state, the geographical area and population of the state increased. The area was more than doubled increasing from 89,200 square kms. to 191,800 square kms., while the population increased from 9.90 million to 19.40 million, according to 1951 census. At the same time, the new state had to face the problem of reformulating the Second Five Year Plan for the new state and even its budget had to be revised as the earlier budget covered only the erstwhile Mysore state for about eight months. The newly formed Mysore state introduced uniform tax laws in all parts of the state. The land revenue settlement was long overdue in many parts of the state. Resurvey and resettlement were started during this year. The state government suffered some loss of revenue in that year also owing to transfer of certain sources of revenue like tax on prize competition and abolition of frontier and interior toll gates.

The foregoing account of the historical evolution of tax policy of the state is intended to highlight the major changes in the structure of the revenue composition and also the impact of the integration of the erstwhile Mysore state into the Indian Union and the reorganisation of the state to become Karnataka. Obviously, these changes have had their influence on tax administration not only on the size of the tax administrative machinery but also on its efficacy and effectiveness. It should be remembered in this context that some of the regions which were integrated to form Karnataka came from such disparate areas ranging from highly efficient states like Bombay and Madras, and the weak administrative set-up of former Hyderabad state. Such disparate tax administrative systems had to be integrated and it took quite sometime to make the integrated tax administration in Karnataka even modestly efficient by the standards of Madras and Bombay states.

Today, Karnataka's tax administration is modeled on Tamil Nadu pattern except, perhaps, the land revenue administration. The taxes which are levied and collected by the state government include land revenue, agricultural income tax, sales tax which comprises Karnataka sales tax and Central sales tax, turnover tax, entry tax, luxury tax, entertainment tax, betting tax, profession tax, stamp duties and registration fees, motor vehicles tax, state excise duties and electricity tax. The relative importance of these taxes is presented in Table 4.

Table 4: Present Composition of Tax Revenue in Karnataka

(Rs. in crores)

	Major Sources of Revenue	**Yield in 1994-95**
1.	Land Revenue	19.78
2.	State Excise	713.47
3.	Sales Tax	2,505.76
4.	Stamp Duties and Registration	372.49
5.	Entertainment Tax	407.98
6.	Motor Vehicles Tax	69.69
7.	Electricity Tax	90.91
8.	Agricultural Income Tax	16.82
9.	Profession Tax	92.40
10.	Betting Tax	14.05
11.	Luxury Tax	16.43
12.	Entry Tax	117.00
	Total	**4,436.78**

Since this paper is concerned with the evolution of tax administration, stress is laid on the discussion of taxes only. Since tax is a compulsory levy imposed by the government and collected without promising *quid pro quo* to the tax payer, some of the levies like stamps and registration cannot be considered strictly as tax, because they are intended to levy user's charges for rendering certain tangible benefits to the duty payers. Even the land revenue can be interpreted as a benefit levy as it is intended to confer ownership right as well as the right to cultivate the land which belongs to the sovereign government. But, traditionally land revenue has come to be treated as tax revenue as it was a major source of revenue of all the earlier governments. Besides, the present tax administration has evolved and has been influenced over time by the experience of land revenue administration. Even stamp duties have come to assume an element of taxation. Hence, all of them have been treated as taxes only for the purpose of discussing their administration.

Administration of land revenue in Karnataka does not differ much from that in other parts of India (see, for details, Balasubramanian 1963:256-68). Earlier, the village officers, Patel (Gowda) and Shanubhog (Kulkarni) used to keep accounts of land revenue demand, collection and arrears. Shanubhog was also entrusted with the responsibility of reporting to the government about the area of land sown, type of crop grown and improvements made on the lands of his village. The Patel was entrusted with the responsibility of maintaining law and order in his village though these police functions were subsequently withdrawn. He was supposed to enforce timely collection of land revenue. In earlier days, the hereditary village servant namely, Thoti used to summon the villagers to the village Chawdi for the purpose of payment of tax. Thoti was paid by the farmers from their produce. But, the Shanubhog and Patel were paid annual stipends, by the government. Both Shanubhg and Patel were assisted by Thoti, Talwar and Neerganti. These officers have been functioning since over the centuries and were holding hereditary offices. They were paid annual fixed percentage of land revenue collected in their village as **Potige.** The landholders were also expected to make payment in kind to these village servants in addition to the land revenue which they paid to the government. All these officers were part-time government servants. In the districts of former Bombay state, namely, Bijapur, Belgaum and Dharwad and Karwar, the Patel, Talatis and Seth (Sanadis) collected land revenue from the ryots. Some villages had two Patels, one in-charge of land revenue collection, and the other, in-charge of law and order. The Talati (Kulkarni) kept accounts of land revenue. They were full-time government servants and were paid monthly salaries. In South Kanara, there were no hereditary village officers. All village officers were appointed on stipendiary basis. In the districts of former Hyderabad state, namely, Gulbarga, Bidar and Raichur, the Patwari (Kulkarni) administered land revenue at the village level. All the village officers were hereditary but full-time government servants receiving monthly salaries. In Bellary district and Kollegal taluk which were part of former Madras Presidency, similar officers administered land revenue and they were also hereditary officers receiving monthly salaries. In Coorg, there were no separate officers to collect land revenue from each village. Villages were grouped into Hobli and Nad and for every Nad there was a Parupattegar or Patel assisted by staff of Nad clerks and Shanubhogs. The ryots were expected to pay their land revenue to these officers. Only the Patel was a hereditary officer. There were nearly one lakh village officers and servants made up of about 12,000 village officers, namely, Kulkarnis, Patwaris or Shanubhogs, 31,000 Patels, 37,000 Thotis, 15,000 Talwars and 5,000 Neergantis. All these hereditary village offices were abolished in 1975 and replaced by village accountants who are now salaried employees of the state government. They receive monthly salaries and other benefits, keep land records, collect land revenue and remit it to the government. They also report on the cropping pattern of the village.

Above these lower level officers there was, and is, the Revenue Inspector (Shekdar). He is, sometimes, assisted by a Deputy Revenue Inspector, both of whom are appointed by the government and paid salaries on a monthly basis. They are entrusted with the duty of supervising revenue collection of a group of villages called Hobli which was a unit of revenue administration above the village. A group of such Hoblis constituted a Taluk or Tahsil. Amildar or Tahsildar (Mamlatdar) was, and is, the revenue officer of the taluk. Until recently, he was also empowered to maintain law and order. But now, he is merely a Revenue Officer except that he settles minor disputes relating to survey, settlement and land revenue payment. A group of such taluks is called sub-division and is administered by an Assistant Commissioner or Sub-Division Officer. Formerly, he was also a civil officer to settle disputes regarding land revenue settlements. But this function has now been transferred to Civil or Munsiff Court. A group of sub-divisions is a District. The Deputy Commissioner is the head of the land revenue administration of a district. Formerly, he was also a District Magistrate to maintain law and order in his district. He continues to be the same even now though some of his police powers have been transferred to the Superintendent of Police in the district. Besides, some of his judicial powers have also been transferred to the District Judge which has affected his position as the District Magistrate. He was also the Chairman of the District Development Council until the creation of Zilla Parishads in 1987. Since the reorganisation of the state and the formation of the new state of Karnataka, the state is divided into four divisions for administrative convenience, namely, Bangalore, Mysore, Belgaum and Gulbarga Divisions. The Divisional Commissioner is the head of the land revenue administration of the division. At the state level, the Commissioner and Secretary to the Government of Karnataka Revenue Department, is the head of the administration. Above him is the Revenue Minister. Revenue disputes are settled by the Revenue Appellate Tribunal. Subsequently, it was merged with the Sales Tax Appellate Tribunal and a single Karnataka Appellate Tribunal was formed during the 1970s.

The payment of land revenue is completed by the end of fiscal year. However, in the districts of the erstwhile Mysore state, land revenue was paid in four instalments in February, March, April and May in each year. In the districts of Belgaum Division, only two instalments were allowed. In the districts of Bellary and South Kanara and in the taluk of Kollegal, land revenue was payable in three instalments in January, February and March. In Coorg district, land revenue was payable in February and March in respect of lands on which Kharif crops were grown and in October and November, in respect of lands on which rabi crops were grown. In Gulbarga Division, land revenue was payable between 1st January and 21st January in the case of lands growing Khariff crops and in April in respect of lands on which rabi crops were grown. Thus, it may be observed that canon of convenience was ensured for the payment of land revenue. Consequently, except in Bellary and Coorg districts and Kollegal taluk, collection of land revenue was not completed before the close of the financial year on 31st March. This resulted in violation of canons of certainty and economy. The fiscal year used to close on 30th May in the erstwhile Mysore state, on 31st July in Belgaum Division and 21st April in Gulbarga Division. Coorg did not have any separate fiscal year. Therefore, all these different fiscal years had to be merged and made into one. In all districts, land revenue payment will have to be completed by 31st March every year. It should be mentioned in this context that land revenue, which was a prominent source of government revenue, has become insignificant and various attempts to revise and enhance it have failed to materialise because of its archaic design which relates the amount of tax to inelastic land area. The land revenue administration has to be supported from the government's general revenue as the cost of collection of land revenue through the age old revenue administrative set up has increased. This is evident from Table-6. It may be observed that the gross yield from land revenue was Rs 1.29 crores in 1994-95 and the cost of collection was Rs. 60.63 crores. The only justification for supporting this administrative set-up from general revenue is that the Divisional Commissioners, Deputy Commissioners, Assistant Commissioners and Thahsildars are entrusted with other responsibilities, prominent among them being implementation of welfare and development programmes.

The functions, powers and remuneration of the officers of land revenue administration are governed by the **Land Revenue Code** of the erstwhile Mysore State which was passed in 1888 and has been amended many times. This Code empowers the Deputy Commissioner of the district to recover arrears of land revenue first by issuing notice to the defaulters and then by auctioning the crop on land concerned or by decreeing movable property with certain exception and finally, selling land concerned in open auction. Since 1904, provision has been made to suspend the collection of land revenue or remit any portion of it to the farmers in areas where crops failed owing to drought or any other natural calamity.

Other than land revenue, agricultural income tax is another modern tax which is levied on income from agriculture. Agricultural Income Tax was first levied in 1955, on the lines of Madras Agriculture Income Tax, which was made applicable to income from commercial crops only. After the reorganisation of the states in 1957, a new **Agricultural Income Tax Act** was passed repealing all the Acts prevailing in the merged areas. When the Agricultural Income Tax was first introduced in 1955, no separate administrative set up was created to enforce it. It was administered by the Revenue Officers of the district. Initially, it was assessed and collected by the Assistant Commissioners and appeals were heard by the Deputy Commissioners of the districts. However, during the 1970s, the administration of this tax was transferred to the Department of Commercial Taxes. One may argue that since agricultural income tax is related to the income from agriculture, it should have been transferred to the Revenue Department. But the basis and procedure of levying and collecting agricultural income tax are slightly different and involve different set of administrative procedures. Therefore, it has been brought under commercial taxes. Though the **Mysore Agricultural Income Tax Act** of 1955 included income from all crops, later, food crops were excluded and today, only plantation crops are included for the purpose of levying and collecting agricultural income tax. Thus, the attempt to raise some revenue from agricultural sector has not been successful. No doubt, under the planning and protectionist regimes the terms of trade turned against agricultural sector thereby imposing a net implicit tax burden on Indian agriculture. Now, in the wake of liberalisation and the consequential reduction in import duties on non-agricultural products, the terms of trade have started turning in favour of agriculture. Hence, the justification for taxing agricultural income from all crops has strengthened.

Major Taxes in Karnataka: Prominent among the taxes levied and colleected by the state government in Karnataka are commercial taxes which include Karnataka sales tax, Central sales tax, entry tax, profession tax, luxury tax, turnover tax, betting tax, entertainment tax and agricultural income tax. Besides these, the state government also levies and collects state excise duties on liquors, motor vehicles tax, stamps and registration and electricity tax.

Sales tax was first levied in India in 1939 to make good the loss of revenue on account of introduction of prohibition in Madras state. It has now become a predominant source of revenue in the tax structure of most of the state governments. Sales tax is not altogether new to Karnataka. A duty known as 'Kurugupudi' was levied for a long time in the erstwhile Mysore state on all articles sold on wholesale or retail basis. There was an inland customs or transit duty called 'Saic'. There was also a tax on traders and artisans generally called 'Mohaturpha'. Over and above these general duties, there was a high consumption tax levied on betel, tobacco, ganja, bhang and godak in Madras-Mysore border areas and all principal towns of that area. A reform was effected in 1861 by the former British government and several duties which were levied haphazardly on sales were removed from that year. Another tax akin to sales tax, namely octroi, was levied by the municipalities on the entry of goods brought into towns/cities for local consumption. The rates of tax were specific and the tax was collected at the entry points to towns and cities. The revenue was elastic. But the administration of this tax came under severe criticism. Therefore, it was abolished in 1979. In its place, an Entry Tax was introduced initially on the four commodities covered by Additional Union Excise duties, namely, sugar, textiles, tobacco and vanaspati. But, subsequently, it was extended to many other commodities to raise the revenue. In recent years, it has been restricted to a few commodities.

Sales tax as a new measure of taxation was introduced for the first time in 1948 in the erstwhile Mysore state. It was partly intended to make good the loss of revenue on account of prohibition policy. The basis of sales tax was the annual net turnover of the dealers above the exemption limit of Rs.10,000. This tax was levied in the form of multipoint sales tax at the rate of 3 pies in a rupee on the value of sales of all goods. This sales tax rates, exemptions and point of levy, including slabs of turnover, were modified periodically to raise more revenue. Besides this sales tax, the state government was also levying sales tax on inter-state sales. Because of the conflict involved in taxation of inter-state sales, the Union Government took over the responsibility of fixing the rates, and the collection responsibility has been entrusted to the state governments. Over and above these, the state government has started levying a separate tax on the turnover of the dealers. This is intended to tax the net income of the big dealers and hence, is an implicit income tax. Surprisingly, it has survived even judicial scrutiny. Karnataka sales tax which started as a multipoint retail sales tax has evolved over the years and has stabilized in the form of single point (first point) sales tax. The exemption limit also has gone up and the list of commodities exempted is also made very small. Recently in 1996, the number of rates have been brought down to four. This is not only intended to simplify sales tax administration but also to pave the way for the replacement of the present system of sales tax by value added tax (VAT). Though VAT will reduce the revenue in the first one or two years, it will become a money spinning source of revenue in course of time.

Sales tax is administered by the Department of Commercial Taxes. Every registered dealer is liable to maintain sales account either in Kannada, Hindi or English, and submit accounts to the commercial tax officer for assessment. If he is satisfied, the tax will be assessed on reported turnover. If he is not satisfied, he will report to the Assessing Officer. If the Assessing Officer is not satisfied with the assessment and the accounts produced by a dealer, he may assess turnover to the best of his ability. He may check the dealer's accounts and give surprise visits to the shop and godown. If the dealer does not agree with the Assessing Officer, he may appeal to the Deputy Commissioner for revision. If he still disagree with the decision of the Deputy Commissioner for commercial taxes, he may appeal to the Joint Commissioner, Additional Commissioner and Commissioner for Commercial Taxes and then to the Appellate Tribunal and finally, to the High Court. If anybody maintains false sales turnover or net returns and keeps false account, he is liable for punishment. The dealers, who are paying tax under the **KST Act**, are authorised to collect tax from consumers or purchasers. The tax is paid in instalments ranging from monthly to quarterly. Delayed payments invite penalty.

State excise duty is a specific tax levied on the volume and strength of alcoholic liquors produced and sold. Excise duty appears to have been levied in the erstwhile Mysore state as early as 1500 AD on toddy, salt and iron. When the British took over the administration of the erstwhile Mysore state during 1799-1800, they found these excise duties in the name of Abhkari or Panchabab i.e., five items on which excise duty was levied, toddy, arrack, ganja, betel leaf and tobacco. The last two items were transferred respectively in 1838-1839 and 1850-51 to the head of 'Saic' or transit duties. The principal sources of excise revenue, therefore, remained toddy and arrack. Up to 1862, the revenue from toddy, arrack and ganja was derived by the government directly from individual manufacturers or suppliers who were themselves wholesale vendors or retailers in several places. Between 1863 and 1866, Sadar Distillery system was introduced, according to which any person could manufacture arrack and sell it by paying excise duty on it. From 1879, this system was discontinued and outright three year contract was given. This monoploy contract was split into three sections - manufacture, transport and sale. Between 1900 and 1930, the strength of the alcoholic content was increased. The government of the erstwhile Mysore State also introduced a 'tree tax'in 1897-98 on Date tree, Palm tree and Coconut tree. All Date trees growing on government or ryotwari lands, whether occupied or unoccupied, were recorded for the disposal of the government for Abhkari purposes, and tree tax ranging from Rs.1.6 per Date tree to Rs.2.12 per Coconut tree was levied. The rates of tax were revised according to the circumstances. During these years a duty was levied on fermented liquor called Beer made from malted corn and barley malt. In addition, a local cess came to be levied on the usual duty on Beer per gallon. Foreign liquors were imported into the state after paying import duty to the Government of India. In the erstwhile Mysore state they could be sold by those shops which had a three year contract by payment of lumpsum duty to the state government. Excise duty was also levied on intoxicant drugs like ganja and opium before 1947. The cultivation of ganja without permission was prohibited as early as 1886. The minimum guaranteed system by which wholesale vendors guaranteed a certain amount to the government was in vogue. In 1902, this system was abolished and replaced by a system in which government supplied ganja to retailers and this was continued until 1930. Since opium was not cultivated in the state it was imported and the revenue was the difference between the imported price and the selling price less the cost of management. The state government also levied licence fee on opium sellers. The objective of levying excise duty was to raise more revenue and regulate the consumption of these goods. But the British government's policy emphasised the revenue aspect more than the objective of restricting consumption.

After 1947, excise duties in the erstwhile Mysore state consisted of duties and licence fee on producers, distributors, wholesalers and retailers of toddy and other country spirits, malt liquors, foreign liquors and intoxicant drugs, mainly ganja and opium. The erstwhile Mysore state had prohibition until December 1969 when it was removed. Today, the state excise includes the rental charges and licence fees on arrack producers, distributors, wholesale and retail vendors and the duty and licence fee on the manufacturers, distributors and wholesalers of Indian made foreign liquors. The present Janata Dal party government has announced that it will reintroduce prohibition in stages. It has announced that it will ban sale of arrack from April 1997. However, the government has not given effect to this. Though prohibition is a desirable social policy enshrined in the Directive Principles of State Policy, it will create revenue loss to the government in the immediate future and will encourage illicit liquor production and consumption. Therefore, it would be better to confine prohibition to banning production, sale and consumption of arrack and allow at least Indian made foreign liquors to be produced and consumed in the state.

Present Administrative Set-up

a) **Commercial Taxes:** Today, about eight taxes are levied and collected by the Department of Commercial Taxes. They are: Karnataka Sales Tax, under the **KST Act of 1957,** Central Sales Tax under the **CST Act of 1956,** Entertainment Tax under the Karnataka Entertainment Act of 1958, Betting Tax under **the Mysore Betting Act of 1932**, Profession Tax under the Karnataka Tax on Professions, Trades, Callings and Employments Act of 1976, Agricultural Income Tax under the **Karnataka Agricultural Income Tax of 1957,** Entry Tax under the **Karnataka Tax on Entry of Goods Act of 1979,** Turnover Tax, and Luxury Tax under the Karnataka Tax on Luxuries (Hotels and Lodging Houses). These are treated as commercial taxes as these are levied on trade and commerce and there is one administrative set-up for all these taxes. At the state level the Finance Commissioner and Secretary to the Government of Karnataka, Finance Department is the Head of the tax administration. Below him, the commercial taxes department is headed by the Commissioner for Commercial Tax, who is in the rank of super-time scale of IAS. The Commissioner is assisted at the state level by five Additional Commissioners (Policy and law), (Vigilance), (Headquarters-1), (Headquarters-2) and (Intelligence-cum-co-ordination), Deputy Commissioner (Legal), Assistant Commissioners and a number of other officers. Besides, the Commissioner's office has a Legal Cell, Special Cell, Vigilance Cell and an In-house Computer Centre to assist the Commissioner in the respective fields for planning, controlling and co-ordinating the activities of the department.

The state is divided into twelve administrative divisions of the Commercial Taxes Department. Each division is headed by a Joint Commissioner of Commercial Taxes (Administration) and he is responsible for the administration of various Acts of the Department in the division under his jurisdiction with the assistance of Assistant Commissioners and Commercial Tax Officers in his office.

Each division has a number of Deputy Commissioners of Commercial Taxes (Assessment), Assistant Commissioners and Commercial Tax Officers, who carry out the work of registration, assessments, etc. A Deputy Commissioner of Commercial Taxes (Assessment) holds jurisdiction in respect of dealers whose annual tax liability is Rs. 1.5 lakh in Bangalore and Rs. 1 lakh in Mangalore city and Rs. 75,000 in other places. An Assistant Commissioner of Commercial Taxes assesses dealers with annual turnover of Rs. 2.5 lakh and above. The Commercial Tax Officers hold jurisdiction over dealers having a total turnover of less than Rs. 5 lakhs in a year. These Commercial Tax Officers and Assistant Commissioners of Commercial Taxes are also entrusted with the work of administration of **Entry Tax Act, Profession Tax Act, Luxury Tax and Entertainment Tax Act.** There are Agricultural Income Tax Officers, Assistant Agricultural Income Tax Officers, Profession Tax Officers for administering the **Agricultural**

Income Tax Act and Profession Tax Act (in respect of professions) and assist the Joint Commissioner of Commercial Taxes (Administration) in the Division.

There are 8 Intelligence Wings, North-Zone with headquarters at Belgaum, South-Zone with headquarters at Bangalore, West Zone with headquarters at Mangalore and East-Zone with headquarters at Bellary, Mysore-Zone with headquarters at Mysore, Central-Zone with headquarters at Davanagere, Hubli-Zone at Hubli and Shimoga-Zone at Shimoga. These divisional Zones are headed by the Joint Commissioner of Commercial Taxes (Intelligence) both drawn from the IAS cadre and from the Department.

At the divisional level there are separate Joint Commissioners of Commercial Taxes (Appeals) and Deputy Commissioners of Commercial Taxes (Appeals) to dispose of appeals against the assessment orders of assessing authorities. In addition, there is one Joint Commissioner of Commercial Taxes (Vigilance) in-charge of check-posts both stationary and mobile, in Bangalore.

There are three Sales Tax Benches of the Karnataka Appellate Tribunal, each of which has an Additional Commissioner of Commercial Taxes as a sitting member, along with a Judicial Member, who is of the rank of a District Judge.

Computerisation of tax forms and information about the dealers started in the mid-80s. But it did not improve the administrative capacity because of the resistance on the part of the staff for fear of losing employment opportunities in the Commercial Taxes Department. So far, only four divisions in Bangalore City are computerised and the department is planning to take up computerisation of other eight divisions in phases. The officers of the Department, other than IAS officers, are recruited through open competition by the Karnataka Public Service Commission. They are given initial training at the Administrative Training Institute, Mysore, and lower level staff are trained at the district level where Commercial Taxes Department is having its own training centres. Occasionally, senior level officers are deputed for in-service refresher training courses conducted by the national level institutes to update their knowledge about taxation and related matters.

Until recently, the Department of Commercial Taxes was dependent on legal opinion provided by the Law Department of the Government of Karnataka. But, because of increasing number of litigations and complexity of tax cases, the Law Department could not provide the required legal assistance. Hence, the state government has permitted all the major departments to have their own legal cells. Accordingly, the Commercial Taxes Department has got its own legal cell directly under the Commissioner.

All officers belong to common cadre and they may be posted to collect any tax and hence, they are interchangeable. For example, a Deputy Commissioner or an Assistant Commissioner of Commercial Taxes, who is in-charge of collecting sales tax, may be posted to collect agricultural income tax. There is no separate cadre for each of the seven taxes. There is also a small cell for research with a senior statistician but this wing has neither expanded nor improved. This is the present structure of the commercial tax administration in Karnataka.

b) Excise Administration: Mention has already been made of the evolution of excise administration in the erstwhile Mysore state. That administrative set up was dissolved after the introduction of prohibition in 1961. Subsequently, when prohibition was removed in December 1969, the state government had to build up a new administrative structure for excise duty collection. Today, the excise duty administration is headed by a Commissioner at the state level and is assisted by a Joint Commissioner and Deputy Commissioner. At the taluk level, there are excise inspectors whose job is mainly to oversee any violation of excise law by production of spurious liquor, false labelling etc. The Excise Department is also having an intelligence department called Enforcement Wing which enforces the excise law.

Excise duty is levied in the form of a specific duty on the volume-cum-alcoholic strength of Indian made foreign liquor (IMFL). Over and above this, there is a licence fee. On top of it, sales tax is also levied on the sale of IMFL. As for as arrack (country liquor) is concerned, the right to produce and vend is auctioned on district basis annually and the rental amount is collected from the contractors who bid the right to vend. This system led to the formation of cartels of bidders, and with a view to giving opportunities to others, bidding was done on taluk basis. However, this resulted in loss of rental income. So, in order to maximise the rental income district-wise bidding was restored. Sales tax on sale of liquor is administered by the Commercial Taxes Department and other levies are collected by the Excise Department. The earlier tree tax has been abolished and toddy tapping has also been prohibited.

c) Motor Vehicle Tax: The **Motor Vehicles Act of 1984** is the law passed by the Parliament which empowers the state government to regulate, levy and collect taxes on the users and owners of motor vehicles or automobiles. The Transport Commissioner is the head of the Motor Vehicles Tax Administration at the state level. He works under the Home Commissioner. Below him are Regional Transport Officers, who collect the tax on various types of vehicles which are prescribed by the State Legislature. Enforcement is done both by the RTOs and the Police Department. The rates of motor vehicle tax are fixed by classifying the motor vehicles into two wheelers, cars, passenger carrying buses and goods vehicles. Passenger carrying vehicles are taxed on the basis of seating capacity and goods vehicles are taxed on the basis of laden as well as unladen weight of the vehicle. Recently, life-time tax has been introduced on two-wheeler vehicles and cars to prevent evasion and to simplify payment of tax. There is also a State Transport Authority at the state level and Regional Transport Authorities excercising below the state level. They are quasi-judicial authorities with substantive powers regarding the issue of route permits for passenger vehicles.

d) Stamps and Registration: Registration fees and stamp duties are collected by the Registrar and Sub-Registrar of land records who come under the Land Revenue Department. Formerly, the Deputy Commissioners were also District Registrars of Stamps and Registration. Separate District Registrars were appointed during 1970s. At the state level, the Revenue Commissioner is the head of Stamps and Registration. Below him is the Inspector General of Registration and Commissioner of Stamps. Judicial stamp duties are prescribed by the Central Government and collected by the state government through stamp vendors by selling them stamped papers and court fee stamps. Non-judicial stamp duties are levied and collected by the Revenue Department. But the rates are prescribed by the State Legislature. Recently, the state government has decided to do away with stamp vendors and install franking machines in the offices of Registrars and Sub-Registrars to prevent black marketing in stamp papers.

Need for Reforms: It may be noticed that tax administration which prevailed in the erstwhile Mysore state has changed in structure, scope and sophistication. Even the tax administration which prevailed in 1957 immediately after the creation of the new state of Karnataka has undergone many changes in response to the revenue needs of the state government. However, there are certain deficiencies which need to be rectified in order to prepare the state's tax administrative set-up for the 21st century.

First, the method of recruitment to the tax administration has more or less remained the same for a very long time. The minimum required qualification for a gazetted officer is a university degree. The quality and content of a university degree have deteriorated because of various reasons. The state government has not increased the minimum required qualification to master's degree level. This is probably because the Union Public Service Commission (UPSC) itself has not changed the minimum required qualification for recruitment of candidates for Central Services. However, the UPSC screens the candidates by conducting preliminary examinations. The reservation policy and corrupt practices which have become wide-spread at the recruitment level have further lowered the quality, capability and attitude of the candidates recruited to tax administration in Karnataka. Therefore, it is nceecessary to introduce preliminary examination to screen the candidates applying for gazetted posts on the lines of UPSC.

Second, training is equally deficient in the sense that the required task-oriented probationery training is not even comparable to that provided to the candidates selected for Central Services. Afterwards, in-service training is not regular but only ad hoc. The contents of the training courses are equally wanting. They do not reflect the need for changing the attitude, motivation and career goals of the candidates recruited. There is need for reorienting and reforming the probationery as well as in-service training to the candidates related to tax administration.

Third, the research input which has become absolutely necessary in tax administration in recent years is lacking even at the state level both in the Finance Department and in the Commercial Taxes Department. They are dependent on ad hoc Expert Committee's recommendations. They have not filled the gap left by the absence of a research wing. It is absolutely necessary to have economic and statistical research wing attached to the Commissioner of Commercial Taxes with qualified specialists recruited for this purpose. As an alternative, they can fund and create separate research centres at the autonomous research institutions located in Bangalore. The Union Ministry of Agriculture has established Agro-Economic Research Centres all over the country. The Union Ministry of Health and Family Welfare has established research centres in different research institutions and also, the Union Ministry of Urban Affairs and Employment has established research cells in major cities of the country. The Commercial Taxes Department should immediately fund separate research centres in one or two of the reputed research insitutions to undertake required research exclusively meant for the use of Commercial Taxes Department. That Department should also have a panel of experts in economics, econometrics and tax laws to meet its requirements periodically.

Another set of issues relating to tax administration relates to modernization of tax designing and tax reform processes. The State Finance Minister has prepared the ground for the introduction of VAT in place of sales tax by rationalising the Sales tax structure on the lines suggested by Bagchi Committee. Now, the Commercial Taxes Department has to design VAT to replace Sales Tax. This can be done by a group of experts or by tax administrators themselves. They require research support which is lacking in the Department. Further, it would be ideal to combine the practical knowledge of the tax administrators and the theoretical knowledge of experts in designing a new tax like VAT. This is not happening in the Department. Therefore, it is necessary to develop in-house skills in tax designing with expert assistance from outside. Similarly, once the designed tax is put into operation, its defects and merits will be known after a lapse of one or two years. Monitoring of such defects will have to be done by the research cell or the legal cell, and measures to reform the tax structure as and when required will have to be thought of. This should also be done within the administrative set up with the assistance from experts from outside. This in-house capability is also lacking. Because of all these deficiencies, there appears to be large scale evasion and increase in legal disputes resulting in accumulation of arrears of tax revenue. This is evident from Table-5.

Table 5

Arrears of Tax Revenue in Karnataka

(Rs. in lakhs).

Year	Average of Tax Revenue
1987-88	28,091
1988-89	31,202
1989-90	27,640
1990-91	37.708
1991-92	42,284
1992-93	46,861
1993-94	64,440

Note: The figures for 1993-94 do not include those in respect of Taxes on Vehicles as the information was not forthcoming from the Department concerned.

Source: Reports of the Comptroller and Auditor General, Report on Karnataka 1992 and 1994, Bangalore, 1994.

Another aspect of tax administration which requires some attention is attending to the grievances of tax payers. This is, no doubt, attended by issuing periodical notifications and clarifications by the Department of Commercial Taxes. But, day to-day grievances cell will have to be attached to the Intelligence Wing which should also become a sort of Ombudsman over the tax Assessing Officers. On the recommendation of the Taxation Enquiry Commission (1953-54), Sales Tax Advisory Board was created to periodically interact with traders to solve their problems. But this Board was not reconstituted for almost one and half decades. Recently, the Finance Minister has announced the reconstitution of the Karnataka Sales Tax Advisory Board. It is hoped that it will meet frequently to solve the day-to-day problems of dealers.

Tax payer's education is another aspect which is lacking. Both these aspects were attempted to be met by the Sales Tax Advisory Board. However, a new institution or organisation for redressing the tax payer's grievances and educating them about all aspects of tax compliance may be created.

Finally, the efficiency of tax administration, as indicated by the cost of collection and arrears of revenue, has ben going down. The cost of collection of many taxes has been increasing. This is evident from Table-6. No doubt the cost of collection as proportion of gross revenue has been declining in the case of commercial taxes. But, this is not happening in the case of other taxes. The cost of compliance for the tax payer is also increasing though no quantitative estimates are available. This needs to be minimised as for as possible to win the confidence of tax payers. Tax payers should not be treated as proverbial suspects. They are the **Kamadhenu** of the state government. Such attitudinal change is required in the adminstrative set-up and personnel of the tax administration.

Table-6
Cost of Tax Collection of Major Taxes in Karnataka

(Rs. in lakhs)

Year	Land Revenue	Stamp Duty and Registration	State Excise Tax	Sales Tax	Tax on Vehicles	Duties	Other Taxes on Fiscal Services	Other Total Fiscal Services
1960-61	131.13	16.02	22.54	26.54	7.17	108.00		311.40
1961-62	345.26	16.98	20.23	30.05	8.88	14.18		435.58
1962-63	140.75	18.92	19.84	32.65	12.99	5.79		230.94
1963-64	174.29	17.41	20.26	33.78	16.43	3.82		265.99
1964-65	189.62	18.75	21.12	37.76	11.80	10.47		289.52
1965-66	197.96	30.17	22.17	45.77	13.20	11.36		320.63
1966-67	217.38	36.05	24.15	53.36	15.61	10.75		357.30
1967-68	201.62	39.14	46.03	61.34	17.09	11.01		376.23
1968-69	220.63	45.411	100.67	69.81	18.96	14.81		470.29
1969-70	243.72	53.71	114.13	79.81	24.78	14.42		530.57
1970-71	311.68	59.75	139.71	97.91	27.28	18.66		654.99
1971-72	336.36	62.54	175.17	115.62	29.12	18.75		737.56
1972-73	661.45	74.32	211.63	141.68	41.51	22.17		1,107.76
1973-74	470.35	72.23	241.36	142.40	35.55	23.06		984.95
1974-75	500.35	96.95	288.23	180.29	40.81	24.93	14.06	1,145.62
1975-76	542.40	100.26	309.17	226.29	46.04	29.84	18.40	1,272.40
1976-77	686.33	109.29	300.52	241.56	54.37	40.10	34.18	1,466.35
1977-78	668.23	147.31	399.40	241.85	73.48	27.26	21.00	1,578.53
1978-79	727.50	161.29	463.91	266.78	91.85	25.70	20.29	1,757.32
1979-80	851.72	156.41	459.17	284.21	114.75	48.08	25.91	1,940.25
1980-81	1,139.46	194.17	646.37	335.26	128.80	52.86	29.72	2,526.64
1981-82	1,197.93	202.14	339.46	400.40	151.90	61.33	30.84	2384.00
1982-83	1,452.46	253.74	419.30	508.61	201.11	100.15	9.33	2,984.70
1983-84	1,538.51	271.33	430.29	588.92	219.60	109.49	62.68	3,220.82
1984-85	1,871.73	329.26	538.67	701.43	273.56	118.52	91.41	3,924.58
1985-86	1,946.62	349.41	576.22	808.79	308.35	134.24	40.08	4,263.71
1986-87	2,344.35	402.20	640.70	939.64	364.11	131.77	08.17	5,030.94
1987-88	3,100.67	491.26	838.42	1,312.20	444.47	144.88	262.92	6,638.92
1988-89	3,144.22	582.01	844.07	1,552.21	511.52	168.29	342.68	7,145.00

Contd.

1989-90	3,499.48	643.85	979.86	1,848.60	608.75	191.22	635.86	8,357.62
1990-91	3,584.74	682.49	1,083.76	1,903.59	672.09	176.67	373.92	8,477.26
1991-92	4,239.67	906.54	1,179.11	2,311.00	812.66	216.70	459.04	10,124.72
1992-93	4,613.64	978.33	1,426.00	2,631.16	942.55	246.44	679.50	11,517.62
1993-94	5,572.37	1,008.62	1,891.00	3,187.92	1,172.98	298.64	737.02	13,868.55
1994-95	6,062.74	1,239.90	1,985.14	3,458.46	1,144.45	169.16	5,037.09	190,76.94
1995-96	6,104.95	1,150.12	2,182.84	4,068.32	1,356.72	298.19	3,300.68	18,461.82
1996-97	7,414.34	1,348.07	2,681.64	4,758.09	1,598.95	360.53	2,348.54	20,510.16

REFERENCES

Balasubramanian, K. (1963). Revenue Administration in Mysore. In

G.S. Halappa (ed.) , **State Administration/** Dharwar: **Karnataka Universtiy.**

Government of Mysore (GOM) (1949). **Budget Speech 1949-50.** Bangalore: Government Press.

Rao, C. Hayavadana (ed.). (1984) **Mysore Gazetteer, Vol IV.** Delhi: B.C. Publishing Corporation.

Thimmaiah, G. (1978) **Perspectives on Tax Design and Tax Reform.** New Delhi: Ashish Publishing Company.

V

ENVIRONMENTAL ADMINISTRATION

- M.V. Nadkarni with G.S. Sastry

Introduction: Environmental administration in Karnataka can be understood only in an all-India perspective and in terms of national policies in relation to environment. The Constitution **(Forty-Second Amendment Act of 1976)** gave Parliament the power to enact laws on virtually any entry in the State list, and through Article 253 brought environmental regulation under the concurrent list. While the focus of this paper is on Karnataka, it is discussed in an all-India framework.

Environmental concern in India rests not so much on aesthetic and health grounds as on survival and livelihood issues. The former are important, but the latter issues concerned with the daily life of the people lend greater urgency to environmental policy in developing countries. This is because the poor depend greatly on natural resources for their livelihood. A deterioration in the quality of environment hits the poor hardest. It is true that economic growth itself creates livelihood opportunities. However, the perception that benefits of economic growth far outweigh its adverse environmental impact has to be moderated by the fact that people benefiting may be quite different from the people losing. The loss of the latter cannot be offset by the gain of the former. This requires that prevention of adverse impact is built into the design of development strategies and projects, and if adverse impact does occur, there has to be an effective mechanism for adequately compensating the affected people or rehabilitating them. In this regard, "Polluter pays Principle" has been universally accepted which holds the polluter responsible for observing anti-pollution laws, who has also to bear the related expenses and undertake to compensate the victims of pollution if it is not prevented. This concern has to be reflected in policies and in their implementation, which indeed is the primary task of environmental administration.

India has increasingly institutionalised its environmental concern after the United Nations Conference on Human Environment at Stockholm in 1972. To serve as a guideline to the governments, both Central and state, Article 48A was added to the Directive Principles of State Policy in 1976, which said, "The state shall endeavour to protect and improve environment and safeguard the forests and wildlife of the country". In a new chapter entitled 'Fundamental Duties', Article 51A(g) imposed a similar responsibility on every citizen to 'protect and improve the natural environment including forests lakes, rivers and, wildlife and to have compassion for living creatures' (As quoted in Rosencranz et al 1991:53). The Supreme Court of India has held 'whenever a problem of ecology is brought before the Court, the Court is bound to bear in mind Art. 48A of the Constitution (Rosencranz et al 1991:54). This commitment to environment has been reflected in many of the pieces of legislation covering forests, wildlife, industrial pollution, hazardous wastes and so on. Quite a few of them were in operation even before the Stockholm Conference. It is not necessary to review them all here, though some important legislations will be referred to as the regulatory framework is designed accordingly.

Instruments of environmental policy are classified into three broad categories (Opschoor and Turner 1994:10). (1) 'Communicative instruments', like publicity and moral persuasion, are aimed at voluntary adaptation of individual, group or corporate behaviour in an environment-friendly direction. Voluntary commitments by industries and agreements between them and the[1] government can also be put under

1. These agreements are a conspicuous feature of environmental administration in the Netherlands. They impose stringent standards, so that the more able can treat or prevent pollution most effectively (Nadkarni *et al* 1995)

this category. (2)'Economic Instruments' affect market conditions and influence the decision making through market or economic incentives, such as, the effluent charges, noise charges,subsidies, tradeable permits, and deposit provision of infrastructure and facilities like collection and refund systems. (3) 'Direct Regulation' is through (a) prohibition, restrictions, and obligations, like imposing emission standards, and (b) disposal of solid waste, treatment of effluents, separate cycle tracks and parks.

All the three categories of environmental policy instruments are used in India, including Karnataka, but 'Direct Regulation' is used much more than the first two. And in using all the three, the government plays an active role, though it is much more direct and dominant in the case of 'Direct Regulation'. The government uses communicative instruments by spreading environmental consciousness among the public, in general, and also by providing information on clean technologies to industries. It encourages and supports voluntary associations if they also can do the same job, and helps institution building. Recent steps in the country as a whole, and also, in Karnataka to promote Joint. Forest Planning and Management can be clubbed with communicative instruments. There are obvious limitations to this category of instruments because people acting in the short-run self interest are not always persuaded to care for the community and long term concerns. That is why they have to be complemented by the other two categories of instruments. There are occasions when only communicative instruments work, such as when it is too costly to monitor the behaviour of all individuals and an appeal to their civic sense is necessary. When there is need for immediate action, as for example, in the case of extremely hazardous smog levels in cities, communicative instruments play the most useful role.

Though economic instruments operate through the market, the government must give legitimacy to them through legislative and institutional support. The most popular economic instrument with economists is a charge on pollutants released in air and water, which has to be designed in such a way that it is cheaper for polluting firms to prevent or treat pollution than to pay the charges. The formula is to fix the charge at the level of the marginal cost of treating pollution at the standard fixed by law or agreement. It is to be noted that a pollution charge, to be effective, has to be on all pollution released even if it is within the permissible limits fixed by the standard. The case for pollution charge rests on the fact that they provide an incentive to abate pollution even beyond the standard fixed and lower the cost of pollution control. Moreover, direct regulation is a very time-consuming process, particularly when the defaulting parties have to be penalised. The penalty under pollution charges is immediate and automatic. But this also has to depend on administration, because some agency has to monitor in a foolproof fashion how far industrial units are releasing pollutants into environment and paying charges, though in principle and bylaw, it is for the industrial units to monitor it themselves and pay charges immediately and automatically. The pollutant charges, however, are levied only in extremely few countries like the Netherlands (in the case of water only, and not air), mainly due to resistance from industries. As per the Policy Statement for Abatement of Pollution by the Government of India (Feb. 1992), the government is interested in the near future to assign a greater role to economic instruments than before. Though pollution charges are not yet tried in India, a few economic instruments like water cess have been tried.

Presently, however, the overwhelming reliance is on direct regulation. In this, India is not alone. Let alone the developing countries, the developed countries have also placed almost all their eggs in one basket of direct regulation. Direct regulation makes no difference between a more efficient abater of pollution and less efficient. It places too large a burden on the resources of the government, as it requires more extensive monitoring and control. It depends very much on judicial processes, in spite of increased administrative powers given recently to Pollution Control Boards. The judicial process is very slow, making the implementation of regulation tardy and inadequate. However,in the case of activities hazardous to health or of situations which have to be tackled urgently, or if non-attainment of standards fixed leads to be very risky, hazardous or uncertain situations, there is no alternative to a full reliance on strict and direct regulation.[2]

2. For a detailed discussion of strength, and limitations of the three categories of instruments, see chapter 2 in Nadkarni *et al* 1995

The first systematic attempt at institutionalising environmental concern in Karnataka was through the establishment of State Environmental Board (SEB) in 1972, with the Chief Minister as its Chairman. This was following a central initiative, whereby in February 1972, a National Committee on Environmental Planning and Co-ordination (NCEPC) was set up as a part of the Department of Science and Technology, Government of India. The SEB had the functions of: (a) acting as a nodal agency for initiating, reviewing and monitoring state environmental matters: (b) proper siting of industries and incorporating environmental safeguards into the development projects: (c) undertaking environmental education and creating awareness; (d) appraising projects at an early stage from an environmental angle; and (e) serving as a liaison with the Department of Science and Technology, NCEPC, and related Departments and research institutions. Karnataka is one among six states where SEBs played an active role (Rosencranz **et al** 1991:43-4). Till 1980, the environment related functions were co-ordinated and monitored at the national level by the Department of Science and Technology. The functions of SEB were taken over by the newly constituted State Department of Ecology and Environment in 1981, following the setting up of a separate Department of Environment (DDE) in 1980 at the national level. The DDE was upgraded into a full Ministry in 1981.

Since then, the apex policy making body in environmental matters is the Ministry of Environment and Forests (MEF) at the national level, and the Department of Forests, Ecology and Environment at the state level in Karnataka. In addition, there is the Department of Science and Technology. The Secretary for the Department is assisted by Special Secretaries in charge of Forests, and Ecology and Environment respectively, and by a Director (Technical cell). All development projects which originate from different government departments have to be submitted to the Department of Forest, Ecology and Environment for clearance from an environmental angle under the provision of **Environment (Protection) Act 1986.** For this, there is a separate Environment Clearance Committee headed by the Special Secretary, Ecology and Environment. The Committee consists of representives from Commerce and Industries, Health and Social Welfare Departments, Chief inspector of Factories and Boilers, Chairman of the Karnataka State Pollution Control Board (KSPCB) and environment experts. Projects of significance from the point of view of air and water pollution are handled by the KSPCB. and other projects of significance from the point of view of impact on forests, biodiversity etc., are handled by the Departments of Ecology and Environment and Forests. In principle, all projects have to be cleared by the Environmental Clearance Committee and the Ministry of Forests, Ecology and Environment. Some 29 types of specially notified projects of crucial environmental significance have to be cleared by the Central MEF (GOI 1994).

That the Union Government dominates over states in environmental regulation may not be liked by those in favour of a high level of autonomy for the states. For curbing temptation on the part of the states to indulge in unfair competition with other states in attracting investment and to give in to populist pressures to convert forest lands for other uses, a certain minimum uniformity in standards and a minimum agreement about environmental objectives are necessary. This can be achieved better by the present arrangement than through increased state autonomy in environmental policy. The states, however, have a free role in the implementation of national policies.

Here, a review of how environmental regulation is administered and with what instruments in two cases, viz., control and prevention of industrial pollution, and conservation and improvement of forests, is presented.

Prevention and Control of Industrial Pollution: Karnataka is a fairly well industrialised state with quite a few heavy industries. It is particularly notable that the growth of highly polluting industries - howsoever measured - is taking place at a faster rate in Karnataka than that of other less polluting industries, as can be seen from Table-1 below. Some 18 industries have been categorised as highly polluting, which are : sugar, fertiliser, cement, distillery, aluminium, petrochemical, thermal power, caustic soda, oil refinery, sulphuric acid, cluster of tanneries, copper smelter, zinc smelter, iron and steel, pulp and paper, dyes and dye intermediate, pesticide manufacturing and formulation, and pharmaceutical manufacturing and formulation. This group is growing faster in Karnataka than in the country as a whole, and also as compared to other industries. This makes the task of controlling industrial pollution more difficult, and also reflects on the nature of economic growth taking place. It also shows how compelling it is to prevent and control industrial pollution.

Table 1:

Growth of Highly Polluting Industries vis-a-vis Other Industries (percentage change between 1980-81 and 1988-89)

Particulars		Highly Polluting Industries		Other Industries	
		India	Karnataka	India	Karnataka
i)	Number of Industrial Units	31.6	34.4	5.7	3.2
ii)	Fuel Consumption	252.2	367.8	209.0	250.5
iii)	Value of input	238.9	271.6	181.6	198.8
iv)	Value of output	244.4	241.4	178.2	193.7

Note: The rate of growth in (ii), (iii) and (iv) is in money terms, not adjusted for inflation.

Source: Annual Survey of Industries.

At the national level, the Ministry of Environment and Forests (MEF), Government of India, is the apex body for the prevention and control of industrial pollution too, as in other environmental matters. The main functions of the MEF are : (i) co-ordination of activities of various central and state authorities: (ii) laying down emission/effluent standards for various industrial activities: (iii) getting information about the industrial processes and to inspect the plant, premises, records and other necessary materials including seizure of documents; (iv) giving directions for closure, prohibition of/or regulation of industrial processes as necessary; and (v) stoppage or regulation of the supply of water and electricity or any other services to industries violating pollution standards. These powers have been assigned to MEF by the **Environmental (Protection) Act, 1986,** which is an umbrella legislation, empowering the government to deal with all aspects of environment. It is not necessary for the MEF to act directly, though the overall control is vested with it.

The MEF acts through the Central and State Pollution Control Boards for implementing anti-pollution laws. Set up earlier to handle only water pollution under the **Water (Prevention and Control of Pollution) Act 1974,** the jurisdiction of these Boards was extended to cover air pollution too under the **Air (Prevention and Control of Pollution) Act of 1981.** The Boards have a two-tier administrative structure to carry out their functions under law. At the first tier, the Boards are constituted by the concerned governments (the Central government in the case of CPCB, and respective state governments in the case of SPCB) by nominating two other executive members - the Chairman and the Member Secretary, and 15 other members - both official and non-official or honorary. These Boards are autonomous in nature and meet once in three months to guide the executive functionaries in their perspective, programme and policies. At the second tier, the day-to-day activities of the Boards are carried out by the appointed regular staff - both technical and administrative, under the guidance of the Chairman and Member Secretary. While the Chairman of the Central Board (CPCB) is a full-time member, the Chairman of the State Boards (SPCBs) may be either full-time or part-time. The Pollution Control Boards have no elected members, as it is supposed to be a professional body. There is no representation to voluntary agencies or NGOs, and environmental activists may or may not find representation depending on who are nominated. The constitution of CPCB, however, is such that the problems of the states are articulated through the representatives of SPCBs, which also helps in proper co-ordination of policies.

The MEF has several zonal offices, the office for South Zone being located in Bangalore. Similarly, the CPCB also has zonal offices, including one in Bangalore. They oversee the activities and operations of SPCBs, co-ordinate with them and provide necessary guidance and information. The SPCBs are under dual control of both CPCB and respective state governments, but they are autonomous bodies. Their

Chairman and Member-Secretary are nominated by the respective state governments and can also be removed by them. The SPCBs are answerable also to CPCB and through it to MEF, Government of India. The main function of carrying out the inspection of industries, monitoring their pollution level and implementing standards is done by SPCBs. This is done by CPCBs too in territories where there are no SPCBs. The CPCB provides technical assistance to SPCBs to carry on and sponsor investigation and research on pollution problems. Both CPCB and SPCBs plan and organise training and awareness programmes on pollution prevention and control. They also collect and publish technical and statistical data and prepare such publicity materials which may be useful in pollution prevention activities.

The Karnataka State Water (Prevention and Control of Pollution) Board was constituted in September 1974 under the **Water Act 1974** referred above. Its scope was widened later to deal with air pollution following the **Act 1981,** and it was consequently renamed as Karnataka State Pollution Control Board (KSPCB) in 1985. Now, it acts as an agency to enforce the **Environment (Protection) Act 1986** as well. Apart from these Acts, it also enforces the Hazardous Waste (Management and Handling) Rules 1989, and Hazardous Chemicals (Export, Import and Storage) Rules 1989. It also enforces like the other SPCBs, the **Water Cess Act of 1977** requiring industries to pay cess on water consumption. This cess was expected to meet the expenses of the Board. The Water Cess, however, has been effective neither in fulfilling this expectation nor as an economic incentive in inducing firms to prevent and/or treat pollution of water.[3] The regulatory powers of the Board remain as the major instrument of environmental policy.

KSPCB uses the following regulatory instruments in the task of preventing and controlling industrial pollution: (a) No Objection Certificate (NOC); (b) Consent; (c) Standards; and (d) Punitive Measures.

---

3. The Water Cess gives some rebate if water pollution treatment plants are installed and pollution standards are met. The water cess, however, has not been an effective economic instrument to control water pollution, as its burden is nominal. It is cheaper to pay the cess than to install pollution treatment plants and operate them.

NOC is required in the case of new industries, which is essentially a certificate of site clearance. To obtain it, an entrepreneur has to submit an application along with the details of the project and its location and prescribed fees to the Member Secretary, KSPCB. The Board issues the NOC only after considering the impact of the proposed project on the environment, topographical and climatic features, biological diversity in the area, compatibility with land use, proximity to protected areas (ancient monuments, archaeological sites, wildlife sanctuaries, national parks) and human settlements. This certificate is obtained once in the life span of an industrial establishment. The Environmental Impact Assessment (ECA) is mandatory for NOC for 29 types of highly sensitive or fragile projects, which have to be cleared only by the MEF, Government of India (GOI 1994). NOC, in the case of other projects, can, however, be issued by the SPCB.

Consent is required before starting the production process of a new industrial unit and to continue production. This is a permit issued by the KSPCB subject to installation of pollution control measures prescribed by the Board. In the case of industrial units already in existence, time limits are prescribed for installing pollution control system and meeting the standards prescribed. The Consent is required to be renewed every year in the case of highly polluting industries. It is renewed only if pollution standards are complied with. The Consent could be conditional, and may be refused or withdrawn in the case of inadequate pollution control measures. Running an industry without proper consent is punishable with imprisonment of not less than two years, extendable up to six years, in addition to a fine. Consent fees contribute towards the expenses of the Board.

In addition to monitoring by the SPCBs, the Health Departments of respective Municipal Corporations (MC) are involved in monioring the industrial units to see if any of them cause health hazard to the public. Thus, as per the **Karnataka Municipal Corporation Act 1976,** all industrial units should obtain a licence from the Health Department, which is to be renewed annually. If KSPCB can effectively monitor them, is it desirable to have, in addition, the requirement of obtaining a licence from MCs as well? Would it not amount to considerable duplication and impose unnecessary hassles and transaction costs on industries? If, however, the Health Departments of MCs monitor only those which are not monitored by KSPCB, it is a different matter and there would be no duplication, but sharing of responsibilities.

Standards refer to specific parameters previously quantified with respect to measures for disposal, discharge and emission of solid, liquid and gaseous wastes into the environment. The standards form the basis for enforcement of any legislation for the abatement of pollution. The main consideration in evolving the standards are: (i) available technology; (ii) the cost of available technology; and (iii) assimilating capacity of the environment. These standards are precise and representative, and have been adopted by the GOI at the national level as Minimum National Standards (MINAS) to abate pollution. The SPCBs are expected to adopt, monitor and implement them. While they have no powers to relax MINAS, they can make them more stringent depending on local conditions.

The implementation of industry specific MINAS needs periodic inspection of industries. The MEF has categorised all industries into Red, Orange and Green, according to the descending order of the level of severity of pollution generated. The frequency of inspection is fixed according to the ascending order of pollution severity (see Table-2). All large industries as well as highly polluting industries are under the 'Red' category. It is to be noted that industries even under the 'Green' category are not totally pollution free. Industries not involving pollution and not requiring monitoring and inspection, are excluded from the three categories.

Table 2
Frequency of Inspection by SPCBs

Size of Industry	Category	Frequency of Inspection
Large	Red	Once a month, or once in six months depending on the severity of pollution
Medium	Red	Once in 3 months
	Orange	Once in 6 months
	Green	Once in a year
Small	Red	Once in 6 months
	Orange	Once in a year
	Green	Once in 2 years

Note: The size of the industry is as per the Fixed Capital. The 'Large' have a Fixed Capital of above Rs 50 million, 'Medium' have Rs 3.5 million to 50 million; and 'Small' up to Rs. 3.5 million.

The Boards are vested with the necessary powers to monitor and regulate pollution problems, and to obtain information for the purpose. On their own also, the Boards have the powers to conduct stream surveys to identify the flow and its characteristics. The Boards can give direction to any person taking water from any stream or well or discharging effluents into any stream or well to give the required information about it. If it is not given, it is a punishable offence, which includes fine and imprisonment.

Punitive Measures can be taken by the KSPCB under various environmental laws. Punishments given to industries running without proper consent have been referred to earlier. Similarly, persons causing pollution of air and water beyond the standards fixed are punishable with imprisonment of not less than one-and-half years and up to six years with a suitable fine. The Boards are empowered to take up the prescribed work in the firms seeking consent, and recover the expenses incurred in installing anti-pollution equipment from the persons or companies concerned.

The process of taking action was lax before the mid-1980s, as the SPCBs had little scope for direct administrative action. They had to approach a magistrate to enjoin the polluter. The Amendments to the **Air Act in 1987** and to the **Water Act** in 1988, not only strengthened penal provisions of these laws, but also empowered the enforcement agencies to close down polluting industries and to discontinue their electricity and water supply (Rosencranz **et al** 1991:2). However, the Boards still have no powers to exact fines, order imprisonment or compel compliance with their directions, for which they have to depend on the courts of law.

Environment is too important a matter to be left only to the government agencies. If the agencies, for various reasons, do not take proper action against the polluter, the citizen has a judicial choice in India in the form of three civil remedies: (a) a common law tort action against the polluter: (b) a writ petition to compel the agency to enforce the law: and (c) a citizen's suit to enforce statutory compliance (Rosencranz ***et al*** 1991: 77). With the emergence of Public Interest Litigation (PIL), whereby even citizens not directly affected by pollution can launch litigation in public interest, the role of higher judiciary (the High Courts and the Supreme Court) has undergone a radical and creative transformation. They have even embarked on necessary administrative action such as appointing expert Committees, and based on their findings, giving direction for closure to polluting industries. These provisions for PIL etc., have made the SPCBs more alert and active.

The discussion above relates mainly to source-oriented pollution coming from individual industrial units. The CPCB has also laid down effect-oriented or ambient quality standards for air and water, which are monitored by SPCBs. These standards are tried to be met by stricter enforcement of source-oriented standards. Where water pollution is due to the failure of municipalities and industries to treat water, bodies and mechanisms are evolved for co-ordinated action for an area, a conspicuous example of which is the Ganga Action Plan in northern India. Such co-ordinated plans are yet to emerge significantly on the Karnataka scene. Recently, however, steps have been initiated for preparing feasibility reports for Action Plans for Cauvery and Tungabhadra rivers. KSPCB has been regularly monitoring ambient air and water quality in several stations and publishing these findings in its Annual Reports.

Though policy and legislation may look stringent on paper, there is many a slip between the cup and the lip. The implementation of pollution control in the 1990s is certainly much more effective than it used to be in the 1980s and far more so compared to the situation in the 1970s. But, in the meanwhile, the number of industries and sources of pollution also have multiplied. A given rate of shortfall has far more adverse effect today than it had before. Nevertheless, there is some indication of how far pollution control laws are put into effect. This can be seen from Table - 3 below for three recent years which gives the proportion (%) of industrial units wit 4 treatment plants in operation in Karnataka.[4]

4. The remaining proportion consists of units where treatment plants are either under construction and planning, and also of defaulters who did nothing in this respect or let out effluents into drainage.

Table 3

Proportion (%) of Industrial Units with Pollution Treatment Plants in Operation in Karnataka.

	As on 31.3.91	As on 31.3.93	As on 31.3.94
Water Pollution Control			
Large Industries	65.8	70.3	72.3
Medium Industries	65.0	53.0	67.1
Small Industries	NA	52.5	46.3
Air Pollution Control			
Large Industries	33.8	62.6	73.5
Medium Industries	33.5	60.1	76.4
Small Industries	NA	34.5	65.9

The Table shows that during the three year period 1991-94 there was a considerable increase in the proportion of industrial units with pollution treatment plants in operation. Unfortunately, comparable figures are not available for earlier years. According to KSPCB officials, however, the situation is far better today than in the 1980s.

The decline in the proportion in the case of medium industries in 1993 for water pollution control is mainly due to starting many new units which were yet to install effluent treatment plants. The situation was to some extent corrected by 1994. It is interesting that air pollution control which was lagging behind till 1993 could catch up with and even fare better than water pollution control by 1994. Small industries, however, have fared worse than other industries, particularly in the case of water pollution control. Often, they cannot afford to install and operate them, and enforcement authorities also tend to go soft in their cases. It is, however, heartening to find a new institutional development in the form of common treatment plants by small industries which cannot afford its own separate facilities. KSPCB has helped in promoting such plants. Half of the cost of pollution control is shared on mutually agreeable principles among industrial units, and the other half is given as subsidy by the Central government to such plants. One such plant is there for tanneries in Kadugondanahally in Bangalore. This, however, is not a widespread phenomenon and many industries which do not have their own treatment plants dump effluents either in municipal drainage or into streams. The municipalities have to treat polluted water on its behalf and have every right to collect user charges to recover its expenses from defaulting units. The matter is more difficult when there are scattered units which let out effluents into streams, as is being done by coffee pulper plants. Effective enforcement is necessary in their cases too.

It is regrettable that enforcement is inadequate even in the highly polluting category of industries. As per the KSPCB Annual Report for 1992 -93, among the 99 units in this category, only 38 complied with the standards. The situation has, however, improved later, since, according to the Report for 1993-94 , 46 have complied with the requirements out of 85 units identified. An indication of how sparingly KSPCB has been using its powers is that since inception it has issued closure orders to only 12 industrial units under the **Water (Prevention and Control) Act 1974** and to 10 units under the **Air (Prevention and Control) Act 1981.** (KSPCB Annual Report 1993-94: 25). Compared with the corresponding figures in the 1992-93 Report, it seems that a significant number of closure orders were issued during 1993-94 (7 and 6 under the two Acts respectively). The trend is towards greater strictness.

There are a few impediments in the way of KSPCB becoming more effective in dealing with pollution. An important one among them is the inadequate budget and staff. Its total revenue increased no doubt from a mere Rs.2.19 lakhs in 1981-82 to Rs 41.42 lakhs in 1993-94. On the other hand, the number of industrial units coming under the pollution control laws has also increased, standing at 6,088 for water pollution control and 4,483 for air pollution, as at the end of 1993-94 (KSPCB Annual Report for 1993-94:12-3). Clubbing them together, KSPCB had, on an average, Rs. 3,925 to spend during 1993-94 for monitoring and dealing with each unit. This included not only salary and travel allowances, but also purchase of equipment and other fixed assets needed, laboratory maintenance and other expenses incurred during the year. The strength of working staff during 1993-94 was only 203, as against the sanctioned strength of 356. Of the total receipts of Rs.414.2 lakhs during 1993-94, the highest share came from Consent and NOC fees and sale of related farms (Rs. 232.28 lakhs). Water cess reimbursement[5] contibuted Rs. 37.8 lakhs, the state government Rs 26.5 lakhs, The Central Government only Rs.9.2 lakhs, and CPCB, another Rs. 13.6 lakhs. Other sources are fines, earnest money deposits/ security deposits, interest etc.

In addition to the problem of finances and staff strength, the Board has also to assume the burden of indicating what technology to adopt to reduce pollution. such a technology has also to be economically viable. A deterrent charge on effluents and emissions would force the firm to seek a proper technology from consultants in the field and adopt it. If the Board is unable to indicate an economically viable technology, then it feels obliged to be indifferent to the environmental degradation that goes on. In the absence of such a deterrent charge, there is no incentive also to evolve and adopt such a technology.

There is also one more problem. Most of the present standards are based on concentration of pollutants in effluents and emissions. The standards can be met simply by diluting the concentration with the help of more water. Not only are the mass of pollutants not reduced, this leads to wastage of water too. A shift to mass based standards is now mooted to solve this circumvention of standards, but it may take some time.

One of the most glaring lacunae is in checking vehicle emissions. Though the concerned authorities try to catch cars and two wheelers, that too occasionally, the bigger offenders like public transport buses, lorries and autorickshaws are left free. The transport vehicles are not designed to reduce air pollution. Unleaded petrol is reported to have

5. Since water cess is levied under the Central Act, the collection is first credited to the Central Government which is later reimbursed to SPCBs.

been introduced recently, and it will take some time to pick up. There is a similar disregard for pollution at the consuming end in other respects too. For example, several drugs and pesticides banned in other countries are allowed to be manufactured and sold in India. The use of low quality detergents polluting water continues to add to the problem of sewerages.

One of the heartening signs, however, is some increase in the awareness both on the part of industry and government to shift from end-of-pipe treatment or clean-up technologies to clean technologies. In other words, there is a trend towards shift of emphasis from control to prevention of pollution. Policy statements of the Government of India in respect of environment, in general, and industrial pollution, in particular, have voiced the need for such a shift. It is realised that the clean-up technologies merely transfer pollution from one medium to another, and may not enable an overall view, apart from being costlier. However, we have still a long way to go before clean technologies are adopted on a wide scale. The net result of making environmental laws more stringent, building up institutions for monitoring and implementation, increasing possibility of recourse to PIL and a more active role of the judiciary, is that they have compelled industries to take into account environmental consideration in their project design and decision-making process.

Conservation and Improvement of Forests: A reference has been made earlier to the Department of Forests headed by a Secretary, as a part of the Ministry of Forests, Ecology and Environment. The operational part of the Forest Department is under the Principal Chief Conservator of Forests, who is directly in charge of forest conservation and improvement. It is manned by the Indian Forest Service personnel and their subordinate staff. They are answerable to the Secretary for the Department of Forests and to the Ministry of Forests, Ecology and Environment. In terms of staff strength, it is a fairly big department. As on 31.12.1995, it had 7,288 permanent staff, and 3,799 temporary staff in Karnataka (GOK 1995:101).

About one-fifth of the geographical area of the state- as many as 38,724 sq.kms. - are under the direct control of the Forest Department. No other Department has so much area to manage. Not all of this area is under forest cover. Only about 11 per cent of the geographical area of the state, or a little over half of the area under the Forest Department is well wooded (GOK 1995:6). It is the task of the Department not only to conserve the area but also to improve the rest of the area which is in different stages of degradation. Additionally, it also has the task of developing and taking care of road-side plantations in cities and villages, and of promoting tree growing on private lands.

This onerous task is further complicated by the fact that there are competing claims on the use of forests and forest areas. At the global level, forests are needed for carbon sequestration and conservation of biodiversity. This is in the national interest too, but at the national level, the commercial use of forests dominates more as a vested interest. Development projects often involve sacrificing forests, which is another form of demand on forest areas by the growing economy. At the local level, people depend on biomass from the forests - fodder, fuel and even food. The locals also press on the forests for extending the area under cultivation, for which they often get support from local political leaders and the state governments. Periodically, Karnataka too has been regularising encroachments into forest and other public lands. These competing claims are not decided by one decision maker weighing pros and cons from his angle, but often by a political struggle between competing interest groups. This makes the task of the foreest manager rather[6] complex and even confusing.[6]

This needs clear guidelines from policy statements of the government. Forest policies are formulated at the national level, which have from time to time set out priorities. The first Forest Policy Statement

6. For a fuller discussion of the political economy of forest use, see, Nadkarni et al 1989 and Nadkarni 1996.

made in 1894, under the colonial regime, sought to resolve competing claims by demarcating different forests for different purposes. It classed the forest area under the following headings: (a) Forests, the preservation of which is essential on climatic or physical grounds; (b) Forests which afford a supply of valuable timbers for commercial purposes; (c) Minor forests ; and (d) Pasture lands. Forest areas in the first class were to be on hill-slopes and such other ecologically sensitive areas and were meant only for conservation and improvement, and not for exploitation. The forests in the second class were meant for commercial exploitation and for raising the revenue of the state, but 'every reasonable facility' was to be afforded to local people to meet their needs of firewood, grass, manure etc., subject to the restriction that'cultivation must not be allowed to so extend as to encroach upon the minimum area of forest which is needed in order to supply the general forest needs of the country....' (Lok Sabha Secretariat 1985:49). The 'minor forests' and pasture lands were meant essentially for meeting the local needs. On the whole, the 1894 policy placed much greater emphasis on the fulfillment of the needs of the people than of other interests. Its approach continues to have relevance even today. In practice, however, the 1894 policy was not faithfully implemented since commercial needs got priority particularly after the Second World War started.

The 1952 Policy Statement departed from the 1894 policy and was more in conformity with how forests were managed during the Second World War and thereafter. The 1952 Policy conceded that "village communities in the neighbourhood of forest will naturally make greater use of its products", but also warned that "such use, however, should in no event be permitted at the cost of national interests" (Lok Sabha Secretariat 1985:57) The national interests were interpreted more as commercial interests in practice, rather than conservation interests. Independent India, till the late 1980s, subordinated local and conservation needs to commercial needs even more than the earlier colonial government.

Fortunately, the resistance of the people to such a policy and rising consciousness about the need for conservation, led to the formulation of a new National Forest Policy in 1988 which revised the earlier priorities. It declared: "The principal aim of Forest Policy must be to ensure environmental stability and maintenance of ecological balance including atmospheric equilibrium which are vital for sustenance of all life forms, human, animal and plant. The derivation of direct economic benefits must be subordinated to this principal aim" (para 2.2).

It has also to be noted that 'meeting the requirements of fuel wood, fodder, minor forest produce and small timber of the rural and tribal populations' is one of the basic objectives of the National Forest Policy (para 2.1). For meeting the commercial needs, the policy statement suggests using private land of 'individuals' (farmers) instead of forest areas, and recommends credit support and technical advice to them in meeting raw material needs of industries.

The conflicts are far from being resolved even today, specially between local needs and needs of conservation. It is widely felt that it is difficult to do so under an institutional set up of exclusive state control and management of forests. It is true that historically the forests have been owned by the state, which has its own justification. Since the main function of forests is recognised as the provider of environmental goods and services, as in the National Forest Policy of 1988, forests acquire the characteristics of a public good. These services are of utmost importance for the survival of mankind, and hence, the ownership of such a good cannot be left to the caprice of a private individual or corporation or even a local community. No doubt, forests also provide private goods, but this capacity can be accommodated within the framework of public ownership, while the capacity to provide public good cannot be so easily accomodated within the framework of private ownership.

Though the state should have the ownership of forests for these reasons, there has also to be an institutional mechanism whereby private goods produced by forests are sustainably exploited by the people. People have traditionally enjoyed access[7] to government forests including the Reserved forests, but they were alienated from the management of forests. This resulted in **a Tragedy of Commons a la Hardin (1968).** Giving a stake to people in the sustainable use of forests and involving them in their management could avert this tragedy. This is now a widely acknowledged principle, and Joint Forest Management is moving in this direction.

Steps were taken in this direction first in West Bengal, widely known as the Arabari experiment. Its spread in the state gave rise to a lot of optimism, and a circular was issued by the Secretary, Environment and Forests, Government of India, on Ist June, 1990, to Forest Secretaries of all states setting out the new policy on "involvement of Village Communities and Voluntary Agencies in the Regeneration of Degraded Forests". With some lapse of time, different states issued Notifications to introduce this new organising principle. Karnataka issued the Notification on 12th April 1993[8]. The scheme is known in Karnataka as Joint Forest Planning and Management (JFPM).

---

7. The **Indian Forest Act of 1878** recognised three categories of forests- The Reserved Forests, Protected Forests and Village Forests. The government held absolute right of ownership in reserved forests, and their products were not to be used by locals unless specifically permitted. Protected forests were those which were yet to be surveyed and settled, but the locals access and privileges were permitted except in those cases whereby they were specifically prohibited (as in the case of cutting valuable timber yielding trees). It was in the case of village forests that the rights of locals were conceded in respect of grazing, fuel needs, requirement of small wood for implements and own house construction but not for sale or barter. The distinctions between the three categories have survived to date. The village forests and protected forests are, by and large, most degraded since the extent of area under them was very small and the pressure on them was high. The reserve forests are, by and large, much better maintained, though degraded in places where pressures for exploitation both for local and commercial use could not be contained (Nadkarni et al 1989; chs.3 and 4). During 1994-95, there were 28,611 sq.kms. of area under Reserved Forests in Karnataka (74 per cent of total forest area), 3,932 sq.kms. under protected forests (10 per cent of total forest area), the remaining proportion being under unclassed, village and private forests (GOK 1995:67).

8. See, SPWD (1993) for a documentation of GOI Circular (1990) as well as the Notification issued by different states.

The scheme is confined only to degraded forests and their regeneration, and is not extended to the management of the already wooded areas as in Reserved Forests. Such of the Reserved Forests which are degraded can also come under this scheme. Presently, forests which have a canopy cover of less than 25 per cent alone are covered by JFPM, though some NGOs are pressing for covering other already rich forests. The principle in official circles appears to be that prople should be allowed to share the benefits only from the forests they have helped to raise, and that extending joint management to forests already rich could lead to over exploitation.

Anyway, JFPM is not just one scheme, but a new organising principle. The land still belongs to the Forest Department, as it should, but people share the forest produce - both major and minor - and participate in planning and management. Regeneration is planned from the beginning by the people themselves. It is they who take decisions about what species of trees to plant, and not the Forest Departmennt. The management is done through a Village Forest Committee, of which the Member-Secretary and Convener will be the local Forester from the Forest Department. The Committee organises how the grasses, leaves and fuel wood from the designated forest area are to be collected and distributed among beneficiaries. Regarding other Minor Forest produce, timber and fuelwood, the first priority is given to meeting the local needs for self consumption, and the surplus would be disposed off through public auction. The proceeds, after deducting expenses incurred, would be shared between the Village Forest Committee (25 per cent for the Committee's Village Forest Development Fund, and 25 per cent for distribution among beneficiary members as per the rules framed by the Committee,) and the Forest Department (50 per cent).

JFPM has already been introduced in Uttara Kannada and Shimoga districts with Overseas Development Agency (ODA) support and also independently in a few more districts on a more limited scale. A recent study of Uttara Kannada showed a rather mixed response to the scheme, but on the whole, the small and marginal farmers and the landless (who comprise the bulk of rural workers here), felt that they would benefit from it and came forward to support it. A difficulty arises when, as in forest regions, there are no nuclear villages but scattered hamlets and all are not equi-distant from the forest areas taken up for improvement (Pasha 1996).

It would be sad if JFPM ends up merely creating a few show-pieces here and there, instead of launching a widespread movement for sustainable use of forests. There are examples of peoples' management where they have merely diverted grazing pressure and extraction of fuel wood to nearby reserve forests while land under their management is protected, and scarcely used. The effort should rather be directed to sustainably meet the needs of the people within the limits of the forest area taken up for management. As a matter of general principle, all the areas expected to face people's pressure should be brought under JFPM provided that the Village Forest Committee (VFC) finds it feasible to manage it for sustainable use. Taking only parts of areas needed exposes other areas to unsustainable use (Nadkarni 1996).

We cannot take for granted that once forests are handed over to the people for management they will be used sustainably. In the earlier days, this was easier for the people because they did not have to cope with the pressures of commercialisation and population as much as now. Fears are expressed that under the continuation of these pressures, JFPM may break down and lapse into open access regimes. JFPM is a better model than one of exclusive management by the people, because the Forest Department can, as a partner with the people, act as a watchdog on the sustainability of forest use. The draft Forest Bill, circulated by the MEF, rightly provides for a mechanism to wind up VFC and enable the Forest Department to take over the concerned forest when there is unsustainable use of and encroachments into the forest. Certain precautions can be taken to avoid arbitrary action, but there should certainly be a provision for mechanisms to warn against and prevent misuse. It is not yet clear what role the Panchayats will play in JFPM, or for that matter, in enriching and safeguarding natural resource base under their jurisdiction. Their co-operation would be vital to the state government in a sustainable management of environment.

Social forestry schemes were introduced in Karnataka more than a decade before JFPM was launched. While JFPM is initiated in forest areas, social forestry projects were undertaken mostly in what were earlier revenue lands used for grazing livestock. But, only a small fraction of uncultivated lands available for development have been covered by social forestry, so far. In most of these cases, at least in

Karnataka, social forestry projects have been managed by the Forest Department itself rather than by local people. Consistency requires that the principles followed in JFPM are followed here too. Social forestry projects particularly need to give a proper priority to raising grass and other fodder as per the wish of the people, avoiding the usual obsession with trees alone (Nadkarni and Pasha 1991).

There are attempts to promote tree growing on private lands. The **Tree Preservation Act of 1976** specifies the number of trees which should be grown on different types of lands and sites. But the prohibition of tree cutting without permission under the same Act comes in the way of giving incentives to tree growing. People may not like to grow trees on private lands unless they are sure that they are free to cut trees when they want. But in genuine cases, permission to cut is given, though people are afraid of hassles, delay and bribery. There are no restrictions on cutting trees in private lands in the case of trees like eucalyptus and casuarina.

Problems are far from being resolved even in areas which are already under good forests where the need is for protection or conservation rather than improvement. The problem is particularly grave in the national parks and wildlife sanctuaries where there are pockets of human habitation. Plans are on the anvil to take out such human population from protected areas and resettle them on the fringes. This has not been quite welcome to these people as they have been accustomed to live within the forests. Making matters difficult, people living within the protected areas are not allowed to collect minor forest produce and cultivate inside the parks. This has led to great bitterness and conflicts, some times leading to burning down vast stretches of forests. It seems to be extremely difficult and costly to protect the parks and sanctuaries without the co-operation of forest dwellers. It may be wiser to co-opt them into the task of forest protection itself, giving them enough economic incentives for the purpose, instead of taking them out and bring in outsiders to protect the parks[9]. Moreover, schemes of rehabilitation also have to be effective, wherever they are carried out, so that they feel convinced that it makes them better off by moving out of the forests.

9. I owe this idea to Dr. P.J. Dilip Kumar in a personal discussion.

Concluding Remarks: Environmental protection is far from achieved in Karnataka. It needs the honest commitment of both the administration in charge of it and political leadership to achieve this task. There is an extensive institutional and legislative framework already to help this task. May be, we have also to think of evolving economic incentives and disincentives to supplement regulatory mechanisms, to make environmental protection more effective. One of the most heartening signs on the environmental front is the growing awareness of environmental degradation and building up of public opinion in favour of environmental protection. This has made the environmental administration also more alert and responsive.

REFERENCES

Government of India (GOI) (1994). **The Environmental Impact Assessment Notification.** New Delhi: Government of India.

Government of Karnataka (GOK) (1995) **Annual Report of the Forest Department: 1994-95.** Bangalore: Government of Karnataka.

Hardin, G. 1968 The Tragedy of Commons. **Science,** 162.

Lok Sabha Secretariat, (1985). **National Forest Policy.** New Delhi: Lok Sabha Secretariat.

Nadkarni, M.V. (1996). Forests, People and Economies. Presidential Address delivered at the 55th Annual Conference of the Indian society of Agricultural Economics held at IRMA, Anand, November 23. **Indian Journal of Agricultural Economics,** January- March.

Nadkarni, M.V. and Syed Ajmal Pasha. (1991). Developing Uncultivated Lands: Some Issues from Karnataka Experience. **Indian Journal of Agricultural Economics,** 46(4): 543-54.

Nadkarni, M.V.(With Syed Ajmal Pasha and L.S. Prabhakar) (1989). **Political Economy of Forest Use and Management.** New Delhi: Sage

Nadkarni, M.V, G.S. Sastry, Onno Kulk, Frans Oosterhuis and Ackerman (1995). **Best of Both Worlds: A Comparative Assessment of Environmental Policy Approaches in India and the Netherlands** A collaborative study carried out by the Institute for Social and Economic Change, Bangalore, and Institute for Environmental Studies, Amsterdam, under IDPAD. Mimeo.

Opschoor, J.B. and R.K. Turner (1994). **Economic Incentives and Environmental Polices: Principles and Practice.** Dordrecht/ Boston/London : Kluver Academic Publishers.

Pasha, Syed Ajmal. (1996) **Livelihood Systems and Pressure on the Forests of Uttara Kannada, Karnataka.** Bangalore: ISEC. Mime.

Rosencranz, Armin, Shyam Divan and Martha L. Noble (1991). **Environmental Law and Policy in India: Cases, Materials and Statutes.** Bombay : Tripathi.

SPWD (Society for Promotion of Wastelands Development) (1993). **Joint Forest Management Updated.** New Delhi: SPWD.

VI

LAW AND ORDER ADMINISTRATION*

S. Krishnamurthy

A. Brief Overview:

Introduction: The people of Karnataka enjoy a reputation concerning their immense hospitable nature. And yet, problems of crime or problems of law and order have been and as of now are matters of serious concern for the administration. Of course, the burgeoning population and the increase in the influx of people from other parts of the country adds to the increasing crisis zones of police work. Rapid industrialization and urbanisation and increased application of science and technology in the day to day lives of the people have slowly altered the pace and style of life and as a result of that clearly visible transition, the load and variety of problems confronting the police of to-day is indeed becoming very complex. Modernization and urbanization have compounded the issues and the bustling metropolis of Bangalore, currently known as the fastest growing city of Asia, with a population bursting at its seams. The city has to cater to the civic needs of over five million people. As a natural result, the problems of crime and the challenges of law and order assumes enormous significance.

* This paper reflects the personal views of the author, not of the government.

The police of Karnataka account for nearly 65,000 men in Khaki Uniform, inclusive of officers of the Indian Police Service, the State Police Service and the ranks. The sweep of the police is indeed vast in terms of over 750 police stations and over 250 out-posts established over the length and breath of the state for the purposes of serving the people. Civil Police, Armed Police and Special Armed Police are the three main arteries of the force and this outfit is headed by a Director General and Inspector General of Police, stationed in the capital, i.e., at Bangalore.

Present Set Up: The duties and tasks performed by the Karnataka Police are as per the **Karnataka Police Act**, which is itself modeled after the **Indian Police Act, 1861**. Further, the police fulfil the task of law enforcement and the prevention and detection of crimes as per the Code of Criminal Procedure 1973, and other special and local penal legislations. In addition, the police are called upon to fulfil various other socially relevant and service oriented functions, the details of which are too exhaustive to be enumerated. Though, it may not be useful to compare the current day workload of the Karnataka State Police with that of the situation as it existed in the year 1956, it would be still appropriate to have a brief understanding of the present day crime prevention and detection tasks that devolve on the police. Of course, it may not be easy to reflect comprehensively the law and order commitments or the traffic enforcement responsibilities and the substantially increasing social service and other social functions that the police fulfil in the course of their charter of duties.

The Karnataka State Police, as on 1st January 1996, has a fairly big organisational structure with the Director General and Inspector General of Police heading the total manpower of nearly 65,000 personnel. Indeed, this force, way back in the year 1956, at the time of the reorganisation of the states, had a modest manpower of about 23,000 police officers and men of various ranks. The formation of the linguistic state had, in fact, added on to the erstwhile state of Mysore, comprising the nine districts, i.e., Mysore, Bangalore, Hassan, Chickmagalur, Shimoga, Chitradurga, Mandya, Tumkur and Kolar by substantially increasing the geographical as well as numerical dimensions. With the emergence of the unified Karnataka, the police personnel who were serving in the newly merged areas were also seconded to the new state of Mysore which came into being on the first of November 1956, and later was renamed as the State of Karnataka in 1973.

In the reorganised set up there were twenty police districts, excluding Bangalore City (which was jurisdictionally divided as Bangalore North and Bangalore South), the revenue district of Kolar being split into two police districts, Kolar and KGF, which looked after the areas coming under the Kolar Revenue area and the Kolar Gold Field areas respectively. In addition, there was also the Railway Police treated as a separate police district. These twenty districts had been grouped under three ranges, each group being placed in-charge of a Deputy Inspector General of Police (DIG). Initially, there were posts of DIGs at Bellary (covering the districts of the old Mysore area) and at Belgaum. These were reorganised by abolishing the post at Bellary and regrouping the districts as under:

1. Central Range: Districts of Bangalore (including Bangalore City), Kolar, K.G.F, Tumkur, Chitradurga and Bellary.

2. Southern Range: Districts of Mysore, Mandya, Hassan Chickmagalur, Shimoga, Dakshina Kannada and Coorg.

3. Northern Range: Districts of Belgaum, Dharwar, Bijapur, Uttara Kannada, Gulbarga, Raichur and Bidar.

Further, each district was divided, for purposes of police administration, into Sub-divisions, Circles, Police Stations and Out-posts. There have been over the years no change in the number of police districts, even though the number of sub-divisions and circles as well as police stations and police out-posts increased. As at the end of the year 1995, the Karnataka State Police Administration had 20 Police Districts (excluding Bangalore City, Mysore City and Hubli-Dharwar). They are divided into 112 Sub-divisions, 228 Police Stations and 309 Out-posts. Over the years, the workload as well as manpower have also increased warranting the streamlining of the administration periodically. Quality of supervision has become a very important task in that regard. Many posts at the district and sub-division levels have been sanctioned and this has necessitated the imperative of reorganising the regional supervision. New ranges have been established by restructuring the existing districts so that better and quality supervision by an officer of the rank of DIG is available. North-Eastern Range was established in the year 1967 by virtually bifurcating the erstwhile Northern Range. A new Range called the Western Range with its headquarters at Mangalore was created, and another range, called as the Eastern Range with its headquarters at Davanagere, was set up in the year 1980. Bangalore City was the first city in 1963 to have a Police Commissioner to provide policing in that jurisdiction (in 1963). Mysore City and Hubli-Dharwar twin cities were also sanctioned the posts of Police Commissioners (in the rank of a DIG) in the year 1990.

Thus, the broad overview of the State Police ranges (as it exists now) can be briefly stated as under:

Police Commissionerates

1. Bangalore City: Commissioner of Police in the rank of the Additional Director General of Police.

2. Mysore City: Commissioner of Police in the rank of Deputy Inspector General of Police.

3. Hubli-Dharwar City: Commissioner of Police in the rank of Inspector General of Police.

Police Ranges:

1. Central Range - Bangalore Rural, Tumkur, Kolar and KGF.
2. Southern Range - Mysore Rural, Mandya, Kodagu and Hassan.
3. Eastern Range - Chitradurga, Shimoga and Bellary.
4. N-E Range - Gulbarga, Bidar and Raichur.
5. Northern Range - Belgaum, Dharwar Rural and Bijapur.
6. Western Range - Daksina Kannada, Chickmagalur and Uttara Kannada.

In addition, the Railway Police also constitute a separate police entity as the others above.

The strength of the police force at the time of the states reorganisation (1956) may be seen below:

Area	Area in Sq,miles	Population	Gazetted officers	Non Gazetted officers	Junior ranks
Mysore State (including Bellary)	33,000	9,900,000	51	599	12,30
Bombay Districts	21,600	5,130,000	13	194	6,131
South Kanara & Kollegal Taluk	4,300	1,331,000	4	48	
Coorg District	1,500	330,000	3	22	
Hyderabad Districts	13,300	2,700,000	16	175	3,721
Total	73,700	19,391,000	87	1,03	23,122

The strength of Karnataka State Police, as at the beginning of 1995, may be seen below:

Sr. No.	Post/Rank Total	Civil	Women	Armed	KSRP	Wireless	Total
1	DG & IGP	1	1				
2	DGP	3					3
3	ADGP	11					11
4	IGP	8					8
5	DIGP	21			1	1	23
6	SP/Comdt	90		8	10	11	119
7	DY.SP	230		33	35	5	303
8	PI/RPI	809	16	86	92	12	1,015

(Contd.)

Sr. No.	Post/Rank Total	Civil	Women	Armed	KSRP	Wireless	Total
9	PSI/RSI	1,613	34	336	226	92	2,193
10	ASI/ARSI	1,896	12	413	78	185	2,584
11	HC/AHC	7,950	313	2,281	1,762	421	12,727
12	PC/APC	24,299	993	9,882	7,296	307	42,777
13	Followers			284	933		1,217
	Total	**36,931**	**1,368**	**13,213**	**10,435**	**1,034**	**62,981**

Increased population, pressures of modern life, poverty, unemployment, broken homes and several other causative factors account for the increasing workload on the police in so far as their crime prevention and crime detection tasks are concerned. Enormous increase in automobiles has very substantially contributed towards increasing the workload of traffic regulation as well as accident prevention and accident investigation and prosecution etc. Greater social conflicts have compounded the police tasks especially those relating to ushering the new ethos and constitutional values. Illustrations of these can be seen in the police tasks connected with the problems relating to untouchability, dowry, exploitation of women and children, problems relating to labour and other land and economic reforms. To sum up, the crimes have shown a steady increase over the last four decades. It may be useful to have a bird's-eye view of the current day work load on the Karnataka police.

The duties and tasks performed by the Karnataka Police are as per the Karnataka Police Act, which itself is modelled after the **Indian Police Act, 1861**. Further, the police fulfil the task of law enforcement and the prevention and detection of crimes as per the **Code of Criminal Procedure, 1973** and other special and local penal legislations. In addition, the police are called upon to fulfill various other socially relevant and service oriented functions, the details of which are too exhaustive to be enumerated. Though, it may not be useful to compare the current day workload of the Karnataka State police with that of the situation as it existed in the year 1956, it would be still appropriate to have a brief understanding of the present day crime prevention and detection tasks that devolve on the police. Of course, it may not be easy to reflect comprehensively the law and order commitments or the traffic enforcement responsibilities and the substantially increasing social service and other social functions that the police fulfil in the course of their charter of duties. During the year 1995, a total of 120,334 cognizable cases were registered under the Indian Penal Code. The details of cases registered under various heads are as under:

1.	Murder for gain	62
2.	Dacoity	307
3.	Robbery	1,081
4.	House breaking and ordinary thefts	1,84,855
5.	Cattle thefts	10
6.	Receiving stolen property	7
7.	Cheating	1,984
8.	Counterfeit coins and currency notes	77
9.	Criminal breach of trust	607
10.	Murder other than for gain	1,672
11.	Rioting	9,665
12.	Fatal motor accidents	4,697
13.	Culpable homocide not amounting to murder	57
14.	Admission of stupefying drugs	4
15.	Kidnapping	575
16.	Rape	262
17.	Other I.P.C. cases	70,060
	Total	**120,334**

Cases under Special and Local Laws: In all, 578,442 cases were reported during the year 1995 under the Special and Local Laws. The details of cases reported are as under

1.	Antiquity and Art Treasure Act	2
2.	Arms Act	127
3.	Prohibition of Child Marriage Act	1
4.	Dowry Prohibition Act, 1961	227
5.	Essential Commodity Act	169
6.	Excise Act	1,797
7.	Explosive Act	76
8.	Gambling Act	4,802
9.	Indian Passport Act	3
10.	Indian Railway Act	9
11.	N.D.P.S.Act	181
12.	Prevention of Food Adulteration Act	1
13.	Prohibition Act	21
14.	Registration of Foreigners Act	18
15.	Other Special and Local Laws	571,008
	Total	**5,78,442**

From a historical perspective, it would be appropriate to note that many pioneering efforts were initiated and completed in those formative years to bring uniformity and cohesiveness to the new police system by endeavouring to evolve a common Police Act; a common Police Manual (1958) as well as several other penal legislations relevant to public order and connected matters. Yet, it is a fact that the roots of the current day set up can be found in the massive and sustained efforts of the police forerunners and the political leaders of that era.

As a first step after the formation of the new state, the police administration took upon itself the arduous task of reorganisation of nearly almost all the district police set ups and the first of such changes were effected in the year 1959. The police all over the country celebrated the police centenary during the year 1961 and closely following that event was the historic liberation of Goa during the year 1962 where a fairly big contingent of officers and men were deputed from the state to assist the liberated Goa administration in the maintenance of law and order and also in policing the capital of Goa, Panaji.

Bangalore City Police: After the formation of the new state, several far-reaching proposals were sanctioned in 1963 with regard to the area and jurisdiction of Bangalore City. As a consequence, the post of Commissioner of Police of the rank of the Deputy Inspector General of Police and the placement of four Deputy Commissioners of Police to assist the Commissioner were created. The city was divided into functional areas of police work. Further, 13 police sub-divisions and two traffic divisions were set up. The establishment of the City Armed Reserve Police (CARP) with a Deputy Commissioner to head that unit and creation of a Special Branch with a DCP to supervise that area of work were other important changes. The Bangalore City Police was given a modest wireless facility and a control room was also set up. The second reorganisation took place in 1978 when its jurisdiction was enlarged. The third reorganisation of the Bangalore City Police was done in the year 1984 with the creation of one more post of the Deputy Commissioner for the Central Armed Reserve Police(CARP) at Audugodi.

The functional division of work at the Deputy Commissioner of Police level was restructured in the year 1992 and the jurisdictional distribution of work was the new pattern. Currently, the post of the Commissioner of Police, Bangalore, is held by an officer of the rank of an Additional Director General of Police and is assisted by three Additional Commissioners of Police (all in the rank of DIG) and the police network has been streamlined during the years 1990 and 1993. A new police control room is envisaged in the year 1996 and is in the process of implementation. The creation of an exclusive women's police station and other special arrangements to look into the complaints of women is another feature of the 90s.[1]

1. The present day police staff pattern for the Bangalore City are Commissioner of Police-1; Additional Commissioner of Police-3; Deputy Commissioner of Police-13; Assistant Commissioner of Police-41 Police Inspectors-80; Police Sub-Inspectors-206; Assistant Sub-Inspectors-192; CHCs-1,448; and CPCs-4,089. Armed Wing consisting of ACPs-11, PIs-23; RSIs-68, ARSIs-123, ACHs-549; and ACPs-2,476.

The Criminal Investigation Department of the State Police: Long before the unified state of Mysore came into being in the year 1956, the Mysore State Police had a Criminal Investigation Division which was reorganised as the CID (Central Crime Branch) in the year 1958. Political Intelligence was being handled by the Special Branch. Similar arrangements to collect, collate and utilise Criminal Intelligence to prevent as well as detect crimes were in vogue in the erstwhile Hyderabad-Karnataka and Bombay-Karnataka Districts. Likewise, districts like Daksihna Kannada and Bellary carried with them similar experiences. Kodagu (Mercara district) had its own indigenous brand of police experience and after the reorganisation of 1956, uniformity was perhaps one of the most important efforts of the police leadership. Amongst such endeavour, the evolution of the common police manual deserves mention and this task was completed by the middle of the 60s. The reorganisation of the Auxiliary units functioning under the Deputy Inspector General of Police CID and Railways - which included the Scientific Laboratory at Bangalore and the Central Crime Branch was done in the year 1958 besides augmenting the strength of the CID. After nearly a decade's experience, the need to streamline the CID was felt and after a systematic study and planning, a blueprint was evolved to establish a new outfit under the CID to tackle important and specialised crimes. The persistent efforts to bring into life this system gave results in the year 1974 with the sanction to set up the Corps of Detectives.

The Corps of Detectives: The Corps of Detectives was established in 1974 and it is popularly known by its acronym COD. The primary objective in setting up the COD was to vest with that unit the responsibilities of investigating economic offences, cases involving grave financial irregularities, other major and complicated cases, which would be given a better and comprehensive attention by the skilled and knowledgeable personnel who would be chosen specially keeping in mind their aptitude and abilities. Initially, the COD was commissioned with four main sub units called by the name of squads: homicide, burglary, counterfeit and arms and fraud. With the rise of special problems like the dowry menace engulfing various sections of the society, an Anti-Dowry Cell in the COD headed by an officer of the rank of a Superintendent of Police, was established in the year 1987. Closely following it was the establishment of the Anti-Dacoity Squad in the year 1988.

Keeping in view the need for specialised and quality output from the COD, it was designed such that only the government or the DGP or the head of the COD could decide on taking up a case for investigation. Later, it became necessary to assign tasks and jobs which not only warranted very skilled handling, but also the cases in which the public interest was focussed. As a result the COD was directed to take up **suo moto** cases and instances of custodial deaths, Dowry deaths and Gun running and Counterfeit Currency offences. The special enquiries squad was constituted and, time and again, called upon to take up delicate and sensitive matters for a thorough probe and report, and many of the cases handled by the COD has had to investigate matters involving bureaucrats and senior level officials, individuals, politicians and highly placed persons in the social hierarchy and public standing. It must be mentioned here that a number of specialised cells have been constituted under the COD to deal with problems such as, unearthing and prosecuting the culprits.

Science and Police Works: Karnataka was one of the pioneering states to have steadily and systematically internalised a scientific approach to police work. A historical perspective of the growth and development of the application of science to police work would surely provide an interesting backdrop.

Forensic Science Laboratory: The first effort to reorganise a scientific laboratory was made in 1958 and at present, the department has a more or less self-contained Forensic Science Laboratory. This unit has steadily grown in its area of work and has occupied a very vital and crucial place in the efforts of the department to fight crime. Over the years the unit has acquired many sophisticated equipments and is also manned by well qualified Technicians and other professionals in the organisation. This unit has now become capable of every kind of analysis relating to DNA finger printing.

The Karnataka government intends to have regional forensic laboratories in all the police range headquarters and already. Forensic

Laboratories have become functional in Davangere (1994) and Mangalore. Mobile forensic units have also been operating since 1992-93, which assist the scientific aids staff to make a preliminary opinion at the scene of incident or crime and thus speed up the criminal justice processes.

In addition to the facilities mentioned above, 'Investigator's kit box' has been provided to the police stations since 1972. However, due to certain administrative and other constraints the scheme really failed to get well settled. To remedy this situation, a new Scientific Investigator's Kit Box has been brought out during the year 1996 and has been supplied to nearly half of the police stations in the state. The success of this scheme can be gauged by the fact that there has been a very widespread and serious requests from many of the states in the country for the supply of kit boxes for their police stations as well.

The Finger Print Bureau (FBB) existed in the state of Karnataka (erstwhile state of Mysore) even prior to 1930. and by the time of State reorganisation, a fully equipped Finger Print Bureau had been organised. Currently, the Central unit of the Finger Print Bureau of the state is based at Bangalore and has a single officer units at all the district headquarters and also the Police Commissionerates at Hubli-Dharwar and Mysore City. The FPB is headed by an officer of the rank of a Superintendent of Police and has staff supporting the unit head with a sanctioned strength of nearly 150 personnel. It is worth noting that, as on date, there are over one lakh finger prints and is the data base. Consequent to the realisation that identification processes occupy a primary importance in police work, the department is in the process of acquiring a computer based system that can enable the personnel to automatically register, store, compare and identify finger prints. It can be mentioned that during the year 1995, the FPB had nearly 75,000 finger print record slips and had over 133,000 single digit cards on record and has been able to establish identity in over 400 cases during the year.

Computer Centre: The Karnataka State Police started switching over to computerisation of records and data in the country way back in the year 1973 itself. The centre has been modernised with latest computers.

All the districts are now having computer facilities and are being used for building up data base as well as for office management. Initially, when the computers were introduced in the police department in 1972, it was primarily for the preparation of the pay-roll, but now the computer application has been steadily covering increasing ambit of police work inclusive of personnel information, motor vehicles inventory, criminal data and stores Inventory etc. Computeration of data has enabled the states as well as National Crime Record Bureau (NCRB) to come up with the Crime in India reports at least within two years after the end of each calendar year and it has helped the police all over the country to plan and prepare for their crime prevention strategies. In this regard the Karnataka Police have now got from the NCRB the needed hardware as well as software data and information.

The State Crime Record Bureau:(SCRB) is a very vital data base generating wing of the police department of the state and is, in fact, reflecting the national pattern to prepare the police organisations to collect, collate and prepare criminal intelligence as well as verification of suspects and others in the combined task of fighting crime. With the escalating crime figures all over the country coupled with the emergence of newer types of crimes, the need for a well documented data base was felt at the apex level of the country and as a result a policy was evolved to establish, develop and sustain criminal record networks which can run at tandem to the National Crime Record Bureau. Accordingly, the SCRB was established in the year 1990 and it maintains a close liaison with the NCRB.

Directorate of Civil Rights Enforcement: The Civil Rights Enforcement Cell was established in the year 1974 in the state of Karnataka under the police department. Initially, the Cell was headed by a Superintendent of Police. During the year 1978, a post of a Deputy Inspector General of Police to head this unit was created and in the year 1980, the Cell was reorganised into four regional cells, one each at Belgaum, Gulbarga, Mysore and Bangalore. In the year 1988, a post of IGP was created to head this cell. In the year 1992, the unit was redesignated as the Directorate of Civil Rights Enforcement and a Director General of Police was positioned to guide the activities of the organisation. Two more regional units at Davanagere and Mangalore were also established. Currently, the head of this Directorate is an officer of the rank of Additional Director General of Police.

The main objective of this unit was to ensure stricter enforcement of the provision of the Protection of the **(Civil Rights Act, 1956,)** and to deal with the cases of harassment and atrocities perpetrated against the members of the Scheduled Castes and Scheduled Tribes. In addition, the cell was also expected to closely monitor the progress of investigation of cases registered by the local police in all parts of the state arose. Consequent to the introduction of the **Scheduled Castes and Scheduled Tribes (Prevention of Atrocities) Act,** 1989, the unit was also assigned similar tasks in relation to the new law.

During the year 1975, the Government of Karnataka expanded the scope of activities of the Cell and added the following areas of work in terms of collection of intelligence and to cause investigation in appropriate cases in respect of violation of legislative provisions/ government orders/commissioners officers regarding the following; reservation of posts for SCs and STs, utilisation of funds for the welfare and development of SCs and STs, Land grant rules, eviction of SCs and STs, from general lands, grant of sites, eviction of SCs and STs by the landlords, eviction of SCs and STs by other communities and government agencies, production of false certificates, offences under the **Bonded Labour Abolition Act 1975,** mismanagement and misuse of grants provided by the Social Welfare Department, violation of constitutional safeguards and protection of SCs and STs, and any other matter pertaining to the violation of any law or rule concerning the SCs and STs.

As on date, the Directorate has a strength of one Addl. DGP, one DIGP, three SPs, five Deputy SPS, twentytwo Inspectors of Police and thirtytwo Sub-inspectors of Police and supporting staff, inclusive of ministerial officials.

Statistics of Cases under the Protection of Civil Rights Act 1956

Year	Cases	False	True	PT	UPI	CON	ACE	OD	B/C	UN
		Reported				Reported				
1991	645	62	583	466	—	79	2	36	-	-
1992	456	59	396	336	—	23	3	34	-	-
1993	376	31	345	174	129	2	-	22	16	1
1994	769	6	763	343	360	8	58	24	25	3

Under the Scheduled Castes and Scheduled Tribes (Prevention of Atrocities) Act, 1989,

Year	Cases	False	True	PT	UPI	CON	ACE	OD	B/C	UN
		Reported				Reported				
1991	510	28	482	331	1	117	17	15		
1992	625	51	574	420	4	112	24	14		
1993	906	70	836	606	67	1	107	13	39	
1994*	778	28	750	272	438	-	13	21	4	

(**Note:** indicates details up to September 1994)

The Commissioner for Scheduled Castes and Scheduled Tribes has, in the summary of recommendations, suggested several steps for the effective enforcement of **the Protection of the Civil Rights Act, 1955,** and also the National Commission on Scheduled Castes and Scheduled Tribes, in its report on the atrocities on Scheduled Castes and Scheduled Tribes (1990), has made some useful suggestions for the effective implementation of the **SC/ST (POA) Act, 1989,** and they may be usefully availed for ensuring better enforcement of that law.

Karnataka State Reserve Police: The necessity for having an armed wing to assist the civil police in times of serious law and order situations and other emergencies is indeed beyond question. In fact, even during the time of the alien rule, contingents from the army and other defence forces used to be committed to assist the civil administration during those crisis hours. Slowly, the administration and the police organisation realised the need to raise and maintain such well-trained armed units as a bulwark against breakdown of public order. Accordingly, Special Armed Police units came to be established much before the dawn of independence. In the erstwhile state of Mysore, the first of such units was known by its nomenclature "Provincial Reserve Police' and was redesignated as the "Mysore State Reserve Police" in the year 1950. Following the reorganisation of states, three active companies of the "Hyderabad State Reserve Police" were allotted to the Mysore State. However, the need to raise such a well-trained armed outfit was increasingly felt and such a specialised unit was formally raised in the year 1958. In the year 1961, the government agreed to raise the strength of the KSRP to one and half battalions. But, there was another commitment agreed upon by the southern states to assist each other in times of law and order crisis by making available their respective reserve police for a common force for the southern zone. In the year 1977, the state agreed to raise the overall strength of the KSRP to two battalions and by the year 1977 the increasing pressure of law and order and other inevitable needs made the police organisation envisage a phased growth for the KSRP into a force with five battalions and two of such units were stationed at Bangalore and the other three were located at Mysore.

Now the KSRP (renamed) has a strength of 10,000 with the Battalion of the KSRP having been sanctioned in the year 1993.

Over the years, a need has been felt that the State Reserve Police Battalions which were utilised by the police and state administration for all law and order situations, must be modulated as a specialised force capable of dealing with special and difficult problems rather than allowing it to continue as an available armed manpower for all matters of routine internal security. With that new awareness, the police leadership has ventured to prepare a portion of the KSRP being slowly conditioned to:

i) handle specially sensitive law and order matters; and

ii) deal with situations caused by extremists, other dangerous and deadly gangs like those of dacoits, and other potentially hazardous elements.

In order to prepare the KSRP to effectively function, better training has been provided and higher resource allocation has been made. One Battalion of the KSRP (i.e., IX Battalion) has been designated as the Special Action force (1993-94) and three companies out of this Battalion are specially trained to deal with very sensitive law and order matters, and other three companies are trained to deal with the challenges posed by terrorists, dacoit gangs and other armed elements.

Another major policy decision (1994-95) is to remove the legal and administrative hurdles to enable transfer of personnel from the KSRP units to the district armed forces so that relatively young, physically young and active manpower is sustained in the state reserve police units.

Police Wireless: Means of communication assumes a very significant position in any area of public administration and more so in a police oganisation. A Wireless Signalling Company was established in the year 1946, drawing ex-servicemen in the erstwhile state of Mysore. Initially, they were trained in the Army Signalling Training Centre at Jalahalli, Bangalore, and by the year 1951, all the nine district headquarters were linked with the state headquarters. Morse Code was the means of communication. VHF communication was set up by the year 1958 and voice communication became possible and the initial use of such a facility was made for police arrangements covering VIP visits. By the time the states reorganisation took place, there were nearly 39 Radio Stations spread all over the state. As the need to establish communication with other parts of the state as well, more and more static stations began to be set up, and during the year 1959 the government sanctioned static units at all District headquarters and also at several other important locations. By the year 1961 and 62, Mobile Radio Stations came to be set up. Bangalore City got its first police control room in the year 1963 with a VHF network and had nearly 10 Mobile communicating units. Teleprinters were introduced into the police department by availing the lines made available by the Post and Telegraphs department. Bangalore, Mysore, Gulbarga and Belgaum were the first units which had a dedicated Teleprinter network for the police and by the year 1977, most of the districts were connected by the Teleprinter network. Slowly VHF networks were established in all the district headquarters, and in major cities like Mangalore, Davanagere, Hubli-Dharwad, Belgaum, Mysore, Shimoga, KGF, Bellary, Gulbarga and Bidar. Hill features in Mysore, Bangalore, Dharwad and Chitradurga were availed to establish unhindered communications. Control rooms in smaller towns like Channapattana, Tumkur, Kolar, Mandya, Chickmagalur, Hassan, Raichur, Karwar, Madikere and Bijapur were also set up. To aid prompt and quick maintenance of all communication equipment, workshops were established in places like Tumkur, Kolar, Mandya, Madikere, Chickmagalur, Hassan, Raichur, Karwar and Bijapur. By the year 1975, almost all the districts were provided with HQ and static stations and were also capable of setting up transportable stations in case of urgent need. This scheme was extended to cover communication network with important police stations on the National Highway and further, it was extended to cover all the police stations in the state, a significant task that was completed by the year 1982. A technical cell was set up in the State Police Grid in the year 1982 to aid improvements in the technical aspects of communication in the department.

In the year 1989, Automac set up was established to enable E-mail facility in the department and to ensure secrecy for certain communications and scramblers were introduced in the year 1996. Teleprinter network between Bangalore, Mysore, Mangalore, Belgaum, Dharwar Gulbarga and Davangere (covering all Range Headquarters locations) were made by the year 1996. Hotline facility between Bangalore and all district units was operational in 1994. Control rooms with modern facilities were functional by the 1990s and Internal telephone exchanges were also provided in Bangalore, Mysore, Hubli-Dharwar, Mangalore and entwining the emergency calls with the Fire Services has also been made by the year 1992.

State Intelligence: The State Special Branch was reorganised in the year 1958 and the unit was headed by an officer of the rank of a Deputy

Inspector General of Police, who supervised both the Crime Branch and the State Special Branch. The Special Branch is engaged in the task of collection of intelligence on all matters affecting the law and order and public tranquility in the state. The organisation of the State Special Branch got a fillip in the years 1975 and 1976 by the sanction of additional staff at several levels. A post of DIG (Intelligence) was created in the year 1980 and the entire set up underwent a reorganistion, and the state intelligence machinery got a broad based staff placement and was also spread out geographically by the location of senior level officers at the ranges. In the year 1982, the two wings of the unit, formerly known as the State Special Branch and the Intelligence Branch were integrated and redesignation of posts in the set up were also effected. Over the years, the State Intelligence Branch has grown and is currently headed by an officer of the rank of an Additional Director General of Police.

Railway Police: At the time of reorganisation the state could boast of railway lines which were nearly 2,595 kilometers long and had Broad, Metre and Narrow guages. In the year 1956, the Railway Police which were functional in all the integrated parts were merged and made into four police circles, twelve railway police stations and thirty police outposts served by a police district headed by a Superintendent of police and 457 officers and men of vairous ranks. In the year 1982, the Railway Police came under charge of an officer of the rank of a Deputy Inspector General of Police. The Railway Police has currently under its set up three subdivisions, seven circles, eighteen police stations and twenty five out-posts.

Forest Cell: In order to prevent smuggling of the precious sandalwood in the forests of the state, especially in the districts of Shimoga, Kodagu, Souh Kanara and North Kanara, a special force was set up in the year 1972 with a team headed by an officer of the rank of a Deputy Inspector General of Police. This squad was strengthened in the year 1974. Again, in the year 1980, further increase in staff was made.

Police Training: A police school was established in the year 1867. Landmark changes were seen successively in the years 1892, 1897, 1914, 1917, 1921, 1927 and 1939. At the time of the formation of the greater Mysore State (in the year 1956) the then existing Central Recruits Training Centre at Bidar, and at Mysore were catering to the needs of police training of constabulary for the northern as well as sourthern zones of the state. The school at Bangalore had been relocated at Mysore (1952) and in the year 1958, a college section was constituted as a separate wing designed to train the middle level officers, (i.e., sub-inspectors as well as Gazetted officers). Over the next decade, many innovative and far-reaching changes were seen in the Mysore training unit. In the meanwhile, the department chose to close the Bidar and Mysore schools which were training the constabulary and in its place a new police training school was envisaged (1958). A new location was found in Channapattana to establish a major constable's training centre and it became fully functional in the year 1964. Thus, the training of officers and men was shared by these two institutions at Mysore and Channapattana respectively.

The transition by way of better and more capable trainers came in its wake and over the years, the syllabus for the training also got overhauled in stages. From the year 1965, the Police Training college at Mysore commenced providing refresher courses for the Sub-Inspectors and Inspectors. In addition, the PTC also began providing training for the Motor Vehicles Inspectors and the Regional Transport Officers.

By the year 1977, the number of untrained constabulary had become substantial due to the limited capacity of the KSPTS, Channapattana, and therefore, three temporary police training schools were established at Dharwar, Gulbarga and Mysore to tide over the problem. In the meanwhile, the need for ensuring training for the newly recruited armed force personnel for the district/city armed reserves as well as the Karnataka State Armed Reserve Police battalions was keenly felt and comprehensive proposals were initiated by the Inspector General of Police to establish the needed institutions. The Government of Karnataka formally sanctioned that proposal in the year 1982 to establish the temporary institutions of Mysore and Rayapura (situated between Hubli-Dharwar cities) to train the freshly recruited constabulary and a new insitution at Khanapura in Belgaum district to train the State Reserve Police. However, due to administrative constraints the KSRP school at Khanapur was to be a temporary unit.

Karnataka Police Academy: The training of the officers of the department, viz., the Sub-Inspectors of Police and the directly recruited Deputy Superintendents of Police (State Service) had got established in the year 1958 with the establishment of a Police Training College at Mysore. This premier institution of police learning has grown from strength to strength over the years. Besides, the initial training of the young and freshly recruited Sub-Inspectors of Police as well as the directly recruited Deputy Superintendents of Police (of the state service), the Police Training College commenced the much needed in-service reorientation programmes for the Inspectors of Police from the year 1965. In addition to ensuring the induction training for the officers of the Indian Police Service who got allotted to the Karnataka Cadre, the Police Training College at Mysore slowly enlarged its ambit and area of training by meeting the tasks of training freshly recruited women police constables and also the promotional programmes for the Head Constables and the Assistant Sub-Inspectors of Police (on their promotion to that rank) so that they are able to fulfill the new and increased professional responsibilities.

The most important part of any training relates to the curriculum development and planning syllabus for the trainees. Since decades, most of these institutions were being run on the basis of past experience and a general idea as to the subjects relevant to police and policing. However, the Government of India had appointed a high powered Committee on Police Training (popularly known as the Gore Committee) and the considered recommendations of that body were available in the year 1971. The Government of Karnataka accepted the recomendations in toto and slowly started incorporating the suggestions made by that body covering all aspects of selection, recruitment and training of police personnel at all levels. The training syllabus has been undergoing systematic changes so as to suit the police capabilities to serve an enlightened and egalitarian modern society.

The police training college was redesignated as the Karnataka Police Academy in the year 1991 and has been slated for a reorganisation of the staff and upgradation of the facilties.

As it is obvious that there are various specialised and exclusive areas of police work, the need to establish training centres for each of such activity was natural. Accordinaly, the Special Branch Training Centre was established at Bangalore during the early 1970s. The Wireless Training Centre was set up in the year 1981. Besides, the KPA and the KSPTS at Channapattana, an exclusive training centre to train the Armed Police Constabulary was commenced at the City Armed Reserve Headquarters at Bangalore in 1984.

With the need for ensuring systematic training of freshly entering police constabulary and with the limited capacity of the existing training facilities, temporary police schools were started in all the districts in the year 1993, and in three batches the backlog of 5,000 constables needing training was more or less cleared.

The department has also evolved a 'Training Policy' document (1995) that covers all aspects of police training and relates all areas of police profession.

Traffic Enforcement and Education: The Bangalore City Police, as early as 1962, did initiate a standardised training procedure for the traffic policemen by a scheme known as 'Traffic Training and Propaganda'. The formative years of organising a proper traffic arrangement to enable smooth movement of vehicular traffic was seen in the efforts of the police leaders who held the task of policing the Bangalore City, and indeed, the meagre traffic police strength of around 300 policemen got increased to around 500 policemen in the year 1963. First in the line of change was the establishment of Traffic Co-ordination Committee in the year 1963 comprising of the Bangalore City Corporation, Bangalore Civil Administration and Police officers. By the year 1975, a 'Traffic Training Institute' was established and it was intended to train Sub-inspectors, Head Constables and Police Constables in the matter of prevention of accidents, traffic regulations, tracking down traffic offenders, road safety measures and to acquaint them with the motor vehicle rules and relvant provisions of the law including traffic engineering. In addition, the training schedules covered the areas of scientfic investigation and prosecution of fatal and other major traffic accidents. Another particularly useful area of work done by this Institute relates to the efforts to train Autorickshaw drivers and also BTS drivers in the observance of traffic rules. To these continuing efforts, the government also sanctioned in the year 1975 an accident relief unit to assist immediately the victims of road accidents. In order to educate the members of the public on matters relevant to road use, 'traffic weeks' were also systematically organised since the middle of the 1970s.

Women Police: The women police wing was, for the first time, established in the state in the year 1960 and since then there has been a steady growth of women police. Inititially, the nature and type of work assigned to women police were related to questioning or guarding women prisioners or suspects and for other emergent law and order duties where female population were involved. In addition, they were expected to assist the male police officers in the enforcement of legislations concerning women. Slowly, this position is changing in that they (women police) are undertaking arduous and other general duties. Important changes are seen in the volume of intake of women police and in the '90s, exculsive women police stations were also established in many of the districts of the state. As at the beginning of 1996, there are nearly 1,400 women police officers. This includes officers of the rank of Inspector and below. It is a point to note that there are a fair number of women Indian Police Service Officers working in the state cadre.

Police Research Centre: The idea of establishing a full-fledged research wing in the police department was inspired by the Conference of the Inspectors General of Police held at the national level in the year 1956. However, due to financial constraints the idea could result in a small unit which became functional in the year 1964 and had its workplace situated in the office of the Inspector General of Police at Bangalore. The Police Research Centre has, over the years, undertaken several data collection and study activities, and a substantial amount of work was turned out especially in the '70s and later on. Initially, a post of Deputy Superintendent of Police was sanctioned in the year 1964. The post of the head of the unit was upgraded to the level of

Superintendent of Police in the year 1972 and currently, the post of the chief of the police research centre is held by an officer of the rank of a Deputy Inspector General of Police (since 1982).

Village Defence Parties or the Grama Rakshaka Dala: Since100 years a system of rural police existed, with variations in the different areas of the state' and such an arrangement depended on the functionaries at the village level. In Bombay-Karnataka areas, persons known as Police Patels, assisted by Walikars, were expected to assist the district police in the collection of criminal intelligence and also render help when the executive police visited the villages for all law enforcement duties. Similarly, in the old Mysore areas, the Police Patels, assisted by talwars or thotis performed similar functions. Bellary, Coorg and Mangalore also had somewhat similar set ups and generally the office of the village headman or patel was hereditary. After the advent of the Constitution of India, all these herediatry offices were abolished by law in the year 1963, though they were asked to continue until such time alternatives were made for the discharge of duties hitherto performed by them. In Karnataka, a village Defence system was conceived on the basis of the provisions of the **Karnataka Police Act, 1963,** and a system of village policing evolved. After a careful examination, a new law called the **Mysore Village Defence Parties Act, 1964,** was enacted and rules were also made thereunder. However, a change was envisaged under the new law that the Dalapathy of the village was to be appointed in place of the village police and a voluntary police system raised. In the year 1975, the organisation and control of the village police under the Dalapathis was transferred to the care of the District Superintendents of police and the Inspector General of Police of the state. The VDPs as they are known is a voluntary force, with a strength of around 10 per cent of the population of each village and the Dalapathy of such village defence party is to be a non political person and briefly stated, these voluntary outfits were expected to perform almost all the tasks done hitherto by the village police patels and others mentioned earlier. As on November 1985, there were nearly over 16,636 Village Defence Parties with a total membership of nearly 386,369 members and 12,631 Dalapathis were rendering the much needed service. Rules for the administration of the scheme and guidelines for running the system have been drawn up and the system is considered very useful and relevant from the point of view of rural policing in the state.

Problems relating to Police Administration: In the foregoing paragraphs, the factual position regarding the present day organisation of the Karnataka Police and various aspects of its functioning have been discussed. However, it may be relevant to refer to some problems of Karnataka police administration, a reference to which was made recently by the Karnataka Minister of State for Home. He stated that top priority is being given to improve transport, communication and housing facilities to the police personnel. He mentioned that only 405 police stations, out of 678, had vehicles. He added that only 38 per cent of the police force have been provided housing as against 68 per cent recommended by the National Police Commission headed by Sri Dharam Vira. There was also a need to fill up the vacant posts and to impart in-service training to police personnel to make them physically and mentally better equipped to tackle emergencies. In the border districts, where terrorist and extremist elements were functioning, there was a need to strengthen the district administration by providing adequate and better arms and communication. Referring to the need for improving communication facilities, he mentioned that the wireless sets provided did not function properly and it was proposed to provide sophisticated suitcases to DIGs and SPs which will contain satellite linked modern communication equipment. The modernisation of the communication system, especially for traffic monitoring, though launched formally in June last year, has not taken off due to various reasons. He added that the police also have to be trained in the use of the high-tech equipment. In Bangalore, which has been the fast growing city in India for decades, there is a need for urgently modernising police control room to ensure effective response to law and order problems. There has been delay in modernising the control room and sooner the hightech equipment is installed and people are trained in the use of the equipments, the better it would be for improving the efficiency of the Bangalore city police.

In the all India context, it is also necessary to take note of the contemporary trends in the present day law and order administration.

Since independence, as stated earlier, the police perform many more tasks arising from increasing urbanisation, crime, labour disputes and industrial unrest, agrarian unrest, students agitation and enforcement of a number of economic and social laws and legislations and disturbances from other tensions, as well as from convulsions and changes in the social, economic and political spheres. Further, in recent years, terrorist activities in many parts of the country have led to the increase in violence and spread of possession of illegal arms and explosives. In the pursuit of socio-economic justice, many social tensions are created resulting in law and order problems.

In spite of the changes that are taking place, even today the Indian **Police Act of 1861** is still in force. The Administrative Reforms Commission (1966) stated that there has been no change in the role of the police since 1861. The National Police Commission set up by the Government of India in /1977 concurred that the basic character of the police is not very different now from then, both in the minds of the administration as well as of the public and that this is one major area which requires attention. But even after 50 years of India's independence, the public image about the police is still poor. The public perceive the police as corrupt, inefficient, brutal and vindictive. Merely increasing the police force to keep pace with increase in the volume of work and introduction of modern methods of investigation and crime detection and science and technology in police methods and strategies are no doubt essential, but are not sufficient to improve the image of the police. The National Police Commission in its first report in 1979 pointed out that the basic fundamental problem regarding the police today is to make them function as an efficient and impartial law enforcement agency guided by the objectives of service to the public at large upholding the constitutional rights and liberty of the people.

In today's democratic set up, the outlook of the police has to be people oriented. A sense of security, both for the public and the people has to be created. The police involvement in the handling of social and economic offences as also traffic violation has made increased confrontation with a wholly different class of offenders. The police has to handle such offenders with tact and finesse with due regard to the regulation of law.

Corruption in the police is a major area of concern. As in any other branch of public administration, it is closely linked with the scope for exercise of power to the advantage or disadvantage of someone or the other. This problem has become complex because of the nexus bewteen the officers, politicians including ministers and undesirable elements in the society. Of late, the phenomenon of criminalisation of politics and the presence of large number politicians with criminal record has, to a great extent, led to demoralisation in the functioning of the police and advertsely affected the public-police relations. Instances are not wanting of the use of the police by the ruling parties to sustain and enhance their power and clout. Problems are also created when policy decisions which can provoke law and order problems are not discussed with police officers before they are announced. Indiscriminate transfer of police without any charge of dereliction of duty against them is ample proof of the odd behaviour of the political executive. Cognisable offences committed by politically organised groups are often not pursued.

In this context, the problems relating to the police administration have to be addressed by the Central and state governments without delay. The problem areas and suggested remedial measures are as under:-

i) The duties, power and responsibilities of the police have to be redefined for what they were when the Act of 1861 was passed.

ii) In view of vast changes in the completion of the work they have to do and meet the new challenges of terrorism, subversion, insurgency, gender violence etc, the public relations of the police with the community need improvement. For this, institutional arrangements, as well as training, especially for lower level offices, have to be made to change and modernise the outlook of the police to make it more friendly.

iii) To improve the morale of the police, development of the individuals and career planning, a good personnel policy is needed. There is need to make changes in the qualifications, recruitment, training and scales of pay, especially in the lower cadres. Political interference in promotions, postings and transfers is on the high side in most states in India. These have to be minimised if they cannot be eliminited altogether. Political patronage or lack of it has adversely affected the police morale, accountability and culture. There is need to enlist voluntary and uniform support of the public in the investigation of offences, especially, in areas relating to gender violence, violence against SC and minorities.

iv) In the 50th year of the country's indpendence, police administration is an area which needs to be reviewed for a thorough and radical overhaul of its structure and function. The conditions and the atmosphere in which the police are working today are far worse than what they were 50 years earlier when they were dealing basically with law and order problems and offences such as dacoities, thefts, robbery, murder etc. If public have to have faith and confidence in the working of the police and their ability to maintain peace and protect the citizens, the initiative has undoubtedly to come from the parties in power in the Centre or at the state governments and from the politicians and legislators. It is high time that the Central Government and the Ministry of Home Affairs take the initiative to act on the recommendations of the National Police Commission and evolve a mechanism which insulates the police from political interference, allows it to function without fear or favour, and enables them to subserve the rule of law. Of late, judicial activism has helped the investigating agencies to investigate the offences committed by ministers and politicians. Though such judicial extremism is welcome, it is ultimately for the political executive to learn lessons and to take measures to insulate police from political pressure and interference in their working. This, coupled with the proper personnel policy of the department and development of institutional mechanism for increasing the police interaction with the public, will be mutually beneficial both for the police to function efficiently and speedily and the public at large to accept the policeman as a person in whom they can have trust and confidence.

v) A major handicap in police administration is the absence of an authority to assess its performance. This is due to the fact that the police organisation is being run without requisite management principles. It is necessary, therefore, to formulate actions and operations in line with the latest management principles and practices followed elsewhere. This could be done by constituting an efficient cell of management experts to advise or hire a management consultant.

vii) The modernisation of the police force with the latest communication, transport, weapons and office equipment system and the simultaneous creation of the necessary infrastructure for the operation in advance will alone make the police force rise to the challenges of elite criminals who are armed with sophisticated equipment. India of the 21st century will require its police force to be equipped with helicopters as an aid in emergencies; a genuine and effective effort to achieve modernisation would be indispensable in the future. A face-lift to police stations and office with the latest office equipment and general facilities will be helpful in boosting the morale of the policemen.

viii) The present policing system in India has too much paper work with hundreds of registers maintained in each station or office with many forms filled up at each stage. A detailed study of the paper work should be undertaken to so that time is saved. Computerisation is also a possibility not far way.

In conclusion, it may be stated that irrespective of whatever is done to modernise the police force, improve personnel policy, provide better scales of pay, transport, communication, equipment, the fact remains that no police force can be truly professional and discharge the duties, without fear or favour if there is no political will to stop interference in the working of the police force.

REFERENCES

Annual Administration Reports of the Karnataka Police Department 1980-1995. Bangalore: Government of Karnataka.

Avalokana, Published by the Kannada and Culture Department, Government of Karnataka.

Government of India. (1982). **Karnataka State Gazetteer, Part-I.** Bangalore: Government of Karnataka.

Government of India. (1983). **Karnataka State Gazetteer, Part-II.** Bangalore: Government of Karnataka.

Police Information Booklet, Karnataka Police Department. 1995.

Policing in Karnataka: Growth in a Century. Published by the Government of Karnataka.

Rao, Hayavardana (1984). **Mysore Gazetteer.** Delhi: B.R.Publishing Corporation.

VII

SOCIAL WELFARE ADMINISTRATION

1

ADMINISTRATION OF HEALTH SERVICES

P. Hanumantha Rayappa and T.V. Sekher

Introduction: World Health Organisation (WHO) has defined health as a state of complete physical, mental and social well-being, and not merely the absence of disease or infirmity. C.M.A. Winslow (1951), in defining health, states that it includes "preventing diseases, prolonging life, promoting physical health and efficiency". Thus, the elements of preventive, curative and rehabilitative and promotive aspect of social welfare are involved in the complex gamut of health administration. Public health administration is an area of activity which calls for specialised knowledge and techniques which can help the people to achieve the health care. In the administration of health department, Freeman and Holmes (1960) have put forward the following steps:

(a) Planning, including community diagnosis, forecasting, setting objectives, budgeting and phasing.

(b) Mobilising, including motivation of staff and community staffing, functional team organisation, organisational structure and delegating.

(c) Co-ordinating all different elements and groups engaged in health problem for preventing duplication.

(d) Guiding, including reconciliation of programme, preventing duplication, establishing communication.

(e) Guiding the control of quality and quantity, evaluating outcome, establishing policies and procedures.

(f) Liberating, including discovering worker, developing people, providing diversified experience and opportunity, developing community leadership.

(g) Accounting, including reporting to people or representives of public about fiscal management.

'Better Health' is a goal which everybody aspires for. The health of an individual is influenced by the surrounding environment, his living conditions, the socio-economic background and the community at large. The health of the child is dependent upon the health of the mother, socio-economic conditions of the family, the environmental factors and a host of others. Similarly, community health is influenced by the conscious efforts made by the community itself, surrounding environment and governmental efforts to promote health of the individuals and the community. Therefore, while assessing health situation in any given area one should understand the plans, programmes and strategies carried out by the respective governments to promote individual as well as community welfare. This would include not only the health sector but also other sectors. The efficiency with which the programmes are formulated and implemented by the respective governments will have their effects in the success of the programme.

Health is a function of the overall integrated development of the society and the health status is one of the indicators of the quality of life. How the socio-economic status influences the health status of people is well established in many ways. Therefore, the health development is defined as "the process of continuous progressive improvement of the health status of the population. Its product is rising level of human well-being not only by reduction in the burden of the disease, but also by the attainment of positive, physical and mental health related to satisfactory economic functioning and social integration" (Park and Park 1990).

Health Administration in India: Health care system in India is operationalised on a three-tier system - Central, state and local levels. The responsibility of the centre consists mainly of policy making, planning, guiding, assisting, evaluating and co-ordinating the work of state health ministries. The responsibility for implementing the policies and programmes rest with state governments which are constitutionally bound to provide medical and health care for the people living in their jurisdictions. Actual implementation takes place at the district level with the office of the district medical, health and family welfare serving as the nerve centre for integrating all health activities in rural areas. In urban areas, the health departments of municipalities and corporations are mainly responsible for providing preventive and curative health services.

The Indian Constitution (Article 246) states that subjects like public health, sanitation, hospitals, and dispensaries fall under the state list, implying devolution of responsibilities to states. Subjects like population control, family planning, medical education, adulteration of food stuff and other goods, drugs and poisons, medical profession, vital statistics, are all in the concurrent list where responsibilities are shared by both the Centre and the states. The state ministries receive funds for the programmes on the concurrent list and are responsbile for implementing those that are identified as of national importance, namely, family welfare, primary health care, prevention and control of diseases and such others.

The Union Ministry of Health is headed by a Minister either of the Cabinet or State rank. The Union Health Ministry has two Departments - Department of Health, and the Department of Family Welfare which were created in 1966. The official organs of the health system at the national level consist of (a) Ministry of Health and Family Welfare, (b) The Director General of Health Services, (c) The Central Council of Health and Family Welfare. The Director General of Health Services is the principal advisor to the Union Government on medical and public health matters. The Directorate of Health Services comprises of three main units such as medical care and hospitals, public health and general administration. It is appropriate to mention here that the significant landmark in state health administration was in 1919, when the states (provinces) obtained autonomy concerning matters of public health from the Central Government. As a consequence of this, most of the states had developed some form of public health organisation by 1922. At the state level the management of health consists of State Ministry of Health, and a Directorate of Health and Family Welfare. The state ministry is headed by a minister. The state health secretariat is the official organ of the State Ministry of Health and Family Welfare and headed by a Secretary who is assisted by other staff. The Director of State Health and Family Welfare is the Chief Technical Advisor and Administrator to the State Government on all matters relating to medical, health and family welfare. He is responsible for the organisation and direction of all health activities. A development in recent years is the bifurcation of the directorate of Medical Education mainly in view of increase in the number of medical colleges. The regional and divisional directors inspect all aspects of health within their jurisdiction while functional directors are specialists in the areas of family welfare, maternal and child health, malaria eradication, leprosy control, etc. Public health engineering is a new development which has been treated as a separate department entrusted with the job of providing drinking water in the rural areas.

At the district level, there is a District Health and Family Welfare Officer with a District Surgeon attached to the district hospital. At the primary health centre level there is a medical officer supported by others. At the grass root level, i.e., at sub-centre level, there is one male and female health worker.

Health Planning: Health Planning in India is an integral part of national planning. The guidelines for national health planning were provided by a number of committees dating back to Bhore Committee in 1946. These committees were appointed by the Government of India from time to time to review the existing situation and recommend suitable measures to improve the situation. A brief review of the recommendations of the important committees has been provided below. It is needless to say that these recommendations and their implementation have far reaching consequences on the states.

The first and the most often cited report on health policies and programmes was the Bhore Committee Report. The Bhore Committee (named after Sir Joseph Bhore) put forward, for the first time, comprehensive proposals for the development of a national programme of health services. It observed that the health programme should be developed on a foundation of preventive health along with curative services in an integrated manner. The Bhore Committee report and its recommendations became the basis for most of the subsequent planning in the country. Consequently, the office of the Director General of Health Services was established in the country in 1947. Simultaneously, the Directorates of Health were established in the states as well. In 1948, India joined the World Health Organisation which meant free flow of information, initiation of programme, exchange of personnel, and so on.

After independence the "Health Survey and Planning Committee" was set up in 1959 under the chairmanship of Dr. A. Lakshmanaswamy Mudaliar to have a fresh look at the health needs and resources. The Committee, among others, recommended strengthening of primary health centres and hospitals at the district and lower levels. It also recommended constitution of All India Health Services on the pattern of the Indian Administrative Service. The Chadha Committee, in 1963, mainly looked at the issues relating to National Malaria Eradication Programme. The Mukherjee Committee was appointed in 1965 to review the strategy for the National Family Planning Programme. Among others, the Committee recommended setting up of separate staff for carrying out family planning activities in the country. The N. Jungalwalla Committee recommended in 1967 an integrated health services instead of segmented approach from the highest to the lowest level in the services, organisation and personnel. The Kartar Singh Committee in 1973 opted for a system of multi-purpose workers and a change in their designations and their workload. The most important recommendation of the Shrivastava Committee (1975) was that the primary health care should be provided within the community itself through trained workers so that the health of the people could be placed in the hands of the people.

The Alma Ata declaration in 1978 and the formulation of National Health Policy in 1983 gave a new direction to the health policy and planning in India, making primary health care the central function and main focus of the national health system. The goal is to attain Health for All by 2000 A.D. The Alma Ata International Conference on primary health care re-affirmed 'health for all' as the major social goal and this was to be achieved by providing primary health care at the doorsteps of the people. This conference called upon the governments to formulate national policies, strategies and plans of action to launch and sustain primary health care as part of a national health system. It was left to each country to develop its norms and indicators for providing primary health care according to its own needs and taking into account its resources. In pursuance of the above objective two important reports were prepared: (1) "Health For All - An Alternative Strategy" sponsored by the ICSSR and ICMR (1981); and (2) "Health For All by 2000 A.D.", - a report of the Working Group (1981). Both the reports considered in detail the various issues involved in providing primary health care, and based on these reports, a national health policy was formulated which was approved by the Parliament in 1983.

The National Health Policy was evolved keeping in view the national commitment to attain the goal of "Health for all by 2000 A.D". The policy laid stress on the preventive, promotive, public health and rehabilitative aspects of health care and pointed to the need for establishing comprehensive primary health care services to reach the population in the remote areas and difficult terrains. There was a need to view health and human development as a vital component of overall integrated socio-economic development and decentralised system of health care delivery with maximum community and individual self-reliance and participation. To achieve this, the health policy laid down certain specific goals to be achieved by 1985, 1990 and 2000 A.D.

Karnataka's performance in certain demographic indicators is quite satisfactory. At the same time, the state is lagging behind in certain other aspects. The goals and achievements of the state in the field of health and family welfare as stated by the state government, is presented in Table 1. The information based on the National Family Health Survey (1992-93) is also presented to illustrate the existing situation with regard to various indicators as assessed in an independent survey.

Health Programmes and Strategies: Health programmes initiated in the country and Karnataka state can be grouped into curative care, preventive or communicable disease control, nutritional improvement, public sanitation and environmental protection and population control. Several strategies have been evolved to take these programmes to the nook and corner of the state and they have met with varied success. Among the programmes aimed at prevention and control of communicable diseases, only major ones can be listed. A brief account of these programmes has been given below.

The National Malaria Eradication Programme came into being in 1958 by reformulating the National Malaria Control Programme of 1953. It has remained a vertical programme under the supervision of District Malaria Control Officers. Though this programme met with success during the initial years, the resurgence of malaria since 1970s posed a major hurdle in its total eradication. At present, the PHCs are involved in the collection and examination of blood smears. The National Filaria programme, initiated in 1955, continues to be a partial programme covering a limited number of districts. The National Tuberculosis programme has been in operation even though BCG vaccination programme began as early as 1951. This programme operates through district tuberculosis units. Immunization against BCG has been included as an item under the Universal Immunization programme (U.I.P.). The National Leprosy Eradication programme has been in operation since 1955 and Leprosy services are provided within the framework of existing PHCs. The revised strategy is based on early detection, drug theraphy, health education and rehabilitation. The National Diarroheal Diseases Control Programme was intensified in 1990. The use of ORS and ORT have been promoted on a large scale in recent years. The National programme for the Control of Blindness was launched in 1976 with the aim to control the incidence of blindness through provision of Vitamin 'A' prophylaxis among other measures.

Iodine deficiency disorders have been tackled beginning with Goitre Control programme in 1962. The use of iodised salt has been propogated under this programme for the control of the disease. There are several other programmes which have been launched to tackle problems such as Sexually Transmitted Diseases (AIDS Control), National Diabetes Control, Guinea Worm Eradication Programme. There are other schemes such as Smallpox Eradication programme which was started in 1962, Expanded programme of Immunization in 1974 which has been christened as Universal Immunization programme in 1985 to prevent six childhood diseases and tetanus among pregnant women, which have been effective in controlling these diseases to a great extent. There are a number of area specific programmes which can be added to this list.

The National Water Supply and Sanitation programme was initiated in 1954. After 1975, the Rural Water Supply scheme was given a big boost and most of the villages have been provided with safe drinking water. However, the public sanitation through the provision of latrines has not met with any success.

The primary health care is to be provided by a network of institutions such as community health centres, primary health centres and sub-centres. Apart from these, the other providers of health services include rural hospitals, taluk hospitals, district hospitals, specialist hospitals and teaching institutions. Employees State Insurance scheme, also provides services to state government employees. At the village level, the following schemes are in operation: (1) Village Health Guide scheme, (2) Training of Village Dais, and (3) Integrated Child Development scheme. Village Health Guide scheme, introduced in Karnataka on an experimental basis, has been slowly withdrawn. In order to promote safe deliveries in rural areas, local dais were given training, and in Karnataka, this was done on a large scale. The emphasis has been on conducting home deliveries under hygienic conditions. Under ICDS, there is an anganwadi worker for every 1,000 population. The worker, selected from the community, is expected to provide supplementary nutrition, health care including immunization and pre-school education to children and expectant and nursing mothers.

Family Planning is a centrally sponsored scheme and the states receive 100 per cent assistance from the Central government. Since most of the policy decisions are made by the Centre, the pattern of organisation and system of delivery are standardised at the state level. There is a State Family Welfare Bureau under the Directorate of Health and Family Welfare. The district level set up consists of District Health and Family Welfare Officer, Mass Media Officer, and a Statistician. The Urban Family Welfare Centres are organised to look after urban areas. The Rural Family Welfare Centres are attached to PHCs in the rural areas. The sub-centres are the grass root level centres where health workers provide the required motivation. In addition, family welfare services are also provided by the private sector and voluntary organisations which are partly funded by the government and/or other national or international organisations. The post-partum centres located in different hospitals also cater to women who come for maternal services.

A separate department for Family Planning was created in 1966 in the Ministry of Health (Government of India). In 1972, **Medical Termination of Pregnancy Act** was passed. In 1977, the Department of Family Planning was renamed as Department of Family Welfare.

Health Institutions in Karnataka: Over the years a large number of health institutions have been established in the state to take health and family welfare services closer to the people. These institutions have been established according to the changed norms prescribed by the Union Ministry of Health and Family Welfare. In 1994, there were 213 Community Health Centres (CHCs), 1,357 Primary Health Centres (PHCs) and 7,793 Sub-Centres (SCs) in the state. In addition, there were Anganwadi Centres in 148 blocks which were engaged in providing supplementary nutrition, pre-school education, and maternal and child health services.

Programmes: Karnataka State is aiming at providing comphrehensive health care services to its people by way of implementing various national and State health programmes of public health importance through its network of various types of health and medical institutions.

The Department of Health and Family Welfare Services provide the following health services:

1) Rural Health Component of Minimum Needs Programme;
2) Medical Development Programme;
3) MCH, Family Welfare and Immunization Programme;
4) National Leprosy Eradication Programme;
5) National Tuperculosis Control Programme;
6) National Programme for Control of Blindness;
7) National Malaria Eradication and National Filaria Control Programme;
8) Prevention and Control of other Communicable Diseases like Diarroheal Diseases, Kyasanur Forest Disease, Japanese Encephalitis etc;
9) Health Education and Training Programme;
10) Nutrition Programme - Nutrition Education and Demonstration ;
11) National Goitre Control Programme;
12) Laboratory Service and Vaccine Production Units;
13) Education and Enviornmental Sanitation ; and
14) Curative Serives.

Health Expenditure: Health is a state subject and the primary responsibility of providing health care is with the state governments. State's expenditure accounts for around 90 per cent of all public expenditure on the health sector. Central funds for the states are in the form of grants for particular programmes, e.g., family planning or sponsored programmes. Funding for sponsored programmes is mainly for the national programmes for disease control. For the year 1994-95, Karnataka state's revenue expenditure on health was 5,077 million, which was 6.39 per cent of the total government revenue expenditure (refer Table 2).

Karnataka is among the states which spend more money on health administration. The major expenditure is on the production of doctors and nurses. The state is having a large number of medical colleges. The expenditure on production of doctors and nurses, however, does not reflect their availability although trained at public cost. For every three doctors the government trains for its health services, seven are trained for the private sector at public cost and a good number of them migrate abroad (Duggal **et al** 1995). Table 3 illustrates the expenditure on health administration in the state over a period of time.

The Subject Committee of the Karnataka Legislature on Health and Family Welfare (1994-95) has stated that the amount earmarked in the budget under plan and non-plan of health and family welfare department has not been spent fully. The reasons for this are that the budget has not been released by the government in stipulated time and the department has not taken any immediate action for the utilisation of the released amount within the specified time. This committee also recommended a separate corporation or engineering division for the construction of buildings coming under the health and family welfare department.

Health Administration in the erstwhile State of Mysore: Health administration in the erstwhile state of Mysore was very well ahead of its neighbouring provinces. Prior to 1864, four hospitals and 24 dispensaries of the British administration were in existence and these were handed over to the then Government of Mysore in 1884. A medical school was establishment as early as 1881, for the purpose of training Hospital Assistants (GOK 1983:1927-30).

In 1907, the reorganisation of the health services took place and a Public Health Department was created. In 1913, the head of the Medical Department was designated as the Sanitary Commissioner. In Mysore state, a Board of Health was appointed in 1929 to act as an Advisory Body on public health matters. Mysore state is the first in the country to establish Rural Health Centres in 1931, which can be considered as a milestone in the health administration of the state. The important activites of these centres were improvement of village sanitation, investigation and control of the outbreak of epidemic diseases, immunization services, chlorination of drinking water sources and reporting of births and deaths. A Bureau of Maternal and Child Health, and a Bureau of Malariology were started in 1934 and a Health Training-cum-Demonstration Centre was opened in 1936 (GOK 1983). Mysore was one 8 the earliest states to establish a Health Educator Bureau in the Department of Health in 1929, to promote health consciousness among people.

The erstwhile state of Mysore occupies a unique position in the field of family planning programme. The World's first family planning clinic was established in Mysore in 1930. The University Medical School in Bangalore was started in 1917 and in 1924, the first medical college was opened. In Appendix A, the evolution of health services in the state is portrayed starting from the establishment of an asylum for leprosy patients, as early as 1847.

After the reorganisation of the state with parts of erstwhile Mysore state, Bombay, Madras, Coorg and Hyderabad in 1956, it was felt that there was need to co-ordinate the medical and health services, and accordingly, the medical department and public health department were amalgamated into a single department - The Department of Health Services.

The phasing out of the Indian Medical Service (IMS) of the pre-independence era had a major impact on the administration of health services in the states (Banerji 1985). This had led to considerable erosion in the competence of health administrators at a time when they were required to show much greater initiative, enterprise and administrative vision in the face of the rising expectations and aspirations of the people. In the first instance, health being essentially a state subject, the administrators were expected to develop their own pattern of health services to suit the conditions prevailing in individual states. In the absence of such action, the state officials had to depend on the 'standard pattern' prescribed by the Central government.

There has been a rapid expansion of medical facilities in the state during the last three decades, both in government and private sector. Many specialised health care institutions of national importance have started functioning. They are NIMHANS, Kidwai Memorial Institute of Oncology, National Tuberculosis Institute, Jayadeva Institute of Cardiology, Sanjay Gandhi Institute of Accident Relief, All India Insitute of Speech and Hearing, Rajiv Gandhi Institute of Child Health etc. The recently established Rajiv Gandhi Health University is a step to streamline the rapidly expanding medical education sector in the state. Another important point that deserves mention here is the implementation of India Population Project (IPP) I to VII. The contribution of the Population Centre, Bangalore, and the Population Research Centre, Institute for Social and Economic Change, Bangalaore, in the areas of research, evaluation and training is worth mentioning.

Panchayat Raj Institutions and Health Services: In Karnataka, which is one of the states which implemented the Panchayat Raj system of decentralisation in a more systematic manner in the eighties, the major responsibility of health care services has been transferred to the local bodies. This transfer of services to the Panchayat Raj institutions can be considered as a landmark in the case of health administration in the state. This, to a great extent, will ensure people's participation as well as facilitate the proper functioning and management of these essential services. But, how far it has really improved its utility to common man by providing basic health services needs to be examined. The functions of Gram Panchayat, Taluk Panchayat and Zilla Panchayat with regard to health and sanitation, as per the **Karnataka Panchayat Raj Act,** is presented in Appendix-B.

Health Care and Voluntary Sector: The Seventh Five Year Plan and the National Health Policy recommended that one of the five strategies to achieve the health care goals should be through the involvement of voluntary organisations. The voluntary sector has played an important role in the delivery of primary health care in the face of most difficult situations. They have demonstrated that good health care is not necessarily expensive, and the health status of the communities can be improved within a relatively short span of time (Sahni 1992). A concrete policy for the involvement of voluntary organisations in health care was adopted by the Central Government in 1982. In Karnataka also many initiatives were taken to involve voluntary agencies more actively and a number of programmes were sponsored by the government and implemented through voluntary organisations. This included scheme for setting up of women's Training Centre for the rehabilitation of women in distress, creches, scheme for the rehabilitation of Devadasi Women, scheme of assistance to voluntary organisations for prohibition and drug abuse prevention, street children programme etc. The emergence of the explosive AIDS epidemic and the rising incidence of Sexually Transmitted Diseases (STDs) are posing new challenges in health care and administration. In Karnataka also, NGOs have been at the forefront in combating the AIDS problem.

The ongoing Structural Adjustment Policies (SAP) will have significant repercussions on the health sector. There is an apprehension that the social sector, particularly health, is more vulnerable to cut in public expenditure in the process of the restructuring of the economy. If it is true, it will affect the functioning of already fragile primary health centres and government hospitals. It is a fact that the poorest sections of the society are heavily dependent on public health facilities. Any change in this regard will affect the common man. The increase in the cost of drugs is also another area of concern. It is also expected that user fees are to be introduced in public hospitals. Yet another dimension of the policy changes in this regard is the increasing thrust on private sector health care. All these measures will undermine the already declining role of the PHCs in the total health delivery system. Overcoming these strains and difficulties in the transition phase is going to be a task for health administrators. They should emphasise the need for the protection of health and the improvement of health status as an essential condition for any socio-economic policy.

CONCLUSION

In this paper, an attempt has been made to highlight the various aspects of health care services and administration in Karnataka. As mentioned earlier, most of the schemes and programmes in the health sector were formulated at the national level and implemented by the state government. But it is found that there are 55 schemes currently dealing with health care. A Sub-group on Social Development of Karnataka (1994) recommended that these schemes can be telescoped into 15 on the basis of being within the same focus or for the same target group for better implementation of these programmes.

Another important development in the health care is the "Shushrusha Scheme", for providing free medical check-up to every citizen once in six months. To implement the scheme effectively, District Level Committees have been constituted with the Deputy Commissioner of the District as Chairman. The National AIDS Control Programme is being implemented in the state under the guidance of National AIDS Control Organisation (NACO). The state AIDS cell was established in 1992 in the Directorate of Health and Family Welfare Services to monitor and supervise the activites. The State Level Empowered Committee has been consituted under the chairmanship of State's Chief Secretary.

The most important problem of health care in the country as a whole and in the states, in particular, lies in the field of organisation and management of health services and its efficient utilisation. Poor utilisation of government health services underline the fact that mere expansion of health infrastructure will not yield the desired results. What is required is the improvement in the qualitative aspects of the health care system. The reluctance on the part of health functionaries to work in rural areas is evident from the existing gap between the number of sanctioned posts and the number of positions filled. Appropriate administrative measures can solve this problem to a great extent. The managerial skills of health functionaries also needs to be improved. This can be done through in-service training and refresher courses.

A look at the scenario in Karnataka reveals that the situation is not very different from the general picture, specifically with regard to government health services. But more importantly, an enormous expansion of the profit-seeking private health sector can be observed in the state, especially during the last two decades. The consequent impact is an increasing trend towards privatisation of medical services. This is more so in the case of medical education. The rapid growth of private sector is essentially the natural consequence of an inadequate public health care system. It is, therefore, the responsibility of the government to strengthen the efficiency of our health care services and this calls for better management and planning. In Karnataka, nearly 500 voluntary organisations are working in the area of health care. Involving these organisations in planning and implementation of various health programmes will go a long way in ensuring better health care services which can be effected through greater public awareness and popular participation.

In this context, the health requirements and problems of socially and economically marginalised groups like tribals, dalits, handicapped and slum dwellers need to be addressed specifically. This can be done by effective intersectoral linkages between various government departments and agencies. Taking into consideration the vastness and diversity of our country, national health policies and planning may have limited scope. Hence, regional planning for health on the basis of the patterns of health indicators and specific problems at the regional level is required. This also necessitates adequate information base on various aspects of rural health services for different geographical, social and economic strata of society. In brief, it is necessary to link the health policies with overall socio-economic development.

What is needed today is a better co-ordination of various health programmes with the active involvement of government, private and voluntary sector. The responsibilities and powers handed over to the elected local bodies will certainly help in achieving our health goals by effective administration of health care services at various levels. This is a challenging task for health administrators, wherein they need to use their expertise to evolve suitable strategies for the development of all concerned.

Table 1 :
Goals and Achievements - Karnataka

Sl. No.	Indicators	Goals by 2000 A.D.*	Achievements (1992)*	NFHS study 1992-93**
1	Crude Birth Rate	21	26.2	24.7
2	Crude Death Rate	9	8.5	7.5
3	Infant Mortality Rate	60	73.0	65.4
4	Net Reproduction Rate	1.0	-	-
5	Population Growth Rate	1.20	1.9	-
6	Couple Protection Rate above	60%	50.25	49.1
7	Life Expectancy above	64 Years 63.3 F	62.1 M	-

Source : * Government of Karnataka (1994)
** National Family Health Survey - 1992-93

Table 2 :

Expenditure on Health - Karnataka

Year	Revenue expenditure on health (Rs. in Million)	As a percentage to total government revenue	Expenditure on health per capta in Rupees
1950-51	0.46	0.35	0.02
1960-61	46.36	5.83	1.97
1970-71	159.53	6.32	5.44
1980-81	603.49	6.74	16.28
1991-92	2,953.10	5.96	64.30
1992-93	3,602.05	6.44	76.80
1993-94 RE	4,237.73	6.56	88.49
1994-95 BE	5,077.72	6.39	103.84

RE = Revised Estimate

BE = Budget Estimate

Source: Up to 1985-86 combined finance and revenue accounts, Comptroller and Auditor General of India, respective Years. Other years, demand for grants of respective states (Duggal **et al** 1995:(16).

Table 3:
Expenditure on Health Administration - Karnataka

Years	Expenditure on health administration (Rs.in Million)	As per cent to total health Expenditure
1950-51	0.05	10.87
1955-56	4.19	25.85
1960-61	11.22	24.20
1965-66	20.72	29.02
1970-71	39.19	24.57
1975-76	12.60	3.33
1980-81	22.74	3.77
1985-86	32.57	2.33
1991-92	42.11	1.43
1992-93	33.02	0.97
1993-94 RE	45.10	1.06
1994-95 BE	58.01	1.14

RE = Revenue Estimate

BE = Budget Estimate

Source : Duggal **et al** 1995 : (16).

APPENDIX A

EVOLUTION OF HEALTH SERVICES IN KARNATAKA

1847

Establishment of an Asylum for Leprosy Patients

|

1884

Creation of Medical Department

Appointment of Senior Surgeon

Handing over of Dispensaries by British Administration

|

1887

Recognition of Public Health

Redesignation of Senior Surgeon as Senior Surgeon-Cum-Ex-officio Sanitary Commissioner

|

1907

Expansion of the Public Health Section

|

February 1929

Bifurcation of the Department

|

(Contd.)

Senior Surgeon
Medical Department

Sanitary Commissioner
Sanitary Department

November 1929

Directorate of Medical Service
Medical Department

Director, Department of
Public Health

1956 - Reorganisation
1995

Amalgamation of Department
Directorate of Health Service

1974

Director

Additional Director

1976

(Contd.)

Director

Additional Director (Public Health & F.P.)

Additional Director (Medical Education)

1977

Establishment of Unitary Administrative Control

Director of Health and Family Planning Services

(Redesignated as Director of Health & F.W. Services)

Bifurcation of the Department (December 1978)

Director of Health and F.W. Services

Director (Medical Education)

Source: GOK 1979.

APPENDIX B

FUNCTIONS OF GRAM PANCHAYATS, TALUK PANCHAYATS AND ZILLA PANCHAYATS

A. Gram Panchayat:

a) Public Health and Family Welfare:

1) Implementation of family welfare programmes.
2) Prevention and remedial measures against epidemics.
3) Regulation of sale of meat, fish and other perishable food articles.
4) Participation in programmes of human and animal vaccination.
5) Licensing of eating and entertainment establishments.
6) Destruction of stray dogs.
7) Regulation of curing, tanning and dyeing of skins and hides.
8) Regulation of offensive and dangerous trades.

b) Rural Sanitation:

1) Maintenance of general sanitation.
2) Cleaning of public roads, drains, tanks, well and other public places.
3) Maintenance and regulation of burning and burial grounds.
4) Construction and maintenance of public latrines.
5) Disposal of unclaimed corpses and carcasses.
6) Management and control of washing and bathing ghats.

c) Women and Child Development:

1) Participation in the implementation of women and child welfare programmes.
2) Promotion of school health and nutrition programmes,

(Contd.)

APPENDIX B

B. **Taluk Panchayat**

a) **Health and Family Welfare;**

1) Promotion of health and family welfare programmes.

2) Promotion of immunization and vaccination programmes.

3) Health and sanitation at fairs and festivals.

b) **Women and Child Development:**

1) Promotion of programmes relating to development of women and children.

2) Promotion of school health and nutrition programmes.

3) Promotion of participation of voluntary organisations in women and child development programmes.

C). **Zilla Panchayat**

a) **Health and Family Welfare:**

1) Management of hospitals and dispensaries excluding those under the management of Government or any other local authority.

2) Implementation of maternity and child health programmes.

3) Implementation of family welfare programmes.

4) Implementation of immunization and vaccination programmes.

b) **Women and Child Development:**

1) Promotion of programmes relating to development of women and children.

2) Promotion of school health and nutrition programme.

3) Promotion of participation of voluntary organisation in women and child development programmes.

Source: **The Karnataka Panchayat Raj Act, 1993.**

REFERENCES

Banerji, D. (1985). **Health and Family Planning Services in India** New Delhi: Lok Prakash.

Duggal, Ravi, Sunil Nandraj, and Asha Vadair (1995). Health Expenditure across States - Parts I and II. **Economic and Political Weekly,** XXX (15 & 16).

Freeman, R.B. and M. Edward Holmes, Jr. (1960). **Administration of Public Health Services.** Philadelphia: Saunders.

Government of India, (GOI) (1946). **Health Survey and Developmental Committee (Bhore Committee),** 4 volumes. Delhi: Manager of Publications.

Government of India (GOI) (1962). **Report of the Health Survey and Planning Committee.** New Delhi: Ministry of Health.

Government of India (GOI) (1963). **Report of the Special Committee on the Preparation for Entry of THE NMEP into the Maintenance Phases.** New Delhi: Ministry of Health.

Government of India (GOI) (1966). **Report on Reorganisation of Family Planning Services Administration and Basic Health Services.** New Delhi: Ministry of Health.

Government of India (GOI) (1967). **Report of the Committee on Integration of Health Services.** New Delhi, Ministry of Health.

Government of India (GOI) (1973). **Report of the Committee on Multi-purpose Workers under Health and Family Planning Programme.** New Delhi: Ministry of Health and Family Planning.

Government of India (GOI) (1975). **Report of the Group on Medical Education and Support Manpower.** New Delhi: Ministry of Health and Family Planning.

Government of India (GOI) (1979). **Health and Family Welfare Services in Karnataka, Year Book. 1978-79.** Bangalore: Directorate of Health and Family Welfare Services.

Government of India (GOI) (1981). **Report of the Working Group on Health for All by 2000 A.D.** New Delhi: Ministry of Health and Welfare.

Government of Karnataka (GOK) (1983). **Karnataka State Gazetteer,** part II. Bangalore: Government of Karnataka.

Government of Karnataka (GOK) (1990). **Department of Health and Family Welfare Status Report 1989-90.** Bangalore: Directorate of Health and Family Welfare Services.

Government of Karnataka (GOK) (1994a). **Health and Family Welfare Services: Annual Report 1993-94.** Bangalore: Directorate of Health Family Welfare Services.

Government of Karnataka (GOK) (1994b). Towards a More Efficient Social Development in Karnataka. **Report of the Sub-Group on Social Development of the Karnataka State.** Bangalore: State Planning Board.

Government of Karnataka (GOK) (1994c). **First Report on Demands for Grants for 1994-95.** Subject Committee of Karnataka Legislature on Health and Family Welfare, Ninth Legislative Assembly, 1994-95.

ICSSR and ICMR (1981). **Health for All: An Alternative Strategy.** Report of a Study Group set up jointly by the ICSSR and ICMR. Pune: Indian Institute of Education.

Park, J.E. and K. Park (1990). **Textbook on Preventive and Social Medicine.** Jabalpur: Banarasidas Bhanot Publishers.

Rao, C. Hayavadana (1984). **Mysore Gazetteer** Vol.IV. Delhi: B.R. Publishing Corporation.

Sahni, Ashok (1992). **The Third Force in Health Care - Voluntary Sector.** Bangalore: Indian Society of Health Administrators.

Voluntary Health Association of India (1992). **State of India's Health.** New Delhi: Voluntary Health Association of India.

Winslow, C.E.A. (1951). **The Cost of Sickness and the Price of Health.** Geneva: World Health Organisation.

World Health Organisation (1978). **Primary Health Care Report of the International Conference on Primary Health Care, Alma Ata (USSR).** Geneva: WHO.

2

STATE AND EDUCATION

A.S. Seetharamu

SCHOOL EDUCATION

1833-1955: The beginnings of state interest in modern education can be traced back to the year 1833 when, Sri Krishna Devaraja Wodeyar III, the Maharaja of Mysore[1] started the Rajah School. In the following years, a number of English schools were started, mostly by the missionaries and especially by the Wesleyan and the London Missions. By 1857, which is a landmark year in educational administration in the State, there were 26 English schools, apart from a large number of Vernacular and religious schools. It is significant to note that the state was providing grant-in-aid to many of these institutions.

Mysore state was under the direct control of the British since 1830. Sir Charles Wood, who was the President of the Board of Control of the East India Company, sent a despatch in 1854 which is referred to as the Magna Carta of English Education in India. The Despatch imposed upon the government the task of creating a properly articulated scheme of education from primary school to the university. There was no organised system of education in Mysore state as elsewhere in India at that time.

Following Wood's Despatch, Mr. Devereux, the Judicial Commissioner, drew up a scheme of education for Mysore and Coorg. Sir Mark Cubbon, the then Commissioner for the government, got the approval of the East India Company, the then government of India, and set it in operation in 1857. For the first time, a Department of Public

1. The first English school had been established a year earlier in 1832 in the Fort, Bangalore. This was known as the Ordinance school. But this was not a State supported school then.

Instruction was created with a Director of Public Instruction along with an inspectorate of only one Inspector of Schools for the entire state which had an enrollment in all schools of nearly 1,600 children[2].

In the year 1863, the Department of Public Instruction was separated from the Judicial Commissioner. By 1868, there were around 50 schools including 18 Government Vernacular schools. The year 1868 is a landmark in the history of education in the state. Mr Lewis Rice, who was the then Director of Public Instruction,drew up a scheme for expanding education in a systematic way and streamlined the administration for the same. This scheme was popularly known as the Hobli[3] School Scheme, which was the first attempt of the state for a balanced growth and development of education across the length and breadth of the state. The schools were established in phases. It was a popular scheme with great public demand. While 146 Hobli schools were established during 1868-69 itself, this number rose to 636 by 1879-80. A significant problem all these years was the shortage of qualified and trained teachers. In a large number of Hoblies, where demand was great, branch schools were opened in other villages of the cluster. The Inspectorate was also reorganised and expanded in 1879.

In the year 1881, the British government retransferred the administration of the state to the royal family. The Ruler of Mysore changed the designation of the Director of Public Instruction as Education Secretary to the Dewan. Sri H.J. Bhabha became the first full time Education Secretary in 1890.

Universities at Madras, Calcutta and Bombay had been established in 1857 following the Despatch. College and University education in India grew rapidly including Government Colleges. The universities were conducting examinations even for matriculation, the equivalent of present day school final or SSLC examination. Girls were allowed to appear for the matriculation examination only in 1877 by the Culcutta University. The government did not faithfully implement the

2. As of today, there are over 5.36 million children over 42,000 primarly schools with a primary school inspectorate of 400 inspectors of schools.

3. Hobli, a cluster of around 15 villages within a radius of around 7 kilometres, constituted a unit of jurisdiction for a school. There were 645 hoblies in the eight districts of the state.

grant-in-aid scheme to the elementary schools as provided by the Wood's Despatch. The missionaries who were running a number of English schools and colleges were aggrieved by this. They started an agitation which did not bear fruit. Hence, they started a consortium in London known as the General Council of Education in India, in 1878. This acted as a pressure group on Lord Ripon who constituted the first Indian Education Commission in 1882 with Sir William Hunter as Chairman.

It is significant to observe that the one specific issue placed before the Hunter Commission under its terms of reference was 'Should Government withdraw from direct educational enterprise in favour of missionaries. Officers of the Department and several native gentlemen argued against any withdrawl in favour of missionaries. Moreover, in England, the British government had passed the **Local-Self Government (LSG) Act in 1882.** The Hunter Commission echoed the spirit of the times when it recommended the transfer of primary education to LSG Units, such as the District Boards and Municipalities.

All these developments at the national level and in England had a reverberating impact on educational administration in Mysore state. It is reflected in the annual report of the then Dewan of Mysore in 1882, Sri K. Sheshadri Iyer. He observed that the existing 773 government and 118 aided schools spread over 8 districts of the state were "wanting in their popular element in their Constitution and direction which alone can give them success and I have, therefore, provided that local boards, assisted by village boards, where practicable, will take entire charge of these schools, manage them with the definite funds that will be placed at their disposal, appointing and dismissing the masters at their own discretion, the government interference being limited purely to the prescribing of proper standards of education in them and providing the Board with a good and competent staff"[4]. Village Education Committees were formed through selections and nominations as educated

4. It is significant to note that 100 years after this report was submitted, the Karnataka Panchayat Act, 1983, and later, the Act of 1993 have captured this dream in letter and spirit through democratic decentralisation of educational administration.

people were very few. Much progress was not achieved in the growth and development of school education.

There was already a wave of demand for mass education across the seas. England had adopted a policy of mass education in 1881, while it had no such plans for its colonies like India. Strongly ciriticising this policy, Dadabhai Naoroji had observed: "What is this unBritish policy of the British in India ?". Added to this, neither state effort earlier nor state patronage later to LSGs had helped in the popularisation of elementary education. India entered the 20th Century with a concern for mass education. This concern is relfected in the pursuit of yet another strategy: Compulsory Primary Education. The Princely state of Baroda was the first to enact the Free and Compulsory Education Regulation in 1906.

'Modern' Mysore state watched with keen interest the Baroda experiment. Sri. H.J. Bhabha, the then Inspector General of Education of Mysore state was sent on a mission in 1909 to Baroda state to study the scheme and its implementation. He returned with a recommendation for such a provision in Mysore state. This proposition was further strengthened when Sri Gopala Krishna Gokhale suggested to the British government at the Imperial Legislative Council meeting in 1910 to adopt the Baroda plan to the whole of British India. The outcome of all these developments and several efforts on the educational scenario in Mysore State culminated in the passing of the Mysore Elementary Education Regulation by the State Legislative Council in October 1913. The Regulation provided for compulsory primary education (CPE) in notified areas. Several strict measures were taken to enforce compulsions for schooling - prohibition of child labour, provision for prosecution of a parent for contravention of the regulation, formation of school committees, appointment of attendance officers, and transfer of control of education from Government/Department to Municipalities in urban areas. In spite of all these measures the scheme did not succeed due to lack of adequate finances, administrative laxity, parental poverty, and of a system of census of school-age children etc,. There are recorded instances of prosecutions and even convictions for the violation of the

Regulation. Enrollment of students in schools which increased from 126,664 in 1914-15 to 213,984 by 1917-18 declined thereafter to 160,337 by 1921-22. This called for more imaginative educational efforts.

The then Indian officiating Inspector General of Education Dr.C.R. Reddy, issued a comphrenehsive Government Order in May 1921 which had a far-reaching significance. Formal transfer of primary education to local bodies was one of the highlights of this Government Order. This was later incorporated in the revised **Mysore Elementary Education Regulation Act 1930** and the primary schools were then transferred to local bodies.[5] It is of interest to note that the number of primary schools declined during the period 1920-30, as revealed in the following table and this necessitated the resumption of control of the schools again through the **Elementary Education Act of 1941.**

Number of Primary Schools by Management

Year	Government	Local Bodies	Aided	Unaided	Total
1920	2,417	21	6,934	50	9,422
1930	4,863	149	1,442	1	6,455
1940	26	4,887	1,563	1	6,487
1950	8,229	35	1,494	8	9,776

Immediately after independence in 1947, the Representative Government of Mysore state appointed Dr. C.R.Reddy, retired Inspector General of Education, to examine the educational system and propose reorganisation. His report, published in 1949, had proposed multi-purpose system of schooling much before the A.L. Mudaliar report of 1952. However, a popular government came in 1952. It constituted a

5. Sri. S.N. Subba Rao had become Inspector General of Education on 18.05.1927. With a view to streamlining territorial jurisdiction and secure unity of administration, the departmental administration was reorganised on 01.11.1927. For the first time. District Education Officers (present day DDPIs and till 1970, DEOs) were appointed by upgrading the posts of District Inspectors. The position of Divisional Deputy Director of Public Instruction (present day JDPI) was created.

High Power Committee with the then Chief Minister, Sri K.Hanumanthiah as Chairman and Sri J.B. Mallaradhya, the then Director of Public Instruction, as Member Secretary. The Committee submitted its report in 1953. Introduction of crafts in primary education was among the important recommendations adopted by the state.

1956–1985; At the time of reorganisation of states in India and creation of new Mysore state, school education was under the control of local bodies/District Boards/Municipalities in Bombay and Madras Presidency districts, while the schools in the erstwhile Mysore state, Coorg and Hyderabad regions were under the control of the government departments. Reorganisation was accompanied with a large number and variety of educational problems. Diversity in structures, curriculum, examinations/ standards, text books, management (private/government), inspection and administration, facilities, qualified teachers along with problems of biligualism in border areas are illustrative in this regard.

In order to achieve uniformity and evolve a common pattern of education, the new state of Mysore constituted a high level committee, called the Educational Integration Advisory Committee, with the then Minister of Education as its Chairman. The Committee made comprehensive recommendations in a period of 2 to 3 years which were implemented in a phased manner. Professor A.C. Deve Gowda was appointed as Director of Public Instruction on 25.09.1958 after a series of six IAS Officers from 14.02.1950 to 24.09.1958. Significant changes in Mysore state immediately following the reorganisation of States may be noted here.

Primary education was made free in all government, District Board and Municipal Primary Schools in 1959-60. In fact, this was a step in the realisation of the Constitutional dream of 1950. Article 45 provided for Universalisation of Primary Education (in a period of ten years) and set this under the Directive Principles of State Policy. In effective terms, the new Mysore state came into being only in 1956.

A proposal for prescribing common Text Books for all standards throughout the state was made and preparatory work initiated in the year 1959-60. Incidentally, it is noted that a Directorate of Text Books was created in the year 1969-70 which was later transferred to the Directorate of State Educational Research and Training in 1978-79. This position continues even to-day.

Construction and maintenance of primary school buildings were made an obligatory duty of the Taluk Boards through the **Mysore Village Panchayat and Local Boards Act of 1959.**

A common high school syllabus was introduced in 1960 and implemented fully by 1963. A uniform grant-in-aid code for private high schools came into force in 1961-62. Secondary Education was made free for all those whose parent's annual income was less than Rs.1,200/-. Triple Benefit Scheme to teachers - Pension, Provident Fund and Life Insurance - was introduced in 1963. Teacher's Benefit Fund and Student's Benefit Fund were started in 1962.

The **Karnataka Public Libraries Act** was passed in 1965. The draft bill had been prepared by Dr. S.R. Ranganathan in 1963. At the time of integration, the Hyderabad-Karnataka regions and the Madras-Karnataka regions had their own Acts passed in 1955 and 1948 respectively. There were 39 libraries in erstwhile Mysore state running on an_**ad hoc** basis without any Act. These 39 libraries included the Educational Library and Museum started in 1891-92, Srinivasa Mandiram Library (the first public library) started in 1888-89 at Bangalore, the Oriental Library established in 1891-92 at Mysore, Sir Seshadri Iyer Memorial Public Library opened at Cubbon Park, Bangalore in 1915 and a few other District Central libraries. The library movement got a fillip after 1965. As on today, there are 441 Public Libraries in Karnataka state including branch libraries founded by the state government.

Quinquennial Education Surveys began in the country in 1957-58, and Mysore state, following suit with the issue of the First Educational Survey Report an Educational Survey Unit in 1963. Then onwards, generally, surveys are being conducted beginning from 1967 and reports of the progress of school education are being issued. So far, six educational survey reports have been released.

A State Educational Research Bureau and State Bureau of Educational and Vocational guidance were established in 1958-59 and 1959-

60 respectively. A State Institute of Education and State Institute of Science were started in 1963-64. A number of Advisory Boards such as for Primary Education, Secondary Education, Teacher's Training, Music, Dance and Drama Education, Sanskrit Education, Hindi Education, Arts and Crafts, Physical Education, Girls and Women's Education and Commerce Education were set up.

A Committee for Pre-Primary Education was set up in 1957 which submitted its report in 1961. However, the Department of Public Instruction did not exhibit much interest in Pre-Primary Education. As of now, there are 5,536 pre-Primary Schools in the state whose number was 73 at the time of Reorganisation. These are mostly left to private initiative as well as to the Department of Social Welfare and Department of Women and Children's Welfare. The latter created a large chain of Anganwadis under the ICDS scheme across the state while the former set up Balwadis in tribal areas.

The examination for school final stage was made uniform throughout the state in 1963. The Karnataka State Secondary Education Examination Board was set up for the purpose in 1966 which was reconstituted in 1990. A District-level Common Examination for Primary Schools was implemented in the whole State in 1964-65 which was later discontinued in 1978-79. Now, in 1996, there is again a move by the state for its revival. With all these measures it was possible to give a semblance of uniformity to the State Educational Administration. It is again noted that the period 1956 to 1965 was a time of intense educational activity in the state.

Different regions of integrated Mysore state had their own history in regard to the policy and enforcement of compulsory primary education (CPE). A comprehensive and integrated policy was the need of the day. Being sensitive to this need, the new Mysore state adopted the **Compulsory Primary Education Act** in 1961. As a follow up of this Act, the inspectorate was reorganised in 1961-62. Compulsory attendance was strictly enforced, and attendance officers were appointed for the purpose. Penalties were levied and prosecutions made. However, compulsion met with stiff resistance from the parents who considered a child on the field or farm to be more valuable to the household than a child in the school, the landlords did not like to be deprived of their cheap labour and so also, in general, the community at large. Hence, a shift in the strategy from compulsion to persuasion, wooing and incentives was made. Many of the present day incentive schemes began in 1960s. The Mid-day Meal Scheme, the Attendance Scholarship Scheme for girls, the Free Supply of Text Books Scheme, etc, and the Pre-Matric Scholarship Scheme, which was also included later the this list, began in the 60s.

The Government of India constituted a National Commission to Review Education in the country under the Chairmanship of Dr. D.S. Kothari in 1964. It submitted the report in 1966 which was adopted by the Parliament in 1968. Professor A.C. Deva Gowda was appointed as a Special Officer for school reorganisation in the state in 1968 to suggest modalities for the implementation of recommendations of the National Education Commission. There was a thorough overhaul of educational administration in Karnataka state in October 1970. The post of the Director of Public Instruction (DPI) for the whole state was split up, expanded and diversified as DPI Primary Education, DPI Secondary Education, DPI Text Books as well as DPI, Directorate of State Educational Research and Training (DSERT) (created in 1975) which amalgamated several state units such as State Educational Research Bureau, State Evaluation Unit, State Institute of Education, State Institute of Science, State Educational and Vocational Guidance Bureau, along with the State Directorate of Text Books, DPI Adult Education (later rechristened as Department of Mass Education for which IAS Officers are appointed since 1988), Director of Pre-university Education and lastly, Director of Vocational Education (since 1979). All these DPIs were brought under a Commissionerate of Public Instruction with an IAS Commissioner of Public Instruction since June 1979.

Another important step in the reorganisation of 1970 was the appointment of an Assistant Educational Officer to be in complete charge of Primary Education in all the taluks of the state as well as educational ranges in urban areas.

Apart from these changes, other changes made were the creation of posts of Joint Directors of Public Instruction (JDAI) for four divisions of the state as well as for the headquarters and 21 Deputy Directors of Public Instruction (DDPI) (formerly DEOs and now with increased powers) assisted by two or three Educational Officers (EOS) in every district. In order to improve the academic standards of school education, nearly two or three Graduate Inspectors of Schools (one for 80 villages) per taluk for the Primary Schools and over 100 Subject Inspectors of Schools for Secondary Education were also appointed.

There was again a large-scale reorganisation in 1995 when a Block Education Officer in Junior Class I scale was appointed for each taluk who would be assisted by the Assistant Educational Officer (AEO) and the Inspectors of schools in the taluks. It may be pointed out here that there are only five women among more than 400 Inspectors of Primary schools in the state.

The Fifth Five Year Plan (1974-79) proposed vocationalisation of education at the plus 2 or higher secondary stage. Karnataka was one of the first few states which introduced vocationalisation at the plus 2 stage in the year 1978. As it is in other parts of the country, the vocationalisation experiment has met with limited success in the state. The total graduate enrollment in India in the 1950s and 1960s (BA/BSc/BCom) as a proportion of total enrollment used to be eighty per cent, out of which the enrollment in arts courses itself (BA degree) was of the order of 55 to 60 per cent. It is in this context that the Kothari Commission Report recommended vocationalisation of higher secondary education to wean away 50 per cent of the intake from graduate studies in general education. This was one of the definite ways to arrest the high incidence of educated unemployment and arrest wasteful expenditure. Realizing that this target of 50 per cent enrollment in vocational courses at the plus two stage was unrealistic, the Fifth Five Year Plan document brought it down to 25 per cent. At the time of introduction of vocationalisation, the target was lowered to 10 per cent. Periodical reviews have revealed that it has been difficult even by 1995 to reach this target of 10 per cent. Even now the enrollment in graduate arts courses is around 50 per cent of total enrollment in higher education. There are several problems that impede the progress of vocationalisation.

Non availability of skilled teachers is one of them. Economy of scale does not permit the appointment of full time teachers for a large variety of courses. There is difficulty in offering several courses which may be needed in the employment market but require considerable capital investment for infrastructure facilities (workshop) and equipments. Colleges do not often assume responsibility for guidance and placement services. A State Department of Vocational Education was started in 1979 as a wing of the Commissionerate of Public Instruction.

1986-1996: The decade 1986 to 1996 has been quite eventful in the history of education in Karnataka state. The Panchayat Raj institutions came into existence in 1987. As a consequence, school education was transferred to the PR bodies by the government. The State Commissionerate of Public Instruction continued with the executive functions at the District level under the guidance and control of the PR bodies. Dr. K.S. Krishnaswamy Committee of 1989 lauded the experiment in regard to attendance of students and teachers. However, with the change of government in March 1992 the administration of school education reverted to the State Department of Education.

The 73rd and 74th Constitutional amendments conferred mandatory status to democratic decentralisation of development administration at the District level and in urban areas including school administration. The new **Karnataka Panchayat Raj Act** was passed in 1993 and power was retransferred to PR bodies since April 1995. Entries No.17, 18 and 19 in a direct way and 1, 20, 25 and 26 in a cognate way as they appear in the 11th schedule of Article 243W of 73rd **Amendment** relate to the powers and functions of Panchayats in the field of education. Entry No.13 of 12th schedule of Article 243G of the **74th Amendment** relates to powers and responsibilities of Municipalities in regard to education. Gram Panchayats came into office in December 1993 and Taluk and Zilla Panchayats came into being in April 1995, since when the educational administration in Karnataka state is again in the hands of local self-government bodies.

The decade 1986 to 1996 also happens to be a decade of intense educational activity following the adoption of the National Policy on Education, 1986. A strategy for quality improvement of primary schools, especially single-teacher/single classroom lower primary schools, known as Operation Blackboard (OB) was launched in 1988. A second teacher was provided to all single teacher schools in the first phase. Beginning from 1992, the second phase of OB has been completed wherein a third teacher is also provided. The norm is to move towards one teacher and one instructional room for every standard of instruction. By now, there is no single teacher school in the state as at least two teachers are recruited for every school. However, in reality, a number of single teacher schools still exist, especially in backward regions in rural areas.

The Government of India constituted a Committee under the Chairmanship of Sri R.H. Dave to specify minimum levels of learning (MLL) for the primary stage of schooling which was to be ensured all over the country. The Karnataka Government has done everything to enforce MLL in the state including training of teachers for the same. It has brought out a Kannada version of MLL and distributed it to all the schools. All the primary school teachers have been given special orientation for realising minimum levels of learning.

In order to improve the quality of teachers and quality of teaching-learning process, the state government has adopted a centrally sponsored scheme. Under this scheme, District Institute of Education and Training have been set up in all Districts for quality improvement of primary education while certain selected B.Ed colleges are given the status of comprehensive teacher's colleges with additional resources for quality improvement programme in secondary education.

A review of the implementation of the National Policy on Education (1986) was made in 1992 by the Government of India. The review document is known as Programme of Action, 1992 (POA 1992). The POA 1992 recommended constitution of Village Education Committees (VECs). Following the 73rd Constitutional Amendment the Central Advisory Board of Education (CABE), constituted a Committee in 1993 to suggest ways and means of smooth decentralisation of education.

Incidentally, this Committee also recommended the constitution of VECs. The Commissionerate of Public Instruction has issued orders in December 1995 for the constitution of VECs in all Village Panchayats.

A programme called Social Safety Net has begun to look after the special needs of welfare sectors such as education and health which may get neglected in a whirlwind of liberalisation policies, and funds are provided by the National Renewal Fund for the purpose. The World Bank gave guidelines for the funding support to Primary Education under the Social Safety Net which is around Rs.40 Crores to every selected district in addition to regular funding. Districts with low female literacy were to be selected for improvement of primary education and universalisation of enrollment, retention and attainment levels (minimum competencies) within a time-frame of 5 to 6 years, that is, by 2000 AD. This is known as the District Primary Education Project (DPEP). Karnataka identified Raichur, Belgaum, Kolar and Mandya districts for the purpose. A state-level DPEP Society has been formed with the Education Minister as its President and the State Project Director, an IAS Officer, its Secretary. Perspective plans for universalisation of primary education for the four districts have been finalised. A number of state level quality improvement programmes have been initiated. The project has been in operation in the 4 districts. In the second phase, beginning from 1996, 5 more districts have been included for DPEP treatment. They are Bellary, Bidar, Gulbarga, Mysore and Bangalore Rural Districts.

HIGHER EDUCATION

1833-1915: The Central College was accorded the status of a degree college in the year 1875-76. It was the only college that was preparing students for the B.A. degree examination of Madras University.[6] The Central College had originated in 1857 as a high school and affiliated to Madras University in 1859. In fact, all other colleges in Mysore State affiliated to Madras University at that time

6. There were only 3 universities in the country started in 1857 and located at Bombay, Calcutta and Madras. Students from High Schools/Colleges from Mysore State were appearing for Matriculation/FA/BA degree in Madras University.

had begun as high scools, for instance, the Rajah school that had begun in 1833 was the nucleus of the Maharaja's College. It was in 1893-94 that the Maharaja's College, Mysore, was accorded the status of a First Grade College which could send students of BA degree course for examination at Madras University in January 1896. Likewise, the Government High School, Mangalore (part of Madras Presidency at that time and integrated to new Mysore state in 1956), established in 1868, was upgraded as a second grade college in 1869. Some of the other old colleges (prior to 1919) are St. Aloysius College, Mangalore (1880), St.Joseph's College, Bangalore (1882), Maharani's College for Women, Mysore (1902).

The number of subjects offered by these colleges for the graduate courses were limited. While Central College, Bangalore, specialised in science subjects, the Maharaja's College, Mysore devoted itself to humanities and arts. The three main subjects taught in the Central College for the BA degree course were physics (including Chemisty), Mathematics and Geology even by 1898.

1916 to 1955: Mysore State entered the twentieth century without a university. There were hardly four universitites in the country at the turn of the century. The foresight of the then Dewan of Mysore State, Sir M. Visveswaraya and the benevolent patronage of the then Maharaja Sri Krishna Devaraja Wodeyar brought into being the University of Mysore on 25th July 1916. It was the first University of the state and the first in a princely State outside the British rule. An Engineering College was established during the same year (1916) at Bangalore and the University had 4 colleges at the time of its creation. A Medical College was started in Bangalore in 1924. The University of Mysore was under the direct administrative control of the State Department of Education from 1916 to 1956. It is significant to observe that during these 40 years, under State control, it had both utmost autonomy and a high reputation.

Amendments had been made to the (Mysore University Act of 1916) successively in the years 1919, 1923, 1925, 1928 and 1933. The 1933 amendment is significant as it provided for an Academic Council as well as made the Senate more representive of popular will. Just before the reorganisation of States, the **Mysore University Act** was amended in 1956 when it became autonomous from governmental control.

1956 to 1996: Reorganisation of States in 1956 presented a variety of problems in university education. Bombay-Karnatak region districts had 13 colleges which were part of the Karnatak University, established in 1950 by the Bombay Government. Most of them were private colleges. There were 70 colleges in the state, of which 57 were under Mysore and Karnatak Universities (Table 1). There was variety in structure, courses, grant-in-aid rules, administration, standards across colleges in the different regions of the state.

The Government of Mysore appointed an University Education Integration Committee in 1958 with Dr. A. Lakshmana Swami Mudaliar as Chairman to suggest ways and means of solving the problems and issues of diversity. Following the recommendations of this Committee, a Directorate of Collegiate Education was created in 1961. The jurisdiction of the two existing universities were redefined and the colleges were distributed. Colleges of education were transferred to the Department of Public Instruction. The Engineering Colleges were under a Directorate of Technical Education, headed ex-officio by the Director of Public Instruction. This was separated from the Department of Public Instruction and treated as an independent Directorate in 1959. The government took over the Medical College and placed it under the Director of Medical Services in 1959.

The number of new colleges grew at a fast rate after reorganisation. Bangalore City (and Bangalore district) itself contributed a large number of colleges. With the passing of the **Bangalore University Act**, a new university was created as a City University in 1964 to take control of the Post-Graduate Departments in Central College, 32 colleges and the University Engineering College in Bangalore City. Later, colleges in Bangalore Rural district, Kolar and Tumkur were handed over to Bangalore University. Incidentally, an Agricultural University was also created in the same year at Hebbal, Bangalore.

The University Review Commission of 1948, headed by Dr S. Radhakrishnan, had recommended, among other measures, the extension of two year degree courses by one more year. The two year intermediate, two year degree and three year Honours Courses were abolished in 1957 and replaced by a one year pre-university and three year degree course.

The problems of school and university education which accompanied the integration of the state in 1956 were getting sorted out in the state. It was at this time that the Government of India set up an Education Commission in 1964 with Dr. D.S. Kothari as its Chairman and adopted its report in 1968. The state government fell in line with the recommendations of the National Commission for uniform structures of education and vocationalisation of higher secondary education. The 10+2+3 structure of education was adopted by the state. The status of the plus two courses in the state has continued to be under triple control. A large number of higher secondary schools, controlled by the Commissioner of Public Instruction, Degree Colleges affiliated to different universities and administered by the Directorate of Collegiate Education as well as independent Junior Colleges with only plus 2 courses are under the academic control of the Director of Pre-University Eduation who is advised by a Pre-University Board which also conducts a common examination. The state government had set up a Committee in 1979 under the Chairmanship of Sri D.V. Urs to suggest measures for uniform administration of plus two stage and to bring it under a single umbrella. Even in 1996, the position of triple control continues at the +2 stage.

A positive measure of the state government in 1970 of providing 100 per cent salary grant to private colleges resulted in the unexpected growth of a large number of private colleges over the years. While government colleges increased from 51 in 1970 to 159 in 1991-92, private colleges have grown from 195 to 675, though many of them are run on a self-financing basis. Growth of private colleges in the 70s was also accompanied by deterioration in standards and discipline.

The Karnataka Government felt a pressing need to have a uniform Act for all the then existing 3 universities in the state. This was made possible through the **Karnataka State Universities Act, 1976.** A significant feature of the 1976 Act has been that the final decison for the recognition of a college be vested with the government while the University had recommending powers. In fact, the arrangement gave rise to piquant situations in the past when the government granted recognition to colleges which had been disqualified for affiliation by the universities.

The Government of Karnataka felt the need to get a review of the state Universities under the **Karnataka State Universities Act, 1976,** and hence, set up a Committee for this under the Chairmanship of Dr. K.N. Raj, which submitted its report in August 1980. Hardly a few recommendations of this Commission were followed up by the government, one of which was to hold a joint entrance examination at the state level for professional courses.

Two more universities were started in 1980 at Gulbarga and Mangalore. There was a reorganisation of jurisdiction of universities. Further in 1987, the Kuvempu University was formed to have control over colleges of Shimoga, Chitradurga and Chikmagalur districts. In order to promote research in Kannada and Culture (and also fall in line with the neighbouring Tamil Nadu and Andhra Pradesh states), a Kannada University was set up of Hampi in 1987. An Agricultural University was created at Dharwad in 1983. A university for legal studies known as National Law School of India University came up in 1987. It is the only university in the country established exclusively for legal studies. This was founded by the Bar Council of India. The Manipal Medical College got deemed university status in 1993. The Indira Gandhi National Open University, New Delhi, set up a Regional Centre at Bangalore in 1988. The Karnataka State Open University has been established in June 1996 in Mysore. The Institutes of Correspondence Courses in the existing universities will get amalgamated into the open university.

There were several Acts regulating the establishment and management of educational institutions in the state, including an Act of regulation of private educational institutions. In spite of all these acts, Karnataka has witnessed erratic growth and development of educational institutions, especially the Pre-Primary institutions in urban areas, B.Ed. Colleges and TCH institutions, Engineering Colleges and Polytechnics. A mushroom growth of countless private tutorial colleges has been witnessed. There has been a widely shared view that education has been highly commercialised. It is felt that the state has failed in its regulatory function of education. In view of all these criticisms and also as a generally felt need, the state realised the need for a **Comprehensive Education Act**. While two early attempts in 1970 and 1974 had not yielded results, the state could succeed in getting a bill drafted from a Committee headed by Dr. A.C. Deva Gowda, The Bill of 1983, adopted by the state Assembly in March 1984, finally became an Act in 1995.

With the imbalanced growth of colleges, multiplication of post-graduate centres and universities, increasing pressure on resources, a need was felt to get a review of the functioning of the universities in the state. The state government set up a Review Committee with Professor T. Navneeth Rao as its Chairman to examine the efficiency, effectiveness and relevance of the university system in the state. The Commission submitted its report in 1993. The state government is examining the proposals for implementation. The Review Committee has made certain sensitive recommendations such as abolition of the Syndicate, integration of Academic Council and the Senate as Academic Senate, re-conversion of Bangalore University as a Unitary University, conversion of one of the state universities as a Central University, creation of a Health University, a Technological University and a Horticulture University, creation of a Karnataka State Council of Higher Education (which had earlier been recommended also by the K.N. Raj Committee in 1980 and the National Policy and Education, 1986) etc. The state government established a Health University in June 1996. All medical and dental colleges including those which teach alternative systems of medicine (alternative to Allopathy) will be brought under the purview of the Health University.

PROFESSIONAL EDUCATION

Technical Education:

1962 to 1955: 'School of Engineering', established in 1862 at Mysore, was the first ever institution for technical education in Old Mysore state. This institution, established to train technicians for subordinate services was elevated to the status of a centre for higher learning in 1875. The first Government Industrial School was started at Hassan in 1889, followed by one such at Mysore in 1892. A scheme of Technical Education was approved in 1903 and in 1913, and Sir M. Visveswaraya got a Mechnical Engineering School at Bangalore and the Chamarajendra Technical Institute at Mysore established. In 1909, Sri Jamshedji Tata established the Indian Institute of Science. The Krishnarajendra Silver Jubilee Technical Institute was establised in 1928 at Bangalore. A landmark in the history of technical education was the starting of the Jayachmarajendra Occupational Institute in 1943 which became the Polytechnic of the same name and served as a model for similar institutions in later years. Before independence, two Engineering Colleges came up in the state. One of them was the BMS College of Engineering and Technology at Bangalore and the other, the BVB College of Engineering at Hubli, both of them established in 1946. Two private Engineering Colleges, the National Institute of Engineering (1950), and the BDT College of Engineering (1951) at Davangere, were established.

1956 to 1996: At the time of reorganisation of states in 1956, there were only 6 Engineering Colleges in the state. The Manipal Institute of Technology came up in 1957. Thereafter, it was a case of slow and steady growth of institutions till 1979. There was a spurt of Engineering Colleges in the following decade. It took nearly 40 years for the state to have 6 Engineering Colleges by 1956, 23 years to get 13 more colleges and a total of 19 colleges in the state by 1979. It took, only 10 years for the 19 colleges to rise up to 50 colleges; there was an increase of 31 colleges in a span of 10 years (Table 2). By 1996, the number of Engineering Colleges stood at 54. It is to be noted that only 5 out of these 54 colleges are Government Colleges, while another 11 private colleges are receiving government aid. The remaining colleges are private, unaided, self-financing institutions. It is note-worthy that 27 per cent of all Engineering Colleges and 18 per cent of all Medical Colleges in India are in Karnataka only.

Medical Education:

1911 to 1990: The first Medical School in the state was established in 1911 and the first Medical College in 1924, both at Bangalore. The Medical College was shifted to Mysore in 1930. The Mysore Medical Education Society was formed in 1954 which established a college at Bangalore in the following year. The first private Medical College in the state, established in 1953 was the Kasturba Medical College founded by Dr. T.M.A. Pai at Manipal. The state government took over the Bangalore and Mysore Medical Colleges in 1957 and 1958 respectively, and also established two more colleges in 1958 and 1961 at Hubli and Bellary respectively. Even to this day, there area only 4 Government Medical Colleges in the state. Later on, colleges came up in Gulbarga (1963), Davangere (1965) and Belgaum (1969). In November 1978, the Directorate of Health Services was bifurcated into two wings: Directorate of Health and Family Welfare Services and Directorate of Medical Education. The number of colleges almost doubled during the period 1985 to 1990.

Professional Education has a special place and importance in state administration. The judiciary has been playing an important role in defining the relationship between state, civil society and professional education since 1963. Articles 15(1), 15(2) and 29(2) of the Indian Constitution provided for Equality of Educational opportunities. Reservation for Schedules Castes and Tribes has been made mandatory. Reservation for backward castes is a prerogative of the state governments. After the reorganisation of states, the state government constituted 4 committees, viz., the Nagana Gowda (1961), the Havanur (1970), the Venkataswamy (1933), and the Justice Chinnappa Reddy (1988) Commissions to guide the state in providing educational opportunities to Backward Castes, Classes, Tribes and Communities. None of these commissions has been able to provide fool-proof guidelines. Decisions of the government and enforcement therein based on all these Committee recommendations have been taken both to the Karnataka High Court and the Supreme Court of India. Invaribaly, government decisions have been struck down. As a result, even now the reservation policy in the state is as per a Government ordinance issued on 13th October 1986.

ADULT AND NON-FORMAL EDUCATION

Adult Education

1868 to 1939: The Hobli school scheme drawn up by Lewis Rice in 1868 for the Mysore state included a provision for night schools for those who could not attend the day schools. Significant among the several beneficiaries of the scheme were the police constables of the state in the year 1874-75. Night schools were given grant-in-aid by the state in 1895 as per certain norms. The State Department of Education was monitoring these schools. With a fluctuating record over the years, the number of night schools in the state stood at 72 in 1939-40.

1940 to 1977: Dr. Laubach of the World Literacy Movement visited Mysore in 1940 carrying the slogan 'Each one, Teach one', and the book, **India shall be Literate.** There were several enthusiastic and committed individuals for this movement in the state. Sri Devudu Narasimha Sastry, poet-laureate B.M.Srikantiah, the Mysore University at Mysore and Bangalore, the Wesleyan Mission were prominent among the promoters of the movement. Literacy Campaigns were launched. Success of all these efforts led to the formation of Mysore State Literacy Council. It is also important to note that at the National Level, due to the visionary efforts of Mahatma Gandhi and Dr. Zakir Hussain, the National Adult Education Association had been formed in 1939 which had an influence on the formation of the State Literacy Council which has now become the Karnataka State Adult Education Council. The Council did considerably well in a variety of ways including post-literacy work. From a position of 178 literacy centres in 1941-42, the figure went up to 1,318 by 1956. Inspired by the success stories of 'Folk Schools' of Denmark, the Council started similar schools in the state known as **Vidyapeethas,** first such school was located at Nanjangud, Mysore District, in 1947-48. It was a Non-formal Vocational Training Institute in rural contexts. There are 14 Vidyapeethas spread all over the state at present including one exclusively for women.

Reorganisation of States did not in any way boost adult education. The Government of India did not accept any executive responsibility for adult education till 1978.

1978 to 1985: For the first time, a National Policy on Adult Education was formulated and adopted on April 5, 1977, by the Parliament when the Janatha Government was in power. It led to the adoption of a project approach and launching of projects all over the country on October 2, 1978, including projects in Karnataka. Centrally sponsored projects known as Rural Functional Literacy Projects/RFLP were initiated in the state. The state government also started State Adult Education projects (SAEP) in unserved areas. Post-literacy centres called Jana Shikshana Nilayas were also started in several regions. The Congress government which replaced the Janatha government in 1979 continued the good work but only after adopting the same strategy and policy with a new nomenclature - the National Adult Education Policy, 1980.

1986 to 1996: The National Education Policy 1986 emphasised the distinctive significance of adult education in the country. Following this, a new national strategy was worked out, the 'Literacy Campaigns'. The National Literacy Mission was set up by the Government of India in 1988. This was one of the 5 Technology Missions of the Government of India. District Literacy Campaigns were launched in Karnataka. All the 21 Districts have completed the first phase of Literacy Campaigns and 9 districts are in the second phase of post-Literacy and Continuing Education.

A special feature of the literacy campaigns has been that the state government has shown utmost commitment to the programme. Though the Department of Mass Education, with an IAS Director, manages the programme at the state level, there is a state level Saksharatha Samithi with the Chief Minister of the state as its President. It is run at the district level as if it is a programme to be supported by the entire District government machinery with the Deputy Comissioner providing leadership.

Non-Formal Education (NFE) : Pre-Primary Education, Anganwadi, Balwadi as well as evening/part-time schools for non-enrolled and drop-out children from formal schools, education and empowerment programmes of adult non-literate women, etc, constitute the world of non-formal education.

1906-1955: Pre-Primary education began in the state with the opening of two Kindergaerten schools in Bangalore and Mysore by Miss L.R. Latter, who came to the state from England at the invitation of the government in the year 1907. Over the years it got a fillip through the interest of Professor M.V. Gopalaswamy, Professor of Psychology at Maharaja's College, Mysore (1933), and the continued visit of Madame Montessori to India during 1930s and 40s. In 1935, the government appointed a Nursery Education Committee with Sri Sultan Mohiyuddin as Chairman (then DDPI, Bangalore), who submitted his report in 1936. Apart from running a few nursery schools, the state government was also giving grants-in-aid to private nursery schools. There were 73 nursery schools in the State by 1956. The observation made on nursery schools by the Educational Reforms Committee in 1953 is quite significant as reflective of state's thinking in regard to Nursery Education. It observed that the responsibility for creches and nursery schools should be left to parents and local bodies. The state should conserve its financial resources to provide free and compulsory education as laid down by the Constitution. In fact, even in 1985-86, there were 1,731 Pre-Primary schools run by the Department of Public Instruction which increased to 5,336 by 1992-93.

1956 to 1973: During this period pre primary/non-formal education did not progress as the state was more concerned about school education. However, there was international interest in NFE in the early 70s as a large number of research studies revealed the limitations of formal schooling in Universaliation of Primary Education (UPE) as well as the importance of pre-primary education in the same direction.

1974 to 1996: For the first time, a National Policy for children was adopted by the Government of India on 26th August 1974. Earlier, in its 35th meeting, the Central Advisory Board of Education had recommended the provision of pre-school education all over the country. The Fifth Five Year Plan of the Government of India (1974-1979) provided for both Non-Formal Education (9 to 14 years) and pre-school education as centrally sponsored programmes. The Government of Karnataka began the first Integrated Child Development Services (ICDS) project in the state at T. Narasipur taluk of Mysore district in 1975-76. Incidentally, this was the year when the National Commission on Status of Women had submitted its report. There has been a steady growth of ICDS projects in the state since then. Anganwadias are set up under the project which integrate health and nutrition along with education which would provide a 'head start' to children to adjust to formal primary education.

Of the 196 taluks in Karnataka 1991-92, there were 142 ICDS projects in the state out of which 110 were centrally sponsored and the rest state sponsored, with a coverage of 72.45 per cent area of the state. The Department of Women and Children's Welfare, created out of the Department of Social Welfare in 1986, looks after all ICDS projects.

Non-Formal Education (9 to 14 years) for non-enrolled and drop-out children has a chequered history in the state. Initially, when it was started in 1978, it was part of the Department of Public Instruction which was shifted later to the DSERT and again shifted to the Department of Mass Education. It had a phenomenal rise up to 1984-85 and declined later. By 1988-89, this centrally sponsored, pro-poor, pro-girl child programme was completely given up with the intention of integrating it with Total Literacy Campaigns.

Education Secretariat: One significant feature of educational administration has been the growth of Education Secretariat after the reorganisation of states. Though the erstwhile Mysore state had an experience of 'planning' since 1916 when Sir M. Visveswaraya had formulated a plan of development of Modern Mysore state, and even the Bombay Karnataka districts had experienced planned development through the Bombay Plan of 1943, still, as a part of National Policy of the Quinquennial Planning and Development, the Karnataka state seriously began to plan for welfare sectors including education since the reorganisation of states. Educational Planning at the state level has got specialised in the last 40 years. It is all along managed by senior and middle level officers in the capacity of Secretary, Additional Secretary and Deputy Secretaries assisted by officers. There are four ministries looking after education under four ministers: minister for

Higher Education, Minister for School Education, State Ministers for Medical and Adult Education. The Education Secretariat serves all these ministeries and exercises control within given framework over all aspects of Education.

Conclusion: The role of the state in the education of its people has been changing over the years. It has evolved in three distinct phases: (a) welfarist (b) regulatory; and (c) promotional. Initially, since 1868, with the introduction of Hobli school scheme and establishment of Government High Schools and Colleges, the state assumed a welfare role; Education was considered as an instrument of well-being of the people and welfare of the society. Experiments in local self governments midway in 1930s where the state wanted to assume promotive role failed and the state continued with its welfarist role. The welfare objectives of the state got strengthened with the achievement of independence and adoption of a Constitution which, by and large, reflected the vision of a welfare state. The role of the state in the universalisation of primary education fitted well with the welfarist role. The state took full executive responsibility for the purpose. Regulating role was kept to the minmum with such acts as the **Compulsory Primary Education Act of 1961.** The promotional role of the State was limited to adult education, pre-primary education, music, fine arts and other components of culture.

Primary education gained a momentum in the 1970s which created a demand for secondary education and its expansion. A need for trained secondary school teachers was felt which led to the mushrooming of B.Ed. Colleges. Likewise, with the national policies of the 70s such as Housing for All, Health for All etc, the demand for engineers and doctors went up, resulting in the proliferation of capitation fee colleges. The state had taken only a welfarist interest in professional education through the instrument of reservation for SCs, STs and Backward groups intending to promote social mobility and bring about social change towards an egalitarian society. All of a sudden the state felt the need for assuming a regulatory role through the **Private Educational Institution Act,** later enacted as the **Karnataka State Education Act.** Curiously enough, instead of promoting mass primary education, the state followed a line of least resistence and yielded to political pressures by which it started promoting mass higher education. In a state with more than 50 per cent literacy (by 1989, at the time of drafting the VIII Five Year Plan), there was a degree college in every taluk and it became a status symbol of the region. The state had to assume regulatory role in regard to growth and development of higher education. It has not succeeded so far.

The state has been a forefront runner in the decentralisation of development administration including education. It adopted the **Karnataka Panchayat Raj Act** in 1983 much before the **73rd and 74th Constitutional amendments of 1993** for democratic decentralisation of state administration. The state handed over the responsibility, powers and finances to the district and sub-district local self-government bodies for school education, adult and non-formal education and libraries. The state was content with a promotional role. With a short break of 3 years between 1991 and 1994, the state has again assumed promotional responsibility for school education. It had already assumed such a responsibility for higher education as early as in 1956. In spite of the powers transfarred to local-self governments bodies at the district and sub-district levels, the state continues to fulfil its departmental responsibilities. It has given up its welfarist role in terms of powers and to performing its regulatory and promotional roles along with executive responsibilities. Such a strategy is in keeping with the latest national social philosophy of liberalisation which includes within its framework the shrinking of the state.

TABLE-1

Distribution of Colleges in the State at the Time of Integration in 1956.

Area	Degree Colleges	Professional	Intermediate	Total
Old Mysore State	14	14	14	42
Bombay State	10	5	-	15
Madras State	4	3	-	7
Hyderabad State	4	1	-	5
Coorg District	1	-	-	1
TOTAL	**33**	**23**	**14**	**70**

A Government College of Agriculture, Dharwad (1948), a Government Teachers College, Mangalore (1950), a Government Degree College, Mercara (1949), Colleges run by the Academy of General Education, Manipal, including a Medical College, 2 Degree Colleges in Gulbarga (1952, 1955) are among them.

TABLE-2

Growth of Engineering & Medical Colleges in the State

Year	Engineering Colleges	Medical Colleges
1956	6	3
1961	11	4
1969	16	7
1979	19	9
1985	41	10
1990	50	19
1996	54	22

REFERENCE

Seetharamu, A.S. (1993). Triangular Context in Professional Education. **Deccan Herald**, Bangalore, December 11.

3

WOMEN AND CHILDREN*

Anitha Kaul

Introduction: Women and children, constituting more than 50 per cent of the population, have had to face many problems and difficulties as a result of the attitude of the society towards them. Women, particularly, were discriminated against in all walks of life, and denied equal opportunities with men. This was reflected in unequal access of women and girls to education, health, nutrition and employment. They, not only had no control over the productive resources such as land, house and other assets, but also had no role to play in decision-making. The system was such that they were relegated to the marginal position with men dominating the domestic as well as outside spheres. While this was the situation, the children, especially girl children, were either totally neglected or discriminated against. The male children, of course, were taken seriously since sons were valued and nurtured for their importance in the patriarchal and male-centered society. To remedy this situation and to bring them to the mainstream of society, certain constitutional guarantees were provided during the post-independence era. To achieve this objective, many programmes were initiated by the Central as well as state governments. However, in spite of this, even after 50 years of independence, the gap between men and women still continues in relation to equal opportunities.

Situation of Women and Children in Karnataka: Karnataka has a population of 44,977,201 with 69.1 per cent of them living in rural areas. With this high percentage concentrated in rural areas, the pressure on land is high. The average size of operational holdings is 2.213 hectares in 1990-91 and the per capita land available for

* This paper reflects the personal views of the author, not of the government.

cultivation is 0.27 hectare. The per capita income ranges from Rs. 10,810 in Kodagu to Rs. 3,725 in Bidar.

The income levels and access to land is low in general, but women's access to income and control over land and economic assets is even lower. Women are, therefore, not counted among the labour force and in non-agricultural activities. In Karnataka, the proportion of total workers, main workers and marginal workers has shown an increase in the total female workforce between 1981 and 1991. But, considering the fact that in rural areas agriculture and household industries account for nearly all the economic activities, and women have combined domestic work, child care and other productivity activities, this figure does not adequately reflect the contribution of women to the workforce.

Table 1

Total Workforce : 1981-1991 (in percentages)

	Total Workers		Main Workers		Marginal Workers	
	1981	1991	1981	1991	1981	1991
Total	40.24	41.99	36.76	36.4	53.48	3.54
Male	54.59	54.09	53.90	53.5	30.69	0.56
Female	25.33	29.39	18.95	22.7	36.38	6.66

Source: Census of India.

The occupational structure of females shows a low proportion in cultivators and high proportion in agricultural labourers. The proportion of female cultivators reduced from 22.5 per cent in 1961 to 8.32 per cent in 1991. The reduction in the case of males has not been so drastic. The proportion of female agricultural labourers increased from 9.17 per cent in 1961 to 16.52 per cent in 1971 and reduced to 15.27 per cent in 1991 (Table 2). This has resulted in women being forced to seek work elsewhere and work is not always available.

Table 2:

Proportion of Male - Female Cultivators, Agricultural Labourers and Other Workers (in percentages)

	1961	1971	1981	1991
Cultivators				
M	38.64	31.54	31.21	28.06
F	22.05	9.72	6.32	8.32
Agricultural Labourers				
M	8.91	13.61	13.32	14.48
F	9.17	16.52	12.26	15.27
Other Workers				
M	12.85	12.03	11.88	12.67
F	5.57	4.43	3.70	4.12

Source: Census of India

Education & Literacy: Education and literacy attainment for the state as a whole are on par with the national average; in rural areas the attainments are poor. Karnataka's overall literacy rate is 55 per cent; the male-female differential is high with 67 per cent male literacy and 44 per cent female literacy. Female literacy is highest in Dakshina Kannada with 55 per cent which is far lower than the highest in the states of Kerala, Tamil Nadu, Maharashtra. The disparity between male and female literacy rates is highest in rural areas. Rural female literacy for the state is as low as 28 per cent with some districts such as Gulbarga and Raichur having a rural female literacy rate of 12.71 per cent and 13.05 per cent only respectively. Table-3 gives the comparative increase in the literacy rates for rural males and females. But, while the rates of literacy have been rising, the total number of illiterate persons, especially among women have also been rising.

Table 3
Rural Male-Female Literacy

Sl.NO.	District		1961	1971	1981	1991
1.	Bangalore	M	27.27	34.74	42.74	57.20
		F	7.26	14.10	19.68	39.69
2.	Bangalore (Rural)	M				49.53
		F				28.20
3.	Chitradurga	M	32.54	37.05	43.84	50.96
		F	8.70	15.21	21.14	29.37
4.	Kolar	M	24.93	30.15	37.95	47.54
		F	6.41	10.59	14.86	24.30
5.	Shimoga	M	34.48	40.98	49.05	55.80
		F	12.39	21.65	28.30	37.246.
	Tumkur	M	31.03	36.83	45.18	53.46
		F	7.90	14.93	21.07	31.32
7.	Belgaum	M	33.17	37.33	43.29	50.23
		F	9.34	12.92	17.98	25.50
8.	Bijapur	M	33.98	35.55	40.31	53.04
		F	7.98	10.18	13.61	28.41
9.	Dharwad	M	43.72	46.77	49.56	54.73
		F	14.11	19.22	23.12	30.41
10.	Uttar Kannada	M	40.07	46.36	53.10	61.12
		F	19.39	27.63	33.76	43.34
11.	Bellary	M	28.09	29.67	35.32	41.79
		F	5.56	9.61	12.61	19.36
12.	Bidar	M	20.85	27.35	33.52	42.70
		F	2.76	5.76	8.80	19.44
13.	Gulbarga	M	19.63	23.44	29.96	34.98
		F	2.93	4.75	7.80	12.71

(Contd.)

14.	Raichur	M	23.06	28.06	32.09	34.87
		F	3.30	6.93	9.82	13.05
15.	Chikmaglur	M	34.48	40.78	49.40	57.74
		F	13.05	21.80	30.04	40.35
16.	Dak.Kannada	M	37.19	48.01	58.04	68.95
		F	19.72	30.23	40.45	55.14
17.	Hassan	M	32.32	37.73	45.22	55.23
		F	9.39	15.79	22.06	33.60
18.	Kodagu	M	34.31	47.54	53.78	62.00
		F	15.74	35.37	40.70	49.77
19.	Mandya	M	23.31	28.47	37.40	47.61
		F	5.25	9.99	16.14	27.39
20.	Mysore	M	21.01	24.31	30.06	38.70
		F	5.21	8.83	12.96	21.43
	Total	**M**	**30.49**	**35.40**	**42.06**	**49.80**
		F	**9.19**	**14.54**	**19.77**	**28.77**

Adult literacy is closely linked with the universalisation of elementary education and retention of girls in schools. A girl who stays in school up to the upper primary level is unlikely to relapse into illiteracy. Thus, there is an immediate connection between universalisation of elementary education and adult literacy and the two must be promoted simultaneously.

Elementary Education: Over the years, there has been an improvement in the enrollment of girls and boys in primary schools in the state. The total enrollment in Karnataka in Classes I-V, as per the data available from the Sixth All India Educational Survey (September 1993) was 6.04 million, of whom 2.81 million were girls. Of this, the enrollment in rural primary schools was 4.18 million with 1.92 million being girls. However, the percentage of Class V enrollment as a per cent of Class I enrollment continues to be low at 59.44 per cent. This appears to point to a very high dropout rate. Another way of looking at enrollment and dropout is to look at Gross Enrollment Ratios (GER).

The Sixth All India Educational Survey shows a GER of 119.23 for Classes I-V. The GER for classes VI-VIII, however, sharply drops to 66.95. For girls, the drop is even sharper from 114.09 to 59.31.

Enrollment figures alone do not give an accurate picture of the progress of schooling. There is the problem of irregular attendance, absenteeism and dropout. The poorer enrollment and higher dropout among girls is the result of low priority to girls education, low value attached to female life itself, poverty, involvement of girls in sibling care, domestic chores such as fuel, fodder and water fetching, cattle grazing etc.

Out of School Children - Child Labour: The fact that dropout rates among girls is higher than the dropout rates among boys is indicative of societal attitudes toward the education of girls. Many of these girls are participating in the workforce. The percentage change between 1971 and 1981 in number and workforce participation rates among boys and girls below 14 years for Karnataka indicates that while boys are being freed from the workforce, they are being increasingly replaced by girls, who work on family farms (Table 4). More and more girls are being denied access to schooling.

Table 4

Workforce Participation Rates (WFPR) for Boys and Girls below 14.

Percentage Increase in Numbers			Percentage Increase in WFPR		
Male	Female	Main worker Male	Main worker Female	Cultivator Female	Agriculture Female
2	55	(-)9	41	50	50

Source: Census of India, 1981, Series I Part III B.

Demographic Features: The sex ratio which was 959 per 1,000 males in 1961 rose by only one point to 960 per 1,000 in 1991. Between 1971 and 1981, there was a marginal increase and this increase was expected to rise even further in 1991; but between 1981 and 1991, there was a decline fairly sharply from 1981 to 1991 in all the districts of

Gulbarga Division, viz., Bellary, Bidar, Gulbarga, Raichur, as well as the districts of Kolar, Tumkur, Bijapur, Belgaum and Dharwad. In fact, in the districts of Bidar, Kolar, Bijapur, Mandya, Raichur and Gulbarga, the 1991 sex ratio is even lower than the 1961 levels. The sex ratio has shown marginal increase, between 1981 and 1991 in all districts of the Mysore division as well as Uttar Kannada, Shimoga and Bangalore. The sex ratio in Chitradurga district has 'remained' stagnant at 944 per 1,000 (Table 5). The major cause of this persistent overall adverse sex ratio and demographic imbalance is the high rate of female mortality from infancy to the end of the reproductive period.[1] In addition, there are the traditionally inculcated and 'socially' approved attitudes of self-sacrifice and self denial which reinforce neglect and lack of proper health and nutrition care of women and girls by others in the family.

Table 5
Sex Ratio

Sl.No.	District	1961	1971	1981	1991
1.	Bangalore	917	909	916	903
2.	Bangalore (R)				945
3.	Chitradurga	940	939	944	944
4.	Kolar	968	961	971	965
5.	Shimoga	898	931	947	960
6.	Tumkur	956	957	961	958
7.	Belgaum	951	947	957	954
8.	Bijapur	976	975	982	964
9.	Dharwad	941	946	948	944
10.	Uttar Kannada	946	957	958	966
11.	Bellary	917	967	973	965
12.	Bidar	971	963	968	952
13.	Gulbarga	989	981	981	962
14.	Raichur	985	981	988	979
15.	Chickmaglur	904	937	935	977
16.	Dakshina Kannada	1,082	1,058	1,059	1,063

1. In recent years, there have been reports of the increasing misuse of aminocentesis to abort the foetus if it is female.

17.	Hassan	969	974	987	999
18.	Kodagu	863	910	933	979
19.	Mandya	967	960	960	963
20.	Mysore	951	942	951	953
	STATE	**959**	**957**	**963**	**960**

Female mortality is higher in practically all age groups up to the end of the reproductive period. The difference is particularly high in the age groups 5-9 and 15-34 (Table 6).

A Report on Medical Certification of Cause of Death brought out by the Directorate of Economics and Statistics, Government of Karnataka, states that the age group 15-34 accounted for 28.4 per cent deaths of females as compared to 16.3 per cent of males. Only after age 35 when women have past their peak child bearing years do female mortality rates drop below male rates.

Table 6

Age Specific Death Rates.

Age Group		1976	1981	1986	1987
0-4	M	-	23.6	24.6	24.6
	F	-	24.9	24.3	25.6
5-9	M	5.6	2.1	1.9	1.6
	F	6.5	2.4	2.1	2.1
10-14	M	1.9	1.0	1.1	1.1
	F	1.7	2.4	1.2	1.0
15-19	M	3.5	1.7	1.6	1.4
	F	2.4	2.8	2.3	2.4
20-24	M	2.3	1.5	2.5	1.9
	F	4.5	2.7	1.9	2.5
25-29	M	3.3	2.3	2.0	1.6
	F	5.5	2.4	2.9	2.9
30-34	M	4.3	2.5	2.6	2.4
	F	7.8	4.7	1.9	2.5

(Contd.)

35-39	M	4.4	4.6	3.9	3.8
	F	4.3	2.2	4.4	3.1
40-44	M	10.0	6.1	4.4	5.4
	F	6.2	5.1	4.6	3.9
45-49	M	9.9	9.9	8.3	8.3
	F	8.3	6.5	5.6	4.7

Prenatal deaths include late foetal deaths (28 weeks after pregnancy), stillbirths and deaths among infants less than seven days old. It is a sensitive index of the quality of mother and child care, and the nature of delivery services. In Karnataka, prenatal death rate showed an alarming increase from 48 in 1981 to 54 in 1987. The 1992 SRS shows a further increase to 65.1 as against the national average of 47.5. The infant mortality rate has been fluctuating in Karnataka from 65 to 80 per 1,000 between 1981 and 1994 (Table 7). Infant mortality increased from 71 per cent in 1981 to 73 per cent 1,000 in 1991. However, the 1994 SRS shows a reduction to 7 per 1,000. The maternal mortality rate continues to be a cause for concern at 400 per lakhs considerably higher than the rates of Kerala (120), Maharashtra (180), Tamil Nadu (30), Punjab (200). The poorer the woman the greater the risk. Maternal malnutrition also affects the health of infants.

Table 7

Infant Mortality Rate: 1981-1993

Year	All India	Karnataka
1981	110	69
1982	105	65
1983	105	71
1984	104	74
1985	97	69
1986	96	73
1987	95	75

(Contd.)

1988	94	74
1989	91	80
1990	80	70
1991	80	77
1992	79	73
1993	74	67

National Nutrition Monitoring Bureau (NNMB) data on malnutrition shows that the number of severely and moderately malnourished children has remained stagnant at 8.3 per cent for the period 1988-90. The number of mildly malnourished children has, on the other hand, increased from 48.8 per cent in 1988-90 to 54.5 per cent in 1991-92. Gender specific data are not available, but anyone working closely with the community will admit that gender is an important determinant in the nutritional status of children. It accounts for lower caloric intakes and poorer nutrition among female children. A study conducted in Pura village of Kunigal Taluk in Tumkur district indicates that adult women had a deficit of 100 calories per day, whereas in many cases men had a surplus of 800 calories.

Child marriage, admittedly on the decline, is still prevalent in Karnataka. According to the 1981 census, out of 93,839 married girls in the age group 10-14, 64,606 were concentrated in the five districts of Bijapur, Belgaum, Dharwad, Gulbarga and Raichur. Early marriage of girls is followed by early and too frequent pregnancies, leading to higher mortality and morbidity levels among them.

In Karnataka, as in other parts of the country there are cases of bride burning for non-fulfilment of dowry demands, rape, wife beating, and female foeticide to satisfy the son preferences. The degrading devadasi practice continues to be kept alive despite social legislation against it, especially in Athani, Saundatti, Bellary, Bijapur, Dharwad, Gulbarga, Raichur and Bidar. The dedications under the devadasi system today are covers for commercial sex work. Between 1987 and 1991, there has been a 43.2 per cent increase in cases of violence against women (Table 8). The percentage increase in the number of reported cases of kidnapping, dowry deaths, cruelty and rape has been much higher than the increase for the rest of the country. In addition, there are a large number of cases that go unnoticed, unreported.

Table 8

Cases of Violence against Women

Sl. No.	Case	Karnataka 1987	Karnataka 1991	% Increase	All India 1987	All India 1988	% Increase
1.	Rape	164	177	7.9	7,767	9,793	26.1
2.	Molestation	807	852	5.6	16,292	20,611	26.5
3.	Kidnap	100	264	164.0	9,016	12,300	36.4
4.	Eveteasing	45	42	-6.7	1,352	999	-26.0
5.	Dowry deaths	83	227	173.5	1,012	5,157	169.0
6.	Cruelty	469	826	76.1	11,603	15,949	37.5
	Total	**1,668**	**2,388**	**43.2**	**47,042**	**64,809**	**37.6**

There is little doubt from the foregoing indicators of development that progress of women and children in the state has been poor. This points to inadequacies in the strategies adopted for the implementation of programmes. A better appreciation of the nature of inadequacies will be gained from a look at the major programmes evolved over the years.

PROGRAMMES FOR WOMEN AND CHILDREN IN KARNATAKA

Community Development Programme: Governmental efforts for women in post independent India must first be seen in the context of the Community Development (CD) programme launched in 1952. The CD programme, hailed as the cornerstone of development in our country, saw women essentially in household roles. It gave training to women for looking after family needs, health and family planning, nutrition, food processing, storage, kitchen gardening etc. The CD programme did not perceive women as participants in the development process. It believed in the 'trickle down' theory and thus reached out to the landholding class; it did not pay attention to the economic and social handicaps of women in subsistence level families, engaged in large numbers in dairying, fisheries, agricultural labour, collection of forest produce etc.

During the 1960s, the main focus countrywide was on achievement of self sufficiency in food grain production. Of great significance during this period was the establishment of a cadre of Gram Sevikas to mobilise, educate and train 'farm women' on aspects relating to high yielding varieties, cattle management, and nutrition.

But these programmes failed to take cognisance of the women's inability to get away from the routine and heavy household chores of water, fuel and fodder collection along with child care and other domestic tasks. The 'popular' perception among extension functionaries was that women were 'unwilling to attend' and farm women's training programmes were consequently given low priority. The cadre of gram sevikas was dismantled during the 1970s; the multipurpose Gram Sevika was replaced by a bottom-heavy cadre of unipurpose male Agricultural Assistants.

Mahila Mandals: The Mahila Mandals, under the Community Development Programme, were set up for taking responsibility for implementing village level programmes. A large number of Mahila Mandals were formed throughout the state. But programmes conceptualised for Mahila Mandals did not conform to the original objectives. The Mahila Mandals served as forums through which Gram Sevikas imparted skills such as sewing, knitting and kitchen gardening. In the 1960s, the Department of Industries initiated a programme for training women through Mahila Mandals in home based crafts. Home Industries were defined as doll and puppet making, rattan, cutting and tailoring, mat weaving, embroidery, knitting, spinning, fruit preservation and[2] any other craft that ladies can learn and pursue as may be approved by the Directors of Industries and Commerce. Here again, a strong middle class and male bias was evident. It is interesting that exactly three decades later, the much publicised VISHWA programme launched with great fanfare had much the same programme content.

2. G.O.No. CI 81 RCI 64 dated 29.12.1965.

Land Reforms: The critical importance of land to the wellbeing of the poor needs no emphasis. Land Reforms tribunals were set up for registering lands in the names of actual tillers. The tribunals had a representation of SC/ST persons. No woman was represented on the tribunals. In Karnataka, 496,394 tenants were registered; 338,060 persons were granted ownership rights. Data on the number of women who received ownership rights is not documented. Table 9 below gives the number of women (widows, unmarried women) 'landowners' who lost land in the process. In terms of both number of persons and area, the figures are significantly high in the districts of Bellary, Chickmaglur, Hassan, Mandya, Mysore, Belgaum, Bijapur, Dharwad, Raichur, Dakshina Kannada and Shimoga. Even assuming that lands were deliberately transferred in favour of such categories in order to escape the ceiling laws, the fact remains that the Khathas were in their names, and over time the women could have been empowered to 'own' their lands.

Table 9

Women Landowners Who have Lost Lands and received payment

District	Widows, Minors Unmarried Women, Physically and Mentally Disabled Persons (%) No.	Area in acres
Bangalore	22.07	7.8
Bellary	42.36	42.72
Chickmaglur	27.45	30.32
Chitradurga	8.70	10.79
Kodagu	24.14	26.75
Hassan	27.75	19.94
Kolar	22.00	15.19
Mandya	32.53	33.78
Mysore	37.78	38.44

Contd.

Tumkur	19.50	18.76
Belgaum	25.79	37.54
Bidar	20.92	30.14
Bijapur	25.61	41.72
Dharwad	32.86	33.96
Gulbarga	22.27	33.22
Raichur	29.11	34.18
Uttara. Kannada	21.70	25.63
Dakshin. Kannada	35.82	44.60
Shimoga	38.09	26.42

Source: Pani 1981

T & V Programme: Training & Visit (T & V) was a major agricultural extension programme initiated in 1978. It covered all districts in Karnataka in a phased manner over a period of three years. The system envisaged dissemination of knowledge on latest technologies through the human worker to the extension agencies, wholly male dominated, who themselves did not understand the extensive role and influence of women in the agricultural economy. Initially, the programme completely bypassed women. It was presumed that whatever information women need about agricultural technologies would reach them through their male relatives. At later stages, in accordance with GOI instructions, feeble attempts were made to identify 30 per cent of the women among the contact farmers. A Monitoring-cum-Evaluation Survey, conducted by the Directorate of Agriculture in 1994-95 about the 'contact farmer's knowledge about himself being a contact farmer', indicated that out of a sample of 1,671 farmers in 17 districts only 249 were aware of their role. If such awareness among men contact farmers was so low, it is a moot point, considering that tradition precluded association of women with men, whether the 30 per cent women contact farmers were at all aware of their role as contact farmers, or whether they had been equipped to extend the messages developed by the research institutions to guide each season's field crop production for better yields.

However, a programme in which women's productive role was recognised in agriculture was the DANIDA funded Women and Youth Training and Extension Programme (WYTEP), which began in Karnataka in 1982. Women were recognised as useful members of society and as indispensable contributors to the overall goal of achieving self sufficiency in food. Field visits to individual farm women were combined with short duration institution based training for groups of 30 women selected from small and marginal farm families in improved agricultural practices. They were appointed as extension workers and formed into groups, enabling them to articulate their problems and seek solutions through experience sharing and consensus. This resulted in improving the status of these women in their families. A survey conducted in 1993 showed that WYTEP had reached out to 230,000 women in their villages. But the lessons from WYTEP were not incorporated into other programmes related to land and agriculture.

The initial period was characterised by the thinking that welfare oriented programmes alone would ensure equality between men and women. A gender blindness pervaded development thinking and planning at that time; there was no understanding that women's issues are in fact development issues.

A description of the programme implemented by the Department of Women and Child Development shows that the focus of departmental efforts since inception throughout the 1980s and practically today is on welfare programmes with limited outreach.

Programmes of the Department of Women and Children: The state has seen the emergence of several institutions over the years to support programmes for women and children. The oldest institution is the Karnataka State Social Welfare Advisory Board (KSSWAB), which was set up to promote voluntary effort in social welfare. With the introduction of specific schemes for women and children, the Department of Rehabilitation and After Care Services was established, which was later converted into the Department of Women and Child Welfare. More recently in 1987, the Karnataka State Women's Development Corporation (KSWDC) was constituted with the long term objective of creating greater employment facilities for women.

Karnataka State Social Welfare Advisory Board: The Karnataka State Social Welfare Advisory Board (KSSWAB) functioning under the Central Social Welfare Board (CSWB) was set up in 1954. The KSSWAB disburses grants to voluntary agencies for various welfare activities such as opening creches, balawadis, old age homes, orphanages, and other services for women and children. In 1958, the KSSWAB started a programme of condensed courses of education to open new avenues of employment for women. Its vocational education programme, initiated much later in 1975, offers courses in secretarial services, ayah training, training for house keepers, nursery school teachers, family planning workers, home decorators etc. A few courses are also offered in Radio and TV Mechanic, Laboratory Technicians, Draftsmen, Accounts, but the numbers are few and far between.

Department of Probation and After Care Services: The Department of Probation and After Care Services was established in 1956 as a wing of the Department of Social Welfare. At the inception, the Department was given the responsibility of opening protective Homes (State Homes and Reception Centres) for women under the **Suppression of Immoral Traffic Act, 1956,** Remand Homes and Certified Schools for children under the Children's Act, as well as After Care Homes for Men. Probation Officers were appointed in each district under the **Probation of Offenders Act** to take cognisance of young 'offenders'. A Resettlement Area was identified in Bijapur under the **Habitual Offenders Act.** Liaison Officers of the Department undertook welfare work in the Jails of Belgaum, Bellary and Bangalore. The focus was on establishing 'victimised' or 'neglected' children, and women in 'moral danger'. Apart from this there were no initiatives to tackle, for example, the problem of child labour, despite the establishment of beedi industries or increased burden on women due to degradation of forests, land alienation and sale migration. These issues were not addressed during this period.

Department of Women and Child Welfare: In 1975, following the International Year of Women and the announcement of the International Decade for Women, the Department of Probation and After Care Services was converted into the Department of Women and Child Welfare. The new Department began functioning with three sections, Social: Defence, Women's Welfare and Child Welfare.

Focus on Institutional Care: The first mandate of the newly converted Department was to continue to run the Protective Homes inherited from the erstwhile Department of Probation and After Care Services for safeguarding women and children. Today, there are eight State Homes, 11 Reception Centres, 22 Certified Schools, 20 Observation Homes and four After Care Homes in the state. Literacy Classes are conducted for women in the State Homes, and formal education is imparted to children in the certified schools through specially appointed teachers. Within the institutions the range of activities expanded over the years; but these tended to be sex based. Girls were given training in sewing, embroidering and knitting; boys were given training in printing and carpentry. The focus was on institutional care and support.

Falling within the same category of 'institutionalisation' was the scheme of Destitute Cottages, which came into operation in the mid 1970s. Under the scheme, voluntary agencies were provided funds to run cottages for groups of 25 destitute, orphaned children. Few attempts were made to 'deinstitutionalise' children (especially girls) through rehabilitation by enabling the child's family, economically and through awareness, to take responsibility and care for the child, or through promotion of in-country adoption or foster care. Since both the government run Certified Schools and the Destitute Cottages run by voluntary agencies had an age ceiling, girls often left these institutions only to be admitted to the counterpart institutions for adults as 'destitute' women.

In 1983, an important development took place, namely the promulgation of the **Devadasi (Prohibition of Dedication) Act,** which resulted from the protest movements and rallies at Nippani and Athani by the Joint Women's Forum and other voluntary bodies. In keeping with the Department's approach of safeguarding and protection, a State Home for Women and a Certified School for girls were opened in Athani in the same year.

Monetary Incentive Schemes: By the mid 1980s, several direct welfare schemes were in operation in the state, including Old Age Pension (OAP), Destitute Widow's Pension (DWP) and Physically Handicapped Pension (PHP). A sum of Rs 75 per month is paid to the eligible beneficiaries. In Karnataka, 548,637 women are availing of the DWP, and 730,190 persons are availing of OAP, and 328,261 persons receive PHP. Gender breakup of persons receiving OAP and PHP is not available.

Also, a direct welfare measure implemented by the Department of Health and Family Welfare is the scheme of maternity allowance for rural women for the first two deliveries. The scheme provides Rs. 300 in three equal installments as supplementary wage income in the last stages of pregnancy and the early stages of child birth.

Relatively new welfare measures are the schemes of scholarship to rural girls and for children in difficult circumstances. The scheme of scholarship to rural girls, introduced in 1992, provides Rs 25 and Rs 50 per month to rural girls for a duration of ten months for pursuing studies in Classes V-VII and VIII-X respectively. The scheme of assistance to children in difficult circumstances, introduced in 1991, similarly provides monetary incentives for the education of children whose parents are categorised as 'convicts' or 'sexworkers'. or 'drug addicts' or 'alcoholics'.

There are other schemes of cash incentives, including the schemes of financial assistance for widow or devadasi marriage and the scheme for encouraging marriages of 'institutional inmates'. The former provides a cash incentive of Rs. 7,000, and the latter an incentive of Rs. 3,000. The scheme of 'Thaliya Bhagya', which provided a set of clothes and a 'Thali' to poor women on marriage was also in operation in the state. In addition, financial assistance is available to women for taking up job-oriented courses and for appearing for competitive examinations such as those conducted by the KPSC, SSB etc.

Training and Awareness Generation: The Women's Welfare section of the Department of Women and Child Welfare originally handled the scheme of training for home based industries started by the Department of Industries in the 1960s. It gave training to Mahila Mandals. A Handloom Instructor and a Home based Industries Instructor were appointed for conducting these programmes. The scheme of training for Home based Industries was later re-formulated as the scheme of assistance to Mahila Mandals and voluntary agencies for setting up Training-cum-Production Units. Assistance up to Rupees, one lakh is available under the scheme for organising and training women to take up income generation activity.

A similar scheme of setting up Training-cum-Production Centres is also implemented by the Karnataka State Women's Development Corporation (KSWDC) to enable women to supplement their income from, for example, mat and basket weaving, pottery, screen printing, leather and rexine manufacturing.

To promote skill development of women belonging to the SC category, assistance is available for training in typing, computer operations, electronic components manufacturing, clock assembly etc.

Income Generation: The KSWDC, implements the Mane Belaku scheme (previously named Gruha Kalyana) which provides financial assistance up to Rs. 10,000, including 25 per cent subsidy for self employment activities like tailoring, rope making, small businesses etc.

The KSWDC also takes up income generating programmes for devadasi women in Belgaum and Bijapur districts, enabling women to take up handloom weaving, agarbathi rolling, camphor making and leather articles production.

ICDS—Nutrition, Health and Education: The Special Nutrition Programme, (SNP) originally implemented by the Department of Social Welfare, was transferred to the Department of Women and Child Welfare in 1975. The centrally funded Integrated Child Development Scheme (ICDS) was also launched in the same year, initially, with one project in T-Narsipur block of Mysore district, followed shortly thereafter by Udupi block of Dakshina Kannada district and Dharwad block, funded by the state government. The ICDS programme provides a package of services for children in the 0-6 age group and for pregnant and nursing mothers, including pre-school education, supplementary nutrition, nutrition education, immunisation health care and referral services. Till 1983-84, ICDS projects covered 100 centres and 10,000 beneficiaries in each block. In 1983-84, the scope was expanded to cover all eligible beneficiaries in the block. In the same year, 30 projects, funded by the state government, were also brought on par with the Central Government funding pattern. For some time, SNP and ICDS projects expanded side by side. As the number of ICDS projects grew the SNP projects were integrated with the ICDS. By 1994-95, all blocks in the state were covered under the ICDS programme. At present, the programme has a coverage of 35 lakh beneficiaries.

There has been significant improvement in the immunisation coverage, under ICDS of Children, particularly of the DPI, POWO and BCG vaccines, though the coverage of measles vaccine still remains below standard. The nutrition status of children in the ICDS blocks has improved. Children attending anganwadi centres tend to continue their education in primary schools as against those that do not enter the anganwadi centre. However, the programme has not succeeded in reaching the under threes, who require more intensive care. Consequently, systematic growth monitoring of children in the 1-3 age group, which age group is most vulnerable to the onset of malnutrition, does not take place regularly. Neither have sustainable linkages been established for proper referral services for severely or moderately malnourished children. Similarly, the nutritional supplementation, health care and health nutrition, including provision of iron and folic acid tablets for pregnant and nursing mothers under the ICDS require greater effort on the part of anganwadi workers to motivate and encourage women, particularly those in the low income families.

ICDS has seen over the years several interventions, including the programme of providing Functional Literacy to Adult Women (FLAW) in modern methods of health, nutrition, child care and home management. FLAW was wound up in the 1980s. More recently, however, the ICDS has recognised the need to address the problems of dropout adolescent girls in the 11-18 age group, though again by focussing on nutrition, nutrition education and home management preparatory to motherhood. There is an NFE component in the adolescent girls scheme, but this has not been effectively operationalised. The programme for adolescent girls is functioning in 23 blocks of 4 districts of Kolar, Bellary, Raichur and Gulbarga.

Even more recent is the Centrally funded programme of combining the anganwadi centre with a creche to facilitate care of children of mothers of agricultural labourers. This initiative, though taken up in Karnataka only on a very small scale, will go a long way in freeing older girls from the responsibility of sibling care and improve female school attendance. At the same time it will enhance the time available to the mother for her earnings and increase her productivity.

The Welfare Approach: Women and children have traditionally been identified by the government as one of the target groups, along with other underprivileged groups, for all of whom special social welfare services are considered necessary. This welfare approach which started in the 1950s continued through the 1970s and was adopted as appropriate even when a separate Department of Women and Child Welfare was set up by the Government of Karnataka in 1975. Sometime in the 1980s, the nomenclature of the Department was changed from Women and Child Welfare to Women and Child Development, but the change in nomenclature was not accompanied by any well articulated change in policy, approaches and strategies at the state level. In most respects the welfare approach continues to this day.

The Welfare approach alone cannot lead to the development of women and children to enable them to achieve the Constitutional goal of equality of legal status and opportunity. Programmes in the Department of Women and Children for enabling girls and women to realise their full potential, especially training and income generation, are few in number. Most schemes emphasise their social disabilities. The sums provided under OAP, DWP are too meagre to enable individual beneficiaries to gain control over their lives. The unit costs under many of the schemes are not accessed by women due to their lack of information. Even today, women in the villages are not aware of the scheme of maternity allowance. The scholarship available under the scheme for children in difficult circumstances fails to take cognisance of the social stigma attached to being associated with prison conviction, drug addiction, or alcoholism. The working women's hostels, constructed by private managements, usually male dominated, are now in great demand as a result of more and more educated women entering the job market, but even economically independent adult women are subject to restrictions in these institutions - to be guided, strictly supervised and protected from the depredation of the outside world. Programmes such as assistance for competitive examinations or job oriented courses, cater to the more articulate vocal middle class, rather than to the poor, rural women. Schemes providing financial assistance for marriage emphasise the domestic role of women; moreover, in the absence of empowerment programmes such schemes do not preclude the possibility of emotional exploitation of the 'beneficiary' women in order to corner the cash incentive available to them. Training and awareness generation programmes also emphasise their secondary and domestic roles. Teaching women in sewing, knitting, papad and pickle making may enable them to earn some extra income but the employment opportunities that these skills provide do not reduce women's domestic responsibilities or enable them to negotiate independently with the outside world. Welfare schemes, though well intentioned, do not touch the roots of the causes of discrimination against women and girls. They merely attempt to redress some of the more overt and visible manifestations of subjugation.

Special Component Plan for Women—the First Attempt: It was during 1984-85 that the Department of Women and Child Development, Karnataka, made its first tentative attempt at drafting a Special Component Plan for Women, advocating a minimum one third physical and financial earmarking for women in all beneficiary oriented and training programmes in the sectors of agriculture, horticulture, rural development, housing etc. The effort resulted in some special schemes being drafted for women in the horticulture sector, but in the crucial agriculture (despite the experience of the WYTEP approach), co-operative, animal husbandry and other allied sectors women continued to be regarded as housewives and not as workers. The general male bureaucratic and political apathy prevalent towards women's issues precluded the possibility of any significant changes in policy and approaches towards women. The predominant thinking (myth) in the state was that women are always supported by males, and by improving the economic status of the family and household the status of women will automatically improve.

Poverty Alleviation Programmes: At the Central level, during the late 1970s, a somewhat more comprehensive view of women, took shape when in the Sixth Plan, for the first time, a separate chapter on women, suggesting a three-fold strategy covering education, health and employment was included. It proposed economic independence of women along with joint titles to wives and husbands in all land and site distribution, and access to health care and family planning services.

Several poverty alleviation programmes including IRDP, DWACRA, Rural Employment programmes, initiated during this period peaked in the Seventh Plan which continued the stress on socio-economic development of women. But, access of women to poverty alleviation programmes has been limited by lack of concept clarity among implementing personnel, faults in the delivery system and lack of support structures.

IRDP: The Integrated Rural Development Programme (IRDP) was launched 1979. The programme provides a loan through commercial banks with a subsidy component to households below the poverty line for the purchase of an asset which would enable self employment. The initial 30 per cent earmarking for women was enhanced to 40 per cent in 1991 and 50 per cent in 1994. The target of including women beneficiaries has not been met. In 1984-85, there were only 8.27 per cent women beneficiaries. This increased to 22.62 per cent in 1987-88. but declined to 6.54 per cent in 1988-89. Between 1990-91 and 1994-95, the programme has covered 33 per cent - 36 per cent women beneficiaries annually, but has yet to reach the 40 per cent and 50 per cent target set for itself. But achievement of targets alone does not tell the whole story. Persons closely associated with the implementation of IRDP admit that the selection of women is done in a circuitous and devious manner by first identifying the male borrower and then asking him to bring along his wife for signing/thumb-printing the loan papers. For instance, in the period ending March 1995, women 'beneficiaries' were provided loans for the following, traditionally male activities: Bullock Carts 770, Electric Meters 185, Mineral based Industries 203. No training programmes were conducted to enable women to gain control and 'own' these assets. This roundabout selection of women beneficiaries is regretfully true even of activities in the animal husbandry sector with which women are familiar.

DWACRA: Development of Women and Children in Rural Areas (DWACRA) started as a pilot project in two districts of Bijapur and Chickmaglur in 1982-93, and extended in a phased manner to all districts by 1994-95. DWACRA is a sub-component of IRDP which aims at organising women into groups of 15-20 members for effective utilisation of credit and subsidy under IRDP. DWACRA groups numbering 3,792 have been formed in the state since inception. The group approach in DWACRA is a good method for women to come together for setting up income generation activities. There are several success stories, as in the case of the Adiparashakti group in Gudehosur of Kodagu district, where women have resisted middle men and have transacted business worth Rs. 298,000 in 1990-91 and Rs. 377,000 in 1992-93. But, a weakness of the programme is that often groups are hastily set up, and the processes and methodologies of group formation to establish trust and cohesion among the members and identify common interests or activities are ignored in an attempt by programme personnel to meet targets for the disbursement of income generation subsidy.

TRYSEM: The scheme for Training Rural Youth for Self Employment (TRYSEM) provides technical and enterpreneurial skills. As in IRDP, a 30 per cent earmarking was made for women under TRYSEM. In Karnataka, TRYSEM has reached out to 36.71 per cent women. Of the women trained, 31.33 per cent have been able to establish themselves in self employment activities, and 3.27 per cent in wage employment. Although TRYSEM fulfills its quota of 30 per cent for women, training has tended to be restricted to stereotyped activities, such as knitting, embroidering and tailoring; few efforts are made to train women in non conventional activities for which there may be local employment opportunities and to establish tie up for credit under, for example IRDP, or ensure sustained raw material supply of marketing linkages.

Rural Employment Programmes (NREP, RLELGP, JRY): The National Rural Development Programme (NREP) was launched in 1980. The Rural Landless Employment Guarantee Programme (RLEGP) was started in 1983. Both programmes had similar objectives, viz., to provide employment in rural areas and create durable assets. NREP was funded by the Government of India and the state in a 50:50 ratio and RLEGP was wholly centre funded. In both programmes, directives were issued to give preference to women in wage employment; but there was no supervisory mechanism to monitor the official directive given.

The NREP and RLEGP were amalgamated into the Jawahar Rozgar Yojana (JRY), funded in the 80:20 ratio by the Central and state governments. As in NREP and RLEGP, there was a 30 per cent earmarking for women. The gap between the directive and the actual reality is evident from the figures in Table 10 below:

Table 10

Achievement for Women under JRY

Year	1989-90	1990-91	1991-92	1992-93	1993-94	1994-95
Total Target (in lakh person days)	490.110	526.930	471.010	441.080	718.010	440.000
Achievement for Women (in lakh person days)	79.656	103.844	79.405	81.009	139.772	88.945
Percentage	16	20	17	18	19	20

Source: Annual Progress Reports of RD & PR Department, Government of Karnataka

Poverty alleviation programme such as IRDP, TRYSEM, JRY are important vehicles to reach women. In implementation, half hearted attempts have been made. A woman is debarred from availing an IRDP loan if the husband has defaulted on an earlier loan, even though her husband may have left her for another woman and she may be the main source of sustenance for the children. These programmes must be redesigned to become more women centered, taking into account the special needs and constraints of women in order to reduce the gap of opportunities between men and women.

SOCIAL SECTORS:

Education: Karnataka has provided several incentives to promote primary education. In 1985, the Vidya Vikasa scheme was launched in order to provide free uniforms and text books to scheduled caste and tribe children. In 1991, the state launched the Akshaya Yojana to improve retention of children in schools. Originally, the Akshaya

Yojana envisaged payment at the rate of Rs. 1 per day for each child who had 80 per cent school attendance. The scheme was reformulated in 1993 to provide free uniforms, text books and take-home food to all children in lower primary schools. The reformulated Akshaya Yojana also has components for improving the school environment, providing play fields. In addition, it has provision for 'yatra', taking children on school excursions and 'manoranjana', cultural and recreation activities for children. Within two years of reformulation, regretfully budgetary allocations for 'yatra' and 'manoranjana' have been cut, and the funds allocated to the school buildings construction programme of the Department have also been cut.

District Primary Education Project: A major initiative taken in 1993-94 was the launching of the World Bank funded District Primary Education Programme (DPEP) in four districts of Karnataka. Low female literacy has been one of the criteria for selection of districts. Accordingly, the programme has been taken up in the districts of Mandya, Kolar, Raichur and Belgaum. DPEP makes a special focus on making education accessible to girls through an intense process of communication and interaction by specially trained teachers and motivators with the child's family and the community in which she/he lives. A new intervention by DPEP is a gender scrutiny of existing text books. It is being increasingly acknowledged that gender bias in teaching-learning materials hampers the quality of education for girls and women. Also envisaged under the DPEP is the opening of Non Formal Education (NFE) centres, which stand to benefit girls who are compelled to drop out of formal school.

Total Literacy Campaigns: Karnataka was one of the first states after Kerala to respond to the TLC: two TLCs were launched in 1990-91 in the districts of Bijapur and Dakshina Kannada. Between 1990-91 and 1994-95 all districts in Karnataka had launched TLCs. The TLC was characterised by a massive people's mobilisation and creation of an environment in which educated volunteers came forward to take on the challenge of illiteracy. Mass mobilisation was achieved by thousands of activists in voluntary agencies, members of peoples[2] science movements, cultural groups, government officials and political cadres moving from village to village talking with people, presenting street plays and songs to arouse an interest in teaching and learning. In support of Post Literacy programmes, the Department of Women & Child Development brought out a series of ten booklets in 1993, entitled 'Namma Kanunugalu' (Our Laws) covering a gamut of laws relating to child labour, bonded labour, migrant and contract labour, rape, dowry, property rights etc.

Mahila Samakhya: Mahila Samakhya, a programme for women's empowerment through education, was introduced in 3 districts of Bijapur, Mysore and Bidar in 1989, and further expanded to the districts of Raichur and Gulbarga in 1992. The programme aims at forming women's collectives called mahila sanghas through an intense personal interaction between Sahayoginis and poor women, giving women a time and space to reflect on the causes of their problems and deprivation. The programme aims at changing the self image of the women and increasing their awareness of and access to existing development programmes.

Health: The family welfare programme aims at reducing population growth rates and addressing the needs of the family, particularly women and children. In reality, the programme has concentrated on achieving sterilisation and laparoscopy targets to the neglect of birth spacing methods and other health needs of women.

The maternal and child health (MCH) services were integrated with the family welfare programme in 1965. These are available in Karnataka through 1,875 PHCs/PHUs, 7,793 sub centres, and 239 Community Health Centres and Sub-District and District Hospitals. In 1992, the World Band funded Child Survival and Safe Motherhood (CSSM) programme was launched. CSSM provides for initiatives in the areas of training of dais and Auxiliary Nurse Midwives (VNMs) and setting up of First Referral Units (FRUS) for promotion of safe deliveries. IPP-IX has also been introduced in 13 districts of the state in 1995, with a focus on improved physical infrastructure for sub centres, PHCs and training institutes.

In Karnataka, as in the rest of the country, women's health has become synonymous with mother and child care services, available to women in the reproductive age group (15-45 years) and their under five year children. The ANM is the key functionary for women's health. A major problem faced by her is the requirement of meeting family planning targets. As a result, little or no other MCH work gets done. There is appreciation for meeting family planning targets, and punishments for not meeting them. But there is no system of incentives for TT immunisation to pregnant women, distribution of iron folate tablets, birth spacing methods, ante natal and post natal check up etc.

The non-maternal aspects of health, including respiratory, circulatory, nervous system infections, parasitic and infectious diseases are dealt with by the general health staff rather than the MCH staff. Here also, social and cultural norms prevent women, particularly those in rural areas, from interacting with male health personnel.

Social Legislation: We have, in our state and country, a tradition of legislation, but poor enforcement. There are laws on registration of births and deaths, minimum age of marriage, registration of marriage, prevention of immoral traffic, rape and dowry prohibition. There are laws to prevent employment of children of tender ages in hazardous industries, and to regulate their employment in non-hazardous industries. There are laws to ensure equal remuneration, rights in property. All these laws are disregarded by the society and remain unenforced by government agencies.

In 1976, the **Equal Remuneration Act** was promulgated to meet the demand for equality in employment by working women. In Karnataka, according to the Annual Reports of the Labour Departments, 20,629 inspections were conducted under the Act in the ten year period between 1983-94, but only 88 prosecutions have been launched. No convictions have been made. There is no information on the number of complaints lodged by women themselves being acted upon. Similarly, under the **Maternity Benefit Act**, 44 units have been inspected between Jan-Oct 1995; only 2 convictions obtained and a penalty of

Rs. 275 imposed. No prosecutions have been launched under the **Child Labour Act**, despite 2,508 inspections purported to have been conducted.

The country-wide anti rape movement during the 1980s, and the promulgation of the **Dowry Prohibition Amendment Act, 1984**, led to the constitution of a Special Police Cell, headed by a Superintendent of Police in the Police Department in 1989, to investigate dowry deaths. Details of cases (Table 11) investigated are as follows:

Table 11

Dowry Cases in Karnataka

Year	Reported	Convicted	Acquitted	Pending Trial/ U/Investigation
1986	15	3	7	5
1987	72	9	23	40
1988	100	5	21	74
1989	115	7	27	77
1990	100	10	17	73
1991	87	3	7	77
1992	112	2	6	102
1993	202	3	4	195
1994	164	-	1	183
1995	184	-	-	184

Source: Office of the IGP, COD, Goverment of Karnataka.

Cases of violence reported against women are on the increase in Karnataka (Table 8), but evidently, there has been no increase in the pace of enforcement of laws. Effective enforcement of laws can only be guaranteed by mass pressure. Social legislation must, therefore, be accompanied by systematic programmes to impart awareness and information for organisation of women, and sensitisation of enforcement agencies. In the absence of adequate publicity, effective mass organisations taking up issues affecting women and offsetting the fear of reprisal, most legislations remain paper legislations.

What ails Women and Child Development in Government: The implementation of existing programmes by various departments is beset with problems in the field:

i) Firstly, there is the 'household' approach to development, which posits that by improving the economic status of the family, the status of women and female children will automatically improve. This has been belied by experience. There are innumerable instances which show that improvement in the economic position of the family imposes far greater social and cultural restrictions and taboos on the women, relegating them deeper into the 'inside' of the house.

ii) Secondly, there is the target-achievement approach. In monitoring IRDP, DWACRA, TRYSEM etc; the focus is on physical and financial numbers: numbers of loans given, numbers of beneficiaries, amount of subsidy released, number of training programmes conducted etc. There is scant attention paid to, for instance, the processes of group formation and cohesion, selection of leaders, increase in productivity and earning levels, contribution to group funds in DWACRA, or relevance of training conducted under TRYSEM.

iii) Thirdly, there is the general bureaucratic lack of understanding and conviction to the women's question. Even today doubts and apprehensions are raised in many fora for a proposal for mainstreaming women in governmental programmes for development.

iv) Fourthly, there is the army of untrained (largely male, but including women) government functionaries who have to cover large areas. The little understanding for women issues that exists at senior/ middle levels of the bureaucracy is considerably reduced by the time the programmes are implemented by the grass roots functionaries.

This being the existing scenario, the likely impact of the New Economic Policy (NEP) on the income earning opportunities of poor women, especially in the informal sector, becomes a very major cause of concern.

NEW THINKING : NEW INITIATIVES IN THE 1990s

Women's Development Programme – Policy Statement: A short policy document on Women's development was released in 1992 which stated that development programmes must have a well conceived edge in favour of women. The document projected an inter-departmental, inter-sectoral programme, recognising that women and child development cannot be the responsibility of one government department alone, but that all government departments, voluntary organisations and all sections of the society must participate in it.

The policy statement, followed up by a series of workshops at district level with government officials of different departments, voluntary organisations, women's activists yielded a few (too few) positive measures, among them, as 50 per cent reservation for women in Teachers Training Institutes (TTI) and in recruitment to the posts of Primary School Teachers, 30 per cent reservation for women in Industrial Training Institutes (ITI), initiating of training programmes for untrained dias, involvement of women in the Joint Village Forest Management Committees, and Village level Water and Sanitation Committees was not fulfiled. A Mahila Police Station has been established at Bangalore. Separately, announcements for 25 per cent reservation for women in all government posts and for appointment of more women police personnel were also made, but these have yet to be operationalised. Circular instructions have been issued regarding joint Pattas for women in all housing schemes including, Ashraya, Ambedkar Housing, Indira Awas Yojana, and in regard to all cases of mutations in the record of rights, but these must be accompanied with gender sensitisation of persons implementing the programmes in the field, if the instructions are to be genuinely translated into action.

Following the formulation of the policy document, a separate Sub Plan for Women, entitled Karnataka Mahila Abhivruddhi Yojana (KMAY) was approved in 1995, providing for a minimum one third budgetary and physical earmarking for women in all beneficiary oriented and training programmes in the sectors of agriculture, forests, co-operation, animal husbandry, fisheries, sericulture, rural development, housing, industries, education and health.

State Programme of Action for the Child: A State Programme of Action for the Child, which is an integrated, multi-sectoral decadal plan of action for ensuring survival, protection and development of children, was prepared with a special gender focus built in for the girl child and adolescent girl. The State Programme of Action lays down time bound goals to be achieved by the end of the century, including: control of major childhood diseases, reduction of child malnutrition, reduction of under-5 death rates and maternal mortality, providing universally available family planning services and universalisation of elementary education, with focus on retention of girls and achievement of the minimum levels of learning.

Amendments to give Women Co-parcenary Rights: A significant landmark in 1994 was the amendment to the **Hindu Succession (Karnataka Amendment) Act** to confer equal rights on daughters in co-parcenary property. According to the Act, the daughter of a co-parcener shall, by birth, become a co-parcener in her own right in the same manner as the son, and will have the same rights in the co-parcenary property.

Karnataka State Women's Commission: The Karnataka State Women's Commission (KSWC) which is a statutory constituted body in 1995 has powers of a civil court under the CPC in trying a suit and in respect of summoning witnesses, receiving evidence etc. It investigates and examines all matters relating to safeguards provided for women under the Constitution and other laws, look into issues such as deprivation of women's rights, non-implementation of laws, non-compliance of policy decisions for women's development, investigate specific problems situations such as discrimination and atrocities against women, undertakes research, take measures to enable women to get due representation in all spheres.

POLITICAL PARTICIPATION: PANCHAYAT RAJ

Reservation for Women: The **Karnataka Zilla and Mandal Panchayat Raj Act** came into force in 1983. Elections to the mandal and zilla panchayats were held in 1987. Of significance was the fact that, for the first time, a 25 per cent reservation was made for women at the mandal and zilla levels. Fourteen-thousand and twentyfour women were elected to the mandals, and approximately, 300 women to the zilla panchayats.

Following the landmark **73rd Amendment to the Constitution, the Karnataka Panchayati Raj Act, 1993,** increased the reservation for women to a minimum one-third reservation, across all categories. In the December 1993 election, 35,334 out of a total of 80,653 seats (constituting 43.6 per cent) went to women.

The Department of Women and Child Development responded to this major development by formulating a new scheme of Training and Communication Support to Elected Women Panchayat Raj Members with training seen not as a one time measure, but as a continuous ongoing process, giving women the space and time to share and learn from their experiences.

FUTURE STEPS

Mainstreaming Women for Social Justice and Economic Equity: Some beginnings have been made by the government, and these will have to be effectively harnessed to bring about gender equity and justice.

One major step already taken by the Government of Karnataka is the reservation for women in panchayat raj institutions under the **Karnataka Panchayat Raj Act** in 1993 increasing the reservation for women to a minimum one third reservation. The election of 42.6 per cent women, including women from dalit and scheduled tribe groups, to gram panchayats, and the initiation of programmes for political empowerment of the elected women raises a glimmer of hope and optimism: that this will eventually result in decisions at local levels which take into account the needs and priorities of women. The Department also arranged for training of women Panchayat members. Also, the current demand for similar reservation in the State Legislature, if acceded to, will bring more and more women into the political process, increase the bargaining power of women and focus on enhanced state support for women and girls.

The in-principle approvals given by the Government of Karnataka for joint land-holdings, sites, houses and other assets, together with one third earmarking for women in all beneficiary oriented and training programmes in the sectors of agriculture, animal husbandry, fisheries, co-operation, industries, forests etc., as well as the amendment to the **Hindu Succession Act** to give equal co-parcenary rights to daughters will lead to the economic empowerment of women and improve their productivity, provided that simultaneously a concerted drive is taken for legal awareness, training, conscientisation, mobilisation and building up of women's groups for collective action. Such drives will have to go beyond the text book information on laws, rules and rights, but should deal with the entire structure and process of the delivery system.

These initiatives will have to be accompanied by sustained and long term programmes of education and literacy - which is relevant to girls and women. That education and literacy can bring about change in the living and earning conditions of women has already been demonstrated by experiences from other parts of the country, including Nellore district of Andhra Pradesh, Puddukkottai district of Tamil Nadu, Durgapur district of Uttar Pradesh and Banda District of Rajasthan.

To sum up, it may be said that the few initiatives taken in recent years through special projects, such as WYTEP, DPEP, TLC, Mahila Samakhya, Panchayat raj training to focus on gender may not perhaps give us the final answers to the question of women and child development and equality between men and women, but they do nevertheless, provide directions for us to move along.

REFERENCES

Administrator July-September (1995), Looking Forwards, Looking Back: Special Issue on Gender and Development. **Journal of LBSNAA, Mussoorie,** XL (3).

Desai, N.(ed.) (1991). **A Decade of Women's Movement in India.** Bombay: Himalaya Publishing House.

Dey, S.K. (1964) **Community Development.** Bombay: Asia Publishing House.

Government of India, (1974). **Report of the Committee on the Status of Women in India: 'Towards Equality'.** New Delhi: Government of India.

Government of India, (1988). **Shramshakti Report of the National Commission on Self Employed Women in the Informal Sector.** New Delhi: Department of Women and Child Development.

Government of Karnataka. (1993). **Report on Monitoring cum Evaluation Survey.** Bangalore: Directorate of Agriculture.

Government of Karnataka (1994). **District Socio-Economic Indicators.** Bangalore: Directorate of Economics and Statistics.

Country Report. Washington DC: World Bank.

Krishnaraj, M. (1988). **Women and Development: The Indian Experience.** SNDT Women's University Monographs on Sociology.Bombay: Shubhada Saraswat Prakashare.

NCERT. (1995). **Sixth All India Educational Survey.** New Delhi: National Council of Educational Research and Training.

Pani, N. (1981). **Reforms to Pre-empt Change: Land Legislation in Karnataka.** Indian Institute of Management. Bangalore

WYTEP (1995). **An Insight into the Genesis and Progress of the Project.** Bangalore: Department of Agriculture and Danida.

The Annual Reports, Government of Karnataka, Department Labour and Department of Women and Child Department.

The Five Year Plans. New Delhi: Planning Commission.

UNDP (1995). **Human Development Report.** New Delhi: Oxford University Press

World Bank (1991). **Gender and Poverty in India: A World Bank**

4

OTHER SERVICES: HOUSING, WATER SUPPLY AND SANITATION, AND PUBLIC DISTRIBUTION SYSTEM

N. Sivanna

Introduction: 'Social Services' have been defined as "those organised activities that are primarily and discreetly concerned with the conservation, protection and the improvement of human resource" (Cassidy 1942). Development of human resources depends mainly on the quality of these services provided to the people. This should mean that the services are intended for improving the standard of living of the people, cspecially the poor. Seen in this perspective, services like housing, water supply and sanitation, and food security have a significant impact on the living conditions of the people.

In this paper, an attempt has been made to examine the services like housing, water supply and sanitation and food security with a two-fold objective of looking at these services as they have been provided and their impact on the living standards of the people in the state of Karnataka. Additionaly, the administrative experiences in executing these services, in terms of initiating innovative measures to strenghten them both qualitatively and quantitatively, have also been examined. The paper is organised into four sections: Section I discusses the housing programes; Section II : water supply and sanitation; Section III: food security-public distribution system; and Section IV: gives an overview of these services.

I

HOUSING

Housing: Shelter is regarded as one of the most basic necessitites of life. As stated in the Karnataka Economic Surveys, "Investment in housing is an essential element of human resource development and serves to fulfil several objectives like raising the quality of life..., creating substantial additional employment". Increasing population, pressure on land and infrastructure, and associated high costs, however, have made proper housing inaccessible to the poorer sections of the population thereby necessitating state intervention. Necessary policies and programmes have been formulated to meet the housing requirements of the economically vulnerable sections as well as to create an enabling environment to accomplish the goal, i.e., "shelter for all".

Housing programme in Karnataka has two components: rural housing and urban housing. Under rural housing, there have been a number of schemes implemented by the government/government agencies. The popular schemes are: distribution house sites to landless labourers, people's housing scheme, experimental low-cost housing scheme, housing under tribal sub-plan, Indira awas yojana and ashraya scheme. The sole objective behind all these schemes has been to provide shelter, especially to the people belonging to the weaker sections and the rural poor in general.

In order to cope with the demand for constructing houses for the general public, the 'Mysore Housing Board' was established in June 1956 which succeeded the then Labour Housing Corporation. The main functions carried out by the Board were: a) to relieve the pressure of housing problem by constructing houses; b) to raise the standard of the types of houses to be constructed through the other agencies; and c) to implement such housing schemes of the government from time to time as entrusted to it. To support the Board's activities, the government had created a separate cell called the 'Rural Housing Cell' in 1957 under an Executive Engineer, under the Development Department. The cell was able to lay out building sites, construct houses and extend loans to most deserving persons in the villages affected especially by floods, fire and other natural calamities. The financial assistance was offered by the Government of India and Life Insurance Corportion (LIC); the maximum amount of loan extended to each house was Rs 3,000. Till 1970, the cell had spent Rs 7 lakhs and made available nearly 3,000 sites. Also, nearly 10,772 houses were constructed in 472 villages with the financial help provided by the LIC. However, it is disappointing to note that compared to the estimated shortage of houses (10 lakhs) in 26,826 villages, the achievement made in 15 years was abysmally low (Hudli 1975).

People's Housing Schemes : Considering the poor achievement, the then government transferred the rural housing programme to the State Housing Board in 1970. In spite of the efforts made by the Board's administration, which utilised the services of available engineering staff in districts to improve the housing situation, the progress was not up to the expectation of the government. Keeping the unsatisfactory achievement in the background, the government then introduced two very important schemes:

1) to distribute sites to all the landless labourers in the villages; and

2) build as many houses as possible on these sites.

As a consequence, nearly 3 lakh sites of various dimensions were marked and distributed to the landless labourers. But the beneficiaries were not happy with the sites allotted since the location of these sites and their condition did not attract them. The task of implementing this scheme was entrusted to the Block Development Officer (BDO). During this period, apart from Peoples' Housing Scheme, there were other schemes like Scheduled Caste and Scheduled Tribe Housing Scheme, plantation Labour Housing Scheme, Iron Ore Mining Labour Housing Scheme, etc.

One of the innovative and commendable aspects of the housing programme of this phase was that in order to make the beneficiaries conscious of a rational approach to the growing housing amenities undertaken by the government, it was felt necessary to educate and guide the beneficiaries on proper lines, as also to impart training to the technical personnel like BDO, Executive Officers and Village Level Workers. As a result, a separate 'Rural Housing Wing' was created to train the above personnel in the specialised fields of village planning and housing.

It is worthwhile to recapitulate here that People's Housing Scheme (PHS) was one of the major housing schemes launched by the then government in the year 1973. Karnataka is one of the foremost states to have taken up this scheme, popularly known as "Janatha Housing Programme", which seeks to provide subsidised houses to the poorest, who are defined as those who are siteless and landless earning less than Rs.2,000/- annum. The programme was fully funded lby the government and the beneficiaries were given both subsidy and loan. The beneficiaary had to cocntribute Rs.500 either in the form of cash or voluntary labour for laying the foundation. The scheme was so devised that durable houses of 300 square feet could be provided on free sites with minimal cost and economy. Each house was provided one door, two windows and one room partititoned for the kitchen purpose. There was no provision, however, either for chimney or for toilet facilities.

It is significant to note that in the year 1978-79, the HUDCO (Housing and Urban Development Corporation), a centrally funded financial organisation extended loans to the state government at a nominal interest rate of 4.5 per cent. With the continous flow of funds and due to government's policy of encouraging housing programme for the economically weaker sections of the society, the amount of loan component was enhanced from Rs.3,000 to Rs 4,000 per house, which included Rs 1,500/- from HUDCO, Rs 2,000 as subsidy from the state government and the remaining Rs 500/- as beneficiaries' contribution.

The overall implementation of the scheme was placed under the charge of the Deputy Commissioner of the district. At the block level, the BDO was in charge of the implementation and assisted the Deputy Commissioner in the day-to-day administration of the scheme. The process of implementation of this programme normally commenced with the inter-taluk allocations, followed by hobli-wise and village-wise allocations; generally, ten houses were allotted to selected villages in the form of clusters. One of the important aspects of the housing programme has been that the unit cost per house varied from year to year. For instance, during the year 1988-89, the unit cost per house was Rs.8,000. Correspondingly, additional facilities were provided like 'Astra Oven' at a cost of Rs.134/- per unit (Rs.80 as subsidy and a

HUDCO Bank loan of Rs.54). The available data reveal that so far, that is, until December 1994, 2,401,275 house sites have been distributed and 838,000 houses have been constructed under various rural housing schemes.

Ashraya Scheme: Ashraya Scheme has been the major housing scheme implemented by the government after people's housing scheme. The unique feature of this scheme is that this has been designed independently by the state government. The important aspects of this scheme are: to provide shelter to the economically weaker sections of the society; to eliminate the homelessness by the turn of the century; to rehabilitate the slum dwellers in the city of Bangalore; and to promote the usage of locally manufactured building materials. The main target groups eligible under Ashraya scheme are: the people whose annual income falls below Rs.8,400 in rural and urban areas in the state excluding Bangalore City; the slum dwellers of Bangalore city whose income is between Rs.8,401 and Rs. 18,000 per annum. A point to be noted here is that 50 per cent of the cost of the site in urban areas is to be contributed by the beneficiaries. The Unit cost of a house under the Ashraya Scheme is as follows (Table 1):

Table 1
Unit Cost of the House Under Ashraya Scheme

Area	Unit cost Rs.	Loan Rs.	Subsidy Rs.
Rural	15,000	10,000	5,000
Urban	16,000	14,000	2,000
Bangalore	33,000	28,000	5,000

Source: HUDD 1995.

Construction of houses under Ashraya is being iplemented by the Deputy Commissioners as well as Karnataka Housing Board. The unit cost for the houses in rural areas is Rs 15,000 with a break up of Rs 10,000 as loan and Rs 5,000 subsidy; in urban areas it is Rs 16,000 with Rs 14,000 as loan and Rs 2,000 as subsidy.

As far as the administration is concerned, the Assistant Commissioners are responsible for certifying the value of the land to be purchased both in rural and urban areas. As per the G.O. (No.HUDI HAS (I) 95, dated 18.8.95, Bangalore), the programme of distribution of sites in the rural areas will be the responsibility of the Zilla Panchayats. Thus, the Zilla Panchayats are expected to meet the cost of farming lay outs, development charges and providing external services like water supply, sanitation, electricity, link roads etc., by integrating schemes like JRY, Rural Sanitation, Bio-Gas, Bhagya Jyothi etc. The government has set a target of distributing 75,000 free sites in rural areas measuring 30'x40' for the year 1995-96. A provision of Rs.7 crores has been made available in the budget for the acquisition/ purchase of land.

In urban areas, a target of 70,500 sites measuring 20'x30' has been set for distibution in the year 1995-96. The plan of distribution is as follows: a) 500 sites per town having a population between 20,000 and 49,999 in 87 towns; and b) 1,000 sites for 35 cities having population exceeding 50,000 (as per the 1991 census). The programme will be implemented by the Deputy Commissioner concerned, and a budget provision of Rs. 4 crores has been made available for the purpose of acquisition/purchase of lands in the urban areas. In terms of physical achievement, from 1991-92 to 1994-95 (up to November 1994)' 7.44 lakhs sites have been distributed under the Ashraya Scheme.

New Action Plan: The government, in order to streamline the process of implemnting the housing schemes, conducted a review of the implementation of the above schemes which brought out the following functional flows. Some of these are:

a) non involvement of the beneficiaries/communities in the construction of houses;

b) wrong selection of beneficiaries;

c) construction of houses by contractors rather than by the beneficiares;

d) slow pace of construction;

e) lack of adequate manpower to supervise and also to assist the beneficiaries in technical details; and

f) non-integration of infrastructural services with housing units.

Taking note of these, the Government prepared a new 'action plan' of housing for the economically weaker sections in rural and urban areas for the year 1995-96 under the Ashraya/Ambedkar and IAY Programme (G.O. HUDIHAH 95 (2), dated 18,.8.1995, Bangalore). Accordingly, the unit cost under the Ashraya/Ambnedkar housing scheme has been raised from Rs. 15,000 to 20,000 and the choice of building design is left to the Zilla Panchayats and Karnataka Land Army Corporation. The beneficiaries have been given the advantage of designing their houses, keeping in view the soil, climatic conditions by using local materials with specification. Here, the services of 'Zilla Nirmithi Kendras' should be utilised by the beneficiaries to construct cost-effective houses both in rural and urban areas.

In the implementation of the above housing schemes, three agencies are involved. The Karnataka Housing Board is the nodal agency for preparing the project report for obtaining the loan component from the HUDCO and for placing the funds at the disposal of Deputy Commissioners and Chief Executive Officers of Zilla Panchayats in urban and rural areas respectively. For this a budget provision of Rs 29.78 crores has been made for the year 1995-96, of which Rs 13.41 crores as subsidy at the rate of Rs. 900 per each house.

One of the significant features of the Ashraya housing scheme is that for the Scheduled Castes and Scheduled Tribes, the scheme is implemented free of cost. The Social Welfare Department has estimated Rs.13.80 crores as subsidy for 1,38,000 beneficiaries and there is no loan component. The housing and urban development department's share will be Rs 9,000, the social welfare department's Rs 10,000, and the Department of Rural Development and Panchayat Raj's Rs 1,000, which will be provided for the construction of latrine. Apart from this, the Social Welfare department has made a budget provision of Rs.50 crores for constructing 25,000 houses under the Ambedkar Centenary Housing programme. Also, the Department of Rural Development and Panchayat Raj has made a provision of Rs. 64.78 crores for constructing

41,224 houses under the Indira Awas Yojana. As per the Government Order, the construction of houses under the above mentioned schemes should be entrusted to a single agency for the entire district in order ensure quality and for effective monitoring of the schemes. In urban areas, the implementation of the Ashraya schemes is supervised and monitored by the Deputy Commissioners of the respective districts. The unit cost for the construction of the house has been raised from Rs.16,000 to Rs 24,500. Of the total amount, Rs 19,500 is funded by the HUDCO and the remaining amount of Rs 5,00 contributed by the beneficiary.

One of the significant aspects of the housing schemes such as Ashraya, Ambedkar and IAY is that reservation for different categories is provided: 23 per cent reservation for Scheduled Castes (18 per cent) and Scheduled Tribes (5 per cent), 30 per cent for other Backward Classes and the remaining 47 per cent for general category under the Ashraya scheme, whereas in respect of the Ambedkar housing scheme, hundred per cent reservation for Scheduled Castes, and under the IAY scheme, 60 per cent for Scheduled Castes and Scheduled Tribes and the remaining 40 per cent for the general category. Families whose annual income is less than Rs 11,800 have been identified as beneficiaries for the allotment of sites and houses by the Taluk Panchayats in rural areas and municipal councils in urban areas. More importantly, in order to involve the beneficiaries in the implementation of the schemes, the government has directed that no private contractors should be allowed in the construction of houses, Instead, it should be entrusted to the KLAC or Zilla Panchayat Engineering Division or B D O. The beneficiaries are motivated to contribute in the form of labour and the technical and material assistance will be provided by the agencies like 'Nirmithi Kendras'.

In addition to providing sites and construction of houses under various schemes, the Karnataka government is quite innovative in introducing a new scheme called 'Neralina Bhagya' in 1993-94. The main objective of this scheme has been to replace the thatched roof with tiled ones so that the poor will have all season roof and they need not become the victims of nature's hazards. The unit cost per house is Rs.

3,000. As a step in this direction, during 1993-94, around 13,047 thatched roof houses were converted into tiled roof and it is proposed in the year 1994-95 that around one lakh houses would get this facility.

A close look at the implementation of the above schemes, both in rural and urban areas, reveals that the achievement is far from satisfactory. The available data indicate that the set targets have not been achieved fully. For instance, the physical progress under the rural housing scheme for the year 1995-96 indicates that out of the total target of 60,000 houses under the Ashraya scheme, 16.72 per cent of houses have been completed, 0.04 per cent of houses against the target of 25,000 under Ambedkar and 7,486 houses out of 44,129 houses proposed under the IAY have been completed. In urban areas, during the years between 1992-93 and 1995-96, only 28 per cent of the houses have been constructed for the welfare of the economically weaker sections of the society. It is significant to note that the distribution of sites has always surpassed the target fixed. For example, during the years 1993-94, the target fixed was 10,000 whereas the actually distributed sites were around 21,481. But, this is not the case in urban areas. The reasons put forth are non-availability of land, inordinate delay in the execution of work and unrealistic fixed targets.

The foregoing account reveals that right from inception, the Government of Karnataka has been making an all-out effort to provide shelter to the economically weaker sections of the society, both in rural and urban areas. There have been innovative efforts to strengthen and popularise the housing schemes like Ashraya. Besides the constraints that have been cited in the implementation of the schemes, the housing programme suffers greatly due to lack of independent departments at the district and taluk levels. The housing department, as expressed by the officers of this department, has been finding it very difficult to co-ordinate and monitor the implementation of the schemes; it is often devoid of a good feedback from the field levels. Indeed, this has been a serious drawback of the entire programme. Keeping in view the organisational and managerial constraints, it has become necessary and essential that the present housing department (which is separated from Urban) should be structured on the lines of a Directorate. Considering the number of schemes that have been formulated and implemented, the Directorate becomes a need of the hour.

In addition to the above mentioned administrative requirements, there are some other areas which should be given proper attention by the government in order to strengthen the housing administration. Seen in this context, as revealed from the field, the beneficiaries of the above housing schemes have been hardly participating in the implementation of the schemes. Although the Housing Policy of the state does envisage participation of the beneficiareis, in real terms, the schemes encourage to a large extent the 'dependency syndrome'. As mentioned earlier, the beneficiaries, by utilising the services of local NGOs, should be motivated to contribute both labour and cash so that they would have the feeling of ownership. More importantly, there is need for the involvement of beneficiaries right from the beginning of the programmes/ schemes. In so far as realising this, both Government agencies and NGOs should work as facilitators and motivators. While commenting on the nature and process of housing schemes in Karnataka, one of the officers observed that "often, the rural housing schemes remain unallotted even well after their construction work is completed. Several such houses start decaying by the time the beneficiaries are selected. Further, in this process, the beneficiaries are unable to participate in the construction activity. Therefore, necessary steps should be taken by the implementing agencies to allot the houses well before the foundation work is commenced and encourage the allottees to physically contribute in the construction of their own houses and the common facilities".

One of the important aspects in the successful impoementation of schemes like housing is with regard to the recovery of loan. As expressed by the functionairies of implementing agencies, there prevails a very poor recovery of the loans given to the beneficiaries. In fact, this has given an unfavourable picture as far as the sustainability of the schemes. Absence of an indpendent department at the sub-state level and insufficient field staff are, in a way, have contributed for the poor recovery of the loan. Necessary steps should be taken in this regard by the government to strengthen the field staff.

Notwithstanding all the above, there is need for transparency in the administration. Interface between the beneficiaries and the implementing agencies appears to be a crucial aspect of development administration. There should be continuous dialogues, exchanges and communiation between the above actors, and then only there is a possibility of meeting the objectives of the schemes.

The appraoch towards rural housing should take note of the economic problems of rural housing like - for the rural poor, the need for food and clothing may perhaps come higher in priority than 'self-help housing'. The problem of non-availability of vacant "gramathana" land may pose a blockage for the housing scheme since whatever land available has already been encroached upon which is mainly unauthorised. As a result, the experience of many states, including Karnataka, reveals that housing schemes like people's housing, Ashraya house sites and other housing programes, have had the necessicity spillover from the existing village gramathana land and have led to either the community grasslands and the community forest cover of the village, adjacent to the village, being utilised for housing purposes, or have led to the acquisition of dry lands situated far away from the main village, where the lands of the poorer farmers could be easily acquired for alloting housing sites and construction of houses (Kumar 1994). In order to cope with the problem of shortage of land, the National Policy on Housing has recognised 'group-based' or 'co-operative activity' or 'community associations' as a corrective measure not only to face the shortage of land but also to promote housing activity in future. All these efforts have the sole objective of at least to 'reduce houselessness'.

II

WATER SUPPLY AND SANITATION

Water Supply: Although water is the basic need of human life, it has become a scarce resource in recent times. The government has the prime responsibility of providing water both in urban and rural areas. For this, it has initiated different types of schemes. At present, in Karnataka, both in urban and rural areas, there is an acute shortage of drinking water although the government has been allocating financial resources to meet the demand. Significantly, many international agencies have been supporting the efforts of the government both at central and state levels.

Rural Water Supply: In Karnataka, augmentation and development of ground water have been initiated since 1966 after the establishment of an independent Directorate of Ground Water Survey and Investigation Wing in the Department of Mines and Geology. This wing had the responsibility of identifying potential drilling sites for ground water, and drilling work was done by the Public Health Engineering (PHE) Department for supplying water in rural areas.

The supply of water in rural areas is being planned, designed and implemented by the Department of Public Health Engineering. In the initial phase, the department had two zones headed by a Chief Engineer: One, for the North at Dharwad, and the other, for the South at Bangalore. Now, both these zones have been amalgamated into one zone and it is located in Bangalore (1980), headed by an Engineer-in-Chief. However, it is significant to note that with the setting up of Zilla Parishads and Mandal Panchayats, the entire department was re-organised and the activities of rural water supply and rural sanitation since then transferred to Zilla Parishads for implementation; only planning, monitoring and technical guidance have been retained at the divisional and state levels.

In augmenting the water resources and thereby providing water in rural areas, the efforts of the state government were strengthened by the Central Government with the financial support given under 'Accelerated Rural Water Supply Programme (ARWSP)'. Under this new arrangement, villages were grouped under threee specific categories. The norms specified under each category were: villages with no water source or 50 feet below the ground or distance exceeding 1.60 kilometers (Category I); where water is saline (Category II); and villages affected by epedimics (Category III). A survey was conducted to identify problem villages. As on 1.4.1988, under category I, 16,764 villages were identified, 3,037 under category II and 202 villages under category III; put altogether 20,003 villages were identified as problem villages.

In addition to the above programme, taking into account the magnitude of the problem of drinking water, the Government of India launched the 'National Planning Water Mission' in the year 1986. This mission has been renamed as 'Rajiv Gandhi National Drinking Water Mission (RGNDWM)'. The mission forms part of the State funded Minimum Needs Programme (MNP) and point 7 of the Twenty Point Programme 1986. The Government of India, thus, continues to accord highest priority to the rural water sector through the activities of the Misssion and ARWSP. The RGNDWM aims at covering all ' no source problem' habitatations, to supply 40 LPCD, to evolve cost effective appropriate technology, to create awareness on the use of safe drinking water and to promote community participation.

In Karnataka, under the above mission, a survey of the status of drinking water supply in rural habitations has been completed. This has helped the government not only in knowing the status of the existing water supply in all the rural habitations but in also providing a basis for programming the necessary schemes in order to provide sufficient soft potable drinking water.

Another significant development to be noted here is that from the year 1988-89 onwards, instead of revenue villages, 'habitation' has been given emphasis to identify the scarcity-hit regions. The habitation includes main villages, hamlets, thandas, project camps etc. The revised norms have highlighted the importance of taking population as the unit to provide water supply. As on March 1996, there are around 56,682 habitations in rural Karnataka.

The following Table 2 gives the details of habitations having different service levels in terms of per capita availability of water:

Table 2
Habitations having Different Services Levels in Terms of Per Capita Availability of Water

Service Level (As on March 1996)		Total	% to the Total
0	LPCD	6,086	10.74
1–10	LPCD	2,044	37.94
11–20	LPCD	6,105	37.94
21–30	LPCD	7,971	–
31–40	LPCD	5,384	–
Above 40	LPCD	29,092	51.32
Total		**56,682**	**100.00**

Source: PHE Department, Government of Karnataka.

It is evident from Table 2 that out of the total inhabitated habitations there are still around 6.086 (10.74 per cent) habitations which do not have any source of water. It is also clear from the table that only half (51.32 per cent) of the habitations have been assured of 40 LPCD whereas 37.94 per cent with less than 40 LPCD. A point to be noted is that it has been the policy of the government that the minimum requirement of water per individual is to be 40 LPCD, especially in rural areas. In order to cover all the habitations with the minimum supply of 40 LPCD, the government has been implementing three important schemes in thre rural areas, viz., Piped Water Supply, Mini Water Supply and Installations of Borewell schemes. The sole objective behind this move has been to provide a safe water source which is described as one which is aesthetically attractive, pathologically safe, chemically pure and hygienically fit for human consumption.

The piped water supply schemes are being provided to villages/habitations where the population is more than 1,000 in maidan areas, and 850 and above in Malnad areas. As on March 1995, since the inception of the programme, around 9,612 piped water supply schemes have been commissioned both under the state and the Central sectors.

The Mini Water Supply Scheme has been implemented since 1983-84 covering a population between 500 and 1,000. Under this scheme, a source yielding more than 1,000 gallons per hour and a cistern having the capacity of 2,500 liters are provided. Four taps will be connected for the use of the habitants. One of the advantages of this scheme, according to the Engineers of PHE, is that there will be a continuous and uninterrupted supply of drinking water. This would also discourage goiing for more number of borewells which would quite be expensive in terms of installation and maintenance Initially, the above scheme was taken up under the District-Sub-Plan, however, from 1994-95 onwards the PHE has been shouldering the responsibility of executing the schemes.

The borewells fitted with handpumps have been provided to habitations with a population less than 500. Under this scheme, borewell facility has been given to Scheduled Caste colonies and this is taken up under the special component plan. It has been the policy of the government that in all habitations the first borewell should be installed in SC/ST colonies and the first 'stand post' under the piped water supply scheme. Apart from this, under the Tribal Sub-plan the borewell scheme has been executed in four districts, namely, Chickmagalur, Mysore, Dakshina Kannada and Kodagu. The available statistics, as on March 1996, reveal that there are around 143,344 borewells fitted with handpumps, 9,927 miniwater supply schemes and 10,059 piped water supply schemes; put together, there are 163,330 water source points and through these sources water has been supplied in rural areas. On an average, the population covered by a single source is around 242. During the last decade (1985-86 to 1996-97), the government has spent around 630 crores towards the rural water supply schemes.

In addition to the above schemes, the government has been implementing both rural water supply and sanitation schemes under the Bilateral Assistance Programme. There are three such programmes, namely;

1) Integrated Rural Sanitation and Water Supply Project under Danida Assistnce.

2) Integrated Rural Water Supply and Sanitation Project under Netherlands Assistance.

3) Karnataka Integrated Rural Water Supply and Environment Project with World Bank Assistance.

Under Danida assistance, three pilot taluks - Bagepally in Kolar, Jagalur in Chitradurga and Hungund in Bijapur district-have been selected. The project is of integrated type involving water supply, environmental sanitation, sanitary latrines and afforestation. The project implementation period is four years, involving a cost of 1,290.68 lakhs of which Danida Government's contribution is 90 per cent (i.e., 1,187.07 lakhs).

The project under Netherlands assistance has been carried out in two districts, viz., Dharwad and Bijapur since 1993 and its cost is 6,770.16 lakhs. The project-duration is five years from 1.6.93 to the end of 31.5.98. Under this project, 120 problematic villages in Dharwad, 71 in Bijapur district have been covered including the schemes like drinking water supply, sanitation, environmental sanitation, construction of Anganawadi buildings, water quality testing laboratories.

The Integrated rural water supply and environmental sanitation project with the World Bank assistance aims at covering villages with acute water shortage, with serious health problems - guinea worms, flurosis, cholera, gastroenteritis and hepatitits - with less than 40 LPCD, without adequate ground water source, and villages with sullage drainage problem. The Project covers 12 districts which include seven drought-prone area districts. It covers 1,200 villages and would be implemented in a period of seven years, and the total cost of the project is estimated to be Rs 447.20 crores. The project has come into effect from 1.3.94 onwards. A significant point to be noted is that the Zilla Panchayats have been entrusted with the responsibility of identifying the affected villages.

One of the important aspects of the above project is that the cost of the project is not only borne by the World Bank (78 per cent), state government (15 per cent) but also by the community (to the tune of

(7.1 per cent). The project has four major components: a) Rural Water Supply; b) Environmental Sanitation; c) Institution building and project support and; d) Health Communication. About 53 per cent of the total project cost is incurred on rural water supply supplied mainly through piped water supply schemes (around 1,200), individual (piped schemes). Through these schemes, it is projected to provide 40 LPCD through standpost and 70 LPCD for home connection, and they are designed mainly to cater the prospective demand expected in 2011. More importantly, about 4.8 million persons are expected to benefit from the above schemes. The project also aims at strenghthening the water quality monitoring and surveillance system in rural areas.

The maintenance of assets created is regarded as an important activity in the schemes of water supply and Sanitation. A close look at the facilities provided and their maintenance indicates that of the total 153,154 (as on March 1995) source points, 12 per cent of them either completely failed or have not been functioning due to several reasons. They are: sources which have completely dried up (1.6 per cent); due to technical problems (2.5 per cent); and reduction in ground water (2.5 per cent). A point to be noted here is that around 8.2 per cent of the source points can be rejuvinated or repaired. There is a tendency to go in for new borewells instead of trying to repair, rejuvenate or augment the existing schemes. However, all this depends on the effective and efficient maintenance of the assets created. Does the community undertake the responsibility of maintaining and monitoring of the assets? Answers, especially from the officials, are not encouraging . This is because there is hardly any voluntarism on the part of the community for the proper upkeep of the assets.

It is worth noting here that the World Bank assisted Water Supply and Environmental Sanitation Project as referred to has very much emphasised the participation of the NGOs not only in the implementation of the project schemes but also in the maintenance of the assets created. Under the project, 'Village Water Supply and Sanitation Committees' have been set up to take care of the maintenance and proper up-keep of the assets. As a suggestion, for the fruitful realisation of the above tasks, it is necessary to motivate and encourage women to work as 'caretakers of the assets'.

More than the above, there are some other requirements which need immediate attention from the administration. In terms of management, at present, the maintenance of the rural water supply is under the purview of Zilla Panchayats which is turning out to be an expensive affair and moreover, a time consuming process. This, in a way, is affecting the proper implementation and maintenance of the schemes. Instead, it is better if the same is left with the village panchayats since the latter have a close access to the subjects like water supply in the villages and they can immediately give necessary attention to the problems, thereby making the administrative process a responsive, people-friendly, reciprocative and committed one. This is to make the point that to address a project like rural water supply there is need for a 'single agency' for the effective formulation, implementation and monitoring in the project. An effort should be made in this direction to mobilise or pool the multiple resources to provide optimal benefits.

In the background of reduction in ground water source, efforts have to be made to encourage, on a large scale, water-shed projects through Dry Land Development Board, rain water harvesting, sprinkler irrigation and ground water recharge. This is mainly because, a vast majority of the villages depend on sub-soil water not only for drinking water but also for irrigation purposes.

Urban Water Supply: In order to supply water in urban areas, the government created a designated body called 'The Karnataka Urban Water Supply and Drainage Board' in 1995. The responsibilities entrusted to this Board are planning, designing and execution of water supply and sanitation works in all the urban areas of the state except Bangalore city. Also, the Board is empowered to handle the operation and maintenance of Municipal Water Supply and Drainage schemes. It has the jurisdiction over 172 urban areas covering a population of nearly 90.90 lakhs, as per the 1991 census.

The Board is headed by a Chairman and is supported by a Managing Director on whom the onus of implementing the scheme's rests. He carries his responsibilities with the support of an executive wing consisting of Chief Engineer, Superintending Engineer (Designs), Executive Engineer (Planning and Design), Secretary, Deputy Chief

Engineer (I,II,III) and other executive officers. The four schemes which come under the Urban Water Supply are:

1) Piped Water Supply Scheme.
2) Urban Water Supply Scheme.
3) Board Water Supply Scheme.
4) Underground Drainage Schem.

The government has followed the population criteria for implementing the above schemes. The Piped Water Supply schemes are executed in urban areas where the population in less than 20,000 (as per the 1991 census) and this is being implemented with 100 per cent grant from the government. As per available statistics, since inception. as many as 192 towns have been covered up to the end of November 1994. During the year 1993-94, five towns were covered with an expenditure of Rs 8.06 crores.

The works under Urban Water Supply schemes have also been taken up where the population is above 20,000. Unlike Piped Water Supply Scheme, the works under this scheme are partly financed by the LIC/HUDCO. The local authority is made responsible for the repayment of the loan with interest. The government has evolved a funding pattern for urban water supply schemes(as per G.O. No. HUDCO/UMS dated 11.8.94) as given in Table 3 below:

Table 3:
Details pertaining to Government's Funding Pattern for Schemes under Urban Water Supply

LIC/HUDCO Local Authority	Govt. (in %)	Loan (in %)	Local Body (in %)
Corporation	70 (50)	05 (20)	25 (30)
City Municpalities	70 (50)	15 (25)	15 (25)
Town Municipalities	70 (50)	25 (30)	05 (20)

Note: Figures in parantheses indicate percentage pattern of funding.
Source: Government of Karnataka.

The Schemes under the Water Supply Board are formulated and implemented by the Board itself after having obtained loans from the Government and the LIC. As per the directives of the government, the repayment of loan (with interest) will have to be made by the Board itself. One of the important functions of the Board's administration is that it not only executes the scheme but also maintains the works after their completion. For this, the Board collects 'user charges'. Apart from this, the Board has been taking up independent water supply schemes out of its own resources.

The Underground Drainage Schemes are executed in almost all urban areas, irrespective of their population, and these schemes have been financed by the LIC and HUDCO (based on the pattern as referred to). However, generally, these schemes are taken up in cities having a population of more than one lakh, and cities and towns located on the river banks.

One of the significant aspects of urban water supply is, that under the special component plan, the piped water suppy schemes have been executed only in Scheduled Caste Colonies in all the towns and cities and corporations. The entire expenditure is borne by the government and the scheme is intended only to benefit the people belonging to Scheduled Caste groups.

A close look at the physcial and financial performance of Urban Water Supply schemes reveals that so far under piped water supply, 192 (as on November 94) with a population of around seven lakhs have been given water suppy. Under this scheme, on an average, the per capita availability of water ranges between 45 LPCD and 100 LPCD. Under urban water supply scheme, 47 towns have been covered (as on November 94) and the population covered is around 219,000, the per capital availability of water ranging between 60 LPCD- 110 LPCD. Progress under the Board Supply shows that so far 20 towns have been given water supply by covering a population of 134,000 with a per capita availability of water between 60 LPCD and 110 LPCD. And, 22 towns have been covered under Underground Drainage scheme, covering a population of 625,000.

As far as the financial performance is concerned, the expenditure incurred on the schemes shows an increasing trend against the actual allocation made. For instance, in the year 1993-94, the expenditure incurred under the Piped Water Supply was around Rs.806.42 lakhs as against the allocation of Rs 700 lakhs, and under the Urban Water Supply scheme Rs 3,313.58 lakhs as against Rs 3,020 lakhs.

Bangalore Water Supply and Sewerage Board: It is a well-known fact that with urban growth, in terms of urban population, there is corresponding need and demand for more of services like water supply and sanitation. Seen in this context, Bangalore, with a population 4,130,288, as per the 1991 census, has been experiencing acute water shortage despite the efforts made by the Bangalore Water Supply and Sewerage Board (BWSSB). This Board was constituted in 1964 by an Act of legislature and is an independent organisation with the prime responsibility of providing water supply and sewerage facilities to the city.

The Board, headed by a Chairman with both line and auxiliary staff, has three important functions: a) to ascertain the sufficiency and wholesomeness of water supply within the Bangalore Metropolitan Area; b) to prepare and carry out schemes for the supply of wholesome water for domestic purposes; and c) to prepare and carry out schemes for the sewerage and the disposal of the sewage of the Bangalore Metropolitan Area. The management of the Board is carried out by six members and they are assisted by a 'Technical Committee'. There are two Chief Engineers for maintenance, collection of revenues, establishment, and one for the project wing of the Board. These two Engineers are well supported by adequate technical and ministerial staff at various levels of project work.

Prior to the constitution of the Board, water supply was taken care of by the Bangalore City Corporation and it was done through Hesaraghatta tank and Chamaraja Sagar reservoir, both built across the river Arkavathy, with a potential supply of 22.5 MLD (million litre per day) and 143.0 MLD of water respectively.

However. this was found to be very insufficient since the population of the city has been growing at an alarming rate. In order to meet the ever increasing demand the Board has been innovative in its efforts, especially to plan for long-term solutions by formulating and implementing Cauvery Water supply schemes, Stages I, II and III, for bringing 540 MLD of water to Bangalore city and these schemes have been successfully commissioned in the years 1974, 1982 and 1993 respectively. It has been a great challenge before the Board since the source point from the City is about 100 kilometers and pumped in three stages to a height of more than 160 metres at each stage. Put together, the potential of water availability to the city from the above sources is around 705.5 million litres per day.

The utility and effective implementation of schemes like water supply can be assessed mainly by comparing water availability with demand for water or by comparing water availability with standard norms laid down. Seen in this context, to quote from the BWSSB doucments, "Though during the period of 100 years all out efforts have been made to supply 435.5 MLD of filtered water to Bangalore City, the supply of drinking water has not reached the required standard (fixed by the Government of India) of 140 litres per capita per day due to the alarming rise in population of Bangalore city from 1.18 lakhs during 1891 to 41.30 lakhs during 1991". The estimated per capita availability of water since the beginning of the century is presented in Table 4.

Table 4

Per Capital Availability of Water aganist the Actual Requirement between 1901 and 1995

Actual Requirement Year	Per Capita Availability (in LPCD)	140 (LPCD)
1901	86	-54
1911	74	-66
1921	58	-82
1931	45	-95
1941	100	-40
1951	79	-61
1961	71	-69

(Cont.)

1971	94	-46
1981	102	-38
1991	105	-35
1992	101	-39

Source: 1993. **Handbook of Statistics,** Bangalore Water Supply and Sewerage Board.

Table 4 shows the per capita availability of water against the actual required per capita requirement of water since the beginnning of the century. It is rather disappointing to note that at no stage the required per capita availability of 140 LPCD has been achieved irrespective of seasonal (monsoon) variations over the decades. It is only in the last couple of years that the position appears to be better compared to the earlier years. The accumulation of water supply did not take place, as desired, to match the fourfold increase of population over the decades, the population which was 163,091 in the year 1901 has gone up to 4,310,288 in the year 1992. In Bangalore city, water users are classified into two categories - domestic and non-domestic -consumers using water for household purposes and non-domestic users for commercial purposes. The data for 1992-93 shows that the average consumption of water per day by domestic users is 163.85 ML; Non-domestic 40.30 ML, and 111.71 ML by users of public taps.

A most important related aspect of water supply in Bangalore city has been the maintenance and treatment or sewerlines and manholes. However, the efforts made to supply water does not match the efforts for conveyance of sullage and disposal of sewage. It is significant to note in this connection that due to the well-defined topography of Bangalore, a natural system of drainage without recourse to pumping existed both for sewage flow and storm water flow by gravity beyond city limits. The sanitary system of sewage and waste water through underground drainage system was introduced in 1922.

Although Bangalore city never had a major programme of sewer construction till 1950, now the city has a well designed and regularly maintained underground sewerage system. This arrangement is done by covering four divisions, viz., East, West, North and South. In addition to the above arrangement, there are two sewage treatment plants - one at Vrishabhavathi valley and the other at Koramangala and Challaghatta valley. These plants have been sufficiently located away from the city limits to avoid mosquito menace and air pollution by foul smell to keep the city environment more hygenic. It is important to note that 80 per cent of the water supply is likely to flow back in the form of sewage into the sewarage system. This clearly speaks for the necessity and importance of treatment plants. The treatment capacity of Vrishabhavathi is 123 MLD, with Koramangala and Challaghatta being 163 MLD. These plants have been upgraded to treat both primary and secondary standards.

Income and Expenditure: The funds required by the Board to make the above arrangements are augumented through levy and collection of water charges on no loss and no profit basis; this indeed is a unique feature of the Board's administration. The current rates of water tariff are charged for two types of water used - filtered water and raw water. The details are given in Table 5.

The available data indicate that 80 to 90 per cent of the total revenue receipts come mainly through levy of water rates and water meter charges and the remaining from the miscellaneous receipts. However, as expressed by the Board authorities, the Board has been incurring losses since 1981-82 which is mainly because of the fact that in fixing the water rates, the interest liability on loans from government and other agencies have not been taken into account. To quote from the Handbook of Statistics, published by the Board (BWSSB 1993), "the revenue collection is not commensurate with the increase in revenue expenditure, particularly on account of payment of interest on debt services, increase in power charges and also increase in establishment expenditure due to the revision of pay scales." A much concerned issue in this context is the maintenance cost of water supply.

As revealed from the discussions with the officials, there is no one-to-one correlation with the acutal maintenance cost. This has further resulted in the unsatisfactory maintenance of schemes, which is a social and economic loss.

Table 5
Rates of Water Tariff (1994-95)

Sl.No.	Slab in litres	Rate for 1000 litres (in Rs) Filtered Water	Raw Water
Category I, Domestic			
1.	0 to 25,000	0.80 (minimum Rs 20)	(minimum Rs 7.50)
2.	25,000 to 50,000	2.00	0.50
3.	50,000 to 75,000	5.00	1.20
4.	75,000 to 100,000	6.50	2.00
5.	Above 100,00	9.00	3.00
Category II, Non-domestic			
1.	0 to 10,000	9.00 (Minimum Rs 90)	25.00 (Minimum Rs 25)
2.	10,000 to 20,000	10.00	4.00
3.	20,000 to 40,000	14.50	5.00
4.	40,000 to 60,000	18.00	7.00
5.	60,000 to 1,00,00	19.99	7.00
6.	100,000 to Above 200,000	20.00	10.00
7.	Industries	20.00	10.00
8.	Swimming Pool (BCC)	15.00	–
9.	Bulk Domestic Users	3.50	–
	Sanitary fees 30% (on water charges) ?		

Source: Bangalore Water Supply and Sewerage Board, Annual Report, 1994-95, Bangalore.

Notwithstanding the above, the Board has been making sincere efforts to augment water supply for the Bangalore citizens by implementing the works under Cauvery III and IV Stages.

There is some hope that the city would get the required water and also would be able to reach the required standard of 140 litres per capita per day which is not the case since the beginning of the century.

Sanitation: It is needless to say that any improvement in sanitary condtion would cetainly prevent water borne and human excreta related contaminations; in a way both sanitation and water supply are like two sides of the same coin. Any sanitry related work devoid of water suply is always incomplete and inconclusive.

Creation of a heatlhy environment in society is possible only when the people living in the society carry certain healthy practices of using and keeping not only their lavatory system clean but also their houses and the environment. Each and every house should possess a lavatory and slowly the traditional practices should be put to an end. However, still in rural areas, the facilties of sanitation have hardly been used by certain sections of the population. An attempt is made here to describe sanitation projects undertaken by the government, especially in rural areas.

Rural Sanitation: The rural sanitation programme has been in operation since the year 1984-85; in this period, totally around 1,016 flush, water seal, sanitary latrines with two leach pits - UNDP design were constructed at an expenditure of Rs. 9.75 lakhs and this was against the target of 1,600. During the period 1985-90 (VIIth plan), the PHE, an implementing agency had planned to construct 23,749 sanitary latrines at a cost of Rs. 341.88 lakhs built under various schemes like RLEGP, NREP. However, the progress was not to the desired extent because against the set target of 23,749, only 8,945 units could be completed and the money spent was Rs 188.17 lakhs. To strengthen the efforts made by the state government in promoting and inculcating better sanitary habits amongst the rural people, the Government of India launched a massive rural sanitation programme in 1986 by introducing Central Rural Sanitation Programme (CRSP) with 100 per cent Central assitance, and a provision was made for taking up these works under RLEGP and NREP. An important feature of this scheme was that not only the SC and ST beneficiaries were given priority but also those who were below the poverty line. And this was extended to select anganwadis also. The Karnataka Land Army Corporation has been entrusted with the responsibility of designing and implementing the programmes in the state. The above programmes have been implemented under Central and state sectors and under

CRSP, NREP and RCEGP schemes. In terms of physical and financial progress, as on 31.3.'1995, of the 70,257 latrines targeted to build, 47,992 have been built (68 per cent) which is quite encouraging considering the slow progress between the years 1984-85 and 1993-94. So far, the government has spent Rs 1,111.29 lakhs towards latrine construction.

In addition to the ongoing sanitation schemes, the Government of Karnataka, with the assistance extended by UNICEF, launched a subsidy-oriented programme, namely, 'Nirmala Grama Yojana'. Under this scheme, the beneficiary was given Rs 500 per unit as subsidy. As a pilot project, the scheme was first implemented in Mysore district. Looking at its success, the programme was later extended to cover Mysore, Gulbarga, Kolar and Belgaum districts with UNICEF assistance of Rs.170 lakhs and with a state budget allocation of Rs. 350 lakhs, the share of the then Mandal Panchayats was Rs. 100 lakhs. The cost of construction was estimated to be Rs. 620 per unit. As on January 1996, against the target of 115,950 units, only 61,443 (53 per cent) units have been completed in all the four districts. It is rather discouraging to note that of the total rural population of 31 million people (1991 census), only about 0.60 million have been covered under the rural sanitation programme. The field level experiences reveal that right from the inception the schemes have not been received well by the public and more importantly, due to unsatisfactory implementation process. In quite in a few instances the funds that were sanctioned remained unutilised and lapsed.

With the above schemes not making any significant impact on motivating the rural people for utilising the benefits under the sanitary schems, the Government of Karnataka made a significant move in launching a new shceme under the caption of 'Nirmala Karnataka' on 2 October 1995, coniciding with Mahatma Gandhi Jayanthi. Under this scheme, the government has planned to cover 20 lakh families by the end of 2000 A.D. by investing an attractive and impressive sum of Rs.400 crores. Each village panchayat has been entrusted with the responsibility of covering at least 100 families in a year. The families who are above the poverty line are given Rs. 1,650 while those who are below the poverty line are given Rs 1,200 as subsidy. In order to make the programme 'people-friendly', 10 per cent of the amount is kept for spending, especially, to create awareness among the families. As an innovative measure, the persons who encourage families will be given Rs. 25 each as incentive and two local masons will be offered special training so that the families need not go after masons settled in different areas; the main purpose behind this has been to utilise the locally available physical and human resources.

The government has, through its circulars, urged to treat this programme as a'movement' and in this studpendous task all categories of people-elected representives, officials, NGOs, youths, students and the conscious public should take part and make the programme a 'people's programme'. The people have to be educated and should be made aware of not only keeping their houses tidy but also their environment . The implementing officers, especially the functionaries of panchayats, have a great moral responsibility of motivating the people to treat this programme as their programme and more importantly the scheme should be implemented keeping in view the likes and the dislikes of the people.

The available statistical information, as on 28.9.95, indicates that the government has planned to construct 564,100 latrines in 5,641 village panchayats. For this purpose, the estimated and sanctioned budget is around Rs.9,223.00 lakhs of which Rs 8,300.70 lakhs, will be given as subsidy, and Rs 922.30 lakhs (10 per cent) of the total amount towards creating awareness amongst the beneficiaries of the programme. Field level experiences reveal that despite some initial problems, people have come forward to utilise the benefits offered under this programme. If this spirit continues amongst the communities, certainly the programme will achieve the objective of creating 'Nirmala Karnataka'.

In making 'Nirmala Karnataka' a dream come true, even the externally aided projects have earmarked a part of their project funds towards rural sanitation. For instance, under the Danida assistance, the government has aimed at constructing 181 institutional latrines and 3,912 household latrines in the three taluks - Bagepally, Jagalur and Hungund in Kolar, Chitradurga and Bijapur districts respectively.

And to maintain a tidy environment in the villages, the project has planned to upgrade water points like washing slabs, drains, soakpits, cattle troughs and 182,590 metres of sullage drainage. The World Bank assisted project has invested about 25 per cent of the total project cost on environmental sanitation covering small side-surface drains for sullage, bathing cubicles, cattle troughts, washing platforms, individual latrines, street dust bins and bio-gas pilot plants. Notwithstanding all these measures, there is a need to give greater attention for recycling the solid and non-solid municipal water for the better use of the same, particularly to promote non-conventional energy resources like bio-gas.

The unique feature of the project is that it has the objective of developing new approaches to increase demand and usage and to promote community involvement in their planning, construction and maintenance. More significantly, the beneficiaries have to share 30 per cent of the cost of drainage and bathing cubicles. In order to carry out the above tasks the NGOs have been appraoched by the government and there has been a positive attitude from the communities and beneficiaries as far as upkeeping of the assets and using of latrines and thereby keeping their houses and the surroundings 'tidy' and 'pollution-free'.

III

THE PUBLIC DISTRIBUTION SYSTEM

For realising the various policy objectives, the government through its policy of intervention initiates and introduces various socio and economic legislations and measures, especially to bring in'social equity' and for ensuring the welfare of the poor with their participation in the development process. Of the many such intended policy interventions, the intervention to provide food security to vulnerable sections of the society has been in operation since the days of the Second World War. Since then, the Government of India has been pursuing a policy of public distribution of essential commodities. Generally, the distribution takes place whenever there is a shortage of essential goods and when therre is a rise in the prices of commoditites in the market.

The objective of public distribution of foodgrains is to achieve a more equitable distribution of food grains and more inportantly to meet the minimum food requirements of the low-income consumers at fair and reasonable prices or controlled prices.

Karnataka has a wide network of public distribution service (PDS) covering 9,897,232 (as on January 1996) card holders both in urban and rural areas. Up to the mid-seventies, the PDS in Karnataka mainly catered to the needs of 11 cities and 13 towns covered by informal rationing. Rural areas were supplied with grains in accordance with the demand exerted by the co-operative societies. During this phase the target group appeared to be mainly the urban dwellers. Today, the PDS has been extended to all the districts in Karnataka.

The responsbility of distributing essential foodgrains is with the Department of Food and Civil Supplies and the distribution is monitored by its two organisations, Directorate of Food and Civil Supplies, and the Karnataka State Food and Civil Supplies Corporation. The Directorate, with a Director and two Joint Directors has state-wide jurisdiction. Of the two Joint Directors, one looks after, exclusively, the procurement and PDS matters, and the other, administration and civil supply matters. At the sub-state level, the Deputy Commissioner is in-charge of the PDS matters and is assisted by the Deputy Director (Food) and his extension staff.

The Karnataka Food and Civil Supplies Corporation (KFCSC) is a designated agency for the purchase of paddy under support price operations. It is also involved in the lifting of foodgrains from the godowns of the Food Corporation of India (FCI) and distribute the same to fair price shops. The Deputy Commissioner is an authorised authority to issue authorisations to persons to be dealers both in rural and urban and informal rationing areas of the district. One of the striking features of PDS in Karnataka is that there are no private wholesale nominees and the distributions is undertaken by 273 public whole sale nomiees of which 135 belong to the co-operative sector, and the remaining 138 are managed by the Karnataka Food and Civil Supplies Corporation.

The Directorate of Food and Civil Supplies Corporation has set for itself the objectives like, making the food available to the people regularly, checking the prices of the items and reducing fluctuations, ensuring physical availability of foodgrains in remote, hilly and inaccessible areas, implementation of the policies related to procurement, storage and distribution of foodgrains.

Card Holders: In order to ensure that regular supply of foodgrains reach the needy and vulnerable sections of the society, the Karnataka government had launched a scheme called 'Supply of Foodgrains at Subsidised Rates to Rural Poor' way back in the year 1985 (from 1.11.85 onwards). Under this scheme, the government had arranged to supply rice to the poorest section of the population at Rs 2 per kilogramme with a maximum ceiling of 10 kilogrammes of rice or equivalent cereals per family. The families falling below the poverty line (annual income below Rs. 3,500, were is dentified as beneficiaries of this scheme. The beneficiaries were given 'green cards' and the non-beneficiaries 'saffron cards' with a nominal charge of 0.50 paise per card, in order to record the foodgrains and other commodities issued to the beneficiaries. The categories of population specially covered were: landless agricultural labourers, village artisans, marginal farmers, small farmers, pensioners, stone cutters, Scheduled Castes, Scheduled Tribes, Plantation labourers, beedi rollers and agarbhathi manufacturers.

The PDS, in Karnataka, to start with, comprised two categories of card holders - green and saffron. Recently, the government has introduced 'Tri-colour cards' and Photo-Cards. The tri-colour cards have been introduced mainly to replace existing green cards which included both rural and urban poor, especially living in the slums. The families, with Rs. 6,400 annual income, were identified as beneficiaries. At present, there are three types of cards: Photo cards; Tri-colour cards; and Saffron cards. As on December 95, altogether there are, as mentioned earlier, 9,897,232 card holders in the state; 7,218,053 card holders (72.93 per cent) belonging to rural areas and 2,679,179 (27.07 per cent) to urban areas. The details of the category of card holders are given in Table 6.

Table 6

Number of Card Holders under Different Categories both in Rural and Urban Areas

Sl. No.	Area	Photo Cards	Tri-colour Cards	Saffron Cards	Total
1	Urban	464,867	79,559	-	555,426 (5.5%)
2.	Rural	-	4,962,374	2,255,679	7,218,053 (72.9%)
3.	Informal Rationing	2,007,412	127,341	-	2,134,753 (21.5%)
	Total	**2,472,279 (24.98 %)**	**5,169,274 (52.22 %)**	**2,255,679 (22.79 %)**	**9,897,232 (100%)**

Source: DFCS - 1995.

Note: Figures in paranthesis indicate percentage to the total.

It is clear from Table 6 that out of the total card holders, photo-card holders 24.98 per cent (2,472,279), tri-colour card holders 52.22 per cent (5,169,274) and saffron card holders 22.79 per cent (2,255,679). In urban areas, the scheme is operated through Informal rationing system[1] and rest of the towns under regular public distribution system.

There are around 2,134,753 (21.56 per cent) card holders under informal rationing area and 555,426 (5.50 per cent) under regular PDS. Out of the total rural card holders (7,218,053) there are 4,962,374 coming under tri-colour cards and the remaining 2,255,679 card holders under saffron card scheme.

The unique feature of the green card scheme has been that the government itself has taken over the responsibility of transporting foodgrains from taluk headquarters to the door-steps of fair price shops located in rural areas. In order to cover the eligible families, the income limit has been raised to Rs. 6,400 per annum (now it is Rs 11,000 per

1. This system of rationing is prevalent in urban areas where the population is more than 40,000.

annum). Under the tri-colour card scheme each beneficiary family is entitled to get 6 to 7 kilogrammes rice, 3 to 4 kilogrammes of wheat and 1.25 kilogrammes of sugar, especially in rural areas at a subsidised rates of Rs 4.45 per kilogramme, Rs 2.75 per kilogramme and Rs 9.25 per kilogramme respectively. Families with an annual income above Rs 6,400 are covered under the saffron card scheme and are entitled to get 10 to 15 kilogrammes of rice and 3 to 5 kilogrammes of wheat per family. Under this scheme, even families hailing from hilly regions and drought-prone areas are entitled to get the above quota of ration. The areas coming uder Non-ITDP and DPAP are also covered under this scheme and the families are entitled to get 5 to 12 kilogrammes of rice and wheat, subject to its avilability.

In the informal rationing areas and in other uraban areas each photo-card holder is entitled to get a minmum of 4 to 6 kilogrammes of rice and 2 to 3 kilogrammes of wheat and 3 kilogrammes of sugar. If there is excess of foodgrains each card holder would be given extra 20 kilogrammes. In Bangalore city, the quota of ration is decided on the size of the family: 2 units for adults and 1 unit for minors. Each unit is alloted 1.5 kilogrammes of rice and 0.5 kilogrammes of sugar. As a result, especially in Bangalore, each card holder would get a quota of 21 kilogrammes of rice, 4 kilogrammes of sugar and 2 to 4 kilogrammes of wheat. As for kerosene, in Bangalore, each card holder will get 13 litres, 10 litres in informal rationing area, 8 litres in other urban centres and 3 litres in rural areas. This facility is available to those families which have no LPG connection. There is a provision for distributing 2 litres of kerosene oil even to those who have LPG connections.

Revamped PDS in Karnataka: In addition to the above mentioned schemes, from 1.1.86 onwards, the government has been implementing the ITDP programme especially to supply subsidised foodgrains to the families living in tribal areas. Under this scheme, 21 taluks have been covered in the districts of Chicmagalur, Kodagu, Dakshina Kannada and Mysore. So far, more than 8,5 lakhs families have been covered under this scheme and each family is entitled to draw more than 10 kilogrammes of rice and 5 kilogrammes of wheat per month at the subsidised rates of Government of Indıa. Under the revamped PDS, the government had identified 71 blocks under DPAP spread all over the state. Under this scheme, so far, more than 27 lakh ration cards have been issued and the fair-price shops to the extent of 4,746 have been opened. In order to reach the remote areas, the government has set up mobile fair-price shops and for this, mobile vans are used. These shops are functioning, at present, in the identified areas, namely, Chickmagalur, Mysore, Dakshina Kannada, Kodagu and Raichur.

Fair-Price Shops: One of the important segments of PDS, facilitating efficent distribution, is the fair-price shop or ration shop. In Karnataka, it is interesting to note that if neither KFCSC nor any Co-operative society is willing or able to run a fair-price depot in a particular area, the authorised authority may grant permission to open a retail outlet to assoications and individuals in the order of priority. They are:

a) a society or an association registered under the Karnataka Registration Act;

b) unemployed graduates;

c) ex-servicemen;

d) physically handicapped; and

e) other persons.

The above order of priority should be followed provided that out of the approved authorisations, 15 per cent shall be reserved for persons belonging to Scheduled Castes and 5 per cent to Scheduled Tribes. If persons belonging to these categories are not available, then the authorisation may be issued to other candidates. At present, as on January 1995, there are around 19,124 fair-price shops functioning in the State, of which 13,950 are in rural areas, 2,209 in informal rationing areas, and 1,302 in urban areas. On an average, each fari-price shop covers a population of 2,483.

Procurement of Foodgrains: Among the many importnt aspects of PDS, the public procurement and the distribution constitute the two major components of the system. In Karnataka, the procurement of food grains like rice is being carried out under the provisions of the Karnataka Rice Procurement (levy) order 1984. The procurement prices of paddy and rice (current marketing season) as fixed by the Government of India, are presented in Table 7:

Table 7

Details showing Procurement Prices for Paddy and Rice

	Paddy (per quintal) Rs.	Rice (per quintal) Rs.
Super Fine variety	380.00	598.202.
Fine variety	360.00	568.253.
Common variety	340.00	538.35

Source: DFCS 1993. Government of Karnatatak

The Food Corporation of India (FCI) has been the sole agent of the state government for procuring levy rice and coarse grains under support price operations. An important aspect of the rice procurement policy in Karnataka is that it has banned the movement of paddy outside the state and has allowed the free movement of the same within the state. Generally, the procurement of rice begins from 1st October and ends by 31st Septemeber which is called as 'procurement period'. Each miller is expected to surrender 33 1/3 per cent of the rice milled at the prices fixed by the Government of India. The FCI district officers procure the rice from what is called a 'mill point levy'. The FCI bears the transporataion cost up to 20 kilometres at the rate of Rs 1.60 per kilometre. During this entire process, the FCI is involved in loading, weighing, storing and unloading.

The target for procuring rice for the given one year period is fixed by the Government of Karnataka and the rice procured of two qualities - boiled and raw rice. The information available from the FCI, Regional Office, reveals that the procurement target has been ranging betwen 125,000 metric tonnes and 200,000 metric tonnes over the years. Against this target, the performance of procurement over the years has been dismal; in terms of percentage procurement it varies between 16.5 per cent and 96.92 per cent. The reasons attributed to this kind of dismal performance are drought situation, floods, failure in the yielding crops etc. As a consequence, the rice procurement in Karnataka is observed to be low compared with other states like Andhra Pradesh, Tamil Nadu, Haryana, and Punjab. Karnataka is not a big contributor to the Central food pool. Another important reason for the dismal performance of procurement against the fixed targets has been due to the ineffective functioning of 'Food Enforcement Cell' which is expected to enforce the government laws stringently, in particular, the Essential Commodities Act. It is also necessary to note here that, recently, the government had abolished the 'Food Cell', which had the authority to enforce the rice procurement orders. Considering the imporatnce of such enforcement, there is need to restablish the 'Food Cell', otherwise, the procurement of rice will continue to be sluggish and as a result the desired target cannot be achieved.

Allotment and Off-take: The process of PDS begins with the allotment and off-take of foodgrains meant for the distribution. Considering the fact that Karnataka is not a big contributor to the Central-pool, the allotment made by the Government of India is hardly commensurate with the actual requirements of the state. For instance, State needs rice and wheat, to the tune of 135,000 metric tonnes and 50,000 metric tonnes respectively whereas, during the last two years (1993-94 and 1994-95), the Centre has been alloting only 120,260 metric tonnes of rice and 30,000 tonnes of wheat per month. As far as sugar and kerosene are concerned, the supply has been 19,943 metric tonnes and 54,819 kilolitres respectively, as against the actual requirement of 29,050 metric tonnes of sugar and 67,000 kilolitres of kerosene. With the revamping of PDS, the government has been alloting both rice and wheat to ITDP and DPAP areas which are included in the total allotment made. The average share of the DPAR blocks in the total allotment has been around 30 per cent in rice and 27 per cent in wheat allotment. The PDS share accounts for more than 60 per cent in rice and 65 per cent in wheat in the total allotment.

An important aspect of allotment and off-take has been the apparent mis-match between the actual allotment and actual off-take. This is mainly due to, as expressed by the authorities, unsatisfactory lifting of foodgrains from the godowns and wholesale points. This is being done despite the government circular which specified the validity period for lifting the foodgrains. The validity period has been fixed as 45 days to lift the quota well before the start of the month. The problem of tardiness has ultimately affected the distribution of foodgrains to vulnerable sections of the society.

Operational Aspects of PDS: The PDS is structured on the lines of vertical hierarchy wherein the command/order flows from top to bottom. In addition to the Directorate of Food and Civil Supplies, which is a nodal department, there are other parallel government organisations like KFCSC and TAPMCS participating actively in carrying out the PDS related activites. Both deal with general and technical matters and they have quality controlling officers too. The officals of above organisations and Deputy Director (Food) come under the administrative control of the Deputy Commissioner. However, for all operational purposes, it is the Deputy Director who steers the wheel of operation by exercising his supervision and control over the personnel engaged in the process.

The actual process of distribution starts with the allotment of rice and wheat by the Directorate of Food and Civil Supplies to all the districts in the state. In turn, the Deputy Commissioner reallots the same to each taluk in the district. As per the office communique, the authorities are expected to lift the foodgrains on or before the 15th of every month in urban areas and 20th in rural areas. And the actual distribution should start from the 1st of the month and completed before the end of the month; the same is the case with the allotment and lifting of sugar. The field level information reveals that notwithstanding all these official directives there prevails a considerble degree of 'red-tapism' in following these norms by the concerned functionaries.

The lifted foodgrains - wheat, rice - are brought to KFCSC taluk level branches which, in turn, are distributed to the fair-price shops. As referred to, one of the pertinent features of PDS in Karnataka is the 'doorstep delivery' which is free of cost. For the transportaion of sugar the cost is borne by the dealers themselves. In the organisational network of PDS, the fair-price shop which is the tail-end of the network plays the most significant role in the retail distribution of essential commodities.

Any meaningful review of the PDS should take into account its organisational and functional aspects. Seen in organisational terms, in Karnataka, there is a need to streamline the system through creating independent departments at district and taluk levels to look after the distribution. There is also need to restructure the State level Directorate. By strengthening the organisations at these levels it would be possible to co-ordinate, monitor and review the PDS operation. There exists a dual responsbility in carrying out the PDS related activites, hence, separate departments and desirable at the sub-state levels. In addition to this, as observed in the field, insufficent field staff is one of the contributing factors for the not so impressive performance of the PDS in Karnataka. At the district level, the administrative structure is found to be weak and lacking in adequate powers, considering the muliplicity of functions. As a result, the inspection and supervision have become routine in nature; hence, there is need to strengthen the administrative machinery.

Taking note of the weak administration structure at the sub-state level, it has become necessary that the operation of PDS should be handed over to the panchayats. As enshrined in the **73rd Constitution Amendnment** (Eleventh Schedule, Art. 243G No.28), the PDS is one of the important functions of the panchayats. Even the **Karnataka Panchyat Raj Act of 1993** enjoins the panchayats to shoulder the responsibility of distributing essential commodities to the PDS cardholders. Through this, transparency in PDS operations could be ensured. This would certainly strengthen the administrative machinery as far as the PDS operation is concerned at the sub-state level.

As brought out by research studies (Sivanna 1993; Mooij 1994) and reported in press, there are a large number of complaints about the bad quality of rice and wheat being suplied to the consumers. The bad quality can be indicated in terms of the supply of broken grains due to improper milling, being insect infested, and inferior quality of packing materials used. A much related issue in this regard is the question of quality versus quanity. As a consequence, the supply of poor quality grains has affected the nutritional status of the consumers. Therefore, there is a widespread feeling that 'quality control cells' at all levels of supply and distribution should be opened. This arrangement would definitely help the consumers to improve their nutritional status.

Regarding the economic viablity of fair-price shops, the resource base of the shops is very poor which is mainly due to the insufficient coverage of the commodites. As a result, the shop owners are a discontented lot and they are hardly left with any decent returns. If the shop owners are allowed to sell non-PDS commodities it would improve the viability of the shops and more importantly, it will enable the shops to become a serviceable and accessible marketing point for the consumers. In the present situation the ration shop owners hardly have any motivation to run the business regularly. It has been found that the regular functioining of these shops, especially in rural areas, in terms of the number of days opened, ranged between six and ten days in a month and during the remaining days the shops had closed for want of business.

In order to make the PDS, essentially as pro-poor, suggestions have been made to exclude certain income and professional groups such as tax payers, higher landowning households (more than four hectares) and all self employed professsionals from the purview of PDS benefits. In this direction, some states have already made efforts to exclude the 'creamy-layers' from the purview of the PDS to provide 'food security' to the vulnerable sections of the society. The states like Punjab, Haryana, Rajasthan, Gujarat have excluded income tax payers from the purview of the PDS. The Karnataka government can think of initiating similar measures through transparent and easily understood eligibility norms, to keep the non-poor out of the PDS eligibility.

In spite of all the merits and demerits of having PDS as an important safety net measure, one significant facet of PDS is its capacity to act as an effective 'delivery system' , particularly in rural areas. This is mainly because, anti-poverty programmes like IRDP, JRY suffer from lack of creditble 'delivery system' at the beneficiary level in rural areas. It is considered to be the greatest weakness of our development management. To overcome this weakness, there is a need to redesign the PDS as a permananet strategy to achieve an equitable distribution of foodgrains so that it would serve as a 'supplementary' to the poverty alleviation programme. The new strategy would be the 'public distribution-cum-delivery' which would certainly ensure food security to the poor. This kind of integration would be able to provide an effective and useful public distribution service to the vulnerable sections of the society.

To strengthen the adminstrative machinery and also to meet the demands of the rural people, it is necessary that the services like housing, water supply and sanitation and PDS should be handed over to the panchayat raj institutions. Since these institutions have been regarded as self-governing institutions and an integral part of our policy, there is need to give them independent powers and treat them as a 'single agency' as far as formulating and implementing the above services are concerned. Any interference or encroachment by the higher level institutions would create obstacles in the effective delivery of the above services. The government should come out with a clear cut and well thought out policy in this regard.

Notwithstanding all the above mentioned policy measures, there is need to create awareness, to educate people about the importance of PDS and its usefulness as an important safety net measure of the government. As a support measure, it is necessary, at the fair-price shop level, to constitute a 'vigilance committee' to work as 'watchdog panel' over the functioning of the shops. More importantly, the local organisations should play a vital role in motivating community approach and participation in the PDS operations. The PDS, in the ultimate analysis, should be able to ensure the consumer his entitlement. Howevers it is significant to note that the increasing poverty and rising prices cannot be effectively handed without strengthening the PDS on all fronts - organisational, adminstrative and economic.

IV

AN OVERVIEW

In the previous sections many facets of housing schemes, water supply and sanitation schemes and public distribution system, especially in the background of their organisation and administration have been discussed at length. In this section, an attempt has been made to present an overview of these services and their implications to the overall development of the society.

Although there are well-knit organisational and functional linkages between the organisations, there prevails many functional linkages betwen the organisations, many functional flaws, in terms of administration, which has ultimately hindered the delivery of the services in a more equitable and effective manner. One can draw an inference that the presence of 'red-tapism' and 'formalism' in the administration has affected the effective delivery of the services. Added to this, the prevalance of misgivings between the implementing agencies, near absence of supervision, monitoring, inspection, proper system of inventory control, are, in a way, contributing in nullifying the delivery of services. The cumulative effect of all these can be seen on the users of these services thereby making them to develop a feeling of dissatisfaction towards the entire process. To put it succinctly, it appears that there is a considerable degree of chasm between the promises made and the achievement.

If the services like housing and PDS have to be result-oriented it has become necessary to strengthen the administrative machinery not only for formulating the schemes but also for implementing them effectively. For instance, there are no field level departments both for the housing and the PDS, and as a result, the pace of implementation of these services is found to be slow. It has become difficult for the line departments to monitor these programmes since they have no direct control over the implementing departments and agencies. In the light of this, as referred to, there is an immediate need to establish independent departments at the sub-state levels; three exists dual responsibility in carrying out the activities and the orders.

To strengthen the administrative machinery and also to meet the demands of the rural people, it is necessary that the services like housing, water supply and sanitation and PDS should be handed over to Panchayat Raj Institutions. Since these institutions have been regarded as self-governing institutions and an integral part of our polity, there is need to give them independent powers and treat them as a 'single agency' as far as formulating and implementing the above services are concerned. Any interference or encroachment by the higher level institutions/organisers would create obstacles in the effective delivery of the above services. The government should come out with a clear cut and well thought out policy in this regard.

Notwithstanding the above discussed organisational and functional flaws in the implementation of the schemes, three is some satisfaction when the state level performance is compared with the all India performance of these services. For instance, as revealed from the NSS surveys, in providing water supply both in rural and urban areas, the states' administration scores an edge over the all India performance. Compared to 55.92 per cent (in rural areas, in 1991) of households having safe drinking water at the national level 67.31 per cent of the households in Karnataka have been provided with safe drinking water. And in urban areas the percentage service is almost the same: 81.59 per cent at the all India level and 81.38 per cent at the state level. On an average, in Karnataka, 71.68 per cent of the households have been assured of safe drinking water compared to 62.72 per cent at the all India level. The following Table 8 shows the percentage of households having safe drinking water between 1981 and 1991.

Table 8

Percentage of Households having Safe Drinking Water (1981-1991)

	Total		Rural		Urban	
	1981	1991	1981	1991	1981	1991
Karnataka	33.87	77.68	17.63	67.31	74.40	81.38
India	37.91	62.72	26.34	55.92	74.13	81.59

However, the conditions with regard to sanitation, especially in the rural areas, hardly show any improvement. The NSS data indicate that, during the year 1991, the percentage of households in rural areas having toilet facilities was only 6.85 per cent compared to the all India percentage of 8.84 per cent. Whereas in urban areas compared to rural areas, the situation appears better since 62.52 per cent of the households in Karnataka were found utilising the toilet facilities compared to all India percentage of 63.58. Further, the facilities used by the SC and ST households is much below the all India average especially in rural areas; 2.59 per cent SC households and 2.71 per cent ST households have been found using toilet facilities against the all India average of 5.15 per cent and 4.10 per cent respectively. The following Table 9 presents the percentage of Scheduled Caste, Scheduled Tribe and 'Others' having toilet facilities.

Table 9

Percentage of Scheduled Castes, Scheduled Tribes and Others having Toilet Facilities

	Scheduled Castes			Scheduled Tribes			Others		
	T	R	U	T	R	U	T	R	U
Karnataka	9.24	2.59	34.78	8.40	2.71	40.53	27.66	8.06	66.30
India	11.16	5.19	38.28	7.22	4.10	40.68	28.63	11.52	68.30

Source: Government of India.

Note: T = Total, R = Rural, U = Urban.

It is clear from Table 9 that rural areas are very much devoid of sanitation facilities and it is more so for the households belonging to the vulnerable sections of the society. Seen in this context, the recently launched 'Nirmala Karnataka' Yojana should be able to fill the gap and threby motivate and enable the rural households to develop the right kind of attitude and liking not only to use the toilet facilities but also to keep the environment tidy and hygeenic.

As regard the housing conditions, the compartive figures between Karnataka and India also show an encouraging trend. The following Table 10 gives the percentage distribution of households living in 'pucca', 'semi-pucca', and 'kutcha' houses (1991 figures).

Table 10

Percentage distribution of Households living in Pucca Semi-Pucca and Kutcha Houses

	Pucca		Semi-Pucca		Kutcha	
	Rural	**Urban**	**Rural**	**Urban**	**Rural**	**Urban**
Karnataka	30.45	69.43	49.34	22.16	20.21	08.41
India	31.20	73.10	36.33	17.57	32.46	09.33

Source: Government of India 1990.

Table 10 reveals that compared to all India figures, the position of Karnataka is found to be better as far as housing condition is concerned. Take, for instance, Kutcha houses: the rural situation in Karnataka is better compared to all India rural situation: 20.21 per cent of the rural households in Karnataka are living in Kutcha houses as against 32.46 per cent households elsewhere in India. The situation is even better in urban areas where the percentage distribution of households living in Kutcha houses is 08.41 per cent compared to 09.53 per cent at the all India level. However, the percentage distribution of pucca houses, especially in rural areas, is not all that encouraging. Almost 50 per cent of the households live in semi-pucca houses compared to 36.33 per cent of households for India as a whole. Altogether, the housing situation is not all that bad, but necessary measures have to be initiated to improve the housing related services and thereby achieve the goal of providing shelter for all by 2000 A.D.

A meaningful study of PDS has become necessasry, especially in the background of Structural Adjustment Programme (SAP) and liberalisation process. There is a mounting fear that the PDS services would be slowly withdrawn. The recent steep rice in the prices has left the consumers in a state of despair which is contrary to an important objective of the PDS, i.e., to safeguard the interests of the consumers, particularly the vulnerable sections of the society. Seen in terms of PDS achievements, for the country as a whole, it is not impressive. "An analysis of the distribution of foodgrains through the public distribution system in different states revealed that the distribution has not gravitated in favour of those areas where more people live. Even within a State, foodgrains distributed through the public distribution system have not reached the poor sections of the population" (Tyagi 1990). This has become an all India feature except for one or two states like Kerala. The following Table 11 shows the population below the poverty line and distribution of foodgrains through the PDS.

Table 11

Population below the Poverty Line and Distribution of Foodgrains through the PDS

State	% Population below the Povertline 1983-84	Per capita Distribution for the Quinquennium ending 1988 (Kgs)
Bihar	51.35	9.954
Madhya Pradesh	50.30	0.192
Uttara Pradesh	46.48	7.175
Orissa	44.76	13.340
Tamil Nadu	44.08	13.075
West Bengal	43.84	32.749
Maharashra	41.50	22.701
Andhra Pradesh	38.67	23.286
Rajasthan	36.63	18.587
Gujarat	27.62	21.802
Kerala	26.05	61.893
Haryana	15.19	10.040
Punjab	10.87	9.459
All India	40.40	21.738

Source: Tyagi 1990.

Table 11 indicates that in Kerala where only 26 per cent of the population is below the poverty line, the per capita per annum distribution of foodgrains has been over l61 kilogrammes, whereas in Karnataka, it is about 23 kilogrammes per annum and its population below the poverty line is 37 per cent. In states like Bihar, Orissa and Madhya Pradesh where the proportion of population below the poverty line is around or above 45 per cent, the average per capita distribution has been below 13 kilogrammes per annum. This implies that the per capita distribution of foodgrains is inconsistent with the population below the poverty line. Necessary policy measures have to be initiated to match the food requirements of the population below the poverty line.

The much discussed issue in recent years is that the distribution system has been more extensive in the urban areas than in the rural areas. The average urban dweller, in terms of the quantity consumed, has better accessbility of services, gains more from the PDS than the average rural dweller. Considering this fact, if the PDS is to act as a viable safety net, especially to the vulnerable sections of the society, then, the poor should be given a larger share in subsidised food, thus reducing their market dependence. Also, considering the gravity of the poverty situtation in the rural areas and poor purchasing power of both the rural and urban poor, it is imperative on the part of the state governments (including Karnataka) to make the supply available at least on a fortnightly basis and more importantly so, increase the quantum based on unit-wise allotment to the rural card holders.

The foregoing analysis reveals that there is a need for proper and effective administrative machinery, especially at the Sub-State level, to facilitate co-ordination between the line, auxiliary departments and other organisations and agencies. This demands for a change in the administrative structure. However, mere creation of new structures or incorporating some changes would not be enough because such changes in the structures may not be functional enough for achieving co-ordination in the delivery of the services. Therefore, it is necessary to introduce in the department a 'culture of management' which is more 'problem-oriented' and less concerned with 'status and power'. In doing this, emphasis should be placed on the reorientatation of the attitudes and values of the officals which would facilitate adjustment of development role demands. In support of this, there is an imperative need to strengthen the administrative machinery of housing, water supply and sanitation and PDS departments so that they will be well equipped to meet not only the objectives of their respective organisations such as 'efficiency', 'economy' but also 'social equity'. More importantly, to bring transparency in administration, the administration should be responsive, committed and people friendly. To put it succinctly, the present day adminstration should move towards a "moral administration" (Dwivedi 1994) and also "human face in administration". This is to say that the officials should actively undertake actions that are socially just and moral and also pursue the goals of social justice, equity and human dignity. Then only it is possible to provide justice to the people, who are at the receiving end. All this would certainly improve the delivery of services and goods to the beneficiaries, in particular, and the society, in general.

REFERENCES

Bangalore Water Supply and Sewerage Board (BWSSB) (1993). **Handbook of Statistics 1991-92 and 1992-93** Bangalore: Government of Karnataka.

Bangalore Water Supply and Sewerge Board (BWSSB) (1995). **Annual Report, 1994-95.** Bangalore: Government of Karnataka

Bora, P.M. (1982). **Food Administration in India.** Delhi: Ajantha Publications.

Cassidy, Harry M. (1942). Social Security and Reconstruction in Canada. Quoted in G. L. Madan (1983), **Indian Social Problems,** Vol.1. New Delhi: Allied Publications.

Directorate of Food and Civil Supplies (1994). **Annual Report (1993-94).** Bangalore: Government of Karnataka.

Directorate of Food and Civil Supplies (DFCS) (1995). **Annual Report (1994-95).** Bangalore: Government of Karnataka.

Dwivedi, O. P. (1994), **Development Administration : From Underdevelopment to Sustainable Development.** New York: Macmillan

Government of India (1990). **NSS, 44th Round (July 1988 - June 1989),** Report No. 376. New Delhi: Department of Statistics.

Housing and Urban Development Department (HUDD). (1995). **Annual Report (1994-95).** Bangalore: Government of Karnataka.

Hudli, V.J. (Ed.) (1975). **Housing in Karnataka.** Mysore: ATI.

Kabra, K.N. and A.C. Ittyerah (1992), **The Public Distribution System in India.** New Delhi: Eastern Books.

Kumar, Sudir (1994). Impact of Liberalisation on Housing Sector and Infrastructure Development in Urban Areas. A paper presented at **the Round Table on Economic Liberalisation: Challenges and Resources in the States.** September 10-12, Bangalore. (Unpublished).

Mahadeva, M. (1992). **A Study of the Housing Co-operatives in India with particular reference to Karnataka.** Mysore: Mysore University. (Unpublished).

Mooij, E. Jos (1994), Public Distribution as Safety Net: Who is Saved. **Economic and Political Weekly,** XXIX (3).

Planning Department (1993). **Economic Survey 1992-93.** Bangalore: Government of Karnataka.

Planning Department (1994). **Economic Survey 1993-94.** Bangalore: Government of Karnataka

Planning Department (1995). **Economic Survey 1994-95** Bangalore: Government of Karnataka

Planning Department (1996). **Economic Survey 1995-96.** Bangalore: Government of Karnataka.

Public Health Engineering (PHE) (1988). **Rural Water Suply and Sanitation Prgramme in Karnataka.** Bangalore: Government of Karnataka.

Rural Development and Panchyati Raj Department, Monitoring and Evaluation Cell (1994). **Annual Report (1993-94).** Bangalore: Government of Karnataka

Sivanna, N. (1993). PDS - Structural Changes. **Deccan Herald,** Bangalore, December 6.

Sivanna, N. (1994). **The Public Distribution System in Karnataka: A Study of its Organisation and Management Aspects.** Bangalore: ISEC. (unpublished).

World Bank (1989). **India: Poverty, Employment and Social Services.** Washington D.C, U.S.A.: The World Bank.

Tyagi, D.S. (1990). **Managing India's Food Economy: Problems and Alternatives.** New Delhi: Sage Publications.

VIII

ADMINISTRATIVE REFORMS

1

ADMINISTRATIVE REFORMS IN KARNATAKA*

A.K.M. Nayak

Introduction: Administrative Reforms is an "effort to apply new ideas or combination of ideas to administrative system with a conscious view of improving the system for positive goals of national development". It is also considered as "directed change of the main features of administrative system". The principal objectives of administrative reforms are securing integrity, efficiency, economy and public co-operation.

Much has been said about the need for administrative reforms and the recommendations made by the various Committees constituted for the purpose. In this paper, an attempt has been made to trace the steps taken by the Government of Karnataka from time to time, in the direction of administrative reforms.

The new state of Karnataka was formed on 1st November 1956, by the integration of nine Kannada speaking districts of the former

* This paper reflects the personal views of the author, not of the government.

states of Bombay, Hyderabad, Madras, Coorg, and the ten districts of the erstwhile Mysore state. The four districts of Bombay and the district of Dakshina Kannada from Madras, with their distinct administrative heritage and ethos, thus became part of the new state along with the very backward four districts of Hyderabad. The erstwhile Mysore state, the biggest unit, had a sound administrative pattern and was a pioneer in India starting many welfare schemes especially in the fields of educations an other civic amenities.

For the purpose of general administration, the Bombay State areas were divided into divisions each in charge of a Commissioner. Each division consisted of a few districts. The Commissioner was the channel of communication between the district and the government. The head of the district administration was the Collector. He was also the District Magistrate and, as such, he was the head of the police. The District Superintendent of Police had to carry out his orders. The district consisted of Prants or Sub-Divisions and they were further divided into taluks, Petas or Mahals. The Assistant Collector or District Deputy Collector, known as Prant Officer, was in charge of a Prant (sub-division) consisting of two to four taluks. The Prant Officer was the connecting link between the Mamlatdars or Mahalkaris and the Collector. He was also the Sub-Divisional Magistrate. The Mamlatdar was the officer in the executive charge of taluk and the Mahalkari was in charge of a Mahal (sub taluk). In addition to the revenue duties, he had quasi judicial duties, magisterial duties as a Magistrate of the taluk and he was also the Sub-Treasury Officer. The Circle Officers and Circle Inspectors were in charge of 30 to 50 villages to assist the Mamlatdar in his duties. The Patil or the Village headman was the principal official in the village. The Patil's office was hereditary except in Uttara Kannada district. The Kulkarni or the Talati was the village registrar or accountant. In Uttara Kannada district, the village accountant was called the 'Shanbhog'

In the Madras state area, the Collector was the head of the general administration of the district. The Collector had under him Deputy Collectors in charge of Sub-Divisions. Each taluk was in charge of a Tahsildar and in the larger taluks, there was an Assistant or Deputy

Tahsildar who was stationed at one of the chief towns. The chief Village servants were the Headman (Patel, Reddi, Gowda or Munsiff), the Karnam or Shanbhog, who was the village accountant, and the Nirganti, who was in-charge of the irrigation of the village lands and regulated the supply of water. Vetti or Toti was a village peon (messenger), who was under the village headman. The Talwari was the Village Policeman. This village official was also called Ugrani.

The entire Hyderabad state was divided into Subhas or Divisions and districts. Each Division was placed under a Revenue Commissioner called Subedar. Each district was placed under a Magistrate or Collector who was popularly called 'Talukdar,. The districts were further divided into sub-divisions, each under a sub-Divisional Officer called Second or Third 'Talukdar' on the basis of his grade and service. There were two or three Tahsils in every Sub-Division and a Tahsildar was in charge of each one of them. Every village had a Patel or Headman.

Kodagu was directly administered by the British through a Chief Commissioner, who was assisted by a Commissioner and two Assistant Commissioners. The Commissioner had revenue powers similar to those exercised by a Collector of Madras. The first Assistant Commissioner was also the District Magistrate and exercised supervisory control over the police, and the second Assistant Commissioner presided over the Civil Court and was also in charge of the treasury.

For administrative purposes, the old Mysore was divided into 10 districts and 89 taluks. The Revenue Commissioner was the head of the Revenue Department. Each district had a Deputy Commissioner, corresponding to the Collector of Part 'A' states, Sub-Division Officer, corresponding to the Deputy Collector, and in every taluk there was an Amildar corresponding to the Tahsildar. The Deputy Commissioner was the head of the district administration and co-ordinated the activities of all the departments. For each Firka or Hobli, there was a Revenue Inspector who was aided in his work by the Village Officers - the Patel and the Shanbhog. The village officers were hereditary officers who received potgi (commission) calculated on the revenue demand of each village and were not in receipt of any pay.

After integration, the administrative units were completely revamped in order to establish an effective system of administration. For administrative convenience, the 19 districts (now 20) of the new state were divided into four Divisions, viz., Bangalore Division consisting of Bangalore, Kolar, Tumkur, Shimoga and Chitradurga districts; Mysore Division consisting of Mysore, Mandya, Kodagu, Dakshina Kannada, Chickmagalur and Hassan districts; Belgaum Division consisting of Belgaum, Bijapur, Dharwad and Uttara Kannada districts; and Gulbarga Division consisting of Gulbarga, Bidar, Raichur and Bellary districts. The Division is under the administration of a Divisional Commissioner, the District under the Deputy Commissioner, the Sub-Division under the Assistant Commissioner, the Taluka under the Tahsildar, and the villages grouped into Hoblis or Revenue Circles under a Revenue Inspector.

The Deputy Commissioner is the head of the district administration in the state. He plays a predominant and pivotal role in all aspects of administration. In his capacity as District Magistrate, he is responsible for the maintenance of law and order within the district. He has to co-ordinate the efforts of several departments in the district and see that all government programmes and policies are well executed. The Deputy Commissioner, as ex-officio Chairman of the District Development Council, also used to guide and co-ordinate the developmental activities of several departments in the district and those of the Taluka Developmental Boards in implementing the Community Development Programmes. However, with the coming into existence of the new Panchayat Raj institutions, the implementation of most development programmes and schemes have been entrusted to these bodies and the Deputy Commissioner no longer has any development functions.

Abolition of Hereditary Village Offices: In pursuance of the government policy of abolition of intermediaries, it was considered desirable to abolish all the hereditary village offices, viz., Patels, Shanbhogs, Kulkarnis and inferior village servants in order to put the revenue administration at the point where it touches the people most in consonance with the modern spirit. These offices were replaced by stipendiary Village Accountants. The Village Accountant was also the Secretary of the smaller Village Panchayats.

With a view to fully decentralise the revenue administration and ease the pressure on taluka office, Nada Kacheries at the Hobli level were opened throughout the state from 15th August 1986.

Department for Administrative Reforms: The business of the government in Mysore state, prior to reorganisation, was being transacted in various branches of the Secretariat numbering 30. Each Secretary had one or more branches under his control. Subsequently, these branches were grouped into various secretariat departments which have been reorganized from time to time.

Realising the need to radically change and restructure the then existing set up of General Administration Department for proper handling of matters relating to Administrative Reforms and Personnel Management, the following two Departments were created with effect from 1.6.1976.

(i) Department of Cabinet Affairs ; and

(ii) Department of Personnel and Administrative Reforms

The Administrative Reforms Division is in charge of -

(1) Administrative Reforms;

(2) O & M Activities;

(3) Mechanisation in Administration;

(4) Simplification of Procedures; and Methods;

(5) Form Designing, and

(6) All Training Matters.

The Division has wide overseeing and direct supervisory functions on all matters of administrative reforms. It can set up task forces for identifying the areas of administration where changes and innovations need to be introduced for improving efficiency in administration. It is also responsible for conducting inspections, and for initiating experiments in administrative reforms at several levels of government functioning.

The Training Unit in this Division has overall control of training activities in the state and has to co-ordinates the activities of several Departments and provide leadership and initiative.

The Division also undertakes work study of the Secretariat Departments and Field Offices. It has already got done a work study of the offices of the Secretariat Health and Family Welfare Department, the Directorate of Health and Family Welfare and the Directorate of Medical Education, by M/s A.F. Ferguson and Company. A work study on the reorganisation of the working of the Chief Minister's Office was also entrusted to this Company.

In 1982, there were 18 Secretariat Departments which included the Legislative Secretariat, the merged Departments of Cabinet Affairs and the Department of Personnel and Administrative Reforms,the Department of Ecology and Environment (1981), and the Department of Science and Technology (1981). The Secretariat Departments later increased in number by the creation of the Department of Information, Tourism and Youth Services (1984), Department of Kannada and Culture (1993). In addition, Labour, which was part of the Social Welfare Department, became a separate Department. Ecology and Environment were clubbed with Forest, Transport with Home, while Institutional Finance and Statistics which were formerly with Food (between April and July 1993) were subsequently transferred to Planning Department in 1993. Science and Technology continued to be a separate department. Co-operation, which was earlier part of Rural Development, Panchayat Raj and Co-operation, was made an independent department.

After the reshuffle of the Secretariat Departments in 1993, the total number of Departments increased to 25. In order to formulate appropriate policies, prepare housing projects and implement housing programmes/projects in a definite time-frame, it was considered necessary to constitute a new Department of Housing. Accordingly, the existing Department of Housing and Urban Development was bifurcated into two Departments, viz., Department of Housing and Department of Urban Development (1995).

One of the important recommendations made by the Eleventh All India Whips Conference was to set up in all states/Union territories, a Department of Parliamentary Affairs on the pattern of the Ministry of Parliamentary Affairs in the Government of India, for better co-ordination between government and the legislature, and smooth and timely discharge of the government business in the legislature. Accepting this recommendation a separate Department of Parliamentary Affairs and Legislation was created by bifurcating the existing Department of Law and Parliamentary Affairs (1996).

Executive Departments: At the time of reorganisation, the then Mysore state had about 50 executive departments. The administration of each major Department was carried on under the direction and control of the Head of the Department. Minor Departments, which did not justify the appointment of a separate Head of Department, were attached to one or other major heads of Departments. With the increase in volume, variety and complexity of governmment work, greater emphasis on welfare activities and the need to improve efficiency in administration, the departments were bifurcated or reorganised, and many new departments were created such as Chief Electrical Inspectorate, Departments of Fisheries and Motor Vehicles (1957), Karnataka Gazetteer Department (1962), Department of Town Planning (1959), Drugs Control Department (1962), Department of Horticulture (1963), Department of Employment and Training, Department of Stores Purchase and Department of Treasuries (1964), Department of Small Savings (1965), Department of Public Libraries (1966), Department of Youth Services (1969), Department of Ports and Inland Water Transport (1972), Department of Irrigation and Directorate of Sugar (1973), Department of Tourism (1974), Department of Weights and Measures (1976), Department of Co-operative Audit, Chief Inspectorate of Factories and Boilers, and Department of Kannada and Culture (1977), Department of Backward Classes and Minorities (1978-79), Department of Municipal Administration (1984-85), Department of Archaeology (1986) and Directorate of Welfare of Disabled (1988-89).

Though most of the Departments have their headquarters at Bangalore, a few, like the Department of Irrigation, Administrative

Training Institute, Archaeology and Museums, etc., have their headquarters outside Bangalore. The organisational set up of almost all the departments have district and taluk level offices and a few departments have village level functionaries (Revenue, Education, Agriculture and Rural Development and Panchayat Raj). Some Departments like Karnataka Gazetteer, Directorate of Sugar, etc., have single unit officer at the state headquarters.

Reducing Delay in the Secretariat: In the Revised Secretariat Manual of Office Procedure all dealing hands in the Secretariat are required to dispose off all receipts and files within five days of their receipt, and officers at all levels should attend the cases submitted to them similarly. If this requirement is not fulfilled, the concerned officer/official is required to explain his failure to do so to the next higher authority. Papers which are of immediate/urgent nature are to be dealt with appropriately.

In order to reduce delay, the Manual provides for level jumping, i.e., the Senior Assistants can be authorised to submit cases directly to the Under Secretary. The Section Officer can be permitted to submit certain types of cases direct to the Deputy Secretary, and the Under Secretary to the Joint Secretary or Secretary. Similarly, the Deputy Secretary may, in certain cases, deal direct with the Minister.

When it is necessary to consult more than one Department on a particular case, such consultation is ordinarily required to take place simultaneously by means of a self contained unofficial note. On important cases, where a decision has to be taken urgently, a reasonable date by which the reply is required can be indicated with a proviso that if no reply is received by the specified time limit, it would be presumed that the Department to which the reference has been made agrees with the proposed course of action. Inter-departmental meetings of officers have to be held where it is necessary to elicit the opinion of other Departments on important cases and arrive at a decision within a time limit.

In order to keep a watch over the progress of work of each Assistant and take suitable steps to expedite action on delayed cases and prevent the Section from running into much arrears, a Weekly Arrears

Statement is required to be prepared on the last working day of every week. Similarly, to bring to the notice of officers, the cases which have been pending in the Sections for over a month, and the reasons for pendency, a monthly statement is required to be prepared by the 10th of every month. This not only provides an opportunity to the officers to review the pending cases, but also to give instructions to the subordinate staff to take special action or to obtain specific orders with a view to expedite the disposal of such cases. It is the tempo of disposal of these cases that give a true picture of the efficiency of any office as the ultimate purpose for which the office is established is the final disposal of the public business and not merely meticulous carrying on of correspondence or shifting of files.

With a view to reducing the delay in the disposal of business in the Secretariat, the following steps have also been suggested:

(a) Secretaries to Government should devote one day every month to review and discuss long pending files which are more than four years old with officers in their respective Departments. Additional Secretary/Deputy Secretary will similarly review cases between 2-4 years, and Under Secretary less than two year old.

(b) Where cases are held up for comments or views from other Departments, Secretaries should contact their counterparts in those Departments and arrange personal discussion for the disposal or settlement of points at issue.

(c) In respect of files for which replies/ comments are due from the lower formations or subordinate offices for a long time, similiar discussion would be held with the Heads of Departments with a view to securing speedy disposal. An Under Secretary of the Secretariat Department is required to be deputed once a month to the Heads of Departments under its control after sending the list of pending cases in advance and with due intimation to the concerned Head of the Department.

(d) The Heads of Departments are required to send to the personal address of the Secretary of the Administrative Department the complete gist of all cases pending for orders for over three years in the

Secretariat. Thereafter, the Secretary or his deputy will find out the reasons for pendency and initiate the action required for the issue of final orders.

To verify whether the procedure prescribed is being observed in practice and to give suitable guidance to the branch inspected to raise its level of performance and to increase its efficiency, frequency of inspection to be carried out by the Secretariat officers has been prescribed. Secretaries to government are also required to conduct surprise checks of a few sections to ensure prompt and efficient disposal of the work in the Department. In every Secretariat, Department officers' meetings are to be held every quarter. At these meetings problems concerning the working of the Department are to be discussed and efforts made to find out ways in which the improvements in the working of the Department can be made. These meetings are to be conducted in such a manner that members of the staff feel that they have a share in shaping decisions which are aimed at improving the standards of efficiency.

Delegation of Powers: Common administrative and financial powers have been delegated, from time to time, to all Secretaries to government, Heads of Departments, and other field functionaries. .Special delegation of powers have been ordered in respect of matters which are specific to certain Departments. Instructions have been issued that apart from ensuring that the administrative and financial powers delegated are exercised by the officers at various levels, it would be necessary to ascertain whether exercise of these powers has resulted in quick disposal, speedy implementation and elimination of unnecessary correspondence. Inspecting Officers have been asked to verify whether the powers have been exercised by the concerned officers and whether there are needless references to higher authorities on subjects covered by the delegation.

Training: One of the methods of improving the efficiency of administration is to improve the quality of personnel engaged in it. The state government has provided facilities for training the government servants of all categories in the various Training Institutions in the state. In 1967, an Administrative Training Institute (ATI) was started in Mysore as a residential institute with a Managing Committee headed by the Chief Secretary. The Institute provides institutional training to the directly recruited probationers to the State Civil Services, Orientation Training to officers promoted to higher posts, and refresher and orientation courses to in-service personnel of different departments. The All India Service probationers, allotted to the Karnataka state, have to undergo a 4-week Orientation Course at the Institute.

The Secretariat Training Institute was started in 1969 as one of the measures for toning up administrative efficiency in the Secretariat. The Institute aims at providing job training to the newly recruited personnel of the Secretariat. It also conducts orientation training courses, refresher courses and short-term courses. The Director and the faculty of the Institute have been authorised to undertake inspection of Departments so that the Inspection Reports would serve as a feedback to the training at the Institute, and also to take up studies, wherever required, subject to those being carried out under the overall control and supervision of the Administrative Reforms Division of the Department of Personnel and Administrative Reforms.

With a view to meeting the functional utility and efficiency of the ministerial staff and junior executives in the field, who constitute the bulk of the state administration, it was considered necessary to start Training Institutes called 'District Training Institutes' in all the districts. The main function of the District Training Institute is to provide job training to the newly recruited and also the existing First and Second Division Assistants of all Departments of the state government and also to provide general courses, ad-hoc short duration courses, etc., to in-service personnel of different Departments.

To encourage sustained interest in training and creative thinking, it was decided to award prizes to trainees, who showed best performance in the long term courses conducted by the Secretariat Training Institute, Administrative Training Institute and the District Training Institutes.

Simplification of Administrative Procedures: The provisions of the Revised Handbook of Office Procedure, applicable to all offices of the Heads of Departments and subordinate offices, were brought into force with effect from 1.4.1971. The Revised Handbook incorporates simplified procedures and methods of work, etc. Subsequently, the Karnataka Award of Prizes for useful suggestions for simplifying procedures of the Department of Government Rules, 1979, were framed which provided for the award of following prizes to state government servants for making useful suggestions for improving the existing procedures of the various government departments.

(1) One First Prize of Rs.5,000;

(2) One Second Prize of Rs.3,000

(3) One Third Prize of Rs.2,000; and

(4) Five Consolation Prizes of Rs.1,000 each.

In order to qualify for the Award the suggestion should be accepted by the government for implementation and the said suggestion should result in (i) improving the procedure at the cutting edge level; (ii) elimination of superfluous formalities or introduction of new methods of work which could be done without causing harassment to the public thereby; and (iii) turning out work of better quality or ensuring completion of the work with considerable economy, speed or convenience to the public and eliminate scope for corruption.

Administrative Language: Administrative language is as important as the simplified procedures for rendering services. In pursuance of the policy of the state government to introduce Kannada as the official language of the state, several instructions were issued, from time to time, for the progressive use of Kannada in all government offices to the extent possible. Subsequently, in exercise of the powers conferred by Section 4 of the **Karnataka Official Language Act, 1963,** the state government directed that with effect from 1st November 1979, Kannada shall be used in respect of all official communications to all state government offices. It was also provided that if the population of any linguistic minority in any taluk is not less than 15 per cent :

(i) petition shall be continued to be accepted in the minority language concerned and the replies given in that language as far as possible;

(ii) handouts and publicity material shall continue to be given in such minority language; and

(iii) Government Notices shall continue to be published in such minority language.

Tours and Inspections: Heads of Departments have to visit every district at regular intervals and should normally visit at least two districts in a month so that all the districts are covered in a year. They are required to spend at least 3-4 days in each district, inspect a few offices, review the implementation of the field activities and give guidance to the field officers. During the visit, they have also to look into the adequacy of supervision exercised by the subordinate offices, O & M aspects, personal matters of staff like increments, promotions, seniority, etc., which are held up for unduly long periods affecting their morale. To resolve inter-departmental problems they are required to meet the Deputy Commissioner and other District Officers.

To acquaint themselves with the actual working of the Departments under their control and to ensure that the programmes are implemented properly, Secretaries to government are also required to undertake tours in the district.

Minimum scale of inspections to be undertaken by the officers at different levels have been prescribed. In addition to all Divisional Offices, the Head of Department has to inspect a cross-section of offices at the District, Sub Division and Taluka levels, so as to have a reasonably well informed impression about the working of his Department. He has also to ensure that during the period of 3-4 years he inspects all the district offices in the state.

Public Grievances: Quick redressal of public grievances is essential in any administration. Way back in 1965 itself, Cells for rendering assistance to the public were set up in the offices of Heads of Departments and also in the offices under their control for receiving petitions and representations, to hear the petitioners, and to ensure that suitable replies were given promptly. Officers at the district, Sub-Divisional and Taluka levels are required to be available at the respective headquarters on Shandy days to enable the public to meet them and represent their grievances. To enable the Secretaries to Government, Deputy Commissioners and other Heads of Departments to effectively attend to public grievances, they are not to have any meetings during the hours specified for granting interviews to the public.

Senior officers are also required to undertake night halts in the interior areas, hear the complaints, if any, and arrange to redress the same on the spot, as far as possible, with the assistance of the local officers. Night halts in the interior villages are to be extensively utilised by the officers for discussion either in groups or with individuals about the problems confronting the village folk and their grievances. The weaker sections of the society are to be encouraged to attend such meetings during the night halts and express freely their grievances to the visiting officers. This opportunity is expected to be effectively and extensively utilised for fulfilling the ultimate aim of government in redressing public grievances directly and thus create the image of the officer as an 'ideal public servant'.

Complaint boxes have been installed in the offices of the Tahsildar, Assistant Commissioner, Deputy Commissioner, Divisional Commissioner, Heads of Departments and each Department of the Secretariat. The complaint box is kept in a common place, which is easily accessible to the people so that any person having a grievance pertaining to any Department could, in writing, put in his petition indicating the grievance. The box is required to be opened once a week in the presence of the Head of the office concerned. He should go through the petitions and indicate the Department to which they relate. The receipt of these petitions should be entered in a regular register maintained by the Head of the Office and he should watch the action taken on the petition by the concerned Departmental officer.

Public Opinion: Public administration is more likely to succeed when it is sensitive and properly responds to public opinion. Instructions have been issued that whenever comments or criticisms are voiced in the press regarding the working of any office or procedure of the Department, immediate action must be taken by the concerned officer to know the true picture of the situation and if the comment is justified, to institute measures to remedy the situation. If, on the other hand, the criticism is not correct, the real situation must be explained. In either case arrangements must be made through the Director of Information and Publicity to publish in the same newspaper where the criticism appeared, as a news item or letter to the editor, within a week at the most, detailing the measures taken by the government to redress the grievances or explaining the correct position regarding the allegations.

Corruption: One of the most significant aspects of public administration is the machinery provided for dealing with complaints of corruption. The Government of India, after independence, introduced measures to check corruption, by passing the **Anti- Corruption Act, 1947.** A separate Department called Anti- Corruption and Efficiency Audit, headed by a Director, was created in 1948, in the erstwhile Mysore state. This functioned till the State Vigilance Commission was constituted in the year 1965, following the recommendations of the Santanam Committee. The Commission functioned primarily to investigate and enquire into the complaints against the government servants in respect of corruption, misconduct, lack of integrity or any kind of malpractices or misnomers. Subsequently, the employees of Local Authorities were also brought under the purview of the Commission. In 1986, the State Vigilance Commission was replaced by the Karnataka Lok Ayukta.

The institution of Lok Ayukta has been set up for the purpose of improving the standards of public administration, investigation of complaints, corruption, favouritism and indiscipline. Broadly speaking, the Lok Ayukta and Upalok Ayukta will investigate and report on allegations or grievances arising out of the conduct of public servants who generally fall within the following categories:

(1) The Chief Minister;

(2) A Minister or a Member of the State Legislature;

(3) A Government servant;

(4) The Chairman, the Vice-Chairman or a member of a local authority, a statutory body or a corporation established by or under any law of the State Legislature, including a Co-operative Society, or a Government Company;

(5) A member of a Committee or Board constituted by the government;

(6) Persons in the service or pay of local authority, a Statutory Body, a Corporation or Company owned or controlled by the state government, or a society registered under the **Karnataka Societies Registration Act** and notified in this behalf in the official Gazette; and,

(7) A Co -operative society or a University established by or under any law of the State Legislature.

The Lok Ayukta investigates complaints against public servants and in a case in which the concerned public servant is found to have committed a criminal offence, it may order and initiate his prosecution. In other cases, it would make a recommendation about remedial measures to the government through the concerned administrative authority in case it finds that the allegations subjected to investigation are substantiated. If the government decides not to accept the recommendation, or the action taken by the administrative authority in pursuance of the recommendation is not satisfactory, the Lok Ayukta or the Upalok Ayukta, as the case may be, may send a special report to the Governor who shall then cause a copy thereof, together with an explanatory ' memorandum, to be placed before each house of the State Legislature. Thus, the Lok Ayukta enhances the accountability of the administration to the Legislature.

Mechanisation in Administration: In the conference held in 1968 on the 'Toning up of Administration', it was suggested that the use of more and more mechanical aids will lead to quicker handling of papers and reduce administrative delays considerably. A Committee on Mechanisation in Administration was constituted in August, 1968. The recommendations of the Committee that Franking Machines should be introduced in government offices as it helps prompt disposal of work and that Departments having a minimum workload of 100 or more letters despatched per day, might purchase the machines was accepted by the government. Heads of Departments/Public Sector Companies, Universities, Autonomous Bodies, were required to resort to the use of Postal Franking Machines to the extent possible.

The programme of modernisation in government offices has been taken up from the year 1984-85. The idea is to make the office more efficient and people-oriented. Regulation of public contact, demystification of office procedure, accessibility of documents to both the staff and public, and better working conditions and creation of an efficient environment are the objectives proposed to be achieved under the scheme. The scheme provides for Special Reception Room for visitors, Contact Windows (Counter System) for transactions involving Licences, Certificates, Police assistance, etc. Extracts of the Manual containing the procedures which govern dealings with public are made known to all the applicants; common visitors are to be educated about the mechanism and formalities of the office; and branches having larger public contact are required to put up leaflets and pamphlets in simple language stating the office methodology of different subjects. All the records are to be catalogued. Open areas around government offices are to be covered with garden and the approach roads asphalted to reduce the dust in the open compound. Office buildings are to be kept clean and neat; modern office gadgets like plain paper copier, Intercom, Duplicating Machine etc., are to be provided. Drinking water facilities and lunch rooms, toilets for visitors, staff and officers with regular water supply, deoderisation and the like are to be provided under the scheme.

Computerisation: Karnataka was one of the first states in the country to go in for computerisation. As early as 1971, the Karnataka Government Computer Centre (KGCC) was established as part of the Directorate of Economics and Statistics for data processing and rendering services to various government departments, autonomous bodies and public undertakings. The technical staff required for software development was drawn from the Department of Statistics, based on certain selection criteria and trained by the suppliers of the Computer System, viz., International Business Machines (IBM). Thus, Karnataka was also the first state in the country to have a full fledged Electronic Data Processing Centre (EDPC) of its own. As the workload increased from year to year, KGCS was separated from the Department of Economics and Statistics and was made an independent Department headed by a Director.

In April, 1984, a High Level Committee (HLC) was constituted with the following objectives:

(a) Identification of areas where computers could be used in various Departments to improve efficiency and productivity in administration;

(b) To set up a Priority Plan of computerisation for the state and also for individual Departments.

(c) Oversee the manpower requirement and adequate training personnel for computerisation.

(d) Proper utilisation of the available computer resources.

(e) A forum to sort out inter-departmental problems, e.g., getting necessary infrastructural facilities, budget sanctions etc.

(f) Monitor the progress of Computerisation of individual Departments with the set target. All Departments opting for Computerisation are required to obtain clearance from the HLC before approaching the Finance Department for concurrence.

In May 1985, a Technical Advisory Panel (TAP) for Computerisation was constituted with the following objectives to :

(1) determine the choice of Computer Hardware for the various Departments;

(2) approve rate contract for the various Computer Systems;

(3) advise the Departments regarding the Computer Systems (Hardware) and feasibility of upgrading/replacing of Computer System; and

(4) advise the Departments regarding award of software development of third party developers in respect of language platform cost, etc.

In April, 1989, instructions were issued to all Departments that technical approval of the TAP has to be invariably obtained for the purchase of hardware and software.

Maintenance of Government Offices: The Administrative Reforms Commission, in its report on the 'Machinery of the Government and its Procedure of Work', had recommended that an efficient care taking arrangement should be provided for every office with a view to avoiding shabby physical conditions in most government offices. The state government, after careful examination of the position and also the recommendation, directed that adequate attention in this regard should be paid by every Head of Office. For an efficient caretaking arrangement in every office, an officer/official at the supervisory level has been ordered to be placed in charge of this work. His function is to arrange for proper cleanliness like regular sweeping, disinfecting, prevention of throwing waste paper in and around the building, light and ventilation, proper layout of furniture and office equipment, etc. Heads of Departments and other superior authorities have also been instructed to inspect the premises at regular intervals to look into the adequacy or otherwise of the action taken. In respect of buildings where large number of offices are located, the office occupying the major portion of the building is made responsible for common services, maintenance of building, cleanliness of the common areas, operation of lifts, working of the canteens etc.

It has also been stressed that though the responsibility for maintaining the office building rests on the Public Works Department, it is the primary duty of the Head of the Office to ensure that the maintenance works are carried out, from time to time, and the premises present proper appearance and healthy surroundings. The PWD authorities have also been directed to undertake maintenance work as part of the regular activities at suitable intervals without waiting for requisition from the Heads of Offices.

Staff Welfare: With a view to ensuring close and continuous co-operation between the state, in its capacity as employer, and the general body of civil servants in matters affecting the services, and to promote well being of the employees etc., the establishment of a Central Staff Council and the Departmental Staff Councils, consisting of representatives of government and of the staff in certain Departments was sanctioned in 1957. Subsequently, it was decided to establish a machinery for joint consultation with the object of promoting the welfare of the employees, of increasing the efficiency of the public service and of securing a greater measure of co-operation between the government, as employer, and the General Body of its employees, in matters of common concern. Any matters relating to conditions under which members of the staff are required to work, general principles regulating conditions of service, welfare of the members of staff and improvement of efficiency and standards of work can be brought up for discussion. The State JCM consists of 30 members (including seven government representatives) and the Secretariat JCM of 10 members (including five government representatives).

Provision has also been made for giving employment to dependents of government servants who die while in service. Rules for grant of relief to families of government employees dying on duty, as a measure of staff welfare, issued in February 1966, now provide for payment of Rs.1,000 for the performance of obsequies. In August 1974, the Under Secretary, General Administration Department (General), was appointed as Grievance Officer, to look after the grievances of Secretariat Employees of and below the rank of Section Officers, in matters like pay fixation, drawal of increments, promotions etc. Subsequently, a Deputy Secretary (Administration & Miscellaneous), General Administration Department, was appointed as Welfare Officer to look into the said grievances.

As a staff welfare measure, a scheme for running a canteen called 'The Karnataka Government Secretariat Canteen' was sanctioned with the Deputy Secretary as Chairman of the Managing Committee. Annual Subvention, which is now Rs.30,000, has also been sanctioned to the Karnataka Government Secretariat Club.

Directions have also been issued to see that service problems are settled expeditiously in the framework of rules and general orders of Government and thereby bring about perceptible improvement in the overall efficiency in administration. The Karnataka Administrative Tribunal has also been constituted to enable employees to get speedy judicial relief in service matters.

Transfers: There should be no frequent transfer of officials. They should stay long enough to produce results. Transfers, when required to be done, should be made only in public interest and subject to accepted principles and policies. The state government has, from time to time, issued guidelines for effecting transfers of its employees. These guidelines, among other things, provide for the maximum period of stay at one place, viz., three years minimum and four years maximum for Group A and Group B officers, three years minimum and five years maximum for Group C officials and three years minimum and ten years maximum for Group D officials. Transfers have to be made only in the month of April and May by the lowest authority competent to effect the transfers. Generally, Group D employees are not to be transferred outside the town where they are already working. Group C officials are not to be posted to their native taluks and Group A and Group B officers should not be posted to their native districts. When both husband and wife are state government employees arrangements should be made to enable both of them to work in the same place or at least in nearby places. Requests from retiring government servants for posting to the place of their preference should be generally complied.

Conclusion: Administrative reforms is a continuous process and there is always scope for improvement and innovation. While introduction of modern gadgets and machinery in administration are to be encouraged, there are no substitutes for the time tested methods of inspections and tours. Reforms will succeed only if administrators continue to be in touch with the people and are personally aware of the ground realities. With this in view, organizing of mass contact programmes, Janatha Darshans and the like, rightly continue to receive the necessary emphasis in this state.

REFERENCES:

Administrative Reforms Commission. 1968. **Report of the Study Team on State Level Administration**. New Delhi: Government of India.

Department of Personnel and Administrative Reforms, Government of Karnataka. **Annual Compendium of Important Government Orders (1962 to 1994)**.

Department of Personnel and Administrative Reforms, Government of Karnataka. **Revised Secretariat Manual of Office Procedure.**

Directorate of Economics and Statistics, Government of Karnataka. **Report on the Administration of the State of Karnataka (up to 1991-92).**

Dubhashi, P.R.1986. **Administrative Reforms.** Delhi: B.R.Publishing Corporation.

Government of India. (1982). **Karnataka State Gazetteer. Part-I.** Bangalore: Government of Karnataka.

Government of India. (1982). **Karnataka State Gazetteer. Part-II.** Bangalore: Government of Karnataka.

State Re-organization Department, Government of Karnataka. **Administrative set up of the Existing Mysore State (1956).**

2

THE STUDY OF POLITICAL SCIENCE AND PUBLIC ADMINISTRATION IN KARNATAKA UNIVERSITIES

K.H. Cheluva Raju

Introduction: Public administration is one of the youngest social sciences in India and its growth has been spectacular during the last fifty years. It is emerging as an important field of study either as a sub-field of political science or as an independent discipline in the Indian universities. It is yet to establish its independent status in many universities. As observed by the review committee of the social sciences in India:

"Public Administration in India is of recent origin. As an academic discipline it is still in the formative stages of development (ICSSR 1973:28)."

Before independence, the study of public administration was introduced as one of the papers of political science at the degree and post-graduate levels, first in Lucknow, and later, in Benaras, Agra, Calcutta and other universities or as a Diploma Course in Madras, Allahabad and Patna universities. This was the consequence of the Indianisation of civil services and the transfer of power to the Indians under the Constitutional reforms of 1919 and 1935. It was only after the attainment of independence in 1947 that public administration has been given the pride of place both at the Centre and different regional levels including municipal government (Kogekar and Appadorai 1953: 8. The credit for establishing the first independent Department of Public Administration and Local Self-Government in 1949 goes to Nagpur University.

The Report of Paul Appleby (1953), the establishment of the Indian Institute of Public Administration, the birth of the Indian Council of Social Science Research, and the Report of the Administrative Reforms Commission gave further encouragement to the study of public administration in the Indian universities. No less important was the contribution of the Public Administration Programme of the U.N.O. and UNESCO'S international review of the study of political science, including India.[1] As a result, many universities in India such as Lucknow, Rajasthan, Osmania and Saugar established separate and independent Departments of Public Administration with Graduate and Post-Graduate courses.

The study of, and research in, public administration received further impetus in India in view of certain important developments, particularly the adoption of a democratic Constitution in 1950 with commitment to the ideals of secular, socialist and welfare state, and the launching of development programmes under the Five-Year Plans in 1952. Public administration has been assigned a vital role as an instrument of social and economic change and the creation of a new political order in India. Public administration, with its values of efficiency, economy, integrity, accountability and transparency has become indispensable for the success of democracy and development in India[2].

Though the forces and factors that contributed to the growth of public administration as a discipline had their influence on the universities in Karnataka, it was not to the same extent as in other universities. However, at present, the study of public administration is on the threshold of many significant changes in all the seven universities in Karnataka[3] and it is emerging as an important branch of political science at the Degree and Post-graduate levels.

1. See Kogekar's report on India in Robson 1954.
2. See, Chapter VI - Reform of Public Administration (Planning Commission 1952).
3. (1) Bangalore University, Bangalore; (2) Mysore University, Mysore; (3) Karnataka University, Dharwar; (4) Mangalore University, Mangalore; (5) Gulbarga University, Gulbarga; (6) Kuvempu University, B.R.Project, Shimoga; and(7) Open University, Mysore.

At this stage of growth, it is necessary to review the progress made in the development of public administration in Karnataka. An attempt has been made in this paper to make a brief critical survey of the developments, identify the problems and issues, and also suggest ways and means of strengthening the study of, and research in, public administration in the universities of Karnataka.

Development of the Study of Public Administration: The study of public administration in the Universities of Karnataka is as sub-field over the years.

The oldest university in Karnataka, the University of Mysore, founded in 1916, introduced public administration as one of the papers of political science for the B.A. Course in 1936 on the model of Lucknow and Allahabad universities. It must be mentioned that the disciplines of political science and economics had a common department in Mysore University till 1947 and then a separate department of Political Science was created with B.A. Hons. and M.A. courses.

There were three significant developments which influenced the study of public administration at the universities level during this period. Firstly, based on the Report of Paul H. Appleby (1953), the Prime Minister of India sent a circular to all the state governments including Mysore, in December 1953, to take steps to revitalise the administrative machinery in the states. Secondly, the Report in 1955 by the Special Officer of the Government of Mysore, D. Rajagopal, recommended the constitution of a Commission for administrative reforms in the state (Rajagopal 1955). Lastly, the submission of another equally important Report on the Mysore administration by A.D. Gorwala in 1958 suggested the urgency of reforms in the various department of the state government (Gorwala 1958). In the light of these developments, and in view of the emerging importance of public administration, the state government impressed on all the universities to introduce the teaching of public administration as one of the optional subjects at the degree level.

The credit for opening the first Department of Public Administration in Karnataka goes to the University of Mysore. The new Department was created in 1954 for teaching public administration as one of the optional subjects for the B.A. course at Maharaja's College, the premier Arts College of the University of Mysore.[4] Being a new discipline at the degree level it became popular and attracted more students. However, within a short time the growth of a new Department of Public Administration was stunted by the opposition from the Department of Political Science. In the year 1958, the new Department of Public Administration was merged with the existing Department of Political Science by the authorities of the Mysore University though the study of public administration continued as an optional subject for the B.A. course.[5] Thus, the first attempt made to establish an independent Department of Public Administration in Karnataka was thwarted in the University of Mysore. Interestingly, later, the post-graduate Department of Political Science of the University of Mysore took an important. decision in 1963 to introduce public administration as one of the specialised branches for the M.A. course in political science[6].

The Karnataka University, established in 1950, continued the study of public administration as one of the papers of political science for the B.A. and M.A. courses under the influence of Bombay and Poona Universities.

The opening of a new University of Bangalore in 1964 added further strength to the study of public administration. The new Bangalore University continued the tradition of the Mysore University prescribing public administration as one of the papers for Political Science for the B.A. course and as one of the papers for the M.A. course in Political Science with the opening of the post-graduate Department in 1973. Further, in 1976 the new post-graduate Department of Political Science introduced specialisation in public administration as one of the branches of political science at the M.A. level.[7] An attempt to start a

4. See, Courses of Study and Examinations, University of Mysore, 1953. The author was appointed the first Head of the Department of Public Administration in 1954.
5. Public Administration as an optional subject for the B.A. course consisted of three papers: 1. Machinery of Government; 2.Government Finance; and 3. Indian Administration.
6. 1) Principles of Management; 2) Public Personnel Administration; 3) Administrative Law; and 4) Administration of Community Development and N.E.S. in India (UGC 1967:87).
7. The specialised branch of Public Administration consisted of two Papers: 1. Elements of Public Management; and 2. Indian Administration

Diploma Course in Public Administration at Bangalore University on the model of Madras University was made in 1976, but it had to be given up because of the starting of an evening M.A. Political Science course at the Central College, Bangalore.

The new Universities of Mangalore and Gulbarga, started in 1980, continued the study of public administration as one of the papers of political science for the B.A. and M.A. courses in political science on the model of Madras and Karnataka Universities respectively.

After a brief history of the development of public administration in the universities of Karnataka, one is tempted to raise the question as to why this discipline has not yet achieved the status of an independent department, and as to why M.A. course in public administration has not been introduced so far in Karnataka when it has developed faster as a major discipline in other states and universities in India. There are two factors that have hindered the development of public administration as an independent subject in Karnataka.

(1) In the earlier years, there was opposition from the Department of Political Science in the Mysore University for the opening of Department of Public Administration or M.A. course on the ground that the new Department or the new course would become rival to the development of political science. This narrow and myopic approach prevented the growth of public administration. However, there has been a remarkable change in the outlook of the teachers of political science of new generation and they have been evincing greater interest in the development of public administration. (2) The second factor that prevented the growth of public administration as an independent discipline has been the problem of employment for the new graduates specialised in public administration. There have been limited opportunities in the teaching profession as this discipline has not been offered as an optional subject either at the Pre-University level or at the Degree level in most of the colleges and universities.

Even the post-graduates who qualified themselves in public administration by going to outside universities, have not been preferred even to the teaching posts in the Departments of Political Science in colleges and universities. Further, despite many attempts the Karnataka Public

Service Commission has not taken action so far to introduce public administration as one of the subjects for the competitive examinations of the Karnataka Administrative and other services, as it has been done by the Union Public Service Commission for the All-India and other Central Services Examinations. As a result, the growth of public administration has been hindered in Karnataka and the discipline has not made progress to the expected level as in other universities in India.

Teaching of Public Administration: The main objectives of the education in public administration are:

(1) to prepare the students for employment in public services or civil services of the Central, state and local governments;

(2) to prepare the students for teaching profession in colleges and universities;

(3) to equip the students for research in universities and other research institutions; and

(4) to prepare the youth for better citizenship and leadership in public affairs[8].

Generally speaking, education in public administration can be provided at three levels:

(1) Pre-University level; (2) Degree level; and (3) Post-graduate level.

Pre-University Level: In many states, particularly Andhra Pradesh and Rajasthan, public administration has been offered as one of the optional subjects at the Pre-University level. This broad-based education has led to an extensive study of public administration at the foundation level. Since the Pre-University examination is a terminal examination the largest number of students are getting the benefit of education in public administration at an early stage. This has led to demand for the courses in public administration at the higher levels of education. Unfortunately, public administration is not offered as one of the optional subjects at the Pre-University level in Karnataka. Perhaps, this is one of the

8. See Programmes in Public Administration, Maxwell School of Citizenship and Public Affairs, Syracuse University, New York, U.S.A., 1985.

obstacles to the development of public administration as an independent discipline in Karnataka.

Degree Level: At the degree level, the importance given to public administration varies from university to university in Karnataka (See Appendix 1).

1. In Mysore and Kuvempu Universities, public administration is given more importance by offering it as one of the optional subjects with five papers like History, Economics and Political Science for the B.A. courses.

2. Again, in Mysore, Karnataka, Bangalore, Gulbarga and Kuvempu Universities, it is prescribed as one of the compulsory papers of political science for the B.A.course.

3. In contrast, public administration is offered as one of the optional papers of political science at the B.A. level in Mangalore University. Students can take either public administration or international relations. By denying compulsory status to public administration as one of the papers of political science at the B.A. Level, Mangalore University has shown lesser importance to the subject as compared to other universities in Karnataka.

4. It is significant to note that the Institute of Correspondence Course and Continuing Education of Mysore University is offering the combined advantage by prescribing it as one of the compulsory papers of political science for the B.A. course. As a result, the subject has become popular among the employed persons in governmental and semi-governmental organisations.

Post-Graduate Level: The importance given to the public administration at the post-graduate level again is not uniform in the Karnataka Universities. They can be divided into four categories (Appendix 1).

(1) One common feature of all universities in Karnataka is that public administration is offered as one of the compulsory papers for the M.A. course in Political Science.

(2) Kuvempu University has taken a decision to offer development administration as a specialised paper for the M.A. course in Political Science from the year 1996-97.

(3) Three Universities - Mysore, Bangalore and Karnataka - are offering public administration as one of the specialised branches of M.A. course in Political Science.

(4) The University of Mysore has taken a landmark decision to start an M.A. course in Public Administration at the Department of Political Science and the Institute of Correspondence Courses from the year 1966-97. This decision of the Mysore University, it is hoped, will encourage the other universities in Karnataka to introduce a full-fledged M.A. course in Public Administration.

On the whole, teaching of public administration has progressed considerably from a simple study of one of the papers of political science to a specialised branch, and then to the prospects of opening of an M.A. course in Public Administration. Nevertheless, the teaching of public administration is facing two problems and challenges: (a) problem of revision of syllabus, and (b) problem of text books:

(a) The utility and popularity of the discipline of public administration at the Degree and Post-graduate levels largely depend on the syllabus and its content. One of the criticisms against the syllabus is that it has been traditional and socially not relevant. There is too much dependence on the principles and techniques of the developing nations, specially U.S.A. (UGC 1982). Being an applied social science as well as management science, public administration should have a fair combination of both the approaches. Equally, there should be more emphasis on the professional and practical nature of the subject.

An analysis of the papers of public administration at the Degree and Post-graduate courses in Karnataka universities shows a fair combination of classical and modern ideas, and equal consideration for organisational and managerial aspects. Since public administration is a dynamic subject, it must change with the new ideas, policies and reforms. The urgent need in the Karnataka universities is the revision and modernisation of the syllabi of public administration on the guidelines suggested by the U.G.C.'s Curriculum Development Centres of Political Science and Public Administration (UGC 1990) which have recommended theory-based, research-minded and job-oriented courses. Any revision should also take note of the new developments and new themes of relevance, values, equity and change of the emerging school of 'New Public Administration' of the United States, which are relevant to India as well as Karnataka.

(b) Another problem facing the teaching of public administration is that of text books. There is justification in the criticism that there is too much dependence on foreign books, particularly those of U.S.A., whose many theories and practices are not relevant to India. There is an urgent need for the books, foreign and Indian, which are closer to the Indian reality and conditions including Karnataka. With the introduction of a paper on 'Government and Politics in Karnataka' in a few universities, the need for comprehensive texts and documents on the subject of the state government, politics and administration has increased significantly in Karnataka.

Another important development at the level of University education in Karnataka is the introduction of regional language - Kannada, as a medium of instruction and examination. About 70 to 80 per cent of the students in social science at the Degree and Post-graduate levels are opting for Kannada medium without proper text books in the regional language. There is dearth of standard books for post-graduate courses though a number of text books are available for the degree courses (Maddanna 1986; Urs 1989) As a result, students as well as teachers are put to serious difficulties. It has come to affect adversely the educational standards in the universities of Karnataka. It is high time that the universities, the Karnataka Text-book Authority and the Kannada Development Authority take measures to meet this challenge.

Research in Public Administration: It is a matter of satisfaction that there has been rapid expansion of research courses due to the efforts of the U.G.C. and also because of the importance of research degrees for teaching posts under the new rules. All the six universities in Karnataka are offering opportunities to do research for M.Phil. and Ph.D. Degrees. For more than a decade, 'Karnataka State Government and Administration' has been developed as one of the areas of research at the post-graduate level. The introduction of the study of 'Government and Politics in Karnataka' by Bangalore and Karnataka Universities has further enhanced the opportunities for research on many aspects of the state public administration, Research students are permitted by the Departments of Political Science to select important topics of the state administration, depending on the interest of students and specialisation of the guiding teachers. It can be seen that, generally, the topics chosen for research by the students fall within the scope of the syllabus of public administration of M.A. or M.Phil. courses, as it would help the students as well as the teachers in view of the familiarity of the subject.

The common topics of the state administration chosen for research at the M.Phil. and Ph.D. levels in the universities of Karnataka are: The offices of the State Governor and the Chief Minister, Cabinet Government, the State Civil services and Personnel administration, Government Departments, Boards, Public Undertakings and Corporations, District administration and role of the Deputy Commissioner, Panchayat Raj Institutions, Municipal Government, Administration of Justice, Controls over the state administration, Prevention of corruption and Office of Lok Ayukta, Redressal of citizens' grievances, Centre-State relations, Inter-State relations, Border disputes with the neighbouring states, Planning and Development Administration in Karnataka (see Appendix II).

Most of the dissertations and theses submitted to M.Phil. and Ph.D. Degrees are historical, legal, institutional, analytical, descriptive and case studies in character. There are a few empirical (micro as well as macro) studies also. One cannot expect at this level either problem-resolving or theory-building type of research except in extraordinary cases. There is need for more empirical, comparative and inter-disciplinary type of research in the universities of Karnataka. It is better if the Board of Studies in Political Science in each university of Karnataka prepares a list of priorities for research in public administration for the guidance of the research students and teachers (Halappa 1970; Raju 1980). It is also necessary on the part of the Departments of Political Science/Public Administration of all Universities in Karnataka to prescribe an optional paper on "Government, Politics and Administration in Karnataka" at M.A. or M.Phil. level on the model of Bangalore and Karnataka Universities in order to create interest, and to improve the quality of research in the chosen field.

However, there are a few difficulties and problems experienced by research students in the Karnataka universities.

(1) There is no common research methodology course for all the research students in social sciences in any university in Karnataka. Each Department offers the methodology course as a part of M.Phil. or Pre-Ph.D. course. In some cases, research students have to depend on their teacher-guides. A common methodology course in social sciences would certainly improve the quality of research.

(2) There are limited number of research scholarships or fellowships awarded by the University Grants Commission or by the Indian Council of Social Science Research for M.Phil. and Ph.D. Courses. The financial assistance by the universities in Karnataka is also not very encouraging and this has come to affect the research programmes of the universities.

(3) Many of the theses of Ph.D. and research works of university teachers have not seen the light of the day. They have not been published by the University Prasaranga or Publication Departments for want of adequate financial assistance either from the concerned University or by the U.G.C. A few have been published either by the authors or through the help of private publishers.

(4) Another problem in Karnataka is that there is no co-ordination of research work done in the various universities. One university does not know what research work goes on in another university. There is no directory or list of Ph.D. theses and M.Phil. dissertations prepared and published by a central agency. Though it is the responsibility of the Karnataka Inter-University Board under the **Universities Act,** nothing has been done in this sphere despite many requests (GOK 1976).

(5) Want of specialised and qualified teachers in public administration is also another contributory factor for less research in this field. After the abolition of the Advanced Course in Public Administration

and Research Methodology by the Indian Institute of Public Administration in 1967, there is no opportunity for the college and university teachers for advanced training in the discipline. There are limited opportunities to the teachers to go for Ph.D. programme either within the country or abroad.

(6) In the universities of Karnataka, there has been more emphasis on research by teachers now than in the earlier years. It is realised now that teaching and research cannot be separated because each one enriches the other. However, the output of research in public administration by the teachers has not been to the expected level though a few have presented research papers on state administration at the annual sessions of the Indian Political Science Conference, the Indian Public Administration Association and the Indian Institute of Public Administration.

Three factors hinder research work of teachers in the Karnataka universities: (1) they are overburdened with teaching work and that too in many subjects, examination and administrative work leaving no time for research activities in their chosen field; (2) absence of sabbatical leave exclusively for research, or limited number of U.G.C. or I.C.S.S.R. fellowships or inadequate financial assistance from the state government: and (3) there has been no systematic or serious review of research programmes or research work done in the universities by the review commissions appointed by the Chancellor under the provisions of the **Karnataka Universities Act,** or by the panels of Experts (RCU 1980 and KURC 1993). As a result, no evaluation research work has taken place in the universities of Karnataka.

Conclusion: This brief survey brings out the problems and issues faced in the development of the study of public administration in the universities of Karnataka. In conclusion, a few measures are suggested to improve the status, and strengthening the study of and research in public administration.

1. The Pre-University Board, in co-operation with the Directorate of Collegiate Education, must take steps to introduce public administration as one of the optional subjects at the Pre - University level of Education in Karnataka.

2. Similarly, the Directorate of Collegiate Education, in co-operation with the universities, should make efforts to introduce public administration as one of the optional subjects at the B.A. level along with other social sciences such as history, economics and political science.

3. The universities in Karnataka should take action, with the financial assistance of the state government and the University Grants Commission, to establish independent and separate departments of public administration to offer post-graduate courses like M.A., M.Phil., and Ph.D. in public administration. This step will relieve the burden on the Departments of Political Science, which can give more attention to the development of studies and research in other important areas. Until the establishment of the new departments of public administration, the Departments of Political Science, particularly of Bangalore, Mysore and Karnataka Universities must be encouraged to start diploma and post-graduate courses in public administration since they have the faculty, specialisation, library and other facilities. It is to be noted that the University of Mysore has taken a decision to start an M.A. course in Public Administration from the year 1996.

4. In view of the importance given to Distance Education in recent years, a few universities in Karnataka, which are offering correspondence courses and external examination facilities, can introduce public administration at the Degree and Post-graduate levels specially for the benefit of persons employed in the government organisations. This can be done on the model of the Institute of Correspondence Courses and Continuing Education of the Mysore University which is expected to become shortly the first Open University in Karnataka.

5. The state government, the University Grants Commission, and the Indian Council of Social Science Research, must increase the financial assistance to the universities in Karnataka for teaching and research in public administration and to undertake developmental programmes in the coming years.

6. The Government of Karnataka can even consider the proposal to establish a 'Social Science Research Council' (on the model of the Indian Council of Social Science Research) for directing, funding and

co-ordinating research in all the social sciences including public administration.

7. Lastly, the Indian Institute of Public Administration, New Delhi, and its Regional Branch in Karnataka have a special role to play as a catalytic agent in the development of the study of public administration in Karnataka.

One of the objectives of the Indian Institute of Public Administration is to promote the study of public administration. Its two National Seminars organised in 1956 and 1977, by bringing together the representatives of the Indian universities, to discuss the teaching and research in public administration had a remarkable influence on the development of this discipline (IIPA 1956 and 1977). Many Universities immediately started Degree and Post-graduate courses in public administration and also opened Departments of Public Administration in some Universities. The Institute is the best research centre with its library and documentation centre for researchers in public administration. Its annual conferences and seminars have become important forums for the expression of views on the problems of public administration in India. Its Journal, the **'Indian Journal of Public Administration'**, offers opportunities to scholars and teachers to publish their research articles on contemporary issues. The Institute has received national as well as international recognition for its contribution to the development of public administration both as a profession and a discipline.

On the lines of the Indian Institute of Public Administration, its Karnataka Regional Branch has to play a positive role in promoting the study of, and research in, public administration by taking the following steps:

(i) It must establish better rapport with the universities in Karnataka and persuade the Vice-Chancellors to give better status to the discipline of public administration by opening Degree and Post-graduate courses, and starting the Departments of Public Administration. They can jointly organise conferences and seminars to discuss the contemporary issues of the state administration.

(ii) It can develop a Regional Branch which can serve as a nodal agency to promote continuous interaction between academicians and administrators, both serving and retired officers of All-India Services and K.A.S. cadres for fruitful exchange of ideas and experience on problems of public administration in Karnataka.

(iii) It can develop a regional library with a documentation centre to promote and assist research on Karnataka Public Administration.

(iv) It can publish an annual Bulletin or a Journal highlighting the developments in the Karnataka administration and also research work done in the universities of Karnataka on the subject.

(v) It can organise an advanced training course or a refresher course on policy and administrative issue for the senior civil servants of the Karnataka Government in collaboration with other academic and social science institutions such as Bangalore University, National Law School of India University, Indian Institute of Management, Institute for Social and Economic Change, and Institute of Advanced Studies, Bangalore.

(vi) The Regional Branch should work as a pressure group for the advancement of the study of, and research in, Public Administration by lobbying with all the concerned bodies in Karnataka.

(vii) The Regional Branch cannot play its assigned role unless it develops its own infra-structure with the assistance of the Indian Institute of Public Administration and the Government of Karnataka.

It is appropriate to conclude with the optimistic note of Paul Appleby:

"Public Administration will grow in importance and significance in India. Its growth should be as much intellectual and methodical as it is physical'' (1995 : 65).

APPENDIX 1

List of Papers in Public Administration offered in Karnataka Universities

BANGALORE UNIVERSITY

B.A.Course - Political Science (Optional Subject).
Third Year - Paper - Public Administration (Compulsory).

M.A. Course - Political Science
First Year - Paper - Administrative Theory and Management (Compulsory)
Public Administration Group:
Paper I - Indian Administration.
Paper II - Bureaucracy and Development Administration.
Government and Politics in Karnataka (another Optional Paper)

MYSORE UNIVERSITY / OPEN UNIVERSITY
B.A. Course - Political Science (Optional Subject).
Third Year - Paper - Public Administration (Compulsory).

B.A. Course - Public Administration (Optional Subject)
First Year - Paper I - Theory and Practice of Modern Government.
Second Year - Paper II - Principles of Public Administration.
Third Year - Paper - III - Financial Administration.
IV - Local Government in Modern States.
V - Indian Administration.

M.A. Course - Political Science
Public Administration Group
First Year - Paper I - Organisation and Management.
Paper II - Major Issues in Indian Administration.
Second Year - Paper III - Development Administration with reference to India.
Paper IV - Public Personnel Administration.
Note: It is proposed to introduce an M.A. Course in Public Administration from the year 1996 in both the Universities.

KARNATAKA UNIVERSITY

B.A. Course - Political Science (Optional Subject).

Third Year - Paper - Public Administration (Compulsory).

M.A. Course - Political Science

First Year - Public Administration Group.
Development Administration in India.
or
Public Personnel Administration in India.
Government and Politics in Karnataka (Optional).
SecondYear -Paper-Theories of Public Administration (Compulsory)

Public Administration Group

Local Government Institution in India.
or
Problems of Indian Administration.

MANGALORE UNIVERSITY

B.A. Course - Political Science (Optional Subject).

Third Year - Paper - Public Administration (Optional).

M.A. Course - Political Science

First Year - Paper - Administrative Theory (Compulsory).
Paper - Development Administration (Optional).

KUVEMPU UNIVERSITY

B.A. Political Science (Optional Subject).

Third Year - Paper - Public Administration (Compulsory).

B.A. - Public Administration (Optional Subject).

First Year - Paper I - Theory and Practice and Modern Government.
Second Year - Paper II - Principles of Public Administration.
Third Year - Paper III- Indian Government and Administration.
Paper IV - Public Financial Administration.
Paper V - Local Government of Modern States.

M.A. - Political Science

Second Year - Public Administration (Compulsory).

Note: It is proposed to introduce "Development Administration" as one of the Optional Papers for the M.A. Course from the year 1996.

GULBARGA UNIVERSITY

B.A. Course - Political Science (Optional Subject).

Third Year - Paper - Public Administration (Compulsory).

M.A. Course - Political Science

Second Year - Paper - Public Administration (Compulsory).

Note:

Based on the information provided by the Heads of Departments of Political Science of the Universities in Karnataka.

APPENDIX II

List of Ph.D. Theses on Topics of State Administration in Karnataka Universities

Name of the Candidate	Guide	Title of Thesis	Year
BANGALORE UNIVERSITY			
N. Muthuraghavan	Dr. K.H. Cheluva Raju	Management of Training Programme in Public Sector Industries in Bangalore.	1984
D. Jeevan Kumar	Dr. K.H. Cheluva Raju	A Study of Organi-sation and Working of the Directorate of Backward Classes and Minorities in Karnataka.	1988
M.G. Krishnan	Dr. K.H. Cheluva Raju	New Pattern of Panchayat Raj in Karnataka.	1989
Sandeep Sastri	Dr. K.H. Cheluva Raju	Public Accounts Committee of Karnataka Legislature.	1992
O.K. Richard	Dr. R.L.M. Patil	Lok Ayukta in Karnataka	1994
Jasantha Dorairaj	Dr. D. Jeevan Kumar	Legislative Control over Delegated Legislation in Karnataka.	1996

MYSORE UNIVERSITY

Laxminarayana	Dr. K.H. Cheluva Raju	The Tungabhadra Board: A Case Study of Administrative Organisation and its Working.	1981
L. Sujatha	Dr. K.B.Y. Thotappa	Karnataka Electricity Board: A Critical Study of its Administrative Aspects.	1983
U. Gurumurthy	Dr. B.S. Bhargava	Panchayat Raj and Weaker Sections: A Case Study of Mysore District in Karnataka.	1984
N. Sivanna	Dr. B.S. Bhargava	Role of Taluk Develop ment Boards in Rural Development: Case Study of a Taluk in Karnataka.	1989
R. Harish	Dr. H.M. Rajashek-hara	Role of Panchayat Raj in Rural Development: A Case Study of Mysore District.	1991
K. Subha	Dr. B.S. Bhargava	Women and Urban Local Government : A Case Study of a Municipal Corporation in Karnataka.	1993
Midatala Rani	Dr.M. Umapathy	The Language Policy of Karnataka.	1994

R. Somappa	Dr. H.M. Rajashek-hara	MunicipalAdministra-tion in Karnataka: A Study of Mysore Municipal Corporation.	1995
K.C. Vidya	Dr. B.S. Bhargava	Women and Panchayati Raj Institutions: Case Study of a District in Karnataka.	1995

KARNATAKA UNIVERSITY

R.R. Kulkarni	Dr. K.V. Viswanth-aiah	Administrative Problems of reorganised Karnataka State.	1979
V.S. Chougule	Dr. K. Raghavendra Rao	Working of Karnataka Public Service Commission: A Functional Assessment.	1984
S. Parameshwara	Dr. R.T. Jangam	Impact of Develop-ment Agencies on the Process of Modernisation: A Case of Backward Classes of Athani.	1986
A.T. Kittur	Dr. V.T.Patil	WorkingofPanchayati Raj Institutions in Karnataka with refere-nce to Dharwar District.	1990
V.N. Torgal	Dr. V.T.Patil	Administrative Innovations in Rural Develop-ment Societies in the two Districts of Karnataka.	1992

GULBARGA UNIVERSITY

K. Mallappa	Dr. K.V. Viswanathaiah	District Administration in Hyderabad Karnataka.	1982

MANGALORE UNIVERSITY

S. Abdul Javed	Dr. K. Ragavendra Rao	Mangalore City Corporation - A Case Study.	1990
Ambrose Pinto	Dr. Valerian Rodrigues	State and Higher Education: The Case of Bangalore University.	1992

Based on the information provided by the teachers and Heads of Departments of Political Science of the Universities in Karnataka.

REFERENCES

Appleby, Paul (1953). **Public Administration : A Report.** New Delhi: Government of India.

Gorwala, A.D. (1958.). **The Mysore Administration: Some Observations and Recommendations.** Bangalore. Government Secretariat

Government of Karnataka. (GOK) (1976). **Karnataka State Universities Act 1979.** Bangalore: Government Press.

Halappa, G.S. (1970). **Studies in State Administration.** Dharwar: Karnataka University.

ICSSR (1973). **Social Sciences in India: Retrospective and Prospective**. A Report of the Social Science Research Review Committee. New Delhi.

IIPA (1956). **Report of the Seminar on the Study of Public Administration in Indian Universities**. New Delhi: Publisher.

IIPA (1977). **Report of the Seminar on Teaching of Public Administration**. New Delhi, IIPA

Kogekar, S.V. and Appadorai (1953). **Teaching of Political Science in India.** Delhi: Premier.

Maddanna, Mali (1996). **Public Administration in Karnataka**. Bangalore: Kala Prakashana.

Planning Commission (1952). **First Five Year Plan.** New Delhi : Government of India.

Rajagopal, D. (1955). **The Development of Public Administration in Mysore State**. Bangalore: Government Secretariat.

Raju, K.H. Cheluva (1980). **Government and Politics in Karnataka.** A Working Paper on areas of research. Mysore: University of Mysore.

Report of the Review Committee of Universities Karnataka (RCU). (1980). Bangalore.

Report of the Karnataka Universities Review Commission (KURC) 1993. Bangalore.

Robson. W.A. (1954). **The University Teaching of Social Sciences-Political Science**. Paris: UNSESO.

University Grants Commission (UGC) (1967). **Report of the Review Committee on Political Science in Indian Universities.** New Delhi.

University Grants Commission (UGC) (1982). **Report on Political Science in India: State of the Discipline and Agenda for the Future**. New Delhi

University Grants Commission (UGC) (1990). **Report of the Curru-culum Centre in Political Science.** New Delhi.

Urs. M.N. Nanjundaraje, (1989) **Public Administration** (in Kannada). Mysore: Adi Shakti Prakashan.

3

TRAINING IN KARNATAKA*
An Analytical Framework

S.K. Hajra and V.S. Angadi

Introduction: Rapid economic development with social justice has been the major thrust of our Five Year Plans. Eradication of poverty and unemployment, reduction of inequalities in income and wealth and improving the quality of life of people have been the major objectives of planned development. A cadre of competent, devoted and dedicated civil servants and managers with determination to achieve results and vision to meet the challenges of a changing world is required for this purpose. Effective implementation of development plans and programmes depends, to a large extent, on the efficiency and effectiveness of the civil servants. This, in turn, needs imaginative and intensive training programmes and career development plans. Here lies the importance of human resource development which, of late, has attracted the attention of policy makers.

Training as an instrument of change is a dynamic activity through which capabilities of personnel can be improved to meet the present and future performance needs in terms of knowledge, skills and attitudes. Civil services have to be equipped to track the political, social, technical and economic problems. Civil services have to be staffed by men and women who are truly professional. Japan and other East Asian countries have achieved spectacular development through regular

* This paper reflects the personal views of the authors, not of the government. Major material in this paper comes from the personal experience of the authors in managing a state level training Institute in Karnataka. Interaction with other training institutes in India, participation in conferences, workshops and study tours have also been of immense help in preparing this paper.

training of manpowr in various fields. Most of these countires earmark a substantial portion of their budget for training to professionalise the civil services. Training is considered as any investment in human capital formation and very rightly so.

Theoretical Framework for Training: Many studies of economic growth in advanced countries confirm the importance of investment in human resources. Capital formation in a country is generally identified with the net increase in land, structures, durable equipment, commodity stocks and foreign claims. But capital stock needs to be interpreted more broadly to include the body of knowledge and skills possessed by the population and the capacity and training of the population to use them effectively. Investment in training enhances productivity by raising the quality of performance of the population and these outlays yield a continuing return in the future.

It is being increasingly accepted that improvement in the quality of people as productive agents is the fundamental objective of development policies. Personnel working for any organisation are assets, and have to be carefully acquired, nurtured and developed. Training Institutes which are centres for diffusion of knowledge, skill and attitudinal reorientation, can play a vital role in developing people on the job.

In this context, the administration has a special responsibility for promoting creative abilities and developing innovational attitudes of the personnel for fostering motivation and commitment for change on a continued basis. Therefore, a well designed, effective, frequent training programme conducted at the training institutes should prepare the administrators of our country as 'Change Designers' and 'Change Pushers'. They can push forward the frontiers of development in all its varied dimensions.

Historical Background: The Ministry of Food, Agriculture, Community Development and Co-operation (Department of Community Development), Government of India, started an Orientation and Study Centre in Mysore in 1959. This was one of the 11 centres established in different parts of India to train District and Block Level Officers and Non-officials working in the Community Development Programme.

The Orientation and Study Centre, Mysore, like all other centres, was a Regional Training Centre imparting training to officials and non-officials in the sourthern states of Karnataka, Tamil Nadu, Andhra Pradesh, Kerala and Maharashtra. The Government of Karnataka took over the Centre and reorganised it as the Administrative Training Institute (ATI), Mysore, in 1967. Apart from the Administrative Training Institute as an apex training Institute, there are 86 other training institutes in Karnataka.

Karnataka State Government's Commitment to Training: Karnataka is one of the states which has recognised the importance of training from the very beginning. The ATI, as an apex training institute, has been engaged in training officials at various levels since 1967. In addition, District Training Institutes (DTIs) in 18 Districts of the state have been functioning in a phased manner to meet the training needs of personnel at the cutting edge of administration.

Realising the importance of human resources development in public administration, the Government of Karnataka has initiated a policy to train all civil servants of varying categories at least once in five years. On an average, 2,500 officers undergo training every year in ATI and its sister institution, Addul Nazir Sab State Institute for Rural Development (ANS SIRD), and 20,000 District and Divisional level officials in DTIs.

Though a good deal has been done in providing training to the civil servants at all levels in Karnataka, much needs to be done to make it systematic, effective and responsive, in tune with the changes sweeping the world. In this context, the following deserve special attention.

Identification of Training Needs: Before undertaking any training programme there needs to be clarity about the goals and objectives of a department. Job analysis and task analysis need to be properly done at the organisational level, departmental level and at the levels of the individuals. This facilitates identification of the performance problems of the officials at various levels.

The identification of performance problems forms the basis for organising the training needs. Training should basically be aimed at removing the felt or perceived deficiencies of an organisation. At present, the identification of training needs is scarcely done. By and large, the training programmes are offered on the perception of the training institutes about what the organisations need without making a comprehensive analysis of the organisational needs by the organisations themselves for the achievement of their objectives. The attempts made at present just do not match the requirement. Conducting training programmes in the absence of such an exercise will not be effective. And this is what is being done in most training institutes. This must be viewed very seriously by all those concerned, particularly the deputing organisations. Since the organisations know where the shoe pinches, it is better they initiate this exercise. It may not be out of place to mention here that the Department of Personnel and Administrative Reforms (DPAR), Government of Karnataka, has initiated a study of 'Training Needs Analysis of State' with which the ATI, Mysore, and the Secretariat Training Institute, Bangalore, are associated.

Formulation of Training Objectives: Formulating training objectives is a difficult task entangled in the field of pedagogy, curriculum development and training techniques. It is, therefore, not surprising that the training objectives are often unspecified and ill-defined. The objectives should be defined in measurable terms to assess how far they have been achieved. There should also be a clear distinction between the training objectives and performance objectives.

Training objectives should be clear, measurable and realistic. The courses should invariably be designed on the basis of determined objectives. Such a systematic exercise will help the identification of performance problems of an organisation and focusing the training efforts on mitigating them. The training institutions in the state need to take up this activity very seriously in consultation with the training co-ordinators of different Departments.

Methodology: Methodology adopted in the training institute has an important bearing on the achievement of objectives of a training programme. In most cases lecturing method is adopted which more often than not fails to hold the attention of the trainees. Methods like action training, brain storming sessions, group exercises, case studies, discussions, role playing etc., should be increasingly used in addition to lectures. Audio visual aids need greater emphasis for stimulating the interaction between trainers and trainees. In other words, a judicious use of training methodology in right combination keeping in view the objectives and the learning styles of the participants will have to be attempted.

Trainers: This is another area of serious concern. Professionally competent and committed trainers make a lot of difference to a training institute. The training institutes, apart from other things, are judged by the quality of the teaching staff. Therefore, selection of the faculty with the right aptitude deserves top priority. Most trainers feel comfortable as lecturers but not as facilitators. Yet, facilitating is precisely the role they should be playing in the development of training. Trainees need to be equipped with the necessary training skills and methodologies of training. It is extremely important that a trainer acts as a role model for the trainees. It is very important to have the right persons selected as trainers who are professionally competent and who have real aptitude for training, teaching and research. It should also be ensured that the expertise acquired by a person while working as a faculty in a training institute is not wasted even after his return to his parent department. They can be used as training managers in their departments and resource persons. It is also desirable to have a team of core faculty which can provide continuity. The selection of the faculty is, therefore, highly crucial to the success of the training function.

Training of Trainers: Training is a continuous process which needs sustained effort. Experienced and committed officers in the Departments form an important component in the process. Training techniques and methodology are constantly undergoing rapid changes. In order to keep the trainers updated they need to be trained in training skills. They would also need to be imparted training at regular intervals. At present, the ATI, Mysore, which has been reorganised as one of the five Regional Training Centres in the country, has a group of trainers who, over the years, have acquired capability in Training of Trainers, and Design of Training modules. The ATI runs regular courses on these subjects both for national and state level trainers. Training modules have been developed under Gender Sensitisation Project for officers of Education, Industries and Commerce and Forest Departments.

Incentives: The job of the trainers needs to be given additional respectability and importance. It would be unrealistic to expect the successful field managers to opt for an assignment as a trainer in a formal faculty post in a training institute leaving behind a sense of importance, prestige, perks, status, power etc., associated with most of the field jobs. It is, therefore, necessary that a suitable scheme of incentives which, at present, is non-existent, is offered to attract the talented officers and academicians to work as faculty members. Reasonably attractive special pay, housing facilities are the minimum incentives one could think of. They could also be given preference in matters of long term training courses, and sabbatical both inside the country and abroad. A similar career development scheme in respect of core faculty should be implemented.

Inventory of Guest Faculty: Training institutes depend on guest faculty for their training programmes. The guest faculty provides the necessary knowledge and expertise which supplement the training capability of the faculties of the institutes. A combined effort by core faculty, officers on deputation from different departments, and from academic world, and guest faculty is an ideal one. However, it should be ensured that the guest faculty has a clear idea of the particular needs of the training institutes, the trainees and the sponsoring government organisations. They should also have knowledge about relevant training skills and methodologies.The training institutes, therefore, have to build an inventory of regular guest faculty depending on the needs of various training programmes. However, the dependence on guest faculty should be minimal. This calls for proper development of internal faculty.

Training Manager: If training is to improve the organisational effectiveness, it is necessary that training becomes an integral part of the personnel management system. For achieving this, each department should have an officer designated as 'Training Manager'. He should preferably be next to the head of the department in the hierarchy. He should be actively involved in various activities such as analysis and identification of training needs, the design of training programmes, selection of trainees for training programmes, selection of the training institutes and the evaluation of training. He should be a person who can advise the Departmental Head about the right kind of intervention for tackling the performance problems. In other words, he will have to act as a bridge between the departments and the state government in the training institutes. The Training Manager should be chosen with care and trained in training skills.

Special Management of Training (SMoT): SMoT focuses attention on systematic training involving identification of training needs, design, implementation and evaluation. On an experimental basis, this exercise was carried out in the Commercial Taxes Department, Government of Karnataka, in collaboration with the ATI, Mysore, under the guidance of a Faculty member of the ATI, Mysore, and the Training Manager of the Department trained abroad. This experiment showed an increase in the revenue collection of the department from Rs.27 lakhs to Rs. 40 lakhs within three months of the implementation of the module in one of the zones in Bangalore. Such consultancy and action research activities need to be extended to other departments.

Training for the Cutting Edge: All categories of government functionaries working interface with the general public fall within this group. Employees in this category are crucial in implementing the government programmes and activities. The broad objectives of the training system at the grass roots level should aim at improving the technical and professional competence; making them perceive the development process in its totality; making them understand the development approach and strategy; and upgrading their skills for identifying and formulating development projects and activising them for better co-ordination at the field level. The training of these persons who constitute about 90 per cent at the grass root level will enable the state in terms of better work.

Since the duties at this level are often repetitive in nature, the training of the functionaries should focus on sharpening their skills, professional knowledge, and attitudinal re-orientation with reasonable investment. Karnataka, with a network of District Training Institutes (DTI's) at the district level to cater to the requirement of this category, has taken a major step to train the personnel at the cutting edge of administration. At present, 20,000 officials, on an average, are trained in 18 DTIs put together.

On the job training and training through distance learning techniques will have to be adopted. This could be done by selecting a core group of personnel from each functional area to be trained first. They can be sent back to their work units to train their peers and subordinates. The distance training through Satellite communication system for 1,800 functionaries and farmers, sponsored by the Women and Children Welfare Department, the Health and Family Welfare Department, and the Watershed Development Department, during February 1995, was acclaimed as a pioneering venture. Likewise, during January 1996, a Satellite based interactive communication training for about 1,800 Primary School Teachers of Education Department was a great success.

Skill Updating: In many jobs, skills and knowledge often become obsolete over a period of time. Technological advances and frequent complicated changes in Acts and Rules cause skills obsolescence within a few years. Administrators need to equip themselves constantly to respond with a special innovation to changing administrative environment. The present emphasis on the New Economic Policy and Democratic Decentralisation, demands new capabilities and changed outlook. The advancement of an individual within the organisation to new levels of responsibility requires new administrative, legal and managerial knowledge and skills, and reorientation of attitudes. There is, therefore, need for systematic arrangement to impart training on a continuous basis to officials at all levels so that they become facilitators and innovators instead of regulators. It may be mentioned here that the ANS SIRD and the District Training Institutes conducted a series of training programmes both for elected members and the executives of Taluka Panchayats. (This will be extended further by training members of the Gram Panchayats for which preparatory steps have been initiated.)

Evaluation of Training: This is a crucial aspect in training and yet the most neglected. It is necessary to evaluate the impact of training on the trainees and thereby on the organisation. Evaluation should come after the completion of the programme, preferably after a time span. This will help assess the effect of the programme on the performance of the trainee and the organisation. A comprehensive exercise in evalution should involve the organisations, the trainees and the training institutes. This exercise in evaluation must take the training programme as a whole, the climate of training, the methodology adopted, the effectiveness or otherwise, of the programme, the impact of training on the participant as an individual, upon his work in the organisation, and upon the organisation as a whole.

Unfortunately, both training institutes and the concerned Departments neglect this important aspect. Needless to say, the major responsibility in this area is that of the organisation. Of course, the training institutes should also play a critical role. An effective evaluation of the training programme will provide guidelines for formulating future training programmes.

The Role of Training Institutes in Attitudinal Transformation: Attitude plays a very important role in the performance level of individuals through commitment. The satisfaction of the customer which is the final objective can be achieved through possession of right attitudes apart from appropriate knowledge and skill. However, attitude is the most difficult of the attributes to inculcate.

The question whether attitudes under the present environment can be influenced through training intervention is highly debatable. However, it should be possible to tackle this important dimension through practical intervention. The training institutes should make use of case studies highlighting the importance of civil servants in the success or failure of government programmes. If the role models are available at work place, it becomes reasonably easy to bring some transformation in the attitudes of the trainees. Constant efforts by the training institutes and the departments can produce some results in this vital area.

Regional Imbalance in Training Coverage: A study of the district-wise officers trained in the ATI reveals that districts like, Bijapur, Bidar, Raichur, Gulbarga and Bellary, have received least attention. The utilisation of facilities in the ATI from Dharwad, Belgaum, and Uttara Kannada districts, is also not very encouraging. Dakshina Kannada, Coorg, Chickmagalur, Kolar, Shimoga, Tumkur, and Chitradurga, are relatively better placed in terms of utilisation of facilities of the ATI. Mysore, Bangalore, Mandya, and Hassan districts have an edge over other districts. A large number of officers from these four districts attended different training programmes.

One reason for such a regional variation in the utilisation of training facilities could be attributed to the location of the ATI. Secondly, training is not being taken seriously by the concerned departments. In order to bridge this regional imbalance in the coverage of training of officers in categorios 'A' and 'B', it is necessary to open a Regional Training Centre either at Dharwad or Belgaum to take care of 7-8 districts with similar functions of the ATI, Mysore. This will be under the administrative control of the ATI, Mysore. It would then be possible to cover 6,000-7,000 government employees under categories 'A' and 'B' in a year. This, in turn, will take care of the policy of the government in terms of imparting training to an officer once in five years.

Data Management and Training: Officials at various levels need to be sensitised to the importance of data management in the domain of administrative and public services. Data flow from the field level which forms the basis for policy decisions at the top for programme identification and planning is generally irregular, lacks consistency and is, at times, totally unreliable. The information base is virtually non-existent in many areas necessitating a heavy reliance on sample surveys at the macro-level which do not provide a reliable basis for micro-level planning. A sound management information system is the basis for good planning and decision making process, and collection of administrative, socio-economic, demographic data, and their monitoring is essential to enable planners and decision makers to set up realistic targets, implement, monitor and review plans and schemes. Officials at all levels, therefore, need to be trained in scientific methods of handling data.

Networking among Training Institutes: There are a large number of training institutes in the state. At present, there is no co-ordination among them resulting in the duplication of activities leading to wastage of resources. The state government should maintain a proper inventory of the activities of the training institutes in the state. Such co-ordination among the training institutes will become cost effective.

Training Budget: If HRD through training intervention is to be viewed seriously, a separate budgetary provision for training should be made for each department. The Heads of the Departments should be made accountable for the training of officers of their departments. Such a measure would take care of deputation of officers to various training institutes. In respect of the quantum of financial allocation, it is suggested that five per cent of the salary component of every department should be earmarked for training.

Controlling Authority: A strong, well informed and committed Governing Board can be invaluable. The objectives of the Board can be threefold: to provide policy guidelines and overall advice; to ensure that the Institute produces results; and to support the Institute. The Board members should assist the Director in obtaining scarce resources such as personnel, capital and recurring finance, equipment, transport etc. The decisions taken by the Managing Committee/Board should be accepted by the government without further examination at different levels.

Cost of Training: The cost of training consists of five components: (a) building infrastructure like classrooms, hostels, administrative block, library etc.: (b) training and administrative hardware and other teaching equipments, audio-visuals, furniture, library books, documentation and retrieval facilities etc. (c) administrative overheads like salaries to employees (both teaching and non-teaching), board and lodging charges (if not borne by the trainees themselves) and other recurrent costs; (d) administrative expenses on the course itself like transport for guest faculty, preparing and distributing course material preparing audio-visual software, stationery consumed in the courses etc; and (e) preparing distance learning material and sending it to the correspondents and setting up guidance for helping them to use distance learning packages.

Government employees in Karnataka are divided into four categories, namely, groups A, B, C, and D. The number of employees in group A, which was 8,943 in 1981, stood at 10,142, in 1986 representing a growth rate of 19 per cent. The number in group B, which was 9,613 in 1981, stood at 23,077 in 1986, representing a growth rate of 140 per cent. The number of employees in group C, which was 301,462 in 1981, stood at 353,112 in 1986,representing a growth rate of 17.5 per cent. The number in group D, which was 52,671 in 1981, stood at 51,360 in 1986, representing a decline of 2.5 per cent. The total number of government employees in these four categories which was 372,239 in 1981, stood at 437,691 in 1986, representing a growth rate of 17,5 per cent.

The total number of government employees which was 576,130 during 1993-94, represented a growth rate of 31.62 per cent over 1986. Of this, about 35,000 employees belonged to groups A and B. Keeping the norm of training an employee at least once in five year means training 7,000 employees a year. The remaining 541,130 employees in categories C and D need to be trained in the DTIs and other training institutes. Maintaining the same norm means training one lakh government employees a year in this category. This is an enormous task and requires investment of a very high order. Expenditure on salaries in Karnataka increased from Rs. 464 crores in 1983-84 to Rs.1,904 crores in 1992-93. Five per cent of this component to training function means a provision of Rs.95 crores. At present, it could be roughly estimated at around Rs. 100 crores. An allocation of Rs. 100 crores at the moment may not be a feasible proposition. To ensure proper utilisation of scarce resources, a modest provision of Rs. 50 cores per year may be considered.

Role of the Department of Personnel and Administration Reforms (DPAR): The DPAR can play a very important role in framing the training policy of the state government. It should build up a comprehensive data base pertaining to different institutions, their activites, their capacities and so on. It must evaluate the training needs in different training institutes and offer policy suggestions. It should also co-ordinate work relating to faculty exchange, faculty placement and liaise with the departments and other organisations of the government to ensure that each department gives top priority to training. This calls for the creation of a separate training wing to be manned by a suitable person with training background.

Role of ATI: The ATI is the apex training institute of the state and the nodal agency for co-ordination in the field of training. It has not only to organise Foundation, Induction and Refresher Training Programmes for group 'A' and 'B' officers but also to co-ordinate the training efforts of all the departments of the government for effective implementation of the training policy of the state. In respect of various training institutes in the state, the ATI has to act as a resource institution, particularly in the case of Training of Trainers for which no facilities are currently available in the state. The ATI will also have to undertake research studies involving identification and evaluation of training needs of various departments.

The ATI needs to develop research capabilities, particularly in the field of action research, relevant to the specific requirements of various government departments. It is also necessary to develop appropriate training modules, case studies etc. It should take up action research on training. In fact, no training should take place without proper action research. If the ATI has to achieve these goals, it is necessary to strenthen its infrastructure. The ATIs will have to strengthen the teaching, research and other staff. Some of the departments such as Engineering, Police, Co-operation, Education and Rural Development etc., have their own institutions. Some of the major departments should also set up their own training institutions. In that case they would be able to cater to almost 90 per cent of the target population. The ATI will have to plan for training the remaining 10 per cent.

Conclusion: Despite the growing concern for training of public personnel, it is being increasingly realised that development of administrators has been either inadequate or **ad hoc.** Even where the matter has received attention in the recent past, the nature and degree of efforts have not been commensurate with the quantitative and qualitiative changes of the time. The number of administrators needing intervention inputs for development has been steadily increasing with planned development. The environmental context of job performance by the senior administrators has also been changing requiring training intervention. The expectation from public servants is manifold. Public officials and senior administrators need appreciation of technology as a key determinant in the dynamics of decision-making and of change as a key factor in administration at the policy level.

The multi-dimensional activities need well developed training facilities in the form of well equipped training institution instead of **ad hoc** provisions of training. This calls for a comprehensive and well thought out training policy of the government. Therefore, it is desirable to give serious attention to this vital issue affecting human resources development.

4

STATE POLICY AND SOCIAL SCIENCE RESEARCH*

P.V. Shenoi and A.S. Seetharamu

Institute for Social and Economic change (ISEC) was the brain-child of the internationally well-known Economist, Professor V.K.R.V. Rao, who founded the famous institutions, such as, Delhi School of Economics and Institute of Economic Growth. ISEC was set up by Professor Rao with a major objective of assisting the state government of Karnataka by undertaking systematic studies for assessment of natural resources, mobilisation of financial and real resources, identification of factors retarding growth and measures for overcoming them, identification of regional and other inequalities and measures for redressal of imbalances and perspective planning. In other words, the focus was in undertaking research and other studies in areas pertaining to the development of the administration of the state of Karnataka. The research, which has been done at the Institute, over the last 25 years, has demonstrated that the Institute has lived up to the expectations of the Founder, Professor Rao. It has been periodically conducting seminars, brain-storming sessions, review and discussion meetings on policy, planning and administration in Karnataka. The Faculty of ISEC have served as chairpersons or members of various state-level committees, commissions, task groups which examined issues and problems of policy and planning in the state.

---

* This article is based on research studies conducted by the Institute for Social and Economic Change, Bangalore, in the area of policy planning an public administration in Karnataka State.

Training programmes in the areas of planning, strategy-formulation and programmes of development have also been organised. Research outputs of the faculty have been used as inputs in all these activites. However, in this paper the focus is on the contribution of ISEC through research studies for policy planning and public administration. Theoretical researches, model-building and simulation exercises, projections and forecasting studies are not included in this paper.

Schemata: Research studies at the ISEC may be classified under two broad categories when they are viewed from the perspective of their relevance for policy, planning and administration. They are: (a) studies which are directly related to policy formulation, planning strategies, plan implementation, evaluation of development programmes of the state, concurrent evaluation of on-going projects and programmes, preparation of perspective plans, examination of state policies, and the like; and (b) research studies which throw up insights for policy and planning. The first category of studies may be called as Policy Oriented Studies while the second category of studies may be called as Policy Relevant Studies. While this is not a generalisation, policy oriented studies have been, by and large, sponsored by the Government of Karnataka or the Government of India. Studies with policy relvance are self-initiated studies, in general. A review of both types of studies has been made in this paper. It is to be noted that the review made here is confined to only studies relating to Karnataka, excluding a wide range of studies with national and international foci. The studies have been classified, for convenience, in two ways: those which are related to macro-economic issues of Karnataka state such as those relating to federal fiscal arrangements, state finances, resource mobilisation, public expenditure analysis, impact of economic reforms, tax reforms etc. The other type of studies are related to sectoral issues and problems such as those relating to agriculture, industry, health, housing, education, social welfare etc; or in other words, economic as well as social sector policies and planning. There are also many issues and problems of development which are treated as integral to this classification such as those of employment, environment, decentralisation, women's status, welfare of scheduled and weaker sections etc, though it is conceded that there may be alternative ways of taxonomy. With this schemata, the studies proper are presented in the following sections.

Policy Oriented/Relevant Studies: At the outset, the studies which are addressed to the macro-economic and social issues and problems have been identified and their contribution to policy, planning and administration discussed.

Macro Issues: Quite a few studies were completed on the state's finances which had implications for fiscal policy of the state and its budgetary plans. Burden of Union loans on the states (including Karnataka), revenue potential and revenue efforts of southern states (including Karnataka), a study of economic feasibility of controls on alcohol consumption, state lottery and horse-racing, centre-state financial relations and finances of local-self governments are some of the studies. Apart from these studies, some collective efforts were also made: 'Planning for Change: Issues in Mysore's Development', 'Planning in Perspective: Policy Choices in Planning for Karnataka', and 'Dimensions of Social Change'.

It is not necessary to develop one to one correspondence between specific recommendations borne out of research studies for a myriad of programmes and strategies under policy and planning. However, it is worthwhile to recount that the studies have adovcated rationalisation of tax structures, identified new avenues of revenues, and have advised the state to incorporate values of equity and justice with the goal of economic growth.

Sectoral Studies: Among all the economic and social sectors on which research studies have been completed in ISEC, the pride of place is occupied by the agricultural sector. This is but natural for a variety of reasons. India, and Karnataka within India, is basically an agricultural economy. Seventy per cent of the population live in rural areas and, nearly two-thirds of our working population are engaged in agriculture and allied activities. Agriculture also holds the key to India's prosperity. For this reason, the Union Ministry of Agriculture has set up a full-fledged and large research unit at the ISEC, known as Agricultural Development and Rural Transformation Unit (ADRT), which is one among the several Agro-Economic Research Centres (AER) in the country. The ADRT has a mandate to work on problems of agriculture in the region mostly using published data. A large number of researches in the Institute have been in the field of agriculture. Likewise, there is also a Population Research Centre (PRC) in the Institute set up by the Ministry of Health and Family Welfare of the GOI. They also have a research mandate to work in the areas of population, health and family welfare. Mostly, they conduct field based studies. The Reserve Bank of India has set up a Chair in Social Services Management which is at the moment redefined to do work in the area of monetary economics. The several other units, viz., Economics, Rural Economics, Ecology Economics, Quantitative Economics, Development Administration, Sociology and Education have been conducting studies of sectoral and inter sectoral issues and problems.

Studies on Infrastructure for Development: The infrastructure studies are of two types, viz., economic infrastructure and social infrastructure. Social infrastructure also includes studies of social and political institutions. Power and energy, credit, markets, irrigation, transportation and communication are some of the important components of economic infrastructure required for development. ISEC has undertaken studies in all these areas. Agricultural finance by commercial banks, rural energy-agriculture interaction in the state, an evaluation of margin money-cum-subsidy for irrigation borewell schemes in Karnataka, a study of differential rates of interest scheme for the weaker sections, studies on tank, well and canal irrigation and their relation to the social universe around them, ex-post evaluation of dugwell investments in hard rock areas of Karnataka, factors promoting and inhibiting the access of small farmers to lift irrigation in Karnataka, institutional constraints in eco-development, a study of pilot project of NABARD in credit delivery system and current status of common property resources in relation to population growth are some of the studies in the area of economic infrastructure.

There are also studies on social infrastructure for development. Growth and distribution of schools in the state, facilities available in hospitals for medical termination of pregnancy, contraceptive use for family planning programmes, panchayat raj institutions, mahila samakhya, public distribution systems, hostel facilities for students etc., are some of the social infrastructure studies.

Studies on infrastructure facilities highlighted, among other issues, the need for balanced distribution of facilities. The studies identified the regional disparities in development of infrastructure facilities, inadequacy of facilities in relation to needs, demand and use, the need for integrated use of water resources for agriculture, paucity of forward and backward linkages for development such as those relating to credit, extension, storage facilities, markets, transport, energy requirements for industrial and agricultural development and the significance of infrastructure facilities in development and especially the quality of services therein.

Agricultural and Rural Development: Time-series analysis of agricultural development in Karnataka state as well as a district-wise analysis, regional analysis of distribution of gains in agricultural development, changes in cropping patterns - problems in cultivation of commercial crops such as coconut, cardamom, pepper and cashewnut, economics of bi-voltine silk worm rearing and estimations of demand and supply for foodgrains in Karnataka are some of the studies in the area of agricultural development in the state.

Studies on the adoption of new agricultural technology in the state with respect to paddy, cotton and jowar unravelled the dynamics of preferences of farmers for local varieties. Rainfall and climate, prices, fertiliser friendliness, credit, market friendliness etc., were the variables identified in this dynamics. Other studies deal with issues like sociological aspects of modern farm technology, the significance of ragi, a millet, in dry land development, use of farm power for HYV crops, a state-wise analysis of fertiliser consumption by major crops, a crop-wise and region-wise analysis of agronomic factors influencing fertiliser consumption, studies of support system for promoting production of oilseeds and pulses and economic viability of tobacco crop in comparative contexts, and policy implications of shifts in cropping patterns.

There are studies on labour absorption and employment potential in agriculture. Dimensions of agricultural labour, labour utilisation in agriculture, employment and income in sericulture and potential of marginal and small farms for agricultural employment are some of these studies.

Some studies have been conducted on markets: case study of regulated markets and marketing of silkworm cocoons. There are also studies on water use efficiency in agriculture, agricultural use of sewage/sullage water and organisational structures for silkworm seed.

A significant contribution of the ISEC in agriculture is in the form of detailed exercises in agro-climatic regional planning (ACRP). Issues in relation to investment, employment and profitability of the ACRP have also been worked out in the case of certain districts.

Rural change and development is another important area where significant contributions have been made by the ISEC right from its inception. One of the earliest large-scale and interdisciplinary research studies had been engineered by Professor V.K.R.V. Rao himself, known as Tumkur Project. It was an attempt at building a model of integrated rural development keeping a backward district as a unit of development. Beginning with a detailed and comprehensive profile of all the taluks in the district the study tested the feasibility of cluster approach to rural development wherein balanced rural growth could be promoted through dispersal of rural infrastructure facilities among a cluster of villages as against the development of villages through nodal village and peripheral villages model. The study covered 30,000 households in 300 villages. Rural life and economy, village development, social and economic stratification in village-life, dynamics of rural under-development were studied using cluster approach. The wealth of data generated from this study have been used for a variety of analyses of rural change. They also served as benchmark data for longitudinal studies on quality of life, state's performance in supply of basic needs, growth and decline in regard to education and schooling processes etc.

Apart from the Tumkur Project, a large number of studies have concentrated on rural sector. Agrarian structure, land reforms, minor irrigation, dry land development, rural industries, green revolution, programme and sector-wise rural response to development initiatives by the state, integration of education in agricultural and non-a gricultural rural development projects of the state, were some of these areas. A notable finding in a study of land reforms was that though concentration in ownership of holdings declined, land based rural power structure did not decline as there emerged a concentration in operational holding through the strategy of lease of lands. Another study on land reforms by a Study Group of the Institute on Land Reforms set up by the National Commission on Rural Labour in 1989 impressed upon a policy for provision to rural poor and labour the access to agricultural and common lands. Studies on dry land agriculture exposed the limitations of the planning process in these areas as compared to their relative success in irrigated areas. A review of researches on interventions for the poor by the state since the 1970s in the areas of employment generation, technology extension, credit-assets-skills, and welfare highlighted the potentials and exposed the limitations of the state as a promoter of rural change.

Quite a number of studies have been completed on decentralised planning and administration. Issues and problems covered under various research projects include organisational and administrative aspects of rural development programmes and institutions such as the SFDA, minor irrigation, land army, TRYSEM, grass roots leadership in the state, panchayat raj system in Karnataka, working of town panchayats, the panchayat raj experiment of 1987 in the state, institutional aspects of Lok Ayukta, profile of Taluk Development Board, the Karnataka experiment in decentralised planning as well as structural and managerial shifts in educational management due to panchayat raj system etc.

Studies have been conducted on a few areas allied to the sectors on agriculture and rural development, such as those of irrigation, animal husbandry, sericulture, forestry, rural industries etc. The more important may be enumerated: cross-breed cattle development programme, supply and demand of bovine feed, CPRs in animal husbandry, small ruminants in Drought Prone Areas of the state, socio-economic implications of farm forestry, economics of rural industries, social forestry projects in the state, development of uncultivated lands, political economy of forest use and management etc.

Major projects have been completed in the areas of irrigation as well as sericulture. Benchmark surveys of command areas in irrigation projects of the state, concurrent evaluation studies and issues of social and economic development in command areas studies on the impact of irrigation schemes have been completed for several river basins such as those of Malaprabha, Ghataprabha, Hemavathi, Harangi, Kabini and Upper Krishna. These studies on irrigation had been sponsored by the Government of Karnataka as long-term projects and for immediate and direct use by planning and implementing agencies by the state.

Likewise, with the large scale expansion of sericulture in the state with the support of the World Bank, long-term research projects on sericulture have been taken up and completed. During its first phase of work, studies in sericulture concentrated on infrastructure for sericulture development, economics of sericulture, evaluation of sericulture projects in the state. During the second phase, the focus shifted from state initiatives to beneficiary perceptions and perspectives. Quite a number of studies on various social and economic issues in sericulture including gender issues have been addressed during this phase. The Central Silk Board and the State Department of Sericulture have been participating in periodical reviews of implications of these studies for policy, planning and implementation over the years.

One more emerging area of focus in rural development has been the place and participation of non-governmental organisations (NGOs) in rural development. Some major projects have been completed in recent years on the participation of NGOs in the following areas: impact of structural adjustment policies on the rural poor and the role of NGOs, NGOs in sericulture, rural development strategies of NGOs, watershed development, rural credit etc.

One more cognate area of development in general and rural development specifically is employment. Quite a few studies have been completed on employment, employment potential of plan schemes, evaluation of rural landless employment guarantee programme, bonded labour rehabilitation programme, rural non-farm employment, child labour in the state, migrating behaviours for employment, and full employment strategies through agri-business consortiums. Apart from this, several task force studies on rural employment have also been completed.

A significant area of concern in agriculture and rural development is "environment." The ISEC has demonstrated concern for issues and problems of environment-friendly and sustainable development. There is a full-fledged Ecology Economics Unit in the Institute. Sustainable agricultural development, corrective to the green revolution, institutional, economic and agronomic aspects of stable development, dry land areas and watershed development, use of common property resources, development of uncultivated lands, social forestry etc., have been researched on in the area of environmental studies.

The foregoing review of studies on agriculture, rural development and cognate concerns shows that a vast array of research wisdom has been generated in the Institute. Most of them have been directly used as inputs for policy, planning, implementation, monitoring and evaluation while the rest have influenced policy and planning.

Industries Sector: ISEC has completed several studies relating to the industries sector. However, the studies are neither as extensive or comprehensive as in the case of agriculture and rural development. Pride of place to rural sector, limited resources and vastness of industries sector have all contributed to this relatively lower coverage. Critical examination of industrial policies, studies on sub-sectors like electronics, food processing, a study of enterpreneurship and social mobility among scheduled castes, workers' participation in management, management problems of state public sector undertakings, ownership change in small scale industries, industrial investment climate in the state, financial performance of public enterprises, techno-economic survey of fishermen community in Karnataka, industrial enterpreneurship in Karnataka, unit costs, prices and resource allocation in the electrical machinery and transport equipment industry, economics of industrial pollution in Karnataka, sickness in small scale sector - causes and cure, priority sector advances in commercial banks etc., are among completed studies. There are also a few studies on urban problems which have a bearing on urban planning and industrial policy: growth of cities and towns in Karnataka during 1961 - 1981, industrialisation and population growth in Bangalore, retail trade structures in Bangalore City, a study of transportation planning for Bangalore City, travel behaviour and mass transport in Bangalore City, slums in Bangalore City etc. Many of these urban studies have also emerged out of a large scale project on Bangalore City as an emerging metropolis. By and large, the studies in the industries and urban development sector have been discrete though they are all useful for policy and planning.

Social Sectors: The ISEC has a few units entirely devoted to studies in social sectors. Education, health and family welfare, housing, social welfare are some of the sub-sectors on which researches have been completed. Studies on anti-poverty programmes and rural employment have been covered earlier under other sectors. Hence, they are not included here.

The thrust areas in education sector are primary education, education as an input in development process and literacy while there have been studies in other areas also such as pre-primary education, secondary education, higher education, teacher education and non-formal education. Perspective plans have been prepared for universalisation of primary education for a few districts in the state under the World Bank funded District Primary Education Project. A Task Force report commissioned by the Government of Karnataka had been prepared in 1986 on education in the state by 2001 for a policy perspective document on Karnataka 2001. A master plan for the universalisation of primary education for Sixth and Seventh Plan periods for the state as a whole had been prepared. Other studies in primary education include a study of growth and stagnation of schools in the state, structural and organisational determinants of schooling, a taluk-level analysis of regional disparities in educational development, dynamics of school participation both in rural areas and urban slums, utilisation of incentives and facilities offered by the state for school children and preparation and field try out of tests required for national norms of Minimum Levels of Learning in Primary schools.

Both the project approach to adult education and the campaign approach of the National Literacy Mission in Karnataka state have been evaluated. Non-formal education for non-enrolled and dropout children have been studied.

Education as an input in rural response to development programmes, integration of education in extension education in agriculture as well as sericulture, study of returns to women's education, role of education in social mobility and social change among women, role of education in the promotion of modernity as well as scientific temper have been studied.

Performance of secondary education as well as vocational education in the state, study on rural immigrants in higher education, school broadcasts, private candidates in SSLC examinations, educational play materials, pre-primary education and teacher training and communication for decision-making in the department of education have been some of the other studies in the education sector.

There are a number of studies in the area of population, health and family welfare. They include health, nutrition and FPP under ICDS programme, evaluation of health and family planning, indigenous health care system, cultural factors associated with child mortality and morbidity, feasibility of health insurance for rural population, public health expenditure, universal immunisation programme, environmental sanitation and supply of drinking water. Recently, a significant state-wide, large-scale sample survey of health and family welfare in Karnataka state has been completed as a part of the National Family Health Survey.

There have also been studies on the role of incentives in family planning programmes, child labour and fertility, evaluation of FP &

MCH Services, cost-benefit analysis of family planning, determinants of fertility behaviour, situational analysis of child in Karnataka etc. There are a few studies on labour migration which have already been referred to.

There are also a few studies on housing and related aspects. Economics of urban water supply, evaluation of hand pump programmes in rural Karnataka and class differences in urban housing etc, may be mentioned.

There are a number of studies on various social groups in the state. Studies on specific castes and sub-castes, poverty and backwardness among them, social amenities for the rural poor, women as a group, gender disparities, deprived castes, have all been insightful in understanding social life and social change in the state.

APPENDIX 1

Administrative Divisions

Sl. No.	Districts	Sub-Divisions	Taluks	Hoblies	Grama Panchayats	Municipalities Corporation
1	2	3	4	5	6	7
1.	BANGALORE (U)	1	3	17	115	5
2.	BANGALORE (R)	2	8	35	227	8
3.	CHITRADURGA	2	9	30	280	5
4.	KOLAR	2	11	53	309	10
5.	SHIMOGA	2	9	52	371	7
6.	TUMKUR	3	10	50	325	6
I	BANGALORE DIVISION	12	50	237	1,627	41
7.	BELGAUM	3	10	35	473	17
8.	BIJAPUR	4	11	36	365	18
9.	DHARWAD	4	17	44	442	19
10	UTTARA KANNADA	3	11	35	212	8
II	BELGAUM DIVISION	14	49	150	1,492	62
11.	BELLARY	2	8	31	222	10
12.	BIDAR	2	5	30	77	5
13.	GULBARGA	3	10	48	339	13
14.	RAICHUR	3	9	57	302	8
III	GULBARGA DIVISION	10	32	166	1,040	36
15.	CHIKMAGALUR	10	32	166	1,040	36
16.	DAKSHINA KANNADA	3	8	26	356	21
17.	HASSAN	2	8	38	261	6
18.	KODAGU	1	3	16	101	1
19.	MANDYA	2	7	31	233	6
20.	MYSORE	3	11	49	366	10
IV	MYSORE DIVISION	13	44	192	1,547	50
	STATE	49	175	745	5,706	189

SOURCE: **Karnataka at a Glance1994**, (1995), Bangalore, Directorate of Economics and Statistics.

APPENDIX 2

Area, Population and Literary Rates of Karnataka State

Sl. No.	District	Area (00 Sq.Kms)	Population (000) 1991 Total	Male	Female	Population (000) 1991 Rural	Urban	Growth rate (percentage) 1981-91	Literacy Rate (%) 1991 Census Males	Females	Total
1	2	3	4	5	6	7	8	9	10	11	12
1.	BANGALORE (U)	22	4,839	2,543	2,296	670	4,169	38	82.94	68.81	76.27
2.	BANGALORE (R)	58	1,673	860	813	1,370	303	15	61.51	38.15	50.17
3.	CHITRADURGA	109	2,180	1,122	1,058	1,591	589	23	66.88	43.36	55.48
4.	KOLAR	82	2,217	1,128	1,089	1,700	517	16	62.69	37.75	50.45
5.	SHINOGA	106	1,910	974	936	1,404	506	15	71.24	51.42	61.53
6.	TUMKUR	106	2,306	1,177	1,129	1,924	382	16	66.49	41.93	54.48
I	BANGALORE DIVISION	483	15,125	7,804	7.321	8.659	6,466	20	71.59	51.05	61.66
7.	BELGAUM	134	3,584	1,834	1,750	2,742	842	18	66.56	38.69	53.00
8.	BIJAPUR	171	2,928	1,491	1,437	2,239	689	21	69.69	40.00	55.13
9.	DHARWAD	137	3,503	1,802	1,701	2,279	1,224	19	71.37	45.20	58.68
10.	UTTARA KANNADA	103	1,220	621	599	296	294	13	76.39	56.77	66.73
II	BELGAUM DIVISION	545	11,235	5,748	3,487	8,186	3,049	18	69.93	43.54	57.04
11.	BELLARY	99	1,890	962	928	1,326	564	27	58.71	31.97	45.57

(Contd.)

12.	BIDAR	54	1,256	643	613	1,010	246	26	58.97	30.53	45.11
13.	GULBARGA	162	2,582	1,316	1,266	1,972	610	24	52.08	24.49	38.54
14.	RAICHUR	140	2,310	1,167	1,143	1,830	480	29	49.53	22.15	35.96
III	GULBARGA DIVISION	455	8,038	4,088	3,950	6.138	1,900	26	54.37	26.89	40.85
15.	CHIKMAGALUR	72	1,017	515	502	845	172	12	70.56	51.31	61.05
16.	DAKSHINA KANNADA	84	2,694	1,306	1,388	1,931	763	13	84.40	67.96	75.86
17.	HASSAN	68	1,570	785	785	1,297	273	15	68.87	44.90	56.85
18.	KODAGU	41	489	247	242	411	78	5	75.35	61.22	68.35
19.	MANDYA	50	1,644	838	806	1,377	267	16	59.18	36.70	48.15
20.	MYSORE	120	3,165	1,621	1,544	2,225	940	22	56.23	37.95	47.32
IV	MYSORE DIVISON	435	10,579	5,267	8.086	2,493	14	67.78	49.31	58.56	
	STATE	1,918	44,977	222,952	22,025	31,069	23,908	21	67.26	44.34	56.05

SOURCE: Karnataka at a Glance 1994-95 (1995), Bangalore, Directorate of Economics and Statistics.

APPENDIX 3

Land Utilisation (Hectares)

Sl. No.	District	Geographical area	Forest	Land not available for cultivation	other uncultivated land	Fallow land	Area Sown
1	2	3	4	5	6	7	8
1.	BANGALORE (U)	2.17.410	3,303	64,127	24,376	31,424	1,01,937
2.	BANGALORE (R)	5,85,431	81,268	88,641	48,425	50,533	3,37,717
3.	CHITRADURGA	10,15,505	90,839	90,648	1,24,359	66,540	7,84,431
4.	KOLAR	7,79,467	70,324	1,37,028	1,23,953	63,701	4,19,203
5.	SHIMOGA	10,57,554	3,27,433	1,17,678	2,07,072	54,521	4,15,560
6.	TUMKUR	10,64,755	44,984	1,48,980	1,49,025	1,18,929	6,42,762
I	BANGALORE DIVISION	47,20,122	6,18,141	6,47,102	6,77,210	3,85,648	27,01,610
7.	BELGAUM	13,44,382	1,90,424	1,12,685	34,817	96,379	10,20,303
8.	BIJAPUR	17,12,348	83,103	1,10,628	12,643	7,54,066	14,97,393
9.	DHARWAD	13,78,200	1,15,303	84,416	27,671	50,756	13,63,184
10.	UTTARA KANNADA	10,24,6679	8,29,613	36,545	28,418	12,892	1,35,508

(Contd.)

II.	BELGAUM DIVISION	54,59,609	12,18,443	3,44,274	1,04,549	3,14,093	40,16,388
11.	BELLARY	9,56,220	1,19,247	1,39,444	37,916	90,288	6,70,985
12.	BIDAR	5,41,765	25,092	43,449	45,254	56,163	4,45,475
13.	GULBARGA	16,10,765	68,759	1,18541	51,488	1,69,715	13,58,062
14.	RAICHUR	13,88,338	47,618	96,136	63,270	2,24,584	11,13,828
III	GULBARGA DIVISION	44,96,531	2,60,716	3,97,570	1,97,928	5,40,750	35,88,350
15.	CHIKMAGALUR	7,22,075	2,00,485	69,360	1,47,353	15,757	3,19,149
16.	DAKSHINA KANNADA	8,33,595	2,26,916	1,61,005	1,93,850	29,678	2,97,909
17.	HASSAN	6,62,602	54.029	1,05,044	75.311	50,350	4,13,132
18.	KODAGU	4,10,775	1,34,597	54,701	67,597	6,24,3	1,50,398
19.	MANDYA	4,98,244	23,765	82,316	80,539	61,987	3,13,146
20.	MYSORE	12,46,283	3,38,461	1,56,027	1,15,331	1,03,175	6,32,340
IV	MYSORE DIVISION	43,73,574	9,78,253	6,28,453	6,78,981	2,67,190	21,26,074
	STATE	1,90,49,836	30,75,553	20,17,399	16,59668	15,07,681	1,24,32,422

SOURCE : **Karnataka at a Glance 1994-95. (1995),** Bangalore, Directorate of Economics and Statistics.

APPENDIX 4

Net Area Irrigated 1993-94 (Hectares)

Sl. No.	District	Canals	Tanks	Wells	Borewells	Other Sources	Total
1	2	3	4	5	6	7	8
1.	BANGALORE (U)	—	3,602	1,608	9,298	—	14,508
2.	BANGALORE (R)	2,794	19,427	14,158	29,117	1,345	66,841
3.	CHITRADURGA	57,841	7,250	19,171	38,136	6,017	1,28,715
4.	KOLAR	—	21,501	24,335	38,436	—	77,986
5.	SHIMOGA	72,095	57,479	4,534	7,974	12,182	1,54,264
6.	TUMKUR	270	30,456	24,591	26,654	231	82,202
I	BANGALORE DIVISION	1,33,000	1,39,715	88,397	1,43,629	19,775	5,24,516
7.	BELGAUM	87,698	5,597	64,327	34,890	89.750	2,82,262
8.	BIJAPUR	69,281	9,357	1,21,165	12,526	96,029	3,08,358
9.	DHARWAD	61,058	29,105	15,813	46,312	24,408	1,77,696
10.	UTTARA KANNADA	—	9,682	4,910	166	8,953	23,711
II.	BELGAUM DIVISION	2,18,037	53,741	2,06,215	93,894	2,20,140	7,92,027
11.	BELLARY	1,10,743	6,124	20,291	24,579	15,613	1,77,350

(Contd.)

12. BIDAR	138	932	26,894	3,,998	1,027	32,989
13. GULBARGA	84,197	6,941	29494	904	1,122	1,22,568
14. RAICHUR	1,86,755	5,092	35,235	7,247	7,931	2,42,260
III. GULBARGA DIVISION	3,81,833	19,089	1,11,824	36,728	25,693	5,75,167
15. CHIKMAGALUR	6,600	8,132	2,494	3,217	7,049	27,492
16. DAKSHINA KANNADA	—	3,523	34,327	1,722	57,234	96,806
17. HASSAN	23,354	26,355	2,293	10,115	7,637	69,754
18. KODAGU	2,227	141	21	—	1,346	3,735
19. MANDYA	86,471	8,353	6,633	986	1,526	1,03,969
20. MYSORE	82,953	13,676	35,243	628	1,227	1,33,727
IV. MYSORE DIVISION	2,01,605	60,180	81,011	16,668	76,019	4,35,483
STATE	9,34,475	2,72,725	4,87,447	2,90,919	3,41,627	2,327,193

SOURCE : **Karnataka at a Glance 1994-95**. (1995), Bangalore, Directorate of Economics and Statistics.

APPENDIX 5

Area Under Important Crops 1993-94 (Hectares)

Sl No.	District	Paddy	Ragi	Jowar	Sajje	Maize	Wheat	Other Cereals	Total Cereals
1	2	3	4	5	6	7	8	9	10
1.	BANGALORE	7,944	51,739	—	—	1,704	3	40	61,430
2.	BANGALORE (R)	21,143	1,39,916	—	—	5,447	5	494	1,67,005
3.	CHITRADURGA	75,543	89,689	77,011	8,141	42,112	348	18,106	3,10,950
4.	KOLAR	33,614	1,10,777	—	471	10,594	39	2,754	1,58,249
5.	SHIMOGA	1,91,205	35,164	22,751	6	17,099	221	692	2,67,138
6.	TUMKUR	37.851	1,86,883	12,306	924	4,293	60	7,833	2,50,150
I.	BANGALORE DIVISION	3,67,300	6,14,168	1,12,068	9,542	81,249	676	29,919	12,14,922
7.	BELGAUM	74,749	1,072	2,28,540	44,435	85,370	48800	8,698	4,91,664
8.	BIJAPUR	842	—	5,21,294	74,794	50,524	58171	1,701	7,07,326
9.	DHARWAD	97,977	9,098	2,57,760	2,862	42,389	85986	26,766	5,22,838
10.	UTTARA KANNADA	92,897	368	497	—	62	—	—	93,844

(Contd.)

II. BELGAUM DIVISION	2,66,465	10,558	10,08,091	1,22,091	1,78,345	1,92,957	37,165	18,15,672
11. BELLARY	53,494	25,788	1,52,857	10,026	27,372	2,146	20,706	2,92,389
12. BIDAR	15,656	—	1,19,953	12,811	285	6,757	1,941	1,57,403
13. GULBARGA	14,142	33	3,52,039	59,663	1,407	21,113	4,258	4,52,655
14. RAICHUR	1,63,591	—	2,54,376	83,919	5,807	13,313	23,133	5,44,141
III GULBARGA DIVISION	2,46,883	25,821	8,79,225	1,66,419	34,871	43,329	50,040	14,46,588
15. CHIKMAGALUR	54,017	51,858	20,348	—	370	75	645	1,27,313
16. DAKSHINA KANNADA	1,48,185	—	—	—	—	—	—	1,48,185
17. HASSAN	55,762	1,40,076	5,570	—	4,306	12	80	2,05,806
18. KODAGU	44,860	856	—	—	1,480	—	—	47,196
19. MANDAYA	74,658	73,502	4,160	—	19	—	94	1,53,433
20. MYSORE	1,15,716	1,09,669	56,046	1,945	16,890	75	273	3,00,614
IV MYSORE DIVISION	4,93,198	3,77,961	86,124	1,945	23,065	162	2,092	9,83,547
STATE	13,73,846	10,28,508	20,85,500	2,99,997	3,17,530	2,73,124	1,18,216	54,60,729

APPENDIX 5
(CONTINUATION)

Gram	Tur	Other Pulses	Total Pulses	Groundnut	Sugarcane	Cotton	High Yielding
11	12	13	14	15	16	17	18
17	1,083	11,491	12,591	1,436	36	—	61,340
133	5,098	34,978	40,209	27,221	1,357	—	1,58,406
2,780	10,750	47,762	61,292	1,98,365	7,269	30,821	2,50,327
104	16,241	25,204	41,369	1,07,572	4,242	66	1,49,164
422	1,824	19,402	21,648	17,763	16,244	39,018	2,19,229
1,240	9,996	65,366	76,602	1,85,708	2,898	732	1,91,988
4,696	44,992	2,04,023	2,53,711	53,38,065	32,046	70,637	10,30,454
22,050	10,504	48,596	81,150	95,533	1,07,053	77,880	2,34,134
42,201	14,903	62,993	1,20,097	78,436	50,766	17,539	1,64,958
51,996	18,168	85,160	1,55,324	1,38,721	90,26	2,09277	1,95,086
90	143	6,871	7,104	2,004	2,004	4,321	54,421
1,16,337	43,718	2,03,620	3,63,675	3,18,489	1,68,849	3,09.017	6,48,599
5,042	43,718	22,128	40,867	78,918	6,877	71,477	2,25,129
31,742	48,506	1,03,144	1,83,392	5,256	18,425	3,160	56,199

(Contd.)

1,03,043	1,66,954	52,922	3,22,919	1,15,299	4,918	2,600	2,64,072
18,861	29,379	37,593	85,833	1,11,401	3,133	73,636	8,27,270
1,58,688	2,58,556	2,15,787	6,33,031	3,10,874	33,353	1,50,873	8,27,270
5,465	882	24,846	32,193	8,000	2,056	1,195	1,O5,150
-----	----	18,222	18,222	3,309	3,927	-----	1,05,150
1,351	3,298	50,367	55,016	5,311	9,227	4,011	1,86,008
----	-----	800	800	43	44	1	31,504
110	1,902	64,894	66,996	18,873	32,265	2	1,48,529
2,891	7,467	89,083	99,441	40,337	20,018	35,179	2,73,992
9,817	13,549	2,49,302	2,72,668	75,873	67,537	40,388	8,51,123
2,89,538	3,60,815	8,72,732	15,23,085	12,43,310	3,01,785	5,70,915	33,57,446

SOURCE : **Karnataka a a Glance 1995-96**, (1995) Bangalore, Directorate of Economics and Statistics.

APPENDIX 6

Industries

Sl. No.	District	Number of Factories					Employees (00)	Industrial Estates	Industrial Estates
		Textiles	Chemical	Engineering	Others	Total			
1	2	3	4	5	6	7	8	9	10
1.	BANGALORE (U)	478	196	1,115	1,819	3,608	4,053	14	1,824
2.	BANGALORE (R)	24	16	47	80	167	192	5	182
3.	CHITRADURGA	43	3	52	230	328	232	4	157
4.	KOLAR	8	12	14	104	138	174	10	152
5.	SHIMOGA	4	6	31	105	146	258	5	173
6.	TUMKUR	--	5	22	230	157	107	7	120
I.	BANGALORE DIVISION	557	238	1,281	2,468	4,544	5,016	45	2,608
7.	BELGAUM	110	10	171	93	384	450	10	318
8.	BIJAPUR	138	3	5	90	236	126	7	134
9.	DHARWAD	196	19	93	301	609	616	9	550
10.	UTTARA KANNADA	1	3	5	59	68	131	6	106

(Contd.)

II. BELGAUM DIVISION	445	35	274	586	1,297	1,323	32	1,108
11. BELLARY	46	5	23	166	240	167	2	96
12. BIDAR	3	14	6	41	64	65	4	88
13. GULBARGA	10	--	13	93	166	220	8	125
14. RAICHUR	132	14	8	173	327	144	5	70
GULBARGA	191	33	50	473	797	596	19	379
15. CHIKMAGALUR	--	4	5	44	53	40	2	32
16. DAKSHINA KANNADA	18	14	53	444	529	438	8	328
17. HASSAN	4	11	2	52	69	70	5	92
18. KODAGU	--	--	6	27	33	23	2	30
19. MANDYA	1	7	6	49	63	102	5	96
20. MYSORE	50	59	84	237	430	568	7	501
VI. MYSORE DIVISION	73	95	156	853	1,177	1,241	29	1,079
STATE	1,266	401	1,761	4,337	7,765	8,180	125	5,176

SOURCE : Karnataka at a Glance 1994-95 (1995), Bangalore, Directorate of Economics and Statistics.

APPENDIX 7

Education

Sl. No	District	Primary Schools (1993-94)		High Schools (1993-94)		Pre-university (1992-93)		General Education		Polytechnic	
		Number	Children	Number	Students (000)	Number	Students (000)	Number	Students (000)	Number	Students (000)
1	2	3	4	5	6	7	8	9	10	11	12
1.	BANGALORE	2.397	781	655	182	160	66	102	520	50	13,825
2.	BANGALORE (R)	2.324	282	183	59	37	23	12	56	1	401
3.	CHITRADURGA	2.256	360	432	74	113	32	45	161	8	1,519
4.	KOLAR	3.016	426	212	73	44	22		121	10	2,5508
5.	SHIMOGA	2.340	331	300	67	63	29	31	120	7	1,551
6.	TUMKUR	3.080	386	408	95	119	27	30	174	6	1,608
I.	BANGALORE DIVISION	15.413	2.566	2.190	550	536	199	242	1,152	82	21,240
7.	BELGAUM	2.616	600	423	112	100	32	47	169	11	3,499
8.	BIJAPUR	2.293	513	384	87	101	46	2	245	7	1,644
9.	DHARWAD	2.201	613	391	114	121	41	65	235	13	3,194
10.	UTTARA KANNADA	1.646	208	201	39	36	17	19	90	6	1,410

(Contd.)

II	BELGAUM DIVISION	8.756	1.934	1.397	352	358	136	172	739	37	9,747
11.	BELLARY	1.377	333	170	49	42	16	17	105	6	2,135
12.	BIDAR	943	293	169	35	58	19	25	95	6	1,317
13.	GULBARGA	2.064	421	290	79	77	19	41	142	7	1,588
14.	RAICHUR	2.601	318	135	39	48	12	21	60	4	666
III	GULBARGA DIVISION	6,985	1,365	764	202	225	66	102	402	23	5,706
15.	CHIKMAGALUR	1.397	223	173	35	37	14	13	53	3	610
16.	DAKSHINA KANNADA	1.777	557	279	107	113	57	66	243	8	3,805
17	HASSAN	2.401	283	328	55	62	16	20	92	3	1,198
18.	KODAGU	423	79	71	17	21	8	5	18	2	520
19.	MANDYA	1.876	272	166	64	41	17	19	72	2	390
20.	MYSORE	2.647	478	364	88	20	40	170	12	2,474	
IV.	MYSORE DIVISION	10.530	1.892	1.381		366	132	163	648	30	8,997
	STATE	41.684	7.732	5.732	1.470	1.458	533	679	2,941	172	45,690

APPENDIX 7

(Continuation)

Engineering		Medical Allopathy		Indian Svstem of Medicine		Dental		Universities Libraries	
Number Students	Students (p)	Number	Students			Number	Students	Number	
13	14	15	16	17	18	19	20	21	22
14.	23.074	5	3.634	3	519	2.825	3	115	
1	1.009		—	—	—	—	—	-	66
3	4.608	1	1.779	1	122	3	1.009	—	128
2	1.627	1	739	—	—	1	120	—	73
1	1.220	—	—	1	41	1	80	1	85
4	5.669	1	1.025	—	—	1	80	—	78
25	37.207	8	7.177	5	682	22	4.114	4	545
2	2.159	1	1.031	5	771	2	436	—	105
3	2.526	2	2.214	5	441	2	302	—	133
4	4.371	1	813	11	876	1	420	2	151
1	882	—	—	—	—	—	—	—	104

(Contd.)

10	9.938	4	4.058	21	2.088	5	1.158	2	493
1	1.520	1	977	2	184	—	—	1	100
2	2.249	—	—	1	110	2	120	—	73
2	2.249	1	1.151	1	240	2	508	1	101
1	695	—	—	—	—	1	40	—	80
6	7.693	2	2.128	4	534	5	668	2	354
1	952	—	—	1	122	—	—	—	57
4	6.825	2	3.001	3	570	3	1.573	1	102
1	2.346	—	—	1	148	1	142	—	61
—	—	—		—	—	—	—	52	1
	1.879	1	1.166	—	—	—	—	—	73
4	4.453	2	1.777	2	234	2	361	1	73
11	16.455	5	5.954	7	1.074	6	2.076	2	418
52	71.293	19	19.317	37	4.378	38	8.016	10	1,810

SOURCE : **Karnataka at Glance 1994-95** (1995), Bangalore, Directorate of Economics and Statistics.

APPENDIX 8

Health

Sl. No.	District	State Government		Other Agencies		Indian system of Medicince		Primary Health Centres	
		Number	Beds	Number	Beds	Number	Beds	Number	Beds
1	2	3	4	5	6	7	8	9	10
1.	BANGALORE	12	4.327	41	3.992	7	371	29	380
2.	BANGALORE (R)	4	210	1	20	4	32	64	702
3.	CHITRADURGA	7	1.665	1	50	3	22	78	788
4.	KOLAR	10	1.127	2	302	2	16	72	696
5.	SHIMOGA	7	722	1	200	2	50	66	582
6.	TUMKUR	4	508	—	—	4	40	86	744
I.	BANGALORE DIVISION	44	8.559	46	4.564	22	531	395	3,892
7.	BELGAUM	9	1.060	—	—	3	22	118	832
8.	BIJAPUR	12	906	1	32	5	6	93	704
9.	DHARWAD	17	1.901	2	187	4	47	91	754
10.	UTTARA KANNADA	11	636	1	25	2	20	56	420

(Contd.)

II. BELGAUM DIVISION	49	4.503	4	244	14	175	358	2,710
11. BELLARY	12	1.350	2	51	5	97	58	429
12. BIDAR	5	443	—	—	—	—	38	282
13. GULBARGA	12	1.190	1	20	4	32	92	658
14. RAICHUR	9	478	—	—	4	32	74	610
III. GULBARGA DIVISION	38	3.461	3	71	13	161	262	1,979
15. CHIKMAGALUR	5	479	1	50	2	16	43	420
16. DAKSHINA KANNADA	10	1.656	1	100	1	6	119	945
17. HASSAN	7	820	—	—	5	57	69	651
18. KODAGU	8	950	—	—	3	30	28	323
19. MANDYA	6	558	2	26	2	31	59	628
20. MYSORE	9	2.207	4	202	7	193	126	1,123
IV. MYSORE DIVISION	45	6,670	8	378	20	333	444	4,123
STATE	176	23,193	61	4,257	69	1,200	1,459	12,671

APPENDIX 8

(Continuation)

Primarv Health Units		Dispensaries		Familv Welfare Centres
Number	Beds	Number	Beds	
11	12	13	14	15
42	35	65	4	47
29	26	7	—	15
49	6	7	—	19
37	31	5	—	22
50	94	14	16	18
40	38	1	—	21
247	230	99	20	142
4	60	4	—	29
34	55	12	32	41
20	20	5	26	17
71	171	37	87	121
24	4	11	—	17
13	37	2	—	13
25	60	11	—	29
8	—	6	23	
70	101	30	—	82
42	44	2	—	14
16	10	15	12	28
53	102	3	—	18
4	—	6	—	6
38	36	4	2	15
59	172	12	—	33
212	364	42	14	114
600	866	208	121	459

SOURCE: **Karnataka at a Glance 1994-95** (1995), Bangalore, Directorate of Economics and Statistics.